FOOTBALL
LEAGUE TABLES
1888-2005

EDITOR
Michael Robinson

British Library Cataloguing in Publication Data
A catalogue record for this book is available from the British Library

ISBN 1-86223-124-9

Printed by The Cromwell Press

THE FOOTBALL LEAGUE – AN OUTLINE HISTORY

1888-89 SEASON   The League was formed with the 12 Original Founding Clubs in one Division.

1891-92 SEASON   The League was enlarged to 14 Clubs in a single Division.

1892-93 SEASON   The League was enlarged to 28 Clubs, comprised of a First Division of 16 Clubs and a Second Division of 12 Clubs.

1893-94 SEASON   The League was enlarged to 31 Clubs by increasing the Second Division to 15 Clubs.

1894-95 SEASON   The League was enlarged to 32 Clubs by increasing the Second Division to 16 Clubs.

1898-99 SEASON   The League was enlarged to 36 Clubs by increasing both the First and Second Divisions to 18 Clubs each.

1905-06 SEASON   The League was enlarged to 40 Clubs by increasing both the First and Second Divisions to 20 Clubs each.

1915-19 SEASONS   The League was suspended for the duration of the Great War.

1919-20 SEASON   The League recommenced and was enlarged to 44 Clubs by increasing both the First and Second Divisions to 22 Clubs each.

1920-21 SEASON   The League was enlarged to 66 Clubs by the creation of a Third Division (of Associate Members) of 22 Clubs. The 22 new clubs were a 'mass' defection from the Southern League.

1921-22 SEASON   The League was enlarged to 86 Clubs by the creation of an additional Third Division of 20 Clubs and the regionalisation of the Third Division into North and South.

1923-24 SEASON   The League was enlarged to 88 Clubs by increasing the 3rd Division (North) from 20 to 22 Clubs.

1939-46 SEASONS   The League was suspended for the duration of the Second World War.

1946-47 SEASON   The League recommenced as previously.

1950-51 SEASON   The League was enlarged to 92 Clubs by increasing both the Third Divisions (North and South) to 24 Clubs each.

1958-59 SEASON   The Third Divisions were deregionalised by the creation of Third and Fourth Divisions of 24 Clubs each.

1987-88 SEASON   The First Division was reduced to 21 Clubs and the Second Division was increased to 23 Clubs.

1988-89 SEASON   The First Division was reduced to 20 Clubs and the Second Division was increased to 24 Clubs.

1991-92 SEASON   The First Division was increased to 22 Clubs and the Fourth Division was reduced to 22 Clubs.

1992-93 SEASON   The First Division split from the Football League to join a new F.A. Premier Division. The remaining Second, Third and Fourth Divisions were retained in the same format but renamed the First, Second and Third Divisions respectively.

1995-96 SEASON   The F.A. Premier League was reduced to 20 Clubs and the Football League Third Division (formerly Fourth Division) was increased to 24 Clubs.

2004-05 SEASON   The Football League First, Second and Third Divisions were renamed The Championship, League One and League Two respectively.

1872 F.A. Cup

Semi-finals

Wanderers vs Queen's Park	0-0
Royal Engineers vs Crystal Palace	3-0

Final

Kennington Oval, 16 March 1872

Wanderers 1 (Betts)
Royal Engineers 0

Attendance 2,000

1873 F.A. Cup

Semi-finals

Queen's Park vs Oxford University	†

(Wanderers received a bye)
† After playing Oxford, Queen's Park scratched from the final because they could not afford to travel to London.

Final

Lillie Bridge, 29th March 1873

Wanderers 2 (Kinnaird, Wollaston)
Oxford University 0

Attendance 3,000

1874 F.A. Cup

Semi-finals

Oxford University vs Clapham Rovers	1-0
Royal Engineers vs Swifts	2-0

Final

Kennington Oval, 14th March 1874

Oxford University 2 (Mackarness, Patton)
Royal Engineers 0

Attendance 2,500

1875 F.A. Cup

Semi-finals

Royal Engineers vs Oxford University	1-0
Old Etonians vs Shropshire Wanderers	1-0

Final

Kennington Oval, 13th March 1875

Royal Engineers 1 (Scorer Not Known)
Old Etonians 1 (aet.) (Bonsor)

Attendance 3,000

Replay

Kennington Oval, 16th March 1875

Royal Engineers 2 (Renny-Tailyour, Stafford)
Old Etonians 0

Attendance 3,000

1876 F.A. Cup

Semi-finals

Wanderers vs Swifts	2-1
Oxford University vs Old Etonians	0-1

Final

Kennington Oval, 11th March 1876

Wanderers 1 (Edwards)
Old Etonians 1 (Bonsor)

Attendance 3,500

Replay

Kennington Oval, 18th March 1876

Wanderers 3 (Hughes 2, Wollaston)
Old Etonians 0

Attendance 3,200

1877 F.A. Cup

Semi-finals

Wanderers vs Cambridge University	1-0

(Oxford University received a bye)

Final

Kennington Oval, 24th March 1877

Wanderers 2 (Heron, Kenrick)
Oxford University 1 (Kinnaird (og))

Attendance 3,000

1878 F.A. Cup

Semi-finals

Royal Engineers vs Old Harrovians	2-1

(Wanderers received a bye)

Final

Kennington Oval, 23rd March 1878

Wanderers 3 (Kenrick 2, Kinnaird)
Royal Engineers 1 (Scorer Not Known)

Attendance 4,500

1879 F.A. Cup

Semi-finals

Old Etonians vs Nottingham Forest	2-1

(Clapham Rovers received a bye)

Final

Kennington Oval, 29th March 1879

Old Etonians 1 (Clerke)
Clapham Rovers 0

Attendance 5,000

1880 F.A. Cup

Semi-finals

Oxford University vs Nottingham Forest	1-0

(Clapham Rovers received a bye)

Final

Kennington Oval, 10th April 1880

Clapham Rovers 1 (Lloyd-Jones)
Oxford University 0

Attendance 6,000

1881 F.A. Cup

Semi-finals

Old Carthusians vs Clapham Rovers	4-1

(Old Etonians received a bye)

Final

Kennington Oval, 9th April 1881

Old Carthusians 3 (Page, Wynyard, Parry)
Old Etonians 0

Attendance 4,500

1882 F.A. Cup

Semi-finals

Old Etonians vs Great Marlow	5-0
Blackburn Rovers vs The Wednesday	0-0, 5-1

Final

Kennington Oval, 25th March 1882

Old Etonians 1 (Anderson)
Blackburn Rovers 0

Attendance 6,500

1883 F.A. Cup

Semi-finals

Blackburn Olympic vs Old Carthusians   4-0
Old Etonians vs Notts County   2-1

Final

Kennington Oval, 31st March 1883

Blackburn Olympic 2   (Matthews, Costley)
Old Etonians 1 (aet.)   (Goodhart)

Attendance 8,000

1884 F.A. Cup

Semi-finals

Blackburn Rovers vs Notts County   1-0
Queen's Park vs Blackburn Olympic   4-1

Final

Kennington Oval, 29th March 1884

Blackburn Rovers 2   (Brown, Forrest)
Queen's Park 1   (Christie)

Attendance 4,000

1885 F.A. Cup

Semi-finals

Blackburn Rovers vs Old Carthusians   5-0
Queen's Park vs Nottingham Forest   1-1, 3-0

Final

Kennington Oval, 4th April 1885

Blackburn Rovers 2   (Forrest, Brown)
Queen's Park 0

Attendance 12,500

1886 F.A. Cup

Semi-finals

Blackburn Rovers vs Swifts   2-1
West Bromwich vs Small Heath Alliance   4-0

Final

Kennington Oval, 3rd April 1886

Blackburn Rovers 0
West Bromwich Albion 0

Attendance 15,000

Replay

Racecourse Ground, Derby, 10th April 1886

Blackburn Rovers 2   (Brown, Sowerbutts)
West Bromwich Albion 0

Attendance 12,000

1887 F.A. Cup

Semi-finals

Aston Villa vs Glasgow Rangers   3-1
West Bromwich Albion vs Preston North End   3-1

Final

Kennington Oval, 2nd April 1887

Aston Villa 2   (Hunter, Hodgetts)
West Bromwich Albion 0

Attendance 15,500

1888 F.A. Cup

Semi-finals

West Bromwich Albion vs Derby Junction   3-0
Preston North End vs Crewe Alexandra   4-0

Final

Kennington Oval 24th March 1888

West Bromwich Albion 2   (Woodhall, Bayliss)
Preston North End 1   (Dewhurst)

Attendance 19,000

FOOTBALL LEAGUE 1888-89

Preston North End	22	18	4	0	74	15	40
Aston Villa	22	12	5	5	61	43	29
Wolverhampton Wanderers	22	12	4	6	50	37	28
Blackburn Rovers	22	10	6	6	66	45	26
Bolton Wanderers	22	10	2	10	63	59	22
West Bromwich Albion	22	10	2	10	40	46	22
Accrington	22	6	8	8	48	48	20
Everton	22	9	2	11	35	46	20
Burnley	22	7	3	12	42	62	17
Derby County	22	7	2	13	41	61	16
Notts County	22	5	2	15	40	73	12
Stoke	22	4	4	14	26	51	12

1889 F.A. Cup

Semi-finals

Preston North End vs West Bromwich Albion   1-0
Wolverhampton Wands. vs Blackburn Rovers   1-1, 3-1

Final

Kennington Oval, 30th March 1889

Preston North End 3   (Dewhurst, J. Ross, Thompson)
Wolverhampton Wanderers 0

Attendance 22,000

FOOTBALL LEAGUE 1889-90

Preston North End	22	15	3	4	71	30	33
Everton	22	14	3	5	65	40	31
Blackburn Rovers	22	12	3	7	78	41	27
Wolverhampton Wanderers	22	10	5	7	51	38	25
West Bromwich Albion	22	11	3	8	47	50	25
Accrington	22	9	6	7	53	56	24
Derby County	22	9	3	10	43	55	21
Aston Villa	22	7	5	10	43	51	19
Bolton Wanderers	22	9	1	12	54	65	19
Notts County	22	6	5	11	43	51	17
Burnley	22	4	5	13	36	65	13
Stoke	22	3	4	15	27	69	10

1890 F.A. Cup

Semi-finals

Blackburn Rovers vs Wolverhampton Wanderers   1-0
Bolton Wanderers vs The Wednesday   1-2

Final

Kennington Oval, 29th March 1890

Blackburn Rovers 6   (Townley 3, Lofthouse, John
Southworth, Walton)
The Wednesday 1   (Bennett)

Attendance 20,000

FOOTBALL LEAGUE 1890-91

Everton	22	14	1	7	63	29	29
Preston North End	22	12	3	7	44	23	27
Notts County	22	11	4	7	52	35	26
Wolverhampton Wanderers	22	12	2	8	39	50	26
Bolton Wanderers	22	12	1	9	47	34	25
Blackburn Rovers	22	11	2	9	52	43	24
Sunderland	22	10	5	7	51	31	23
Burnley	22	9	3	10	52	63	21
Aston Villa	22	7	4	11	45	58	18
Accrington	22	6	4	12	28	50	16
Derby County	22	7	1	14	47	81	15
West Bromwich Albion	22	5	2	15	34	57	12

Sunderland deducted two points

1891 F.A. Cup

Semi-finals

Blackburn Rovers vs West Bromwich Albion   3-2
Sunderland vs Notts County   3-3, 0-2

Final

Kennington Oval, 21st March 1891

Blackburn Rovers 3   (Southworth, Dewar, Townley)
Notts County 1   (Oswald)

Attendance 23,000

FOOTBALL LEAGUE 1891-92

Sunderland	26	21	0	5	93	36	42
Preston North End	26	18	1	7	61	31	37
Bolton Wanderers	26	17	2	7	51	37	36
Aston Villa	26	15	0	11	89	56	30
Everton	26	12	4	10	49	49	28
Wolverhampton Wanderers	26	11	4	11	59	46	26
Burnley	26	11	4	11	49	45	26
Notts County	26	11	4	11	55	51	26
Blackburn Rovers	26	10	6	10	58	65	26
Derby County	26	10	4	12	46	52	24
Accrington	26	8	4	14	40	78	20
West Bromwich Albion	26	6	6	14	51	58	18
Stoke	26	5	4	17	38	61	14
Darwen	26	4	3	19	38	112	11

1892 F.A. Cup

Semi-finals

West Brom. Albion vs Nottingham Forest   1-1, 1-1, 6-2
Aston Villa vs Sunderland   4-1

Final

Kennington Oval, 12th March 1892

West Bromwich Albion 3   (Nicholls, Geddes, Reynolds)

Aston Villa 0

Attendance 25,000

DIVISION 1 1892-93

Sunderland	30	22	4	4	100	36	48
Preston North End	30	17	3	10	57	39	37
Everton	30	16	4	10	74	51	36
Aston Villa	30	16	3	11	73	62	35
Bolton Wanderers	30	13	6	11	56	55	32
Burnley	30	13	4	13	51	44	30
Stoke	30	12	5	13	58	48	29
West Bromwich Albion	30	12	5	13	58	69	29
Blackburn Rovers	30	8	13	9	47	56	29
Nottingham Forest	30	10	8	12	48	52	28
Wolverhampton Wanderers	30	12	4	14	47	68	28
The Wednesday	30	12	3	15	55	65	27
Derby County	30	9	9	12	52	64	27
Notts County	30	10	4	16	53	61	24
Accrington	30	6	11	13	57	81	23
Newton Heath	30	6	6	18	50	85	18

DIVISION 2 1892-93

Small Heath	22	17	2	3	90	35	36
Sheffield United	22	16	3	3	62	19	35
Darwen	22	14	2	6	60	36	30
Grimsby Town	22	11	1	10	42	41	23
Ardwick	22	9	3	10	45	40	21
Burton Swifts	22	9	2	11	47	47	20
Northwich Victoria	22	9	2	11	42	58	20
Bootle	22	8	3	11	49	63	19
Lincoln City	22	7	3	12	45	51	17
Crewe Alexandra	22	6	3	13	42	69	15
Burslem Port Vale	22	6	3	13	30	57	15
Walsall Town Swifts	22	5	3	14	37	75	13

1893 F.A. Cup

Semi-finals

Wolverhampton Wanderers vs Blackburn Rovers   2-1
Everton vs Preston North End   2-2, 0-0, 2-1

Final

Fallowfield, Manchester, 25th March 1893

Wolverhampton Wanderers 1   (Allen)

Everton 0

Attendance 45,000

DIVISION 1 1893-94

Aston Villa	30	19	6	5	84	42	44
Sunderland	30	17	4	9	72	44	38
Derby County	30	16	4	10	73	62	36
Blackburn Rovers	30	16	2	12	69	53	34
Burnley	30	15	4	11	61	51	34
Everton	30	15	3	12	90	57	33
Nottingham Forest	30	14	4	12	57	48	32
West Bromwich Albion	30	14	4	12	66	59	32
Wolverhampton Wanderers	30	14	3	13	52	63	31
Sheffield United	30	13	5	12	47	61	31
Stoke	30	13	3	14	65	79	29
The Wednesday	30	9	8	13	48	57	26
Bolton Wanderers	30	10	4	16	38	52	24
Preston North End	30	10	3	17	44	56	23
Darwen	30	7	5	18	37	83	19
Newton Heath	30	6	2	22	36	72	14

DIVISION 2 1893-94

Liverpool	28	22	6	0	77	18	50
Small Heath	28	21	0	7	103	44	42
Notts County	28	18	3	7	70	31	39
Newcastle United	28	15	6	7	66	39	36
Grimsby Town	28	15	2	11	71	58	32
Burton Swifts	28	14	3	11	79	61	31
Burslem Port Vale	28	13	4	11	66	64	30
Lincoln City	28	11	6	11	59	58	28
Woolwich Arsenal	28	12	4	12	52	55	28
Walsall Town Swifts	28	10	3	15	51	61	23
Middlesbrough Ironopolis	28	8	4	16	37	72	20
Crewe Alexandra	28	6	7	15	42	73	19
Ardwick	28	8	2	18	47	71	18
Rotherham Town	28	6	3	19	44	91	15
Northwich Victoria	28	3	3	22	30	98	9

1894 F.A. Cup

Semi-finals

Notts County vs Blackburn Rovers   1-0
Bolton Wanderers vs The Wednesday   2-1

Final

Goodison Park, 31st March 1894

Notts County 4   (Logan 3, Watson)

Bolton Wanderers 1   (Cassidy)

Attendance 37,000

DIVISION 1 1894-95

Sunderland	30	21	5	4	80	37	47
Everton	30	18	6	6	82	50	42
Aston Villa	30	17	5	8	82	43	39
Preston North End	30	15	5	10	62	46	35
Blackburn Rovers	30	11	10	9	59	49	32
Sheffield United	30	14	4	12	57	55	32
Nottingham Forest	30	13	5	12	50	56	31
The Wednesday	30	12	4	14	50	55	28
Burnley	30	11	4	15	44	56	26
Bolton Wanderers	30	9	7	14	61	62	25
Wolverhampton Wanderers	30	9	7	14	43	63	25
Small Heath	30	9	7	14	50	74	25
West Bromwich Albion	30	10	4	16	51	66	24
Stoke	30	9	6	15	50	67	24
Derby County	30	7	9	14	45	68	23
Liverpool	30	7	8	15	51	70	22

DIVISION 2 1894-95

Bury	30	23	2	5	78	33	48
Notts County	30	17	5	8	75	45	39
Newton Heath	30	15	8	7	78	44	38
Leicester Fosse	30	15	8	7	72	53	38
Grimsby Town	30	18	1	11	79	52	37
Darwen	30	16	4	10	74	43	36
Burton Wanderers	30	14	7	9	67	39	35
Woolwich Arsenal	30	14	6	10	75	58	34
Manchester City	30	14	3	13	82	72	31
Newcastle United	30	12	3	15	72	84	27
Burton Swifts	30	11	3	16	52	74	25
Rotherham Town	30	11	2	17	55	62	24
Lincoln City	30	10	0	20	52	92	20
Walsall Town Swifts	30	10	0	20	47	92	20
Burslem Port Vale	30	7	4	19	39	77	18
Crewe Alexandra	30	3	4	23	26	103	10

1895 F.A. Cup

Semi-finals

Aston Villa vs Sunderland	2-1
West Bromwich Albion vs The Wednesday	2-0

Final

Crystal Palace, 20th April 1895

Aston Villa 1   (Chatt)
West Bromwich Albion 0

Attendance 42,560

DIVISION 1 1895-96

Aston Villa	30	20	5	5	78	45	45
Derby County	30	17	7	6	68	35	41
Everton	30	16	7	7	66	43	39
Bolton Wanderers	30	16	5	9	49	37	37
Sunderland	30	15	7	8	52	41	37
Stoke	30	15	0	15	56	47	30
The Wednesday	30	12	5	13	44	53	29
Blackburn Rovers	30	12	5	13	40	50	29
Preston North End	30	11	6	13	44	48	28
Burnley	30	10	7	13	48	44	27
Bury	30	12	3	15	50	54	27
Sheffield United	30	10	6	14	40	50	26
Nottingham Forest	30	11	3	16	42	57	25
Wolverhampton Wanderers	30	10	1	19	61	65	21
Small Heath	30	8	4	18	39	79	20
West Bromwich Albion	30	6	7	17	30	59	19

DIVISION 2 1895-96

Liverpool	30	22	2	6	106	32	46
Manchester City	30	21	4	5	63	38	46
Grimsby Town	30	20	2	8	82	38	42
Burton Wanderers	30	19	4	7	69	40	42
Newcastle United	30	16	2	12	73	50	34
Newton Heath	30	15	3	12	66	57	33
Woolwich Arsenal	30	14	4	12	59	42	32
Leicester Fosse	30	14	4	12	57	44	32
Darwen	30	12	6	12	72	67	30
Notts County	30	12	2	16	57	54	26
Burton Swifts	30	10	4	16	39	69	24
Loughborough	30	9	5	16	40	67	23
Lincoln City	30	9	4	17	53	75	22
Burslem Port Vale	30	7	4	19	43	78	18
Rotherham Town	30	7	3	20	34	97	17
Crewe Alexandra	30	5	3	22	30	95	13

1896 F.A. Cup

Semi-finals

The Wednesday vs Bolton Wanderers	1-1, 3-1
Wolverhampton Wanderers vs Derby County	2-1

Final

Crystal Palace, 18th April 1896

The Wednesday 2   (Spiksley 2)
Wolverhampton Wanderers 1   (Black)

Attendance 48,836

DIVISION 1 1896-97

Aston Villa	30	21	5	4	73	38	47
Sheffield United	30	13	10	7	42	29	36
Derby County	30	16	4	10	70	50	36
Preston North End	30	11	12	7	55	40	34
Liverpool	30	12	9	9	46	38	33
The Wednesday	30	10	11	9	42	37	31
Everton	30	14	3	13	62	57	31
Bolton Wanderers	30	12	6	12	40	43	30
Bury	30	10	10	10	39	44	30
Wolverhampton Wanderers	30	11	6	13	45	41	28
Nottingham Forest	30	9	8	13	44	49	26
West Bromwich Albion	30	10	6	14	33	56	26
Stoke	30	11	3	16	48	59	25
Blackburn Rovers	30	11	3	16	35	62	25
Sunderland	30	7	9	14	34	47	23
Burnley	30	6	7	17	43	61	19

DIVISION 2 1896-97

Notts County	30	19	4	7	92	43	42
Newton Heath	30	17	5	8	56	34	39
Grimsby Town	30	17	4	9	66	45	38
Small Heath	30	16	5	9	69	47	37
Newcastle United	30	17	1	12	56	52	35
Manchester City	30	12	8	10	58	50	32
Gainsborough Trinity	30	12	7	11	50	47	31
Blackpool	30	13	5	12	59	56	31
Leicester Fosse	30	13	4	13	59	56	30
Woolwich Arsenal	30	13	4	13	68	70	30
Darwen	30	14	0	16	67	61	28
Walsall	30	11	4	15	53	69	26
Loughborough	30	12	1	17	50	64	25
Burton Swifts	30	9	6	15	46	61	24
Burton Wanderers	30	9	2	19	31	67	20
Lincoln City	30	5	2	23	27	85	12

1897 F.A. Cup

Semi-finals

Aston Villa vs Liverpool	3-0
Everton vs Derby County	3-2

Final

Crystal Palace, 10th April 1897

Aston Villa 3   (Campbell, Wheldon, Crabtree)
Everton 2   (Bell, Boyle)

Attendance 62,017

DIVISION 1 1897-98

Sheffield United	30	17	8	5	56	31	42
Sunderland	30	16	5	9	43	30	37
Wolverhampton Wanderers	30	14	7	9	57	41	35
Everton	30	13	9	8	48	39	35
The Wednesday	30	15	3	12	51	42	33
Aston Villa	30	14	5	11	61	51	33
West Bromwich Albion	30	11	10	9	44	45	32
Nottingham Forest	30	11	9	10	47	49	31
Liverpool	30	11	6	13	48	45	28
Derby County	30	11	6	13	57	61	28
Bolton Wanderers	30	11	4	15	28	41	26
Preston North End	30	8	8	14	35	43	24
Notts County	30	8	8	14	36	46	24
Bury	30	8	8	14	39	51	24
Blackburn Rovers	30	7	10	13	39	54	24
Stoke	30	8	8	14	35	55	24

DIVISION 2 1897-98

Burnley	30	20	8	2	80	24	48
Newcastle United	30	21	3	6	64	32	45
Manchester City	30	15	9	6	66	36	39
Newton Heath	30	16	6	8	64	35	38
Woolwich Arsenal	30	16	5	9	69	49	37
Small Heath	30	16	4	10	58	50	36
Leicester Fosse	30	13	7	10	46	35	33
Luton Town	30	13	4	13	68	50	30
Gainsborough Trinity	30	12	6	12	50	54	30
Walsall	30	12	5	13	58	58	29
Blackpool	30	10	5	15	49	61	25
Grimsby Town	30	10	4	16	52	62	24
Burton Swifts	30	8	5	17	38	69	21
Lincoln City	30	6	5	19	43	82	17
Darwen	30	6	2	22	31	76	14
Loughborough	30	6	2	22	24	87	14

1898 F.A. Cup

Semi-finals

Southampton vs Nottingham Forest	1-1, 0-2
Derby County vs Everton	3-1

Final

Crystal Palace, 16th April 1898

Nottingham Forest 3   (Capes 2, McPherson)
Derby County 1   (Bloomer)

Attendance 62,017

DIVISION 1 1898-99

Aston Villa	34	19	7	8	76	40	45
Liverpool	34	19	5	10	49	33	43
Burnley	34	15	9	10	45	47	39
Everton	34	15	8	11	48	41	38
Notts County	34	12	13	9	47	51	37
Blackburn Rovers	34	14	8	12	60	52	36
Sunderland	34	15	6	13	41	41	36
Wolverhampton Wanderers	34	14	7	13	54	48	35
Derby County	34	12	11	11	62	57	35
Bury	34	14	7	13	48	49	35
Nottingham Forest	34	11	11	12	42	42	33
Stoke	34	13	7	14	47	52	33
Newcastle United	34	11	8	15	49	48	30
West Bromwich Albion	34	12	6	16	42	57	30
Preston North End	34	10	9	15	44	47	29
Sheffield United	34	9	11	14	45	51	29
Bolton Wanderers	34	9	7	18	37	51	25
The Wednesday	34	8	8	18	32	61	24

DIVISION 2 1898-99

Manchester City	34	23	6	5	92	35	52
Glossop North End	34	20	6	8	76	38	46
Leicester Fosse	34	18	9	7	64	42	45
Newton Heath	34	19	5	10	67	43	43
New Brighton Tower	34	18	7	9	71	52	43
Walsall	34	15	12	7	79	36	42
Woolwich Arsenal	34	18	5	11	72	41	41
Small Heath	34	17	7	10	85	50	41
Burslem Port Vale	34	17	5	12	56	34	39
Grimsby Town	34	15	5	14	71	60	35
Barnsley	34	12	7	15	52	56	31
Lincoln City	34	12	7	15	51	56	31
Burton Swifts	34	10	8	16	51	70	28
Gainsborough Trinity	34	10	5	19	56	72	25
Luton Town	34	10	3	21	51	95	23
Blackpool	34	8	4	22	49	90	20
Loughborough	34	6	6	22	38	92	18
Darwen	34	2	5	27	22	141	9

1899 F.A. Cup

Semi-finals

Sheffield United vs Liverpool	2-2, 4-4, 0-1*, 1-0
Derby County vs Stoke	3-1

* match abandoned

Final

Crystal Palace, 15th April 1899

Sheffield United 4   (Bennett, Priest, Beers, Almond)
Derby County 1   (Boag)

Attendance 73,833

DIVISION 1 1899-1900

Aston Villa	34	22	6	6	77	35	50
Sheffield United	34	18	12	4	63	33	48
Sunderland	34	19	3	12	50	35	41
Wolverhampton Wanderers	34	15	9	10	48	37	39
Newcastle United	34	13	10	11	53	43	36
Derby County	34	14	8	12	45	43	36
Manchester City	34	13	8	13	50	44	34
Nottingham Forest	34	13	8	13	56	55	34
Stoke	34	13	8	13	37	45	34
Liverpool	34	14	5	15	49	45	33
Everton	34	13	7	14	47	49	33
Bury	34	13	6	15	40	44	32
West Bromwich Albion	34	11	8	15	43	51	30
Blackburn Rovers	34	13	4	17	49	61	30
Notts County	34	9	11	14	46	60	29
Preston North End	34	12	4	18	38	48	28
Burnley	34	11	5	18	34	54	27
Glossop	34	4	10	20	31	74	18

DIVISION 2 1899-1900

The Wednesday	34	25	4	5	84	22	54
Bolton Wanderers	34	22	8	4	79	25	52
Small Heath	34	20	6	8	78	38	46
Newton Heath	34	20	4	10	63	27	44
Leicester Fosse	34	17	9	8	53	36	43
Grimsby Town	34	17	6	11	67	46	40
Chesterfield	34	16	6	12	65	60	38
Woolwich Arsenal	34	16	4	14	61	43	36
Lincoln City	34	14	8	12	46	43	36
New Brighton Tower	34	13	9	12	66	58	35
Burslem Port Vale	34	14	6	14	39	49	34
Walsall	34	12	8	14	50	55	32
Gainsborough Trinity	34	9	7	18	47	75	25
Middlesbrough	34	8	8	18	39	69	24
Burton Swifts	34	9	6	19	43	84	24
Barnsley	34	8	7	19	46	79	23
Luton Town	34	5	8	21	40	75	18
Loughborough	34	1	6	27	18	100	8

1900 F.A. Cup

Semi-finals

Nottingham Forest vs Bury	1-1, 2-3
Southampton vs Millwall Athletic	0-0, 3-0

Final

Crystal Palace, 21st April 1900

Bury 4   (McLuckie 2, Wood, Plant)
Southampton 0

Attendance 68,945

DIVISION 1 1900-01

Liverpool	34	19	7	8	59	35	45
Sunderland	34	15	13	6	57	26	43
Notts County	34	18	4	12	54	46	40
Nottingham Forest	34	16	7	11	53	36	39
Bury	34	16	7	11	53	37	39
Newcastle United	34	14	10	10	42	37	38
Everton	34	16	5	13	55	42	37
The Wednesday	34	13	10	11	52	42	36
Blackburn Rovers	34	12	9	13	39	47	33
Bolton Wanderers	34	13	7	14	39	55	33
Manchester City	34	13	6	15	48	58	32
Derby County	34	12	7	15	55	42	31
Wolverhampton Wanderers	34	9	13	12	39	55	31
Sheffield United	34	12	7	15	35	52	31
Aston Villa	34	10	10	14	45	51	30
Stoke	34	11	5	18	46	57	27
Preston North End	34	9	7	18	49	75	25
West Bromwich Albion	34	7	8	19	35	62	22

DIVISION 2 1900-01

Grimsby Town	34	20	9	5	60	33	49
Small Heath	34	19	10	5	57	24	48
Burnley	34	20	4	10	53	29	44
New Brighton Tower	34	17	8	9	57	38	42
Glossop	34	15	8	11	51	33	38
Middlesbrough	34	15	7	12	50	40	37
Woolwich Arsenal	34	15	6	13	39	35	36
Lincoln City	34	13	7	14	43	39	33
Burslem Port Vale	34	11	11	12	45	47	33
Newton Heath	34	14	4	16	42	38	32
Leicester Fosse	34	11	10	13	39	37	32
Blackpool	34	12	7	15	33	58	31
Gainsborough Trinity	34	10	10	14	45	60	30
Chesterfield	34	9	10	15	46	58	28
Barnsley	34	11	5	18	47	60	27
Walsall	34	7	13	14	40	56	27
Stockport County	34	11	3	20	38	68	25
Burton Swifts	34	8	4	22	34	66	20

1901 F.A. Cup

Semi-finals

Tottenham Hotspur vs West Bromwich Albion	4-0
Sheffield United vs Aston Villa	2-2, 3-0

Final

Crystal Palace, 20th April 1901

Tottenham Hotspur 2   (Brown 2)
Sheffield United 2   (Bennett, Priest)

Attendance 114, 815

Replay

Burnden Park, Bolton, 27th April 1901

Tottenham Hotspur 3   (Cameron, Smith, Brown)
Sheffield United 1   (Priest)

Attendance 20,740

DIVISION 1 1901-02

Sunderland	34	19	6	9	50	35	44
Everton	34	17	7	10	53	35	41
Newcastle United	34	14	9	11	48	34	37
Blackburn Rovers	34	15	6	13	52	48	36
Nottingham Forest	34	13	9	12	43	43	35
Derby County	34	13	9	12	39	41	35
Bury	34	13	8	13	44	38	34
Aston Villa	34	13	8	13	42	40	34
The Wednesday	34	13	8	13	48	52	34
Sheffield United	34	13	7	14	53	48	33
Liverpool	34	10	12	12	42	38	32
Bolton Wanderers	34	12	8	14	51	56	32
Notts County	34	14	4	16	51	57	32
Wolverhampton Wanderers	34	13	6	15	46	57	32
Grimsby Town	34	13	6	15	44	60	32
Stoke	34	11	9	14	45	55	31
Small Heath	34	11	8	15	47	45	30
Manchester City	34	11	6	17	42	58	28

DIVISION 2 1901-02

West Bromwich Albion	34	25	5	4	82	29	55
Middlesbrough	34	23	5	6	90	24	51
Preston North End	34	18	6	10	71	32	42
Woolwich Arsenal	34	18	6	10	50	26	42
Lincoln City	34	14	13	7	45	35	41
Bristol City	34	17	6	11	52	35	40
Doncaster Rovers	34	13	8	13	49	58	34
Glossop	34	10	12	12	36	40	32
Burnley	34	10	10	14	41	45	30
Burton United	34	11	8	15	46	54	30
Barnsley	34	12	6	16	51	63	30
Burslem Port Vale	34	10	9	15	43	59	29
Blackpool	34	11	7	16	40	56	29
Leicester Fosse	34	12	5	17	38	56	29
Newton Heath	34	11	6	17	38	53	28
Chesterfield	34	11	6	17	47	68	28
Stockport County	34	8	7	19	36	72	23
Gainsborough Trinity	34	4	11	19	30	80	19

1902 F.A. Cup

Semi-finals

Sheffield United vs Derby County	1-1, 1-1, 1-0
Southampton vs Nottingham Forest	3-1

Final

Crystal Palace, 19th April 1902

Sheffield United 1   (Common)
Southampton 1   (Wood)

Attendance 76,914

Replay

Crystal Palace, 26th April 1902

Sheffield United 2   (Hedley, Barnes)
Southampton 1   (Brown)

Attendance 33,068

DIVISION 1 1902-03

The Wednesday	34	19	4	11	54	36	42
Aston Villa	34	19	3	12	61	40	41
Sunderland	34	16	9	9	51	36	41
Sheffield United	34	17	5	12	58	44	39
Liverpool	34	17	4	13	68	49	38
Stoke	34	15	7	12	46	38	37
West Bromwich Albion	34	16	4	14	54	53	36
Bury	34	16	3	15	54	43	35
Derby County	34	16	3	15	50	47	35
Nottingham Forest	34	14	7	13	49	47	35
Wolverhampton Wanderers	34	14	5	15	48	57	33
Everton	34	13	6	15	45	47	32
Middlesbrough	34	14	4	16	41	50	32
Newcastle United	34	14	4	16	41	51	32
Notts County	34	12	7	15	41	49	31
Blackburn Rovers	34	12	5	17	44	63	29
Grimsby Town	34	8	9	17	43	62	25
Bolton Wanderers	34	8	3	23	37	73	19

DIVISION 2 1902-03

Manchester City	34	25	4	5	95	29	54
Small Heath	34	24	3	7	74	36	51
Woolwich Arsenal	34	20	8	6	66	30	48
Bristol City	34	17	8	9	59	38	42
Manchester United	34	15	8	11	53	38	38
Chesterfield	34	14	9	11	67	40	37
Preston North End	34	13	10	11	56	40	36
Barnsley	34	13	8	13	55	51	34
Burslem Port Vale	34	13	8	13	57	62	34
Lincoln City	34	12	6	16	46	53	30
Glossop	34	11	7	16	43	58	29
Gainsborough Trinity	34	11	7	16	41	59	29
Burton United	34	11	7	16	39	59	29
Blackpool	34	9	10	15	44	59	28
Leicester Fosse	34	10	8	16	41	65	28
Doncaster Rovers	34	9	7	18	35	72	25
Stockport County	34	7	6	21	39	74	20
Burnley	34	6	8	20	30	77	20

1903 F.A. Cup

Semi-finals

Aston Villa vs Bury	0-3
Derby County vs Millwall Athletic	3-0

Final

Crystal Palace, 18th April 1903

Bury 6   (Leeming 2, Ross, Sagar, Plant, Wood)

Derby County 0

Attendance 63,102

DIVISION 1 1903-04

The Wednesday	34	20	7	7	48	28	47
Manchester City	34	19	6	9	71	45	44
Everton	34	19	5	10	59	32	43
Newcastle United	34	18	6	10	58	45	42
Aston Villa	34	17	7	10	70	48	41
Sunderland	34	17	5	12	63	49	39
Sheffield United	34	15	8	11	62	57	38
Wolverhampton Wanderers	34	14	8	12	44	66	36
Nottingham Forest	34	11	9	14	57	57	31
Middlesbrough	34	9	12	13	46	47	30
Small Heath	34	11	8	15	39	52	30
Bury	34	7	15	12	40	53	29
Notts County	34	12	5	17	37	61	29
Derby County	34	9	10	15	58	60	28
Blackburn Rovers	34	11	6	17	48	60	28
Stoke	34	10	7	17	54	57	27
Liverpool	34	9	8	17	49	62	26
West Bromwich Albion	34	7	10	17	36	60	24

DIVISION 2 1903-04

Preston North End	34	20	10	4	62	24	50
Woolwich Arsenal	34	21	7	6	91	22	49
Manchester United	34	20	8	6	65	33	48
Bristol City	34	18	6	10	73	41	42
Burnley	34	15	9	10	50	55	39
Grimsby Town	34	14	8	12	50	49	36
Bolton Wanderers	34	12	10	12	59	41	34
Barnsley	34	11	10	13	38	57	32
Gainsborough Trinity	34	14	3	17	53	60	31
Bradford City	34	12	7	15	45	59	31
Chesterfield	34	11	8	15	37	45	30
Lincoln City	34	11	8	15	41	58	30
Burslem Port Vale	34	10	9	15	54	52	29
Burton United	34	11	7	16	45	61	29
Blackpool	34	11	5	18	40	67	27
Stockport County	34	8	11	15	40	72	27
Glossop	34	10	6	18	57	64	26
Leicester Fosse	34	6	10	18	42	82	22

1904 F.A. Cup

Semi-finals

Manchester City vs The Wednesday	3-0
Bolton Wanderers vs Derby County	1-0

Final

Crystal Palace, 23rd April 1904

Manchester City 1   (Meredith)

Bolton Wanderers 0

Attendance 61,374

DIVISION 1 1904-05

Newcastle United	34	23	2	9	72	33	48
Everton	34	21	5	8	63	36	47
Manchester City	34	20	6	8	66	37	46
Aston Villa	34	19	4	11	63	43	42
Sunderland	34	16	8	10	60	44	40
Sheffield United	34	19	2	13	64	56	40
Small Heath	34	17	5	12	54	38	39
Preston North End	34	13	10	11	42	37	36
The Wednesday	34	14	5	15	61	57	33
Woolwich Arsenal	34	12	9	13	36	40	33
Derby County	34	12	8	14	37	48	32
Stoke	34	13	4	17	40	58	30
Blackburn Rovers	34	11	5	18	40	51	27
Wolverhampton Wanderers	34	11	4	19	47	73	26
Middlesbrough	34	9	8	17	36	56	26
Nottingham Forest	34	9	7	18	40	61	25
Bury	34	10	4	20	47	67	24
Notts County	34	5	8	21	36	69	18

DIVISION 2 1904-05

Liverpool	34	27	4	3	93	25	58
Bolton Wanderers	34	27	2	5	87	32	56
Manchester United	34	24	5	5	81	30	53
Bristol City	34	19	4	11	66	45	42
Chesterfield Town	34	14	11	9	44	35	39
Gainsborough Trinity	34	14	8	12	61	58	36
Barnsley	34	14	5	15	38	56	33
Bradford City	34	12	8	14	45	49	32
Lincoln City	34	12	7	15	42	40	31
West Bromwich Albion	34	13	4	17	56	48	30
Burnley	34	12	6	16	43	52	30
Glossop	34	10	10	14	37	46	30
Grimsby Town	34	11	8	15	33	46	30
Leicester Fosse	34	11	7	16	40	55	29
Blackpool	34	9	10	15	36	48	28
Burslem Port Vale	34	10	7	17	47	72	27
Burton United	34	8	4	22	30	84	20
Doncaster Rovers	34	3	2	29	23	81	8

1905 F.A. Cup

Semi-finals

Everton vs Aston Villa	1-1, 1-2
Newcastle United vs The Wednesday	1-0

Final

Crystal Palace, 15th April 1905

Aston Villa 2   (Hampton 2)

Newcastle United 0

Attendance 101,117

DIVISION 1 1905-06

Liverpool	38	23	5	10	79	46	51
Preston North End	38	17	13	8	54	39	47
The Wednesday	38	18	8	12	63	52	44
Newcastle United	38	18	7	13	74	48	43
Manchester City	38	19	5	14	73	54	43
Bolton Wanderers	38	17	7	14	81	67	41
Birmingham	38	17	7	14	65	59	41
Aston Villa	38	17	6	15	72	56	40
Blackburn Rovers	38	16	8	14	54	52	40
Stoke	38	16	7	15	54	55	39
Everton	38	15	7	16	70	66	37
Woolwich Arsenal	38	15	7	16	62	64	37
Sheffield United	38	15	6	17	57	62	36
Sunderland	38	15	5	18	61	70	35
Derby County	38	14	7	17	39	58	35
Notts County	38	11	12	15	55	71	34
Bury	38	11	10	17	57	74	32
Middlesbrough	38	10	11	17	56	71	31
Nottingham Forest	38	13	5	20	58	79	31
Wolverhampton Wanderers	38	8	7	23	58	99	23

DIVISION 2 1905-06

Bristol City	38	30	6	2	83	28	66
Manchester United	38	28	6	4	90	28	62
Chelsea	38	22	9	7	90	37	53
West Bromwich Albion	38	22	8	8	79	36	52
Hull City	38	19	6	13	67	54	44
Leeds City	38	17	9	12	59	47	43
Leicester Fosse	38	15	12	11	53	48	42
Grimsby Town	38	15	10	13	46	46	40
Burnley	38	15	8	15	42	53	38
Stockport County	38	13	9	16	44	56	35
Bradford City	38	13	8	17	46	60	34
Barnsley	38	12	9	17	60	62	33
Lincoln City	38	12	6	20	69	72	30
Blackpool	38	10	9	19	37	62	29
Gainsborough Trinity	38	12	4	22	44	57	28
Glossop	38	10	8	20	49	71	28
Burslem Port Vale	38	12	4	22	49	82	28
Chesterfield Town	38	10	8	20	40	72	28
Burton United	38	10	6	22	34	67	26
Clapton Orient	38	7	7	24	35	78	21

1906 F.A. Cup

Semi-finals

Everton vs Liverpool	2-0
Woolwich Arsenal vs Newcastle United	0-2

Final

Crystal Palace, 21st April 1906

Everton 1   (Young)

Newcastle United 0

Attendance 75,609

DIVISION 1 1906-07

Newcastle United	38	22	7	9	74	46	51
Bristol City	38	20	8	10	66	47	48
Everton	38	20	5	13	70	46	45
Sheffield United	38	17	11	10	57	55	45
Aston Villa	38	19	6	13	78	52	44
Bolton Wanderers	38	18	8	12	59	47	44
Woolwich Arsenal	38	20	4	14	66	59	44
Manchester United	38	17	8	13	53	56	42
Birmingham	38	15	8	15	52	52	38
Sunderland	38	14	9	15	65	66	37
Middlesbrough	38	15	6	17	56	63	36
Blackburn Rovers	38	14	7	17	56	59	35
The Wednesday	38	12	11	15	49	60	35
Preston North End	38	14	7	17	44	57	35
Liverpool	38	13	7	18	64	65	33
Bury	38	13	6	19	58	68	32
Manchester City	38	10	12	16	53	77	32
Notts County	38	8	15	15	46	50	31
Derby County	38	9	9	20	41	59	27
Stoke	38	8	10	20	41	64	26

DIVISION 2 1906-07

Nottingham Forest	38	28	4	6	74	36	60
Chelsea	38	26	5	7	80	34	57
Leicester Fosse	38	20	8	10	62	39	48
West Bromwich Albion	38	21	5	12	83	45	47
Bradford City	38	21	5	12	70	53	47
Wolverhampton Wanderers	38	17	7	14	66	53	41
Burnley	38	17	6	15	62	47	40
Barnsley	38	15	8	15	73	55	38
Hull City	38	15	7	16	65	57	37
Leeds City	38	13	10	15	55	63	36
Grimsby Town	38	16	3	19	57	62	35
Stockport County	38	12	11	15	42	52	35
Blackpool	38	11	11	16	33	51	33
Gainsborough Trinity	38	14	5	19	45	72	33
Glossop	38	13	6	19	53	79	32
Burslem Port Vale	38	12	7	19	60	83	31
Clapton Orient	38	11	8	19	45	67	30
Chesterfield Town	38	11	7	20	50	66	29
Lincoln City	38	12	4	22	46	73	28
Burton United	38	8	7	23	34	68	23

1907 F.A. Cup

Semi-finals

Woolwich Arsenal vs The Wednesday	1-3
West Bromwich Albion vs Everton	1-2

Final

Crystal Palace, 20th April 1907

The Wednesday 2   (Stewart, Simpson)

Everton 1   (Sharp)

Attendance 84,584

DIVISION 1 1907-08

Manchester United	38	23	6	9	81	48	52
Aston Villa	38	17	9	12	77	59	43
Manchester City	38	16	11	11	62	54	43
Newcastle United	38	15	12	11	65	54	42
The Wednesday	38	19	4	15	73	64	42
Middlesbrough	38	17	7	14	54	45	41
Bury	38	14	11	13	58	61	39
Liverpool	38	16	6	16	68	61	38
Nottingham Forest	38	13	11	14	59	62	37
Bristol City	38	12	12	14	58	61	36
Everton	38	15	6	17	58	64	36
Preston North End	38	12	12	14	47	53	36
Chelsea	38	14	8	16	53	62	36
Blackburn Rovers	38	12	12	14	51	63	36
Woolwich Arsenal	38	12	12	14	51	63	36
Sunderland	38	16	3	19	78	75	35
Sheffield United	38	12	11	15	52	58	35
Notts County	38	13	8	17	39	51	34
Bolton Wanderers	38	14	5	19	52	58	33
Birmingham	38	9	12	17	40	60	30

DIVISION 2 1907-08

Bradford City	38	24	6	8	90	42	54
Leicester Fosse	38	21	10	7	72	47	52
Oldham Athletic	38	22	6	10	76	42	50
Fulham	38	22	5	11	82	49	49
West Bromwich Albion	38	19	9	10	61	39	47
Derby County	38	21	4	13	77	45	46
Burnley	38	20	6	12	67	50	46
Hull City	38	21	4	13	73	62	46
Wolverhampton Wanderers	38	15	7	16	50	45	37
Stoke	38	16	5	17	57	52	37
Gainsborough Trinity	38	14	7	17	47	71	35
Leeds City	38	12	8	18	53	65	32
Stockport County	38	12	8	18	48	67	32
Clapton Orient	38	11	10	17	40	65	32
Blackpool	38	11	9	18	51	58	31
Barnsley	38	12	6	20	54	68	30
Glossop	38	11	8	19	54	74	30
Grimsby Town	38	11	8	19	43	71	30
Chesterfield Town	38	6	11	21	46	92	23
Lincoln City	38	9	3	26	46	83	21

1908 F.A. Cup

Semi-finals

Wolverhampton Wanderers vs Southampton	2-0
Newcastle United vs Fulham	6-0

Final

Crystal Palace, 25th April 1908

Wolverhampton Wanderers 3   (Hunt, Hedley, Harrison)

Newcastle United 1   (Howie)

Attendance 74,967

DIVISION 1 1908-09

Newcastle United	38	24	5	9	65	41	53
Everton	38	18	10	10	82	57	46
Sunderland	38	21	2	15	78	63	44
Blackburn Rovers	38	14	13	11	61	50	41
The Wednesday	38	17	6	15	67	61	40
Woolwich Arsenal	38	14	10	14	52	49	38
Aston Villa	38	14	10	14	58	56	38
Bristol City	38	13	12	13	45	58	38
Middlesbrough	38	14	9	15	59	53	37
Preston North End	38	13	11	14	48	44	37
Chelsea	38	14	9	15	56	61	37
Sheffield United	38	14	9	15	51	59	37
Manchester United	38	15	7	16	58	68	37
Nottingham Forest	38	14	8	16	66	57	36
Notts County	38	14	8	16	51	48	36
Liverpool	38	15	6	17	57	65	36
Bury	38	14	8	16	63	77	36
Bradford City	38	12	10	16	47	47	34
Manchester City	38	15	4	19	67	69	34
Leicester Fosse	38	8	9	21	54	102	25

DIVISION 2 1908-09

Bolton Wanderers	38	24	4	10	59	28	52
Tottenham Hotspur	38	20	11	7	67	32	51
West Bromwich Albion	38	19	13	6	56	27	51
Hull City	38	19	6	13	63	39	44
Derby County	38	16	11	11	55	41	43
Oldham Athletic	38	17	6	15	55	43	40
Wolverhampton Wanderers	38	14	11	13	56	48	39
Glossop	38	15	8	15	57	53	38
Gainsborough Trinity	38	15	8	15	49	70	38
Fulham	38	13	11	14	58	48	37
Birmingham	38	14	9	15	58	61	37
Leeds City	38	14	7	17	43	53	35
Grimsby Town	38	14	7	17	41	54	35
Burnley	38	13	7	18	51	58	33
Clapton Orient	38	12	9	17	37	49	33
Bradford Park Avenue	38	13	6	19	51	59	32
Barnsley	38	11	10	17	48	57	32
Stockport County	38	14	3	21	39	71	31
Chesterfield Town	38	11	8	19	37	67	30
Blackpool	38	9	11	18	46	68	29

1909 F.A. Cup

Semi-finals

Manchester United vs Newcastle United	1-0
Bristol City vs Derby County	1-1, 2-1

Final

Crystal Palace, 24th March 1909

Manchester United 1 (A. Turnbull)
Bristol City 0

Attendance 71,401

DIVISION 1 1909-10

Aston Villa	38	23	7	8	84	42	53
Liverpool	38	21	6	11	78	57	48
Blackburn Rovers	38	18	9	11	73	55	45
Newcastle United	38	19	7	12	70	56	45
Manchester United	38	19	7	12	69	61	45
Sheffield United	38	16	10	12	62	41	42
Bradford City	38	17	8	13	64	47	42
Sunderland	38	18	5	15	66	51	41
Notts County	38	15	10	13	67	59	40
Everton	38	16	8	14	51	56	40
The Wednesday	38	15	9	14	60	63	39
Preston North End	38	15	5	18	52	58	35
Bury	38	12	9	17	62	66	33
Nottingham Forest	38	11	11	16	54	72	33
Tottenham Hotspur	38	11	10	17	53	69	32
Bristol City	38	12	8	18	45	60	32
Middlesbrough	38	11	9	18	56	73	31
Woolwich Arsenal	38	11	9	18	37	67	31
Chelsea	38	11	7	20	47	70	29
Bolton Wanderers	38	9	6	23	44	71	24

DIVISION 2 1909-10

Manchester City	38	23	8	7	81	40	54
Oldham Athletic	38	23	7	8	79	39	53
Hull City	38	23	7	8	80	46	53
Derby County	38	22	9	7	72	47	53
Leicester Fosse	38	20	4	14	79	58	44
Glossop	38	18	7	13	64	57	43
Fulham	38	14	13	11	51	43	41
Wolverhampton Wanderers	38	17	6	15	64	63	40
Barnsley	38	16	7	15	62	59	39
Bradford Park Avenue	38	17	4	17	64	59	38
West Bromwich Albion	38	16	5	17	58	56	37
Blackpool	38	14	8	16	50	52	36
Stockport County	38	13	8	17	50	47	34
Burnley	38	14	6	18	62	61	34
Lincoln City	38	10	11	17	42	69	31
Clapton Orient	38	12	6	20	37	60	30
Leeds City	38	10	7	21	46	80	27
Gainsborough Trinity	38	10	6	22	33	75	26
Grimsby Town	38	9	6	23	50	77	24
Birmingham	38	8	7	23	42	78	23

1910 F.A. Cup

Semi-finals

Newcastle United vs Swindon Town	2-0
Barnsley vs Everton	0-0, 3-0

Final

Crystal Palace, 23rd April 1910

Newcastle United 1 (Rutherford)
Barnsley 1 (Tufnell)

Attendance 77,747

Replay

Goodison Park, 28th April 1910

Newcastle United 2 (Shepherd 2 (1 pen))
Barnsley 0

Attendance 69,000

DIVISION 1 1910-11

Manchester United	38	22	8	8	72	40	52
Aston Villa	38	22	7	9	69	41	51
Sunderland	38	15	15	8	67	48	45
Everton	38	19	7	12	50	36	45
Bradford City	38	20	5	13	51	42	45
The Wednesday	38	17	8	13	47	48	42
Oldham Athletic	38	16	9	13	44	41	41
Newcastle United	38	15	10	13	61	43	40
Sheffield United	38	15	8	15	49	43	38
Woolwich Arsenal	38	13	12	13	41	49	38
Notts County	38	14	10	14	37	45	38
Blackburn Rovers	38	13	11	14	62	54	37
Liverpool	38	15	7	16	53	53	37
Preston North End	38	12	11	15	40	49	35
Tottenham Hotspur	38	13	6	19	52	63	32
Middlesbrough	38	11	10	17	49	63	32
Manchester City	38	9	13	16	43	58	31
Bury	38	9	11	18	43	71	29
Bristol City	38	11	5	22	43	66	27
Nottingham Forest	38	9	7	22	55	75	25

DIVISION 2 1910-11

West Bromwich Albion	38	22	9	7	67	41	53
Bolton Wanderers	38	21	9	8	69	40	51
Chelsea	38	20	9	9	71	35	49
Clapton Orient	38	19	7	12	44	35	45
Hull City	38	14	16	8	55	39	44
Derby County	38	17	8	13	73	52	42
Blackpool	38	16	10	12	49	38	42
Burnley	38	13	15	10	45	45	41
Wolverhampton Wanderers	38	15	8	15	51	52	38
Fulham	38	15	7	16	52	48	37
Leeds City	38	15	7	16	58	56	37
Bradford Park Avenue	38	14	9	15	53	55	37
Huddersfield Town	38	13	8	17	57	58	34
Glossop	38	13	8	17	48	62	34
Leicester Fosse	38	14	5	19	52	62	33
Birmingham	38	12	8	18	42	64	32
Stockport County	38	11	8	19	47	79	30
Gainsborough Trinity	38	9	11	18	37	55	29
Barnsley	38	7	14	17	52	62	28
Lincoln City	38	7	10	21	28	72	24

DIVISION 2 1911-12

Derby County	38	23	8	7	74	28	54
Chelsea	38	24	6	8	64	34	54
Burnley	38	22	8	8	77	41	52
Clapton Orient	38	21	3	14	61	44	45
Wolverhampton Wanderers	38	16	10	12	57	33	42
Barnsley	38	15	12	11	45	42	42
Hull City	38	17	8	13	54	51	42
Fulham	38	16	7	15	66	58	39
Grimsby Town	38	15	9	14	48	55	39
Leicester Fosse	38	15	7	16	49	66	37
Bradford Park Avenue	38	13	9	16	44	45	35
Birmingham	38	14	6	18	55	59	34
Bristol City	38	14	6	18	41	60	34
Blackpool	38	13	8	17	32	52	34
Nottingham Forest	38	13	7	18	46	48	33
Stockport County	38	11	11	16	47	54	33
Huddersfield Town	38	13	6	19	50	64	32
Glossop	38	8	12	18	42	56	28
Leeds City	38	10	8	20	50	78	28
Gainsborough Trinity	38	5	13	20	30	64	23

1911 F.A. Cup

Semi-finals

Bradford City vs Blackburn Rovers	3-0
Newcastle United vs Chelsea	3-0

Final

Crystal Palace, 22nd April 1911

Bradford City 0
Newcastle United 0

Attendance 69,098

Replay

Old Trafford, 26th April 1911

Bradford City 1 (Spiers)
Newcastle United 0

Attendance 58,000

1912 F.A. Cup

Semi-finals

Swindon Town vs Barnsley	0-0, 0-1
Blackburn Rovers vs West Bromwich Albion	0-0, 0-1

Final

Crystal Palace, 20th April 1912

Barnsley 0
West Bromwich Albion 0

Attendance 54,556

Replay

Bramall Lane, 24th April 1912

Barnsley 1 (Tufnell)
West Bromwich Albion 0 (aet.)

Attendance 38,555

DIVISION 1 1911-12

Blackburn Rovers	38	20	9	9	60	43	49
Everton	38	20	6	12	46	42	46
Newcastle United	38	18	8	12	64	50	44
Bolton Wanderers	38	20	3	15	54	43	43
The Wednesday	38	16	9	13	69	49	41
Aston Villa	38	17	7	14	76	63	41
Middlesbrough	38	16	8	14	56	45	40
Sunderland	38	14	11	13	58	51	39
West Bromwich Albion	38	15	9	14	43	47	39
Woolwich Arsenal	38	15	8	15	55	59	38
Bradford City	38	15	8	15	46	50	38
Tottenham Hotspur	38	14	9	15	53	53	37
Manchester United	38	13	11	14	45	60	37
Sheffield United	38	13	10	15	63	56	36
Manchester City	38	13	9	16	56	58	35
Notts County	38	14	7	17	46	63	35
Liverpool	38	12	10	16	49	55	34
Oldham Athletic	38	12	10	16	46	54	34
Preston North End	38	13	7	18	40	57	33
Bury	38	6	9	23	32	59	21

DIVISION 1 1912-13

Sunderland	38	25	4	9	86	43	54
Aston Villa	38	19	12	7	86	52	50
The Wednesday	38	21	7	10	75	55	49
Manchester United	38	19	8	11	69	43	46
Blackburn Rovers	38	16	13	9	79	43	45
Manchester City	38	18	8	12	53	37	44
Derby County	38	17	8	13	69	66	42
Bolton Wanderers	38	16	10	12	62	63	42
Oldham Athletic	38	14	14	10	50	55	42
West Bromwich Albion	38	13	12	13	57	50	38
Everton	38	15	7	16	48	54	37
Liverpool	38	16	5	17	61	71	37
Bradford City	38	12	11	15	50	60	35
Newcastle United	38	13	8	17	47	47	34
Sheffield United	38	14	6	18	56	70	34
Middlesbrough	38	11	10	17	55	69	32
Tottenham Hotspur	38	12	6	20	45	72	30
Chelsea	38	11	6	21	51	73	28
Notts County	38	7	9	22	28	56	23
Woolwich Arsenal	38	3	12	23	26	74	18

DIVISION 2 1912-13

Preston North End	38	19	15	4	56	33	53
Burnley	38	21	8	9	88	53	50
Birmingham	38	18	10	10	59	44	46
Barnsley	38	19	7	12	57	47	45
Huddersfield Town	38	17	9	12	66	40	43
Leeds City	38	15	10	13	70	64	40
Grimsby Town	38	15	10	13	51	50	40
Lincoln City	38	15	10	13	50	52	40
Fulham	38	17	5	16	65	55	39
Wolverhampton Wanderers	38	14	10	14	56	54	38
Bury	38	15	8	15	53	57	38
Hull City	38	15	6	17	60	56	36
Bradford Park Avenue	38	14	8	16	60	60	36
Clapton Orient	38	10	14	14	34	47	34
Leicester Fosse	38	13	7	18	50	65	33
Bristol City	38	9	15	14	46	72	33
Nottingham Forest	38	12	8	18	58	59	32
Glossop	38	12	8	18	49	68	32
Stockport County	38	8	10	20	56	78	26
Blackpool	38	9	8	21	39	69	26

1913 F.A. Cup

Semi-finals

Aston Villa vs Oldham Athletic	1-0
Sunderland vs Burnley	0-0, 3-2

Final

Crystal Palace, 19th April 1913

Aston Villa 1   (Barber)

Sunderland 0

Attendance 120,081

DIVISION 1 1913-14

Blackburn Rovers	38	20	11	7	78	42	51
Aston Villa	38	19	6	13	65	50	44
Middlesbrough	38	19	5	14	77	60	43
Oldham Athletic	38	17	9	12	55	45	43
West Bromwich Albion	38	15	13	10	46	42	43
Bolton Wanderers	38	16	10	12	65	52	42
Sunderland	38	17	6	15	63	52	40
Chelsea	38	16	7	15	46	55	39
Bradford City	38	12	14	12	40	40	38
Sheffield United	38	16	5	17	63	60	37
Newcastle United	38	13	11	14	39	48	37
Burnley	38	12	12	14	61	53	36
Manchester City	38	14	8	16	51	53	36
Manchester United	38	15	6	17	52	62	36
Everton	38	12	11	15	46	55	35
Liverpool	38	14	7	17	46	62	35
Tottenham Hotspur	38	12	10	16	50	62	34
The Wednesday	38	13	8	17	53	70	34
Preston North End	38	12	6	20	52	69	30
Derby County	38	8	11	19	55	71	27

DIVISION 2 1913-14

Notts County	38	23	7	8	77	36	53
Bradford Park Avenue	38	23	3	12	71	47	49
The Arsenal	38	20	9	9	54	38	49
Leeds City	38	20	7	11	76	46	47
Barnsley	38	19	7	12	51	45	45
Clapton Orient	38	16	11	11	47	35	43
Hull City	38	16	9	13	53	37	41
Bristol City	38	16	9	13	52	50	41
Wolverhampton Wanderers	38	18	5	15	51	52	41
Bury	38	15	10	13	39	40	40
Fulham	38	16	6	16	46	43	38
Stockport County	38	13	10	15	55	57	36
Huddersfield Town	38	13	8	17	47	53	34
Birmingham	38	12	10	16	48	60	34
Grimsby Town	38	13	8	17	42	58	34
Blackpool	38	9	14	15	33	44	32
Glossop	38	11	6	21	51	67	28
Leicester Fosse	38	11	4	23	45	61	26
Lincoln City	38	10	6	22	36	66	26
Nottingham Forest	38	7	9	22	37	76	23

1914 F.A. Cup

Semi-finals

Sheffield United vs Burnley	0-0, 0-1
Aston Villa vs Liverpool	0-2

Final

Crystal Palace, 25th April 1914

Burnley 1   (Freeman)

Liverpool 0

Attendance 72,778

DIVISION 1 1914-15

Everton	38	19	8	11	76	47	46
Oldham Athletic	38	17	11	10	70	56	45
Blackburn Rovers	38	18	7	13	83	61	43
Burnley	38	18	7	13	61	47	43
Manchester City	38	15	13	10	49	39	43
Sheffield United	38	15	13	10	49	41	43
The Wednesday	38	15	13	10	61	54	43
Sunderland	38	18	5	15	81	72	41
Bradford Park Avenue	38	17	7	14	69	65	41
West Bromwich Albion	38	15	10	13	49	43	40
Bradford City	38	13	14	11	55	49	40
Middlesbrough	38	13	12	13	62	74	38
Liverpool	38	14	9	15	65	75	37
Aston Villa	38	13	11	14	62	72	37
Newcastle United	38	11	10	17	46	48	32
Notts County	38	9	13	16	41	57	31
Bolton Wanderers	38	11	8	19	68	84	30
Manchester United	38	9	12	17	46	62	30
Chelsea	38	8	13	17	51	65	29
Tottenham Hotspur	38	8	12	18	57	90	28

DIVISION 2 1914-15

Derby County	38	23	7	8	71	33	53
Preston North End	38	20	10	8	61	42	50
Barnsley	38	22	3	13	51	51	47
Wolverhampton Wanderers	38	19	7	12	77	52	45
The Arsenal	38	19	5	14	69	41	43
Birmingham	38	17	9	12	62	39	43
Hull City	38	19	5	14	65	54	43
Huddersfield Town	38	17	8	13	61	42	42
Clapton Orient	38	16	9	13	50	48	41
Blackpool	38	17	5	16	58	57	39
Bury	38	15	8	15	61	56	38
Fulham	38	15	7	16	53	47	37
Bristol City	38	15	7	16	62	56	37
Stockport County	38	15	7	16	54	60	37
Leeds City	38	14	4	20	65	64	32
Lincoln City	38	11	9	18	46	65	31
Grimsby Town	38	11	9	18	48	76	31
Nottingham Forest	38	10	9	19	43	77	29
Leicester Fosse	38	10	4	24	47	88	24
Glossop	38	6	6	26	31	87	18

1915 F.A. Cup

Semi-finals

Sheffield United vs Bolton Wanderers	2-1
Chelsea vs Everton	2-0

Final

Old Trafford, 24th April 1915

Sheffield United 3   (Simmons, Kitchen, Fazackerley)

Chelsea 0

Attendance 49,557

DIVISION 1 1919-20

West Bromwich Albion	42	28	4	10	104	47	60
Burnley	42	21	9	12	65	59	51
Chelsea	42	22	5	15	56	51	49
Liverpool	42	19	10	13	59	44	48
Sunderland	42	22	4	16	72	59	48
Bolton Wanderers	42	19	9	14	72	65	47
Manchester City	42	18	9	15	71	62	45
Newcastle United	42	17	9	16	44	39	43
Aston Villa	42	18	6	18	75	73	42
The Arsenal	42	15	12	15	56	58	42
Bradford Park Avenue	42	15	12	15	60	63	42
Manchester United	42	13	14	15	54	50	40
Middlesbrough	42	15	10	17	61	65	40
Sheffield United	42	16	8	18	59	69	40
Bradford City	42	14	11	17	54	63	39
Everton	42	12	14	16	69	68	38
Oldham Athletic	42	15	8	19	49	52	38
Derby County	42	13	12	17	47	57	38
Preston North End	42	14	10	18	57	73	38
Blackburn Rovers	42	13	11	18	64	77	37
Notts County	42	12	12	18	56	74	36
The Wednesday	42	7	9	26	28	64	23

DIVISION 1 1920-21

Burnley	42	23	13	6	79	36	59
Manchester City	42	24	6	12	70	50	54
Bolton Wanderers	42	19	14	9	77	53	52
Liverpool	42	18	15	9	63	35	51
Newcastle United	42	20	10	12	66	45	50
Tottenham Hotspur	42	19	9	14	70	48	47
Everton	42	17	13	12	66	55	47
Middlesbrough	42	17	12	13	53	53	46
The Arsenal	42	15	14	13	59	63	44
Aston Villa	42	18	7	17	63	70	43
Blackburn Rovers	42	13	15	14	57	59	41
Sunderland	42	14	13	15	57	60	41
Manchester United	42	15	10	17	64	68	40
West Bromwich Albion	42	13	14	15	54	58	40
Bradford City	42	12	15	15	61	63	39
Preston North End	42	15	9	18	61	65	39
Huddersfield Town	42	15	9	18	42	49	39
Chelsea	42	13	13	16	48	58	39
Oldham Athletic	42	9	15	18	49	86	33
Sheffield United	42	6	18	18	42	68	30
Derby County	42	5	16	21	32	58	26
Bradford Park Avenue	42	8	8	26	43	76	24

DIVISION 2 1919-20

Tottenham Hotspur	42	32	6	4	102	32	70
Huddersfield Town	42	28	8	6	97	38	64
Birmingham	42	24	8	10	85	34	56
Blackpool	42	21	10	11	65	47	52
Bury	42	20	8	14	60	44	48
Fulham	42	19	9	14	61	50	47
West Ham United	42	19	9	14	47	40	47
Bristol City	42	13	17	12	46	43	43
South Shields	42	15	12	15	58	48	42
Stoke City	42	18	6	18	60	54	42
Hull City	42	18	6	18	78	72	42
Barnsley	42	15	10	17	61	55	40
Port Vale	42	16	8	18	59	62	40
Leicester City	42	15	10	17	41	61	40
Clapton Orient	42	16	6	20	51	59	38
Stockport County	42	14	9	19	52	61	37
Rotherham County	42	13	8	21	51	83	34
Nottingham Forest	42	11	9	22	43	73	31
Wolverhampton Wanderers	42	10	10	22	55	80	30
Coventry City	42	9	11	22	35	73	29
Lincoln City	42	9	9	24	44	101	27
Grimsby Town	42	10	5	27	34	75	25

Leeds City were expelled from the League after 8 matches of the season due to financial irregularities. Port Vale took over their fixtures and their final figures include the following statistics from Leeds City

8	4	2	2	17	10	10

DIVISION 2 1920-21

Birmingham	42	24	10	8	79	38	58
Cardiff City	42	24	10	8	59	32	58
Bristol City	42	19	13	10	49	29	51
Blackpool	42	20	10	12	54	42	50
West Ham United	42	19	10	13	51	30	48
Notts County	42	18	11	13	55	40	47
Clapton Orient	42	16	13	13	43	42	45
South Shields	42	17	10	15	61	46	44
Fulham	42	16	10	16	43	47	42
The Wednesday	42	15	11	16	48	48	41
Bury	42	15	10	17	45	49	40
Leicester City	42	12	16	14	39	46	40
Hull City	42	10	20	12	43	53	40
Leeds United	42	14	10	18	40	45	38
Wolverhampton Wanderers	42	16	6	20	49	66	38
Barnsley	42	10	16	16	48	50	36
Port Vale	42	11	14	17	43	49	36
Nottingham Forest	42	12	12	18	48	55	36
Rotherham County	42	12	12	18	37	53	36
Stoke City	42	12	11	19	46	56	35
Coventry City	42	12	11	19	39	70	35
Stockport County	42	9	12	21	42	75	30

DIVISION 3 1920-21

Crystal Palace	42	24	11	7	70	34	59
Southampton	42	19	16	7	64	28	54
Queen's Park Rangers	42	22	9	11	61	32	53
Swindon Town	42	21	10	11	73	49	52
Swansea Town	42	18	15	9	56	45	51
Watford	42	20	8	14	59	44	48
Millwall Athletic	42	18	11	13	42	30	47
Merthyr Town	42	15	15	12	60	49	45
Luton Town	42	16	12	14	61	56	44
Bristol Rovers	42	18	7	17	68	57	43
Plymouth Argyle	42	11	21	10	35	34	43
Portsmouth	42	12	15	15	46	48	39
Grimsby Town	42	15	9	18	49	59	39
Northampton Town	42	15	8	19	59	75	38
Newport County	42	14	9	19	43	64	37
Norwich City	42	10	16	16	44	53	36
Southend United	42	14	8	20	44	61	36
Brighton & Hove Albion	42	14	8	20	42	61	36
Exeter City	42	10	15	17	39	54	35
Reading	42	12	7	23	42	59	31
Brentford	42	9	12	21	42	67	30
Gillingham	42	8	12	22	34	74	28

1920 F.A. Cup

Semi-finals

Aston Villa vs Chelsea	3-1
Huddersfield Town vs Bristol City	2-1

Final

Stamford Bridge, 24th April 1920

Aston Villa 1   (Kirton)

Huddersfield Town 0   (aet.)

Attendance 50,018

1921 F.A. Cup

Semi-finals

Tottenham Hotspur vs Preston North End	2-1
Wolverhampton Wanderers vs Cardiff City	0-0, 3-1

Final

Stamford Bridge, 23rd April 1921

Tottenham Hotspur 1 (Dimmock)
Wolverhampton Wanderers 0

Attendance 72,805

DIVISION 1 1921-22

Liverpool	42	22	13	7	63	36	57
Tottenham Hotspur	42	21	9	12	65	39	51
Burnley	42	22	5	15	72	54	49
Cardiff City	42	19	10	13	61	53	48
Aston Villa	42	22	3	17	74	55	47
Bolton Wanderers	42	20	7	15	68	59	47
Newcastle United	42	18	10	14	59	45	46
Middlesbrough	42	16	14	12	79	69	46
Chelsea	42	17	12	13	40	43	46
Manchester City	42	18	9	15	65	70	45
Sheffield United	42	15	10	17	59	54	40
Sunderland	42	16	8	18	60	62	40
West Bromwich Albion	42	15	10	17	51	63	40
Huddersfield Town	42	15	9	18	53	54	39
Blackburn Rovers	42	13	12	17	54	57	38
Preston North End	42	13	12	17	42	65	38
The Arsenal	42	15	7	20	47	56	37
Birmingham	42	15	7	20	48	60	37
Oldham Athletic	42	13	11	18	38	50	37
Everton	42	12	12	18	57	55	36
Bradford City	42	11	10	21	48	72	32
Manchester United	42	8	12	22	41	73	28

DIVISION 2 1921-22

Nottingham Forest	42	22	12	8	51	30	56
Stoke City	42	18	16	8	60	44	52
Barnsley	42	22	8	12	67	52	52
West Ham United	42	20	8	14	52	39	48
Hull City	42	19	10	13	51	41	48
South Shields	42	17	12	13	43	38	46
Fulham	42	18	9	15	57	38	45
Leeds United	42	16	13	13	48	38	45
Leicester City	42	14	17	11	39	34	45
The Wednesday	42	15	14	13	47	50	44
Bury	42	15	10	17	54	55	40
Derby County	42	15	9	18	60	64	39
Notts County	42	12	15	15	47	51	39
Crystal Palace	42	13	13	16	45	51	39
Clapton Orient	42	15	9	18	43	50	39
Rotherham County	42	14	11	17	32	43	39
Wolverhampton Wanderers	42	13	11	18	44	49	37
Port Vale	42	14	8	20	43	57	36
Blackpool	42	15	5	22	44	57	35
Coventry City	42	12	10	20	51	60	34
Bradford Park Avenue	42	12	9	21	46	62	33
Bristol City	42	12	9	21	37	58	33

DIVISION 3N 1921-22

Stockport County	38	24	8	6	60	21	56
Darlington	38	22	6	10	81	37	50
Grimsby Town	38	21	8	9	72	47	50
Hartlepools United	38	17	8	13	52	39	42
Accrington Stanley	38	19	3	16	73	57	41
Crewe Alexandra	38	18	5	15	60	56	41
Stalybridge Celtic	38	18	5	15	62	63	41
Walsall	38	18	3	17	66	65	39
Southport	38	14	10	14	55	44	38
Ashington	38	17	4	17	59	66	38
Durham City	38	17	3	18	68	67	37
Wrexham	38	14	9	15	51	56	37
Chesterfield	38	16	3	19	48	67	35
Lincoln City	38	14	6	18	48	59	34
Barrow	38	14	5	19	42	54	33
Nelson	38	13	7	18	48	66	33
Wigan Borough	38	11	9	18	46	72	31
Tranmere Rovers	38	9	11	18	51	61	29
Halifax Town	38	10	9	19	56	76	29
Rochdale	38	11	4	23	52	77	26

DIVISION 3S 1921-22

Southampton	42	23	15	4	68	21	61
Plymouth Argyle	42	25	11	6	63	24	61
Portsmouth	42	18	17	7	62	39	53
Luton Town	42	22	8	12	64	35	52
Queen's Park Rangers	42	18	13	11	53	44	49
Swindon Town	42	16	13	13	72	60	45
Watford	42	13	18	11	54	48	44
Aberdare Athletic	42	17	10	15	57	51	44
Brentford	42	16	11	15	52	43	43
Swansea Town	42	13	15	14	50	47	41
Merthyr Town	42	17	6	19	45	56	40
Millwall Athletic	42	10	18	14	38	42	38
Reading	42	14	10	18	40	47	38
Bristol Rovers	42	14	10	18	52	67	38
Norwich City	42	12	13	17	50	62	37
Charlton Athletic	42	13	11	18	43	56	37
Northampton Town	42	13	11	18	47	71	37
Gillingham	42	14	8	20	47	60	36
Brighton & Hove Albion	42	13	9	20	45	51	35
Newport County	42	11	12	19	44	61	34
Exeter City	42	11	12	19	38	59	34
Southend United	42	8	11	23	34	74	27

1922 F.A. Cup

Semi-finals

Huddersfield Town vs Notts County	3-1
Preston North End vs Tottenham Hotspur	2-1

Final

Stamford Bridge, 29th April 1922

Huddersfield Town 1 (Smith (pen))
Preston North End 0

Attendance 53,000

DIVISION 1 1922-23

Liverpool	42	26	8	8	70	31	60
Sunderland	42	22	10	10	72	54	54
Huddersfield Town	42	21	11	10	60	32	53
Newcastle United	42	18	12	12	45	37	48
Everton	42	20	7	15	63	59	47
Aston Villa	42	18	10	14	64	51	46
West Bromwich Albion	42	17	11	14	58	49	45
Manchester City	42	17	11	14	50	49	45
Cardiff City	42	18	7	17	73	59	43
Sheffield United	42	16	10	16	68	64	42
The Arsenal	42	16	10	16	61	62	42
Tottenham Hotspur	42	17	7	18	50	50	41
Bolton Wanderers	42	14	12	16	50	58	40
Blackburn Rovers	42	14	12	16	47	62	40
Burnley	42	16	6	20	58	59	38
Preston North End	42	13	11	18	60	64	37
Birmingham	42	13	11	18	41	57	37
Middlesbrough	42	13	10	19	57	63	36
Chelsea	42	9	18	15	45	53	36
Nottingham Forest	42	13	8	21	41	70	34
Stoke City	42	10	10	22	47	67	30
Oldham Athletic	42	10	10	22	35	65	30

DIVISION 3N 1922-23

Nelson	38	24	3	11	61	41	51
Bradford Park Avenue	38	19	9	10	67	38	47
Walsall	38	19	8	11	51	44	46
Chesterfield	38	19	7	12	68	52	45
Wigan Borough	38	18	8	12	64	39	44
Crewe Alexandra	38	17	9	12	48	38	43
Halifax Town	38	17	7	14	53	46	41
Accrington Stanley	38	17	7	14	59	65	41
Darlington	38	15	10	13	59	46	40
Wrexham	38	14	10	14	38	48	38
Stalybridge Celtic	38	15	6	17	42	47	36
Rochdale	38	13	10	15	42	53	36
Lincoln City	38	13	10	15	38	55	36
Grimsby Town	38	14	5	19	55	52	33
Hartlepools United	38	10	12	16	48	54	32
Tranmere Rovers	38	12	8	18	49	59	32
Southport	38	12	7	19	32	46	31
Barrow	38	13	4	21	50	60	30
Ashington	38	11	8	19	51	77	30
Durham City	38	9	10	19	43	59	28

DIVISION 2 1922-23

Notts County	42	23	7	12	46	34	53
West Ham United	42	20	11	11	63	38	51
Leicester City	42	21	9	12	65	44	51
Manchester United	42	17	14	11	51	36	48
Blackpool	42	18	11	13	60	43	47
Bury	42	18	11	13	55	46	47
Leeds United	42	18	11	13	43	36	47
The Wednesday	42	17	12	13	54	47	46
Barnsley	42	17	11	14	62	51	45
Fulham	42	16	12	14	43	32	44
Southampton	42	14	14	14	40	40	42
Hull City	42	14	14	14	43	45	42
South Shields	42	15	10	17	35	44	40
Derby County	42	14	11	17	46	50	39
Bradford City	42	12	13	17	41	45	37
Crystal Palace	42	13	11	18	54	62	37
Port Vale	42	14	9	19	39	51	37
Coventry City	42	15	7	20	46	63	37
Clapton Orient	42	12	12	18	40	50	36
Stockport County	42	14	8	20	43	58	36
Rotherham County	42	13	9	20	44	63	35
Wolverhampton Wanderers	42	9	9	24	42	77	27

DIVISION 3S 1922-23

Bristol City	42	24	11	7	66	40	59
Plymouth Argyle	42	23	7	12	61	29	53
Swansea Town	42	22	9	11	78	45	53
Brighton & Hove Albion	42	20	11	11	52	34	51
Luton Town	42	21	7	14	68	49	49
Millwall Athletic	42	14	18	10	45	40	46
Portsmouth	42	19	8	15	58	52	46
Northampton Town	42	17	11	14	54	44	45
Swindon Town	42	17	11	14	62	56	45
Watford	42	17	10	15	57	54	44
Queen's Park Rangers	42	16	10	16	54	49	42
Charlton Athletic	42	14	14	14	55	51	42
Bristol Rovers	42	13	16	13	35	36	42
Brentford	42	13	12	17	41	51	38
Southend United	42	12	13	17	49	54	37
Gillingham	42	15	7	20	51	59	37
Merthyr Town	42	11	14	17	39	48	36
Norwich City	42	13	10	19	51	71	36
Reading	42	10	14	18	36	55	34
Exeter City	42	13	7	22	47	84	33
Aberdare Athletic	42	9	11	22	42	70	29
Newport County	42	8	11	23	40	70	27

1923 F.A. Cup

Semi-finals

Bolton Wanderers vs Sheffield United	1-0
West Ham United vs Derby County	5-2

Final

Wembley, 28th April 1923

Bolton Wanderers 2   (Jack, J.R. Smith)
West Ham United 0

*Official Attendance 126,047 (the actual attendance could
have been as high as 200,000)*

DIVISION 1 1923-24

Huddersfield Town	42	23	11	8	60	33	57
Cardiff City	42	22	13	7	61	34	57
Sunderland	42	22	9	11	71	54	53
Bolton Wanderers	42	18	14	10	68	34	50
Sheffield United	42	19	12	11	69	49	50
Aston Villa	42	18	13	11	52	37	49
Everton	42	18	13	11	62	53	49
Blackburn Rovers	42	17	11	14	54	50	45
Newcastle United	42	17	10	15	60	54	44
Notts County	42	14	14	14	44	49	42
Manchester City	42	15	12	15	54	71	42
Liverpool	42	15	11	16	49	48	41
West Ham United	42	13	15	14	40	43	41
Birmingham	42	13	13	16	41	49	39
Tottenham Hotspur	42	12	14	16	50	56	38
West Bromwich Albion	42	12	14	16	51	62	38
Burnley	42	12	12	18	55	60	36
Preston North End	42	12	10	20	52	67	34
The Arsenal	42	12	9	21	40	63	33
Nottingham Forest	42	10	12	20	42	64	32
Chelsea	42	9	14	19	31	53	32
Middlesbrough	42	7	8	27	37	60	22

DIVISION 2 1923-24

Leeds United	42	21	12	9	61	35	54
Bury	42	21	9	12	63	35	51
Derby County	42	21	9	12	75	42	51
Blackpool	42	18	13	11	72	47	49
Southampton	42	17	14	11	52	31	48
Stoke City	42	14	18	10	44	42	46
Oldham Athletic	42	14	17	11	45	52	45
The Wednesday	42	16	12	14	54	51	44
South Shields	42	17	10	15	49	50	44
Clapton Orient	42	14	15	13	40	36	43
Barnsley	42	16	11	15	57	61	43
Leicester City	42	17	8	17	64	54	42
Stockport County	42	13	16	13	44	52	42
Manchester United	42	13	14	15	52	44	40
Crystal Palace	42	13	13	16	53	65	39
Port Vale	42	13	12	17	50	66	38
Hull City	42	10	17	15	46	51	37
Bradford City	42	11	15	16	35	48	37
Coventry City	42	11	13	18	52	68	35
Fulham	42	10	14	18	45	56	34
Nelson	42	10	13	19	40	74	33
Bristol City	42	7	15	20	32	65	29

DIVISION 3N 1923-24

Wolverhampton Wanderers	42	24	15	3	76	27	63
Rochdale	42	25	12	5	60	26	62
Chesterfield	42	22	10	10	70	39	54
Rotherham County	42	23	6	13	70	43	52
Bradford Park Avenue	42	21	10	11	69	43	52
Darlington	42	20	8	14	70	53	48
Southport	42	16	14	12	44	42	46
Ashington	42	18	8	16	59	61	44
Doncaster Rovers	42	15	12	15	59	53	42
Wigan Borough	42	14	14	14	55	53	42
Grimsby Town	42	14	13	15	49	47	41
Tranmere Rovers	42	13	15	14	51	60	41
Accrington Stanley	42	16	8	18	48	61	40
Halifax Town	42	15	10	17	42	59	40
Durham City	42	15	9	18	59	60	39
Wrexham	42	10	18	14	37	44	38
Walsall	42	14	8	20	44	59	36
New Brighton	42	11	13	18	40	53	35
Lincoln City	42	10	12	20	48	59	32
Crewe Alexandra	42	7	13	22	32	58	27
Hartlepools United	42	7	11	24	33	70	25
Barrow	42	8	9	25	35	80	25

DIVISION 3S 1923-24

Portsmouth	42	24	11	7	87	30	59
Plymouth Argyle	42	23	9	10	70	34	55
Millwall Athletic	42	22	10	10	64	38	54
Swansea Town	42	22	8	12	60	48	52
Brighton & Hove Albion	42	21	9	12	68	37	51
Swindon Town	42	17	13	12	58	44	47
Luton Town	42	16	14	12	50	44	46
Northampton Town	42	17	11	14	64	47	45
Bristol Rovers	42	15	13	14	52	46	43
Newport County	42	17	9	16	56	64	43
Norwich City	42	16	8	18	60	59	40
Aberdare Athletic	42	12	14	16	45	58	38
Merthyr Town	42	11	16	15	45	65	38
Charlton Athletic	42	11	15	16	38	45	37
Gillingham	42	12	13	17	43	58	37
Exeter City	42	15	7	20	37	52	37
Brentford	42	14	8	20	54	71	36
Reading	42	13	9	20	51	57	35
Southend United	42	12	10	20	53	84	34
Watford	42	9	15	18	45	54	33
Bournemouth	42	11	11	20	40	65	33
Queen's Park Rangers	42	11	9	22	37	77	31

1924 F.A. Cup

Semi-finals

Newcastle United vs Manchester City	2-0
Aston Villa vs Burnley	3-0

Final

Wembley, 26th April 1924

Newcastle United 2 (Harris, Seymour)

Aston Villa 0

Attendance 91,695

DIVISION 1 1924-25

Huddersfield Town	42	21	16	5	69	28	58
West Bromwich Albion	42	23	10	9	58	34	56
Bolton Wanderers	42	22	11	9	76	34	55
Liverpool	42	20	10	12	63	55	50
Bury	42	17	15	10	54	51	49
Newcastle United	42	16	16	10	61	42	48
Sunderland	42	19	10	13	64	51	48
Birmingham	42	17	12	13	49	53	46
Notts County	42	16	13	13	42	31	45
Manchester City	42	17	9	16	76	68	43
Cardiff City	42	16	11	15	56	51	43
Tottenham Hotspur	42	15	12	15	52	43	42
West Ham United	42	15	12	15	62	60	42
Sheffield United	42	13	13	16	55	63	39
Aston Villa	42	13	13	16	58	71	39
Blackburn Rovers	42	11	13	18	53	66	35
Everton	42	12	11	19	40	60	35
Leeds United	42	11	12	19	46	59	34
Burnley	42	11	12	19	46	75	34
The Arsenal	42	14	5	23	46	58	33
Preston North End	42	10	6	26	37	74	26
Nottingham Forest	42	6	12	24	29	65	24

DIVISION 2 1924-25

Leicester City	42	24	11	7	90	32	59
Manchester United	42	23	11	8	57	23	57
Derby County	42	22	11	9	71	36	55
Portsmouth	42	15	18	9	58	50	48
Chelsea	42	16	15	11	51	37	47
Wolverhampton Wanderers	42	20	6	16	55	51	46
Southampton	42	13	18	11	40	36	44
Port Vale	42	17	8	17	48	56	42
South Shields	42	12	17	13	42	38	41
Hull City	42	15	11	16	50	49	41
Clapton Orient	42	14	12	16	42	42	40
Fulham	42	15	10	17	41	56	40
Middlesbrough	42	10	19	13	36	44	39
The Wednesday	42	15	8	19	50	56	38
Barnsley	42	13	12	17	46	59	38
Bradford City	42	13	12	17	37	50	38
Blackpool	42	14	9	19	65	61	37
Oldham Athletic	42	13	11	18	35	51	37
Stockport County	42	13	11	18	37	57	37
Stoke City	42	12	11	19	34	46	35
Crystal Palace	42	12	10	20	38	54	34
Coventry City	42	11	9	22	45	84	31

DIVISION 3N 1924-25

Darlington	42	24	10	8	78	33	58
Nelson	42	23	7	12	79	50	53
New Brighton	42	23	7	12	75	50	53
Southport	42	22	7	13	59	37	51
Bradford Park Avenue	42	19	12	11	84	42	50
Rochdale	42	21	7	14	75	53	49
Chesterfield	42	17	11	14	60	44	45
Lincoln City	42	18	8	16	53	58	44
Halifax Town	42	16	11	15	56	52	43
Ashington	42	16	10	16	68	76	42
Wigan Borough	42	15	11	16	62	65	41
Grimsby Town	42	15	9	18	60	60	39
Durham City	42	13	13	16	50	68	39
Barrow	42	16	7	19	51	74	39
Crewe Alexandra	42	13	13	16	53	78	39
Wrexham	42	15	8	19	53	61	38
Accrington Stanley	42	15	8	19	60	72	38
Doncaster Rovers	42	14	10	18	54	65	38
Walsall	42	13	11	18	44	53	37
Hartlepools United	42	12	11	19	45	63	35
Tranmere Rovers	42	14	4	24	59	78	32
Rotherham County	42	7	7	28	42	88	21

DIVISION 3S 1924-25

Swansea Town	42	23	11	8	68	35	57
Plymouth Argyle	42	23	10	9	77	38	56
Bristol City	42	22	9	11	60	41	53
Swindon Town	42	20	11	11	66	38	51
Millwall Athletic	42	18	13	11	58	38	49
Newport County	42	20	9	13	62	42	49
Exeter City	42	19	9	14	59	48	47
Brighton & Hove Albion	42	19	8	15	59	45	46
Northampton Town	42	20	6	16	51	44	46
Southend United	42	19	5	18	51	61	43
Watford	42	17	9	16	38	47	43
Norwich City	42	14	13	15	53	51	41
Gillingham	42	13	14	15	35	44	40
Reading	42	14	10	18	37	38	38
Charlton Athletic	42	13	12	17	46	48	38
Luton Town	42	10	17	15	49	57	37
Bristol Rovers	42	12	13	17	42	49	37
Aberdare Athletic	42	14	9	19	54	67	37
Queen's Park Rangers	42	14	8	20	42	63	36
Bournemouth & Boscombe Ath.	42	13	8	21	40	58	34
Brentford	42	9	7	26	38	91	25
Merthyr Town	42	8	5	29	35	77	21

1925 F.A. Cup

Semi-finals

Sheffield United vs Southampton	2-0
Cardiff City vs Blackburn Rovers	3-1

Final

Wembley, 25th April 1925

Sheffield United 1 (Tunstall)

Cardiff City 0

Attendance 91,763

DIVISION 1 1925-26

Huddersfield Town	42	23	11	8	92	60	57
The Arsenal	42	22	8	12	87	63	52
Sunderland	42	21	6	15	96	80	48
Bury	42	20	7	15	85	77	47
Sheffield United	42	19	8	15	102	82	46
Aston Villa	42	16	12	14	86	76	44
Liverpool	42	14	16	12	70	63	44
Bolton Wanderers	42	17	10	15	75	76	44
Manchester United	42	19	6	17	66	73	44
Newcastle United	42	16	10	16	84	75	42
Everton	42	12	18	12	72	70	42
Blackburn Rovers	42	15	11	16	91	80	41
West Bromwich Albion	42	16	8	18	79	78	40
Birmingham	42	16	8	18	66	81	40
Tottenham Hotspur	42	15	9	18	66	79	39
Cardiff City	42	16	7	19	61	76	39
Leicester City	42	14	10	18	70	80	38
West Ham United	42	15	7	20	63	76	37
Leeds United	42	14	8	20	64	76	36
Burnley	42	13	10	19	85	108	36
Manchester City	42	12	11	19	89	100	35
Notts County	42	13	7	22	54	74	33

DIVISION 3N 1925-26

Grimsby Town	42	26	9	7	91	40	61
Bradford Park Avenue	42	26	8	8	101	43	60
Rochdale	42	27	5	10	104	58	59
Chesterfield	42	25	5	12	100	54	55
Halifax Town	42	17	11	14	53	50	45
Hartlepools United	42	18	8	16	82	73	44
Tranmere Rovers	42	19	6	17	73	83	44
Nelson	42	16	11	15	89	71	43
Ashington	42	16	11	15	70	62	43
Doncaster Rovers	42	16	11	15	80	72	43
Crewe Alexandra	42	17	9	16	63	61	43
New Brighton	42	17	8	17	69	67	42
Durham City	42	18	6	18	63	70	42
Rotherham United	42	17	7	18	69	92	41
Lincoln City	42	17	5	20	66	82	39
Coventry City	42	16	6	20	73	82	38
Wigan Borough	42	13	11	18	68	74	37
Accrington Stanley	42	17	3	22	81	105	37
Wrexham	42	11	10	21	63	92	32
Southport	42	11	10	21	62	92	32
Walsall	42	10	6	26	58	107	26
Barrow	42	7	4	31	50	98	18

DIVISION 2 1925-26

The Wednesday	42	27	6	9	88	48	60
Derby County	42	25	7	10	77	42	57
Chelsea	42	19	14	9	76	49	52
Wolverhampton Wanderers	42	21	7	14	84	60	49
Swansea Town	42	19	11	12	77	57	49
Blackpool	42	17	11	14	76	69	45
Oldham Athletic	42	18	8	16	74	62	44
Port Vale	42	19	6	17	79	69	44
South Shields	42	18	8	16	74	65	44
Middlesbrough	42	21	2	19	77	68	44
Portsmouth	42	17	10	15	79	74	44
Preston North End	42	18	7	17	71	84	43
Hull City	42	16	9	17	63	61	41
Southampton	42	15	8	19	63	63	38
Darlington	42	14	10	18	72	77	38
Bradford City	42	13	10	19	47	66	36
Nottingham Forest	42	14	8	20	51	73	36
Barnsley	42	12	12	18	58	84	36
Fulham	42	11	12	19	46	77	34
Clapton Orient	42	12	9	21	50	65	33
Stoke City	42	12	8	22	54	77	32
Stockport County	42	8	9	25	51	97	25

DIVISION 3S 1925-26

Reading	42	23	11	8	77	52	57
Plymouth Argyle	42	24	8	10	107	67	56
Millwall	42	21	11	10	73	39	53
Bristol City	42	21	9	12	72	51	51
Brighton & Hove Albion	42	19	9	14	84	73	47
Swindon Town	42	20	6	16	69	64	46
Luton Town	42	18	7	17	80	75	43
Bournemouth & Boscombe Ath.	42	17	9	16	75	91	43
Aberdare Athletic	42	17	8	17	74	66	42
Gillingham	42	17	8	17	53	49	42
Southend United	42	19	4	19	78	73	42
Northampton Town	42	17	7	18	82	80	41
Crystal Palace	42	19	3	20	75	79	41
Merthyr Town	42	14	11	17	69	75	39
Watford	42	15	9	18	73	89	39
Norwich City	42	15	9	18	58	73	39
Newport County	42	14	10	18	64	74	38
Brentford	42	16	6	20	69	94	38
Bristol Rovers	42	15	6	21	66	69	36
Exeter City	42	15	5	22	72	70	35
Charlton Athletic	42	11	13	18	48	68	35
Queen's Park Rangers	42	6	9	27	37	84	21

1926 F.A. Cup

Semi-finals

Bolton Wanderers vs Swansea Town	3-0
Manchester City vs Manchester United	3-0

Final

Wembley, 24th April 1926

Bolton Wanderers 1 (Jack)

Manchester City 0

Attendance 91,447

DIVISION 1 1926-27

Newcastle United	42	25	6	11	96	58	56
Huddersfield Town	42	17	17	8	76	60	51
Sunderland	42	21	7	14	98	70	49
Bolton Wanderers	42	19	10	13	84	62	48
Burnley	42	19	9	14	91	80	47
West Ham United	42	19	8	15	86	70	46
Leicester City	42	17	12	13	85	70	46
Sheffield United	42	17	10	15	74	86	44
Liverpool	42	18	7	17	69	61	43
Aston Villa	42	18	7	17	81	83	43
The Arsenal	42	17	9	16	77	86	43
Derby County	42	17	7	18	86	73	41
Tottenham Hotspur	42	16	9	17	76	78	41
Cardiff City	42	16	9	17	55	65	41
Manchester United	42	13	14	15	52	64	40
The Wednesday	42	15	9	18	75	92	39
Birmingham	42	17	4	21	64	73	38
Blackburn Rovers	42	15	8	19	77	96	38
Bury	42	12	12	18	68	77	36
Everton	42	12	10	20	64	90	34
Leeds United	42	11	8	23	69	88	30
West Bromwich Albion	42	11	8	23	65	86	30

DIVISION 2 1926-27

Middlesbrough	42	27	8	7	122	60	62
Portsmouth	42	23	8	11	87	49	54
Manchester City	42	22	10	10	108	61	54
Chelsea	42	20	12	10	62	52	52
Nottingham Forest	42	18	14	10	80	55	50
Preston North End	42	20	9	13	74	72	49
Hull City	42	20	7	15	63	52	47
Port Vale	42	16	13	13	88	78	45
Blackpool	42	18	8	16	95	80	44
Oldham Athletic	42	19	6	17	74	84	44
Barnsley	42	17	9	16	88	87	43
Swansea Town	42	16	11	15	68	72	43
Southampton	42	15	12	15	60	62	42
Reading	42	16	8	18	64	72	40
Wolverhampton Wanderers	42	14	7	21	73	75	35
Notts County	42	15	5	22	70	96	35
Grimsby Town	42	11	12	19	74	91	34
Fulham	42	13	8	21	58	92	34
South Shields	42	11	11	20	71	96	33
Clapton Orient	42	12	7	23	60	96	31
Darlington	42	12	6	24	79	98	30
Bradford City	42	7	9	26	50	88	23

DIVISION 3N 1926-27

Stoke City	42	27	9	6	92	40	63
Rochdale	42	26	6	10	105	65	58
Bradford Park Avenue	42	24	7	11	101	59	55
Halifax Town	42	21	11	10	70	53	53
Nelson	42	22	7	13	104	75	51
Stockport County	42	22	7	13	93	69	49
Chesterfield	42	21	5	16	92	68	47
Doncaster Rovers	42	18	11	13	81	65	47
Tranmere Rovers	42	19	8	15	85	67	46
New Brighton	42	18	10	14	79	67	46
Lincoln City	42	15	12	15	90	78	42
Southport	42	15	9	18	80	85	39
Wrexham	42	14	10	18	65	73	38
Walsall	42	14	10	18	68	81	38
Crewe Alexandra	42	14	9	19	71	81	37
Ashington	42	12	12	18	60	90	36
Hartlepools United	42	14	6	22	66	81	34
Wigan Borough	42	11	10	21	66	83	32
Rotherham United	42	10	12	20	70	92	32
Durham City	42	12	6	24	58	105	30
Accrington Stanley	42	10	7	25	62	98	27
Barrow	42	7	8	27	34	117	22

Stockport County had two points deducted

DIVISION 3S 1926-27

Bristol City	42	27	8	7	104	54	62
Plymouth Argyle	42	25	10	7	95	61	60
Millwall	42	23	10	9	89	51	56
Brighton & Hove Albion	42	21	11	10	79	50	53
Swindon Town	42	21	9	12	100	85	51
Crystal Palace	42	18	9	15	84	81	45
Bournemouth & Boscombe Ath.	42	18	8	16	78	66	44
Luton Town	42	15	14	13	68	66	44
Newport County	42	19	6	17	57	71	44
Bristol Rovers	42	16	9	17	78	80	41
Brentford	42	13	14	15	70	61	40
Exeter City	42	15	10	17	76	73	40
Charlton Athletic	42	16	8	18	60	61	40
Queen's Park Rangers	42	15	9	18	65	71	39
Coventry City	42	15	7	20	71	86	37
Norwich City	42	12	11	19	59	71	35
Methyr Town	42	13	9	20	63	80	35
Northampton Town	42	15	5	22	59	87	35
Southend United	42	14	6	22	64	77	34
Gillingham	42	11	10	21	54	72	32
Watford	42	12	8	22	57	87	32
Aberdare Athletic	42	9	7	26	62	101	25

1927 F.A. Cup

Semi-finals

Cardiff City vs Reading	3-0
Arsenal vs Southampton	2-1

Final

Wembley, 23rd April 1927

Cardiff City 1   (Ferguson)

Arsenal 0

Attendance 91,206

DIVISION 1 1927-28

Everton	42	20	13	9	102	66	53
Huddersfield Town	42	22	7	13	91	68	51
Leicester City	42	18	12	12	96	72	48
Derby County	42	17	10	15	96	83	44
Bury	42	20	4	18	80	80	44
Cardiff City	42	17	10	15	70	80	44
Bolton Wanderers	42	16	11	15	81	66	43
Aston Villa	42	17	9	16	78	73	43
Newcastle United	42	15	13	14	79	81	43
Arsenal	42	13	15	14	82	86	41
Birmingham	42	13	15	14	70	75	41
Blackburn Rovers	42	16	9	17	66	78	41
Sheffield United	42	15	10	17	79	86	40
The Wednesday	42	13	13	16	81	78	39
Sunderland	42	15	9	18	74	76	39
Liverpool	42	13	13	16	84	87	39
West Ham United	42	14	11	17	81	88	39
Manchester United	42	16	7	19	72	80	39
Burnley	42	16	7	19	82	98	39
Portsmouth	42	16	7	19	66	90	39
Tottenham Hotspur	42	15	8	19	74	86	38
Middlesbrough	42	11	15	16	81	88	37

DIVISION 3N 1927-28

Bradford Park Avenue	42	27	9	6	101	45	63
Lincoln City	42	24	7	11	91	64	55
Stockport County	42	23	8	11	89	51	54
Doncaster Rovers	42	23	7	12	80	44	53
Tranmere Rovers	42	22	9	11	105	72	53
Bradford City	42	18	12	12	85	60	48
Darlington	42	21	5	16	89	74	47
Southport	42	20	5	17	79	70	45
Accrington Stanley	42	18	8	16	76	67	44
New Brighton	42	14	14	14	72	62	42
Wrexham	42	18	6	18	64	67	42
Halifax Town	42	13	15	14	73	71	41
Rochdale	42	17	7	18	74	77	41
Rotherham United	42	14	11	17	65	69	39
Hartlepools United	42	16	6	20	69	81	38
Chesterfield	42	13	10	19	71	78	36
Crewe Alexandra	42	12	10	20	77	86	34
Ashington	42	11	11	20	77	103	33
Barrow	42	10	11	21	54	102	31
Wigan Borough	42	10	10	22	56	97	30
Durham City	42	11	7	24	53	100	29
Nelson	42	10	6	26	76	136	26

DIVISION 2 1927-28

Manchester City	42	25	9	8	100	59	59
Leeds United	42	25	7	10	98	49	57
Chelsea	42	23	8	11	75	45	54
Preston North End	42	22	9	11	100	66	53
Stoke City	42	22	8	12	78	59	52
Swansea Town	42	18	12	12	75	63	48
Oldham Athletic	42	19	8	15	75	51	46
West Bromwich Albion	42	17	12	13	90	70	46
Port Vale	42	18	8	16	68	57	44
Nottingham Forest	42	15	10	17	83	84	40
Grimsby Town	42	14	12	16	69	83	40
Bristol City	42	15	9	18	76	79	39
Barnsley	42	14	11	17	65	85	39
Hull City	42	12	15	15	41	54	39
Notts County	42	13	12	17	68	74	38
Wolverhampton Wanderers	42	13	10	19	63	91	36
Southampton	42	14	7	21	68	77	35
Reading	42	11	13	18	53	75	35
Blackpool	42	13	8	21	83	101	34
Clapton Orient	42	11	12	19	55	85	34
Fulham	42	13	7	22	68	89	33
South Shields	42	7	9	26	56	111	23

DIVISION 3S 1927-28

Millwall	42	30	5	7	127	50	65
Northampton Town	42	23	9	10	102	64	55
Plymouth Argyle	42	23	7	12	85	54	53
Brighton & Hove Albion	42	19	10	13	81	69	48
Crystal Palace	42	18	12	12	79	72	48
Swindon Town	42	19	9	14	90	69	47
Southend United	42	20	6	16	80	64	46
Exeter City	42	17	12	13	70	60	46
Newport County	42	18	9	15	81	84	45
Queen's Park Rangers	42	17	9	16	72	71	43
Charlton Athletic	42	15	13	14	60	70	43
Brentford	42	16	8	18	76	74	40
Luton Town	42	16	7	19	94	87	39
Bournemouth & Boscombe Ath.	42	13	12	17	72	79	38
Watford	42	14	10	18	68	78	38
Gillingham	42	13	11	18	62	81	37
Norwich City	42	10	16	16	66	70	36
Walsall	42	12	9	21	75	101	33
Bristol Rovers	42	14	4	24	67	93	32
Coventry City	42	11	9	22	67	96	31
Merthyr Town	42	9	13	20	53	91	31
Torquay United	42	8	14	20	53	103	30

1928 F.A. Cup

Semi-finals

Blackburn Rovers vs Arsenal	1-0
Huddersfield Town	2-2, 0-0, 1-0

Final

Wembley, 21st April 1928

Blackburn Rovers 3 (Roscamp 2, McLean)
Huddersfield Town 1 (Jackson)

Attendance 92,041

DIVISION 1 1928-29

The Wednesday	42	21	10	11	86	62	52
Leicester City	42	21	9	12	96	67	51
Aston Villa	42	23	4	15	98	81	50
Sunderland	42	20	7	15	93	75	47
Liverpool	42	17	12	13	90	64	46
Derby County	42	18	10	14	86	71	46
Blackburn Rovers	42	17	11	14	72	63	45
Manchester City	42	18	9	15	95	86	45
Arsenal	42	16	13	13	77	72	45
Newcastle United	42	19	6	17	70	72	44
Sheffield United	42	15	11	16	86	85	41
Manchester United	42	14	13	15	66	76	41
Leeds United	42	16	9	17	71	84	41
Bolton Wanderers	42	14	12	16	73	80	40
Birmingham	42	15	10	17	68	77	40
Huddersfield Town	42	14	11	17	70	61	39
West Ham United	42	15	9	18	86	96	39
Everton	42	17	4	21	63	75	38
Burnley	42	15	8	19	81	103	38
Portsmouth	42	15	6	21	56	80	36
Bury	42	12	7	23	62	99	31
Cardiff City	42	8	13	21	43	59	29

DIVISION 3N 1928-29

Bradford City	42	27	9	6	128	43	63
Stockport County	42	28	6	8	111	58	62
Wrexham	42	21	10	11	91	69	52
Wigan Borough	42	21	9	12	82	49	51
Doncaster Rovers	42	20	10	12	76	66	50
Lincoln City	42	21	6	15	91	67	48
Tranmere Rovers	42	22	3	17	79	77	47
Carlisle United	42	19	8	15	86	77	46
Crewe Alexandra	42	18	8	16	80	68	44
South Shields	42	18	8	16	83	74	44
Chesterfield	42	18	5	19	71	77	41
Southport	42	16	8	18	75	85	40
Halifax Town	42	13	13	16	63	62	39
New Brighton	42	15	9	18	64	71	39
Nelson	42	17	5	20	77	90	39
Rotherham United	42	15	9	18	60	77	39
Rochdale	42	13	10	19	79	96	36
Accrington Stanley	42	13	8	21	68	82	34
Darlington	42	13	7	22	64	88	33
Barrow	42	10	8	24	64	93	28
Hartlepools United	42	10	6	26	59	112	26
Ashington	42	8	7	27	45	115	23

DIVISION 2 1928-29

Middlesbrough	42	22	11	9	92	57	55
Grimsby Town	42	24	5	13	82	61	53
Bradford Park Avenue	42	22	4	16	88	70	48
Southampton	42	17	14	11	74	60	48
Notts County	42	19	9	14	78	65	47
Stoke City	42	17	12	13	74	51	46
West Bromwich Albion	42	19	8	15	80	79	46
Blackpool	42	19	7	16	92	76	45
Chelsea	42	17	10	15	64	65	44
Tottenham Hotspur	42	17	9	16	75	81	43
Nottingham Forest	42	15	12	15	71	70	42
Hull City	42	13	14	15	58	63	40
Preston North End	42	15	9	18	78	79	39
Millwall	42	16	7	19	71	86	39
Reading	42	15	9	18	63	86	39
Barnsley	42	16	6	20	69	66	38
Wolverhampton Wanderers	42	15	7	20	77	81	37
Oldham Athletic	42	16	5	21	54	75	37
Swansea Town	42	13	10	19	62	75	36
Bristol City	42	13	10	19	58	72	36
Port Vale	42	15	4	23	71	86	34
Clapton Orient	42	12	8	22	45	72	32

DIVISION 3S 1928-29

Charlton Athletic	42	23	8	11	86	60	54
Crystal Palace	42	23	8	11	81	67	54
Northampton Town	42	20	12	10	96	57	52
Plymouth Argyle	42	20	12	10	83	51	52
Fulham	42	21	10	11	101	71	52
Queen's Park Rangers	42	19	14	9	82	61	52
Luton Town	42	19	11	12	89	73	49
Watford	42	19	10	13	79	74	48
Bournemouth & Boscombe Ath.	42	19	9	14	84	77	47
Swindon Town	42	15	13	14	75	72	43
Coventry City	42	14	14	14	62	57	42
Southend United	42	15	11	16	80	75	41
Brentford	42	14	10	18	56	60	38
Walsall	42	13	12	17	73	79	38
Brighton & Hove Albion	42	16	6	20	58	76	38
Newport County	42	13	9	20	69	86	35
Norwich City	42	14	6	22	69	81	34
Torquay United	42	14	6	22	66	84	34
Bristol Rovers	42	13	7	22	60	79	33
Merthyr Town	42	11	8	23	55	103	30
Exeter City	42	9	11	22	67	88	29
Gillingham	42	10	9	23	43	83	29

1929 F.A. Cup

Semi-finals

Bolton Wanderers vs Huddersfield Town	3-1
Portsmouth vs Aston Villa	1-0

Final

Wembley, 27th April 1929

Bolton Wanderers 2 (Butler, Blackmore)

Portsmouth 0

Attendance 92,576

DIVISION 1 1929-30

Sheffield Wednesday	42	26	8	8	105	57	60
Derby County	42	21	8	13	90	82	50
Manchester City	42	19	9	14	91	81	47
Aston Villa	42	21	5	16	92	83	47
Leeds United	42	20	6	16	79	63	46
Blackburn Rovers	42	19	7	16	99	93	45
West Ham United	42	19	5	18	86	79	43
Leicester City	42	17	9	16	86	90	43
Sunderland	42	18	7	17	76	80	43
Huddersfield Town	42	17	9	16	63	69	43
Birmingham	42	16	9	17	67	62	41
Liverpool	42	16	9	17	63	79	41
Portsmouth	42	15	10	17	66	62	40
Arsenal	42	14	11	17	78	66	39
Bolton Wanderers	42	15	9	18	74	74	39
Middlesbrough	42	16	6	20	82	84	38
Manchester United	42	15	8	19	67	88	38
Grimsby Town	42	15	7	20	73	89	37
Newcastle United	42	15	7	20	71	92	37
Sheffield United	42	15	6	21	91	96	36
Burnley	42	14	8	20	79	97	36
Everton	42	12	11	19	80	92	35

DIVISION 3N 1929-30

Port Vale	42	30	7	5	103	37	67
Stockport County	42	28	7	7	106	44	63
Darlington	42	22	6	14	108	73	50
Chesterfield	42	22	6	14	76	56	50
Lincoln City	42	17	14	11	83	61	48
York City	42	15	16	11	77	64	46
South Shields	42	18	10	14	77	74	46
Hartlepools United	42	17	11	14	81	74	45
Southport	42	15	13	14	81	74	43
Rochdale	42	18	7	17	89	91	43
Crewe Alexandra	42	17	8	17	82	71	42
Tranmere Rovers	42	16	9	17	83	86	41
New Brighton	42	16	8	18	69	79	40
Doncaster Rovers	42	15	9	18	62	69	39
Carlisle United	42	16	7	19	90	101	39
Accrington Stanley	42	14	9	19	84	81	37
Wrexham	42	13	8	21	67	88	34
Wigan Borough	42	13	7	22	60	88	33
Nelson	42	13	7	22	51	80	33
Rotherham United	42	11	8	23	67	113	30
Halifax Town	42	10	8	24	44	79	28
Barrow	42	11	5	26	41	98	27

DIVISION 2 1929-30

Blackpool	42	27	4	11	98	67	58
Chelsea	42	22	11	9	74	46	55
Oldham Athletic	42	21	11	10	90	51	53
Bradford Park Avenue	42	19	12	11	91	70	50
Bury	42	22	5	15	78	67	49
West Bromwich Albion	42	21	5	16	105	73	47
Southampton	42	17	11	14	77	76	45
Cardiff City	42	18	8	16	61	59	44
Wolverhampton Wanderers	42	16	9	17	77	79	41
Nottingham Forest	42	13	15	14	55	69	41
Stoke City	42	16	8	18	74	72	40
Tottenham Hotspur	42	15	9	18	59	61	39
Charlton Athletic	42	14	11	17	59	63	39
Millwall	42	12	15	15	57	73	39
Swansea Town	42	14	9	19	57	61	37
Preston North End	42	13	11	18	65	80	37
Barnsley	42	14	8	20	56	71	36
Bradford City	42	12	12	18	60	77	36
Reading	42	12	11	19	54	67	35
Bristol City	42	13	9	20	61	83	35
Hull City	42	14	7	21	51	78	35
Notts County	42	9	15	18	54	70	33

DIVISION 3S 1929-30

Plymouth Argyle	42	30	8	4	98	38	68
Brentford	42	28	5	9	94	44	61
Queen's Park Rangers	42	21	9	12	80	68	51
Northampton Town	42	21	8	13	82	58	50
Brighton & Hove Albion	42	21	8	13	87	63	50
Coventry City	42	19	9	14	88	73	47
Fulham	42	18	11	13	87	83	47
Norwich City	42	18	10	14	88	77	46
Crystal Palace	42	17	12	13	81	74	46
Bournemouth & Boscombe Ath.	42	15	13	14	72	61	43
Southend United	42	15	13	14	69	59	43
Clapton Orient	42	14	13	15	55	62	41
Luton Town	42	14	12	16	64	78	40
Swindon Town	42	13	12	17	73	83	38
Watford	42	15	8	19	60	73	38
Exeter City	42	12	11	19	67	73	35
Walsall	42	13	8	21	71	78	34
Newport County	42	12	10	20	74	85	34
Torquay United	42	10	11	21	64	94	31
Bristol Rovers	42	11	8	23	67	93	30
Gillingham	42	11	8	23	51	80	30
Merthyr Town	42	6	9	27	60	135	21

1930 F.A. Cup

Semi-finals

Arsenal vs Hull City	2-2, 1-0
Huddersfield Town vs Sheffield Wednesday	2-1

Final

Wembley, 26th April 1930

Arsenal 2   (James, Lambert)
Huddersfield Town 0

Attendance 92,448

DIVISION 1 1930-31

Arsenal	42	28	10	4	127	59	66
Aston Villa	42	25	9	8	128	78	59
Sheffield Wednesday	42	22	8	12	102	75	52
Portsmouth	42	18	13	11	84	67	49
Huddersfield Town	42	18	12	12	81	65	48
Derby County	42	18	10	14	94	79	46
Middlesbrough	42	19	8	15	98	90	46
Manchester City	42	18	10	14	75	70	46
Liverpool	42	15	12	15	86	85	42
Blackburn Rovers	42	17	8	17	83	84	42
Sunderland	42	16	9	17	89	85	41
Chelsea	42	15	10	17	64	67	40
Grimsby Town	42	17	5	20	82	87	39
Bolton Wanderers	42	15	9	18	68	81	39
Sheffield United	42	14	10	18	78	84	38
Leicester City	42	16	6	20	80	95	38
Newcastle United	42	15	6	21	78	87	36
West Ham United	42	14	8	20	79	94	36
Birmingham	42	13	10	19	55	70	36
Blackpool	42	11	10	21	71	125	32
Leeds United	42	12	7	23	68	81	31
Manchester United	42	7	8	27	53	115	22

DIVISION 2 1930-31

Everton	42	28	5	9	121	66	61
West Bromwich Albion	42	22	10	10	83	49	54
Tottenham Hotspur	42	22	7	13	88	55	51
Wolverhampton Wanderers	42	21	5	16	84	67	47
Port Vale	42	21	5	16	67	61	47
Bradford Park Avenue	42	18	10	14	97	66	46
Preston North End	42	17	11	14	83	64	45
Burnley	42	17	11	14	81	77	45
Southampton	42	19	6	17	74	62	44
Bradford City	42	17	10	15	61	63	44
Stoke City	42	17	10	15	64	71	44
Oldham Athletic	42	16	10	16	61	72	42
Bury	42	19	3	20	75	82	41
Millwall	42	16	7	19	71	80	39
Charlton Athletic	42	15	9	18	59	86	39
Bristol City	42	15	8	19	54	82	38
Nottingham Forest	42	14	9	19	80	85	37
Plymouth Argyle	42	14	8	20	76	84	36
Barnsley	42	13	9	20	59	79	35
Swansea Town	42	12	10	20	51	74	34
Reading	42	12	6	24	72	96	30
Cardiff City	42	8	9	25	47	87	25

DIVISION 3N 1930-31

Chesterfield	42	26	6	10	102	57	58
Lincoln City	42	25	7	10	102	59	57
Wrexham	42	21	12	9	94	62	54
Tranmere Rovers	42	24	6	12	111	74	54
Southport	42	22	9	11	88	56	53
Hull City	42	20	10	12	99	55	50
Stockport County	42	20	9	13	77	61	49
Carlisle United	42	20	5	17	98	81	45
Gateshead	42	16	13	13	71	73	45
Wigan Borough	42	19	5	18	76	86	43
Darlington	42	16	10	16	71	59	42
York City	42	18	6	18	85	82	42
Accrington Stanley	42	15	9	18	84	108	39
Rotherham United	42	13	12	17	81	83	38
Doncaster Rovers	42	13	11	18	65	65	37
Barrow	42	15	7	20	68	89	37
Halifax Town	42	13	9	20	55	89	35
Crewe Alexandra	42	14	6	22	66	93	34
New Brighton	42	13	7	22	49	76	33
Hartlepools United	42	12	6	24	67	86	30
Rochdale	42	12	6	24	62	107	30
Nelson	42	6	7	29	43	113	19

DIVISION 3S 1930-31

Notts County	42	24	11	7	97	46	59
Crystal Palace	42	22	7	13	107	71	51
Brentford	42	22	6	14	90	64	50
Brighton & Hove Albion	42	17	15	10	68	53	49
Southend United	42	22	5	15	76	60	49
Northampton Town	42	18	12	12	77	59	48
Luton Town	42	19	8	15	76	51	46
Queen's Park Rangers	42	20	3	19	82	75	43
Fulham	42	18	7	17	77	75	43
Bournemouth & Boscombe Ath.	42	15	13	14	72	73	43
Torquay United	42	17	9	16	80	84	43
Swindon Town	42	18	6	18	89	94	42
Exeter City	42	17	8	17	84	90	42
Coventry City	42	16	9	17	75	65	41
Bristol Rovers	42	16	8	18	75	92	40
Gillingham	42	14	10	18	61	76	38
Walsall	42	14	9	19	78	95	37
Watford	42	14	7	21	72	75	35
Clapton Orient	42	14	7	21	63	91	35
Thames Association	42	13	8	21	54	93	34
Newport County	42	11	6	25	69	111	28
Norwich City	42	10	8	24	47	76	28

1931 F.A. Cup

Semi-finals

Everton vs West Bromwich Albion	0-1
Birmingham vs Sunderland	2-0

Final

Wembley, 25th April 1931

West Bromwich Albion 2 (W.G. Richardson 2)

Birmingham 1 (Bradford)

Attendance 92,406

DIVISION 1 1931-32

Everton	42	26	4	12	116	64	56
Arsenal	42	22	10	10	90	48	54
Sheffield Wednesday	42	22	6	14	96	82	50
Huddersfield Town	42	19	10	13	80	63	48
Aston Villa	42	19	8	15	104	72	46
West Bromwich Albion	42	20	6	16	77	55	46
Sheffield United	42	20	6	16	80	75	46
Portsmouth	42	19	7	16	62	62	45
Birmingham	42	18	8	16	78	67	44
Liverpool	42	19	6	17	81	93	44
Newcastle United	42	18	6	18	80	87	42
Chelsea	42	16	8	18	69	73	40
Sunderland	42	15	10	17	67	73	40
Manchester City	42	13	12	17	83	73	38
Derby County	42	14	10	18	71	75	38
Blackburn Rovers	42	16	6	20	89	95	38
Bolton Wanderers	42	17	4	21	72	80	38
Middlesbrough	42	15	8	19	64	89	38
Leicester City	42	15	7	20	74	94	37
Blackpool	42	12	9	21	65	102	33
Grimsby Town	42	13	6	23	67	98	32
West Ham United	42	12	7	23	62	107	31

DIVISION 2 1931-32

Wolverhampton Wanderers	42	24	8	10	115	49	56
Leeds United	42	22	10	10	78	54	54
Stoke City	42	19	14	9	69	48	52
Plymouth Argyle	42	20	9	13	100	66	49
Bury	42	21	7	14	70	58	49
Bradford Park Avenue	42	21	7	14	72	63	49
Bradford City	42	16	13	13	80	61	45
Tottenham Hotspur	42	16	11	15	87	78	43
Millwall	42	17	9	16	61	61	43
Charlton Athletic	42	17	9	16	61	66	43
Nottingham Forest	42	16	10	16	77	72	42
Manchester United	42	17	8	17	71	72	42
Preston North End	42	16	10	16	75	77	42
Southampton	42	17	7	18	66	77	41
Swansea Town	42	16	7	19	73	75	39
Notts County	42	13	12	17	75	75	38
Chesterfield	42	13	11	18	64	86	37
Oldham Athletic	42	13	10	19	62	84	36
Burnley	42	13	9	20	59	87	35
Port Vale	42	13	7	22	58	89	33
Barnsley	42	12	9	21	55	91	33
Bristol City	42	6	11	25	39	78	23

DIVISION 3N 1931-32

Lincoln City	40	26	5	9	106	47	57
Gateshead	40	25	7	8	94	48	57
Chester	40	21	8	11	78	60	50
Tranmere Rovers	40	19	11	10	107	58	49
Barrow	40	24	1	15	86	59	49
Crewe Alexandra	40	21	6	13	95	66	48
Southport	40	18	10	12	58	53	46
Hull City	40	20	5	15	82	53	45
York City	40	18	7	15	76	81	43
Wrexham	40	18	7	15	64	69	43
Darlington	40	17	4	19	66	69	38
Stockport County	40	13	11	16	55	53	37
Hartlepools United	40	16	5	19	78	100	37
Accrington Stanley	40	15	6	19	75	80	36
Doncaster Rovers	40	16	4	20	59	80	36
Walsall	40	16	3	21	57	85	35
Halifax Town	40	13	8	19	61	87	34
Carlisle United	40	11	11	18	64	79	33
Rotherham United	40	14	4	22	63	72	32
New Brighton	40	8	8	24	38	76	24
Rochdale	40	4	3	33	48	135	11

Wigan Borough resigned from the League during the season and their record was expunged

DIVISION 3S 1931-32

Fulham	42	24	9	9	111	62	57
Reading	42	23	9	10	97	67	55
Southend United	42	21	11	10	77	53	53
Crystal Palace	42	20	11	11	74	63	51
Brentford	42	19	10	13	68	52	48
Luton Town	42	20	7	15	95	70	47
Exeter City	42	20	7	15	77	62	47
Brighton & Hove Albion	42	17	12	13	73	58	46
Cardiff City	42	19	8	15	87	73	46
Norwich City	42	17	12	13	76	67	46
Watford	42	19	8	15	81	79	46
Coventry City	42	18	8	16	108	97	44
Queen's Park Rangers	42	15	12	15	79	73	42
Northampton Town	42	16	7	19	69	69	39
Bournemouth & Boscombe Ath.	42	13	12	17	70	78	38
Clapton Orient	42	12	11	19	77	90	35
Swindon Town	42	14	6	22	70	84	34
Bristol Rovers	42	13	8	21	65	92	34
Torquay United	42	12	9	21	72	106	33
Mansfield Town	42	11	10	21	75	108	32
Gillingham	42	10	8	24	40	82	28
Thames Association	42	7	9	26	53	109	23

1932 F.A. Cup

Semi-finals

Chelsea vs Newcastle United	1-2
Arsenal vs Manchester City	1-0

Final

Wembley, 23rd April 1932

Newcastle United 2 (Allen 2)

Arsenal 1 (John)

Attendance 92,298

DIVISION 1 1932-33

Arsenal	42	25	8	9	118	61	58
Aston Villa	42	23	8	11	92	67	54
Sheffield Wednesday	42	21	9	12	80	68	51
West Bromwich Albion	42	20	9	13	83	70	49
Newcastle United	42	22	5	15	71	63	49
Huddersfield Town	42	18	11	13	66	53	47
Derby County	42	15	14	13	76	69	44
Leeds United	42	15	14	13	59	62	44
Portsmouth	42	18	7	17	74	76	43
Sheffield United	42	17	9	16	74	80	43
Everton	42	16	9	17	81	74	41
Sunderland	42	15	10	17	63	80	40
Birmingham	42	14	11	17	57	57	39
Liverpool	42	14	11	17	79	84	39
Blackburn Rovers	42	14	10	18	76	102	38
Manchester City	42	16	5	21	68	71	37
Middlesbrough	42	14	9	19	63	73	37
Chelsea	42	14	7	21	63	73	35
Leicester City	42	11	13	18	75	89	35
Wolverhampton Wanderers	42	13	9	20	80	96	35
Bolton Wanderers	42	12	9	21	78	92	33
Blackpool	42	14	5	23	69	85	33

DIVISION 2 1932-33

Stoke City	42	25	6	11	78	39	56
Tottenham Hotspur	42	20	15	7	96	51	55
Fulham	42	20	10	12	78	65	50
Bury	42	20	9	13	84	59	49
Nottingham Forest	42	17	15	10	67	59	49
Manchester United	42	15	13	14	71	68	43
Millwall	42	16	11	15	59	57	43
Bradford Park Avenue	42	17	8	17	77	71	42
Preston North End	42	16	10	16	74	70	42
Swansea Town	42	19	4	19	50	54	42
Bradford City	42	14	13	15	65	61	41
Southampton	42	18	5	19	66	66	41
Grimsby Town	42	14	13	15	79	84	41
Plymouth Argyle	42	16	9	17	63	67	41
Notts County	42	15	10	17	67	78	40
Oldham Athletic	42	15	8	19	67	80	38
Port Vale	42	14	10	18	66	79	38
Lincoln City	42	12	13	17	72	87	37
Burnley	42	11	14	17	67	79	36
West Ham United	42	13	9	20	75	93	35
Chesterfield	42	12	10	20	61	84	34
Charlton Athletic	42	12	7	23	60	91	31

DIVISION 3N 1932-33

Hull City	42	26	7	9	100	45	59
Wrexham	42	24	9	9	106	51	57
Stockport County	42	21	12	9	99	58	54
Chester	42	22	8	12	94	66	52
Walsall	42	19	10	13	75	58	48
Doncaster Rovers	42	17	14	11	77	79	48
Gateshead	42	19	9	14	78	67	47
Barnsley	42	19	8	15	92	80	46
Barrow	42	18	7	17	60	60	43
Crewe Alexandra	42	20	3	19	80	84	43
Tranmere Rovers	42	17	8	17	70	66	42
Southport	42	17	7	18	70	67	41
Accrington Stanley	42	15	10	17	78	76	40
Hartlepools United	42	16	7	19	87	116	39
Halifax Town	42	15	8	19	71	90	38
Mansfield Town	42	14	7	21	84	100	35
Rotherham United	42	14	6	22	60	84	34
Rochdale	42	13	7	22	58	80	33
Carlisle United	42	13	7	22	51	75	33
York City	42	13	6	23	72	92	32
New Brighton	42	11	10	21	63	88	32
Darlington	42	10	8	24	66	109	28

DIVISION 3S 1932-33

Brentford	42	26	10	6	90	49	62
Exeter City	42	24	10	8	88	48	58
Norwich City	42	22	13	7	88	55	57
Reading	42	19	13	10	103	71	51
Crystal Palace	42	19	8	15	78	64	46
Coventry City	42	19	6	17	106	77	44
Gillingham	42	18	8	16	72	61	44
Northampton Town	42	18	8	16	76	66	44
Bristol Rovers	42	15	14	13	61	56	44
Torquay United	42	16	12	14	72	67	44
Watford	42	16	12	14	66	63	44
Brighton & Hove Albion	42	17	8	17	66	65	42
Southend United	42	15	11	16	65	82	41
Luton Town	42	13	13	16	78	78	39
Bristol City	42	12	13	17	83	90	37
Queen's Park Rangers	42	13	11	18	72	87	37
Aldershot	42	13	10	19	61	72	36
Bournemouth & Boscombe Ath.	42	12	12	18	60	81	36
Cardiff City	42	12	7	23	69	99	31
Clapton Orient	42	8	13	21	59	93	29
Newport County	42	11	7	24	61	105	29
Swindon Town	42	9	11	22	60	105	29

1933 F.A. Cup

Semi-finals

Everton vs West Ham United	2-1
Manchester City vs Derby County	3-2

Final

Wembley, 29th April 1933

Everton 3 (Stein, Dean, Dunn)

Manchester City 0

Attendance 92,950

DIVISION 1 1933-34

Arsenal	42	25	9	8	75	47	59
Huddersfield Town	42	23	10	9	90	61	56
Tottenham Hotspur	42	21	7	14	79	56	49
Derby County	42	17	11	14	68	54	45
Manchester City	42	17	11	14	65	72	45
Sunderland	42	16	12	14	81	56	44
West Bromwich Albion	42	17	10	15	78	70	44
Blackburn Rovers	42	18	7	17	74	81	43
Leeds United	42	17	8	17	75	66	42
Portsmouth	42	15	12	15	52	55	42
Sheffield Wednesday	42	16	9	17	62	67	41
Stoke City	42	15	11	16	58	71	41
Aston Villa	42	14	12	16	78	75	40
Everton	42	12	16	14	62	63	40
Wolverhampton Wanderers	42	14	12	16	74	86	40
Middlesbrough	42	16	7	19	68	80	39
Leicester City	42	14	11	17	59	74	39
Liverpool	42	14	10	18	79	87	38
Chelsea	42	14	8	20	67	69	36
Birmingham	42	12	12	18	54	56	36
Newcastle United	42	10	14	18	68	77	34
Sheffield United	42	12	7	23	58	101	31

DIVISION 2 1933-34

Grimsby Town	42	27	5	10	103	59	59
Preston North End	42	23	6	13	71	52	52
Bolton Wanderers	42	21	9	12	79	55	51
Brentford	42	22	7	13	85	60	51
Bradford Park Avenue	42	23	3	16	86	67	49
Bradford City	42	20	6	16	73	67	46
West Ham United	42	17	11	14	78	70	45
Port Vale	42	19	7	16	60	55	45
Oldham Athletic	42	17	10	15	72	60	44
Plymouth Argyle	42	15	13	14	69	70	43
Blackpool	42	15	13	14	62	64	43
Bury	42	17	9	16	70	73	43
Burnley	42	18	6	18	60	72	42
Southampton	42	15	8	19	54	58	38
Hull City	42	13	12	17	52	68	38
Fulham	42	15	7	20	48	67	37
Nottingham Forest	42	13	9	20	73	74	35
Notts County	42	12	11	19	53	62	35
Swansea Town	42	10	15	17	51	60	35
Manchester United	42	14	6	22	59	85	34
Millwall	42	11	11	20	39	68	33
Lincoln City	42	9	8	25	44	75	26

DIVISION 3N 1933-34

Barnsley	42	27	8	7	118	61	62
Chesterfield	42	27	7	8	86	43	61
Stockport County	42	24	11	7	115	52	59
Walsall	42	23	7	12	97	60	53
Doncaster Rovers	42	22	9	11	83	61	53
Wrexham	42	23	5	14	102	73	51
Tranmere Rovers	42	20	7	15	84	63	47
Barrow	42	19	9	14	116	94	47
Halifax Town	42	20	4	18	80	91	44
Chester	42	17	6	19	89	86	40
Hartlepools United	42	16	7	19	89	93	39
York City	42	15	8	19	71	74	38
Carlisle United	42	15	8	19	66	81	38
Crewe Alexandra	42	15	6	21	81	97	36
New Brighton	42	14	8	20	62	87	36
Darlington	42	13	9	20	70	101	35
Mansfield Town	42	11	12	19	81	88	34
Southport	42	8	17	17	63	90	33
Gateshead	42	12	9	21	76	110	33
Accrington Stanley	42	13	7	22	65	101	33
Rotherham United	42	10	8	24	53	91	28
Rochdale	42	9	6	27	53	103	24

DIVISION 3S 1933-34

Norwich City	42	25	11	6	88	49	61
Coventry City	42	21	12	9	100	54	54
Reading	42	21	12	9	82	50	54
Queen's Park Rangers	42	24	6	12	70	51	54
Charlton Athletic	42	22	8	12	83	56	52
Luton Town	42	21	10	11	83	61	52
Bristol Rovers	42	20	11	11	77	47	51
Swindon Town	42	17	11	14	64	68	45
Exeter City	42	16	11	15	68	57	43
Brighton & Hove Albion	42	15	13	14	68	60	43
Clapton	42	16	10	16	75	69	42
Crystal Palace	42	16	9	17	71	67	41
Northampton Town	42	14	12	16	71	78	40
Aldershot	42	13	12	17	52	71	38
Watford	42	15	7	20	71	63	37
Southend United	42	12	10	20	51	74	34
Gillingham	42	11	11	20	75	96	33
Newport County	42	8	17	17	49	70	33
Bristol City	42	10	13	19	58	85	33
Torquay United	42	13	7	22	53	93	33
Bournemouth & Boscombe Ath.	42	9	9	24	60	102	27
Cardiff City	42	9	6	27	57	105	24

1934 F.A. Cup

Semi-finals

Manchester City vs Aston Villa	6-1
Portsmouth vs Leicester City	4-1

Final

Wembley, 28th April 1934

Manchester City 2 (Tilson 2)

Portsmouth 1 (Rutherford)

Attendance 93,258

DIVISION 1 1934-35

Arsenal	42	23	12	7	115	46	58
Sunderland	42	19	16	7	90	51	54
Sheffield Wednesday	42	18	13	11	70	64	49
Manchester City	42	20	8	14	82	67	48
Grimsby Town	42	17	11	14	78	60	45
Derby County	42	18	9	15	81	66	45
Liverpool	42	19	7	16	85	88	45
Everton	42	16	12	14	89	88	44
West Bromwich Albion	42	17	10	15	83	83	44
Stoke City	42	18	6	18	71	70	42
Preston North End	42	15	12	15	62	67	42
Chelsea	42	16	9	17	73	82	41
Aston Villa	42	14	13	15	74	88	41
Portsmouth	42	15	10	17	71	72	40
Blackburn Rovers	42	14	11	17	66	78	39
Huddersfield Town	42	14	10	18	76	71	38
Wolverhampton Wanderers	42	15	8	19	88	94	38
Leeds United	42	13	12	17	75	92	38
Birmingham	42	13	10	19	63	81	36
Middlesbrough	42	10	14	18	70	90	34
Leicester City	42	12	9	21	61	86	33
Tottenham Hotspur	42	10	10	22	54	93	30

DIVISION 3N 1934-35

Doncaster Rovers	42	26	5	11	87	44	57
Halifax Town	42	25	5	12	76	67	55
Chester	42	20	14	8	91	58	54
Lincoln City	42	22	7	13	87	58	51
Darlington	42	21	9	12	80	59	51
Tranmere Rovers	42	20	11	11	74	55	51
Stockport County	42	22	3	17	90	72	47
Mansfield Town	42	19	9	14	75	62	47
Rotherham United	42	19	7	16	86	73	45
Chesterfield	42	17	10	15	71	52	44
Wrexham	42	16	11	15	76	69	43
Hartlepools United	42	17	7	18	80	78	41
Crewe Alexandra	42	14	11	17	66	86	39
Walsall	42	13	10	19	81	72	36
York City	42	15	6	21	76	82	36
New Brighton	42	14	8	20	59	76	36
Barrow	42	13	9	20	58	87	35
Accrington Stanley	42	12	10	20	63	89	34
Gateshead	42	13	8	21	58	96	34
Rochdale	42	11	11	20	53	71	33
Southport	42	10	12	20	55	85	32
Carlisle United	42	8	7	27	51	102	23

DIVISION 2 1934-35

Brentford	42	26	9	7	93	48	61
Bolton Wanderers	42	26	4	12	96	48	56
West Ham United	42	26	4	12	80	63	56
Blackpool	42	21	11	10	79	57	53
Manchester United	42	23	4	15	76	55	50
Newcastle United	42	22	4	16	89	68	48
Fulham	42	17	12	13	76	56	46
Plymouth Argyle	42	19	8	15	75	64	46
Nottingham Forest	42	17	8	17	76	70	42
Bury	42	19	4	19	62	73	42
Sheffield United	42	16	9	17	79	70	41
Burnley	42	16	9	17	63	73	41
Hull City	42	16	8	18	63	74	40
Norwich City	42	14	11	17	71	61	39
Bradford Park Avenue	42	11	16	15	55	63	38
Barnsley	42	13	12	17	60	83	38
Swansea Town	42	14	8	20	56	67	36
Port Vale	42	11	12	19	55	74	34
Southampton	42	11	12	19	46	75	34
Bradford City	42	12	8	22	50	68	32
Oldham Athletic	42	10	6	26	56	95	26
Notts County	42	9	7	26	46	97	25

DIVISION 3S 1934-35

Charlton Athletic	42	27	7	8	103	52	61
Reading	42	21	11	10	89	65	53
Coventry City	42	21	9	12	86	50	51
Luton Town	42	19	12	11	92	60	50
Crystal Palace	42	19	10	13	86	64	48
Watford	42	19	9	14	76	49	47
Northampton Town	42	19	8	15	65	67	46
Bristol Rovers	42	17	10	15	73	77	44
Brighton & Hove Albion	42	17	9	16	69	62	43
Torquay United	42	18	6	18	81	75	42
Exeter City	42	16	9	17	70	75	41
Millwall	42	17	7	18	57	62	41
Queen's Park Rangers	42	16	9	17	63	72	41
Clapton Orient	42	15	10	17	65	65	40
Bristol City	42	15	9	18	52	68	39
Swindon Town	42	13	12	17	67	78	38
Bournemouth & Boscombe Ath.	42	15	7	20	54	71	37
Aldershot	42	13	10	19	50	75	36
Cardiff City	42	13	9	20	62	82	35
Gillingham	42	11	13	18	55	75	35
Southend United	42	11	9	22	65	78	31
Newport County	42	10	5	27	54	112	25

1935 F.A. Cup

Semi-finals

Sheffield Wednesday vs Burnley	3-0
Bolton Wanderers vs West Bromwich Albion	1-1, 0-2

Final

Wembley, 27th April 1935

Sheffield Wednesday 4 (Rimmer 2, Palethorpe, Hooper)

West Bromwich Albion 2 (Boyes, Sandford)

Attendance 93,204

DIVISION 1 1935-36

Sunderland	42	25	6	11	109	74	56
Derby County	42	18	12	12	61	52	48
Huddersfield Town	42	18	12	12	59	56	48
Stoke City	42	20	7	15	57	57	47
Brentford	42	17	12	13	81	60	46
Arsenal	42	15	15	12	78	48	45
Preston North End	42	18	8	16	67	64	44
Chelsea	42	15	13	14	65	72	43
Manchester City	42	17	8	17	68	60	42
Portsmouth	42	17	8	17	54	67	42
Leeds United	42	15	11	16	66	64	41
Birmingham	42	15	11	16	61	63	41
Bolton Wanderers	42	14	13	15	67	76	41
Middlesbrough	42	15	10	17	84	70	40
Wolverhampton Wanderers	42	15	10	17	77	76	40
Everton	42	13	13	16	89	89	39
Grimsby Town	42	17	5	20	65	73	39
West Bromwich Albion	42	16	6	20	89	88	38
Liverpool	42	13	12	17	60	64	38
Sheffield Wednesday	42	13	12	17	63	77	38
Aston Villa	42	13	9	20	81	110	35
Blackburn Rovers	42	12	9	21	55	96	33

DIVISION 2 1935-36

Manchester United	42	22	12	8	85	43	56
Charlton Athletic	42	22	11	9	85	58	55
Sheffield United	42	20	12	10	79	50	52
West Ham United	42	22	8	12	90	68	52
Tottenham Hotspur	42	18	13	11	91	55	49
Leicester City	42	19	10	13	79	57	48
Plymouth Argyle	42	20	8	14	71	57	48
Newcastle United	42	20	6	16	88	79	46
Fulham	42	15	14	13	76	52	44
Blackpool	42	18	7	17	93	72	43
Norwich City	42	17	9	16	72	65	43
Bradford City	42	15	13	14	55	65	43
Swansea Town	42	15	9	18	67	76	39
Bury	42	13	12	17	66	84	38
Burnley	42	12	13	17	50	59	37
Bradford Park Avenue	42	14	9	19	62	84	37
Southampton	42	14	9	19	47	65	37
Doncaster Rovers	42	14	9	19	51	71	37
Nottingham	42	12	11	19	69	76	35
Barnsley	42	12	9	21	54	80	33
Port Vale	42	12	8	22	56	106	32
Hull City	42	5	10	27	47	111	20

DIVISION 3N 1935-36

Chesterfield	42	24	12	6	92	39	60
Chester	42	22	11	9	100	45	55
Tranmere Rovers	42	22	11	9	93	58	55
Lincoln City	42	22	9	11	91	51	53
Stockport County	42	20	8	14	65	49	48
Crewe Alexandra	42	19	9	14	80	76	47
Oldham Athletic	42	18	9	15	86	73	45
Hartlepools United	42	15	12	15	57	61	42
Accrington Stanley	42	17	8	17	63	72	42
Walsall	42	16	9	17	79	59	41
Rotherham United	42	16	9	17	69	66	41
Darlington	42	17	6	19	74	79	40
Carlisle United	42	14	12	16	56	62	40
Gateshead	42	13	14	15	56	76	40
Barrow	42	13	12	17	58	65	38
York City	42	13	12	17	62	95	38
Halifax Town	42	15	7	20	57	61	37
Wrexham	42	15	7	20	66	75	37
Mansfield Town	42	14	9	19	80	91	37
Rochdale	42	10	13	19	58	88	33
Southport	42	11	9	22	48	90	31
New Brighton	42	9	6	27	43	102	24

DIVISION 3S 1935-36

Coventry City	42	24	9	9	102	45	57
Luton Town	42	22	12	8	81	45	56
Reading	42	26	2	14	87	62	54
Queen's Park Rangers	42	22	9	11	84	53	53
Watford	42	20	9	13	80	54	49
Crystal Palace	42	22	5	15	96	74	49
Brighton & Hove Albion	42	18	8	16	70	63	44
Bournemouth & Boscombe Ath.	42	16	11	15	60	56	43
Notts County	42	15	12	15	60	57	42
Torquay United	42	16	9	17	62	62	41
Aldershot	42	14	12	16	53	61	40
Millwall	42	14	12	16	58	71	40
Bristol City	42	15	10	17	48	59	40
Clapton Orient	42	16	6	20	55	61	38
Northampton Town	42	15	8	19	62	90	38
Gillingham	42	14	9	19	66	77	37
Bristol Rovers	42	14	9	19	69	95	37
Southend United	42	13	10	19	61	62	36
Swindon Town	42	14	8	20	64	73	36
Cardiff City	42	13	10	19	60	73	36
Newport County	42	11	9	22	60	111	31
Exeter City	42	8	11	23	59	93	27

1936 F.A. Cup

Semi-finals

Arsenal vs Grimsby Town	1-0
Fulham vs Sheffield United	1-2

Final

Wembley, 25th April 1936

Arsenal 1 (Drake)
Sheffield United 0

Attendance 93,384

DIVISION 1 1936-37

Manchester City	42	22	13	7	107	61	57
Charlton Athletic	42	21	12	9	58	49	54
Arsenal	42	18	16	8	80	49	52
Derby County	42	21	7	14	96	90	49
Wolverhampton Wanderers	42	21	5	16	84	67	47
Brentford	42	18	10	14	82	78	46
Middlesbrough	42	19	8	15	74	71	46
Sunderland	42	19	6	17	89	87	44
Portsmouth	42	17	10	15	62	66	44
Stoke City	42	15	12	15	72	57	42
Birmingham	42	13	15	14	64	60	41
Grimsby Town	42	17	7	18	86	81	41
Chelsea	42	14	13	15	52	55	41
Preston North End	42	14	13	15	56	67	41
Huddersfield Town	42	12	15	15	62	64	39
West Bromwich Albion	42	16	6	20	77	98	38
Everton	42	14	9	19	81	78	37
Liverpool	42	12	11	19	62	84	35
Leeds United	42	15	4	23	60	80	34
Bolton Wanderers	42	10	14	18	43	66	34
Manchester United	42	10	12	20	55	78	32
Sheffield Wednesday	42	9	12	21	53	69	30

DIVISION 3N 1936-37

Stockport County	42	23	14	5	84	39	60
Lincoln City	42	25	7	10	103	57	57
Chester	42	22	9	11	87	57	53
Oldham Athletic	42	20	11	11	77	59	51
Hull City	42	17	12	13	68	69	46
Hartlepools United	42	19	7	16	75	69	45
Halifax Town	42	18	9	15	68	63	45
Wrexham	42	16	12	14	71	57	44
Mansfield Town	42	18	8	16	91	76	44
Carlisle United	42	18	8	16	65	68	44
Port Vale	42	17	10	15	58	64	44
York City	42	16	11	15	79	70	43
Accrington Stanley	42	16	9	17	76	69	41
Southport	42	12	13	17	73	87	37
New Brighton	42	13	11	18	55	70	37
Barrow	42	13	10	19	70	86	36
Rotherham United	42	14	7	21	78	91	35
Rochdale	42	13	9	20	69	86	35
Tranmere Rovers	42	12	9	21	71	88	33
Crewe Alexandra	42	10	12	20	55	83	32
Gateshead	42	11	10	21	63	98	32
Darlington	42	8	14	20	66	96	30

DIVISION 2 1936-37

Leicester City	42	24	8	10	89	57	56
Blackpool	42	24	7	11	88	53	55
Bury	42	22	8	12	74	55	52
Newcastle United	42	22	5	15	80	56	49
Plymouth Argyle	42	18	13	11	71	53	49
West Ham United	42	19	11	12	73	55	49
Sheffield United	42	18	10	14	66	54	46
Coventry City	42	17	11	14	66	54	45
Aston Villa	42	16	12	14	82	70	44
Tottenham Hotspur	42	17	9	16	88	66	43
Fulham	42	15	13	14	71	61	43
Blackburn Rovers	42	16	10	16	70	62	42
Burnley	42	16	10	16	57	61	42
Barnsley	42	16	9	17	50	64	41
Chesterfield	42	16	8	18	84	89	40
Swansea Town	42	15	7	20	50	65	37
Norwich City	42	14	8	20	63	71	36
Nottingham Forest	42	12	10	20	68	90	34
Southampton	42	11	12	19	53	77	34
Bradford Park Avenue	42	12	9	21	52	88	33
Bradford City	42	9	12	21	54	94	30
Doncaster Rovers	42	7	10	25	30	84	24

DIVISION 3S 1936-37

Luton Town	42	27	4	11	103	53	58
Notts County	42	23	10	9	74	52	56
Brighton & Hove Albion	42	24	5	13	74	43	53
Watford	42	19	11	12	85	60	49
Reading	42	19	11	12	76	60	49
Bournemouth & Boscombe Ath.	42	20	9	13	65	59	49
Northampton Town	42	20	6	16	85	68	46
Millwall	42	18	10	14	64	54	46
Queen's Park Rangers	42	18	9	15	73	52	45
Southend United	42	17	11	14	78	67	45
Gillingham	42	18	8	16	52	66	44
Clapton Orient	42	14	15	13	52	52	43
Swindon Town	42	14	11	17	75	73	39
Crystal Palace	42	13	12	17	62	61	38
Bristol Rovers	42	16	4	22	71	80	36
Bristol City	42	15	6	21	58	70	36
Walsall	42	13	10	19	62	84	36
Cardiff City	42	14	7	21	54	87	35
Newport County	42	12	10	20	67	98	34
Torquay United	42	11	10	21	57	80	32
Exeter City	42	10	12	20	59	88	32
Aldershot	42	7	9	26	50	89	23

1937 F.A. Cup

Semi-finals

Sunderland vs Millwall	2-1
Preston North End vs West Bromwich Albion	4-1

Final

Wembley, 1st May 1937

Sunderland 3 (Gurney, Carter, Burbanks)
Preston North End 1 (F. O'Donnell)

Attendance 93,495

DIVISION 1 1937-38

Arsenal	42	21	10	11	77	44	52
Wolverhampton Wanderers	42	20	11	11	72	49	51
Preston North End	42	16	17	9	64	44	49
Charlton Athletic	42	16	14	12	65	51	46
Middlesbrough	42	19	8	15	72	65	46
Brentford	42	18	9	15	69	59	45
Bolton Wanderers	42	15	15	12	64	60	45
Sunderland	42	14	16	12	55	57	44
Leeds United	42	14	15	13	64	69	43
Chelsea	42	14	13	15	65	65	41
Liverpool	42	15	11	16	65	71	41
Blackpool	42	16	8	18	61	66	40
Derby County	42	15	10	17	66	87	40
Everton	42	16	7	19	79	75	39
Huddersfield Town	42	17	5	20	55	68	39
Leicester City	42	14	11	17	54	75	39
Stoke City	42	13	12	17	58	59	38
Birmingham	42	10	18	14	58	62	38
Portsmouth	42	13	12	17	62	68	38
Grimsby Town	42	13	12	17	51	68	38
Manchester City	42	14	8	20	80	77	36
West Bromwich Albion	42	14	8	20	74	91	36

DIVISION 3N 1937-38

Tranmere Rovers	42	23	10	9	81	41	56
Doncaster Rovers	42	21	12	9	74	49	54
Hull City	42	20	13	9	80	43	53
Oldham Athletic	42	19	13	10	67	46	51
Gateshead	42	20	11	11	84	59	51
Rotherham United	42	20	10	12	68	56	50
Lincoln City	42	19	8	15	66	50	46
Crewe Alexandra	42	18	9	15	71	53	45
Chester	42	16	12	14	77	72	44
Wrexham	42	16	11	15	58	63	43
York City	42	16	10	16	70	68	42
Carlisle United	42	15	9	18	57	67	39
New Brighton	42	15	8	19	60	61	38
Bradford City	42	14	10	18	66	69	38
Port Vale	42	12	14	16	65	73	38
Southport	42	12	14	16	53	82	38
Rochdale	42	13	11	18	67	78	37
Halifax Town	42	12	12	18	44	66	36
Darlington	42	11	10	21	54	79	32
Hartlepools United	42	10	12	20	53	80	32
Barrow	42	11	10	21	41	71	32
Accrington Stanley	42	11	7	24	45	75	29

DIVISION 2 1937-38

Aston Villa	42	25	7	10	73	35	57
Manchester United	42	22	9	11	82	50	53
Sheffield United	42	22	9	11	73	56	53
Coventry City	42	20	12	10	66	45	52
Tottenham Hotspur	42	19	6	17	76	54	44
Burnley	42	17	10	15	54	54	44
Bradford Park Avenue	42	17	9	16	69	56	43
Fulham	42	16	11	15	61	57	43
West Ham United	42	14	14	14	53	52	42
Bury	42	18	5	19	63	60	41
Chesterfield	42	16	9	17	63	63	41
Luton Town	42	15	10	17	89	86	40
Plymouth Argyle	42	14	12	16	57	65	40
Norwich City	42	14	11	17	56	75	39
Southampton	42	15	9	18	55	77	39
Blackburn Rovers	42	14	10	18	71	80	38
Sheffield Wednesday	42	14	10	18	49	56	38
Swansea Town	42	13	12	17	45	73	38
Newcastle United	42	14	8	20	51	58	36
Nottingham Forest	42	14	8	20	47	60	36
Barnsley	42	11	14	17	50	64	36
Stockport County	42	11	9	22	43	70	31

DIVISION 3S 1937-38

Millwall	42	23	10	9	83	37	56
Bristol City	42	21	13	8	68	40	55
Queen's Park Rangers	42	22	9	11	80	47	53
Watford	42	21	11	10	73	43	53
Brighton & Hove Albion	42	21	9	12	64	44	51
Reading	42	20	11	11	71	63	51
Crystal Palace	42	18	12	12	67	47	48
Swindon Town	42	17	10	15	49	49	44
Northampton Town	42	17	9	16	51	57	43
Cardiff City	42	15	12	15	67	54	42
Notts County	42	16	9	17	50	50	41
Southend United	42	15	10	17	70	68	40
Bournemouth & Boscombe Ath.	42	14	12	16	56	57	40
Mansfield Town	42	15	9	18	62	67	39
Bristol Rovers	42	13	13	16	46	61	39
Newport County	42	11	16	15	43	52	38
Exeter City	42	13	12	17	57	70	38
Aldershot	42	15	5	22	39	59	35
Clapton Orient	42	13	7	22	42	61	33
Torquay United	42	9	12	21	38	73	30
Walsall	42	11	7	24	52	88	29
Gillingham	42	10	6	26	36	77	26

1938 F.A. Cup

Semi-finals

Preston North End vs Aston Villa	2-1
Sunderland vs Huddersfield Town	1-3

Final

Wembley, 30th April 1938

Preston North End 1 (Mutch (pen))
Huddersfield Town 0 (aet.)

Attendance 93,497

DIVISION 1 1938-39

Everton	42	27	5	10	88	52	59
Wolverhampton Wanderers	42	22	11	9	88	39	55
Charlton Athletic	42	22	6	14	75	59	50
Middlesbrough	42	20	9	13	93	74	49
Arsenal	42	19	9	14	55	41	47
Derby County	42	19	8	15	66	55	46
Stoke City	42	17	12	13	71	68	46
Bolton Wanderers	42	15	15	12	67	58	45
Preston North End	42	16	12	14	63	59	44
Grimsby Town	42	16	11	15	61	69	43
Liverpool	42	14	14	14	62	63	42
Aston Villa	42	15	11	16	71	60	41
Leeds United	42	16	9	17	59	67	41
Manchester United	42	11	16	15	57	65	38
Blackpool	42	12	14	16	56	68	38
Sunderland	42	13	12	17	54	67	38
Portsmouth	42	12	13	17	47	70	37
Brentford	42	14	8	20	53	74	36
Huddersfield Town	42	12	11	19	58	64	35
Chelsea	42	12	9	21	64	80	33
Birmingham	42	12	8	22	62	84	32
Leicester City	42	9	11	22	48	82	29

DIVISION 3N 1938-39

Barnsley	42	30	7	5	94	34	67
Doncaster Rovers	42	21	14	7	87	47	56
Bradford City	42	22	8	12	89	56	52
Southport	42	20	10	12	75	54	50
Oldham Athletic	42	22	5	15	76	59	49
Chester	42	20	9	13	88	70	49
Hull City	42	18	10	14	83	74	46
Crewe Alexandra	42	19	6	17	82	70	44
Stockport County	42	17	9	16	91	77	43
Gateshead	42	14	14	14	74	67	42
Rotherham United	42	17	8	17	64	64	42
Halifax Town	42	13	16	13	52	54	42
Barrow	42	16	9	17	66	65	41
Wrexham	42	17	7	18	66	79	41
Rochdale	42	15	9	18	92	82	39
New Brighton	42	15	9	18	68	73	39
Lincoln City	42	12	9	21	66	92	33
Darlington	42	13	7	22	62	92	33
Carlisle United	42	13	7	22	64	111	33
York City	42	12	8	22	66	92	32
Hartlepools United	42	12	7	23	55	94	31
Accrington Stanley	42	7	6	29	49	103	20

DIVISION 2 1938-39

Blackburn Rovers	42	25	5	12	94	60	55
Sheffield United	42	20	14	8	69	41	54
Sheffield Wednesday	42	21	11	10	88	59	53
Coventry City	42	21	8	13	62	45	50
Manchester City	42	21	7	14	96	72	49
Chesterfield	42	20	9	13	69	52	49
Luton Town	42	22	5	15	82	66	49
Tottenham Hotspur	42	19	9	14	67	62	47
Newcastle United	42	18	10	14	61	48	46
West Bromwich Albion	42	18	9	15	89	72	45
West Ham United	42	17	10	15	70	52	44
Fulham	42	17	10	15	61	55	44
Millwall	42	14	14	14	64	53	42
Burnley	42	15	9	18	50	56	39
Plymouth Argyle	42	15	8	19	49	55	38
Bury	42	12	13	17	65	74	37
Bradford Park Avenue	42	12	11	19	61	82	35
Southampton	42	13	9	20	56	82	35
Swansea Town	42	11	12	19	50	83	34
Nottingham Forest	42	10	11	21	49	82	31
Norwich City	42	13	5	24	50	91	31
Tranmere Rovers	42	6	5	31	39	99	17

DIVISION 3S 1938-39

Newport County	42	22	11	9	58	45	55
Crystal Palace	42	20	12	10	71	52	52
Brighton & Hove Albion	42	19	11	12	68	49	49
Watford	42	17	12	13	62	51	46
Reading	42	16	14	12	69	59	46
Queen's Park Rangers	42	15	14	13	68	49	44
Ipswich Town	42	16	12	14	62	52	44
Bristol City	42	16	12	14	61	63	44
Swindon Town	42	18	8	16	72	77	44
Aldershot	42	16	12	14	53	66	44
Notts County	42	17	9	16	59	54	43
Southend United	42	16	9	17	61	64	41
Cardiff City	42	15	11	16	61	65	41
Exeter City	42	13	14	15	65	82	40
Bournemouth & Boscombe Ath.	42	13	13	16	52	58	39
Mansfield Town	42	12	15	15	44	62	39
Northampton Town	42	15	8	19	51	58	38
Port Vale	42	14	9	19	52	58	37
Torquay United	42	14	9	19	54	70	37
Clapton Orient	42	11	13	18	53	55	35
Walsall	42	11	11	20	68	69	33
Bristol Rovers	42	10	13	19	55	61	33

1939 F.A. Cup

Semi-finals

Portsmouth vs Huddersfield Town	2-1
Wolverhampton Wanderers vs Grimsby Town	5-0

Final

Wembley, 29th April 1939

Portsmouth 4 (Parker 2, Barlow, Anderson)
Wolverhampton Wanderers 1 (Dorsett)

Attendance 99,370

1946 F.A. Cup

Semi-finals

Bolton Wanderers vs Charlton Athletic	0-2
Derby County vs Birmingham City	1-1,4-0

Final

Wembley, 27th April 1946

Derby County 4 (H. Turner (og), Doherty, Stamps 2)
Charlton Athletic 1 (H. Turner)

Attendance 98,000

DIVISION 1 1946-47

Liverpool	42	25	7	10	84	52	57
Manchester United	42	22	12	8	95	54	56
Wolverhampton Wanderers	42	25	6	11	98	56	56
Stoke City	42	24	7	11	90	53	55
Blackpool	42	22	6	14	71	70	50
Sheffield United	42	21	7	14	89	75	49
Preston North End	42	18	11	13	76	74	47
Aston Villa	42	18	9	15	67	53	45
Sunderland	42	18	8	16	65	66	44
Everton	42	17	9	16	62	67	43
Middlesbrough	42	17	8	17	73	68	42
Portsmouth	42	16	9	17	66	60	41
Arsenal	42	16	9	17	72	70	41
Derby County	42	18	5	19	73	79	41
Chelsea	42	16	7	19	69	84	39
Grimsby Town	42	13	12	17	61	82	38
Blackburn Rovers	42	14	8	20	45	53	36
Bolton Wanderers	42	13	8	21	57	69	34
Charlton Athletic	42	11	12	19	57	71	34
Huddersfield Town	42	13	7	22	53	79	33
Brentford	42	9	7	26	45	88	25
Leeds United	42	6	6	30	45	90	18

DIVISION 3N 1946-47

Doncaster Rovers	42	33	6	3	123	40	72
Rotherham United	42	29	6	7	114	53	64
Chester	42	25	6	11	95	51	56
Stockport County	42	24	2	16	78	53	50
Bradford City	42	20	10	12	62	47	50
Rochdale	42	19	10	13	80	64	48
Wrexham	42	17	12	13	65	51	46
Crewe Alexandra	42	17	9	16	70	74	43
Barrow	42	17	7	18	54	62	41
Tranmere Rovers	42	17	7	18	66	77	41
Hull City	42	16	8	18	49	53	40
Lincoln City	42	17	5	20	86	87	39
Hartlepools United	42	15	9	18	64	73	39
Gateshead	42	16	6	20	62	72	38
York City	42	14	9	19	67	81	37
Carlisle United	42	14	9	19	70	93	37
Darlington	42	15	6	21	68	80	36
New Brighton	42	14	8	20	57	77	36
Oldham Athletic	42	12	8	22	55	80	32
Accrington Stanley	42	14	4	24	56	92	32
Southport	42	7	11	24	53	85	25
Halifax Town	42	8	6	28	43	92	22

DIVISION 2 1946-47

Manchester City	42	26	10	6	78	35	62
Burnley	42	22	14	6	65	29	58
Birmingham City	42	25	5	12	74	33	55
Chesterfield	42	18	14	10	58	44	50
Newcastle United	42	19	10	13	95	62	48
Tottenham Hotspur	42	17	14	11	65	53	48
West Bromwich Albion	42	20	8	14	88	75	48
Coventry City	42	16	13	13	66	59	45
Leicester City	42	18	7	17	69	64	43
Barnsley	42	17	8	17	84	86	42
Nottingham Forest	42	15	10	17	69	74	40
West Ham United	42	16	8	18	70	76	40
Luton Town	42	16	7	19	71	73	39
Southampton	42	15	9	18	69	76	39
Fulham	42	15	9	18	63	74	39
Bradford Park Avenue	42	14	11	17	65	77	39
Bury	42	12	12	18	80	78	36
Millwall	42	14	8	20	56	79	36
Plymouth Argyle	42	14	5	23	79	96	33
Sheffield Wednesday	42	12	8	22	67	88	32
Swansea Town	42	11	7	24	55	83	29
Newport County	42	10	3	29	61	133	23

DIVISION 3S 1946-47

Cardiff City	42	30	6	6	93	30	66
Queen's Park Rangers	42	23	11	8	74	40	57
Bristol City	42	20	11	11	94	56	51
Swindon Town	42	19	11	12	84	73	49
Walsall	42	17	12	13	74	59	46
Ipswich Town	42	16	14	12	61	53	46
Bournemouth & Boscombe Ath.	42	18	8	16	72	54	44
Southend United	42	17	10	15	71	60	44
Reading	42	16	11	15	83	74	43
Port Vale	42	17	9	16	68	63	43
Torquay United	42	15	12	15	52	61	42
Notts County	42	15	10	17	63	63	40
Northampton Town	42	15	10	17	72	75	40
Bristol Rovers	42	16	8	18	59	69	40
Exeter City	42	15	9	18	60	69	39
Watford	42	17	5	20	61	76	39
Brighton & Hove Albion	42	13	12	17	54	72	38
Crystal Palace	42	13	11	18	49	62	37
Leyton Orient	42	12	8	22	54	75	32
Aldershot	42	10	12	20	48	78	32
Norwich City	42	10	8	24	64	100	28
Mansfield Town	42	9	10	23	48	96	28

1947 F.A. Cup

Semi-finals

Charlton Athletic vs Newcastle United	4-0
Burnley vs Liverpool	0-0, 1-0

Final

Wembley, 26th April 1947

Charlton Athletic 1 (Duffy)
Burnley 0 (aet.)

Attendance 99,000

DIVISION 1 1947-48

Arsenal	42	23	13	6	81	32	59
Manchester United	42	19	14	9	81	48	52
Burnley	42	20	12	10	56	43	52
Derby County	42	19	12	11	77	57	50
Wolverhampton Wanderers	42	19	9	14	83	70	47
Aston Villa	42	19	9	14	65	57	47
Preston North End	42	20	7	15	67	68	47
Portsmouth	42	19	7	16	68	50	45
Blackpool	42	17	10	15	57	41	44
Manchester City	42	15	12	15	52	47	42
Liverpool	42	16	10	16	65	61	42
Sheffield United	42	16	10	16	65	70	42
Charlton Athletic	42	17	6	19	57	66	40
Everton	42	17	6	19	52	66	40
Stoke City	42	14	10	18	41	55	38
Middlesbrough	42	14	9	19	71	73	37
Bolton Wanderers	42	16	5	21	46	58	37
Chelsea	42	14	9	19	53	71	37
Huddersfield Town	42	12	12	18	51	60	36
Sunderland	42	13	10	19	56	67	36
Blackburn Rovers	42	11	10	21	54	72	32
Grimsby Town	42	8	6	28	45	111	22

DIVISION 2 1947-48

Birmingham City	42	22	15	5	55	24	59
Newcastle United	42	24	8	10	72	41	56
Southampton	42	21	10	11	71	53	52
Sheffield Wednesday	42	20	11	11	66	53	51
Cardiff City	42	18	11	13	61	58	47
West Ham United	42	16	14	12	55	53	46
West Bromwich Albion	42	18	9	15	63	58	45
Tottenham Hotspur	42	15	14	13	56	43	44
Leicester City	42	16	11	15	60	57	43
Coventry City	42	14	13	15	59	52	41
Fulham	42	15	10	17	47	46	40
Barnsley	42	15	10	17	62	64	40
Luton Town	42	14	12	16	56	59	40
Bradford Park Avenue	42	16	8	18	68	72	40
Brentford	42	13	14	15	44	61	40
Chesterfield	42	16	7	19	54	55	39
Plymouth Argyle	42	9	20	13	40	58	38
Leeds United	42	14	8	20	62	72	36
Nottingham	42	12	11	19	54	60	35
Bury	42	9	16	17	58	68	34
Doncaster Rovers	42	9	11	22	40	66	29
Millwall	42	9	11	22	44	74	29

DIVISION 3N 1947-48

Lincoln City	42	26	8	8	81	40	60
Rotherham United	42	25	9	8	95	49	59
Wrexham	42	21	8	13	74	54	50
Gateshead	42	19	11	12	75	57	49
Hull City	42	18	11	13	59	48	47
Accrington Stanley	42	20	6	16	62	59	46
Barrow	42	16	13	13	49	40	45
Mansfield Town	42	17	11	14	57	51	45
Carlisle United	42	18	7	17	88	77	43
Crewe Alexandra	42	18	7	17	61	63	43
Oldham Athletic	42	14	13	15	63	64	41
Rochdale	42	15	11	16	48	72	41
York City	42	13	14	15	65	60	40
Bradford City	42	15	10	17	65	66	40
Southport	42	14	11	17	60	63	39
Darlington	42	13	13	16	54	70	39
Stockport County	42	13	12	17	63	67	38
Tranmere Rovers	42	16	4	22	54	72	36
Hartlepools United	42	14	8	20	51	73	36
Chester	42	13	9	20	64	67	35
Halifax Town	42	7	13	22	43	76	27
New Brighton	42	8	9	25	38	81	25

DIVISION 3S 1947-48

Queen's Park Rangers	42	26	9	7	74	37	61
Bournemouth & Boscombe Ath.	42	24	9	9	76	35	57
Walsall	42	21	9	12	70	40	51
Ipswich Town	42	23	3	16	67	61	49
Swansea Town	42	18	12	12	70	52	48
Notts County	42	19	8	15	68	59	46
Bristol City	42	18	7	17	77	65	43
Port Vale	42	16	11	15	63	54	43
Southend United	42	15	13	14	51	58	43
Reading	42	15	11	16	56	58	41
Exeter City	42	15	11	16	55	63	41
Newport County	42	14	13	15	61	73	41
Crystal Palace	42	13	13	16	49	49	39
Northampton Town	42	14	11	17	58	72	39
Watford	42	14	10	18	57	79	38
Swindon Town	42	10	16	16	41	46	36
Leyton Orient	42	13	10	19	51	73	36
Torquay United	42	11	13	18	63	62	35
Aldershot	42	10	15	17	45	67	35
Bristol Rovers	42	13	8	21	71	75	34
Norwich City	42	13	8	21	61	76	34
Brighton & Hove Albion	42	11	12	19	43	73	34

1948 F.A. Cup

Semi-finals

Derby County vs Manchester United	1-3
Blackpool vs Tottenham Hotspur	3-1

Final

Wembley, 24th April 1948

Manchester United 4 (Rowley 2, Pearson, Anderson)

Blackpool 2 (Shimwell (pen), Mortensen)

Attendance 99,000

DIVISION 1 1948-49

Portsmouth	42	25	8	9	84	42	58
Manchester United	42	21	11	10	77	44	53
Derby County	42	22	9	11	74	55	53
Newcastle United	42	20	12	10	70	56	52
Arsenal	42	18	13	11	74	44	49
Wolverhampton Wanderers	42	17	12	13	79	66	46
Manchester City	42	15	15	12	47	51	45
Sunderland	42	13	17	12	49	58	43
Charlton Athletic	42	15	12	15	63	67	42
Aston Villa	42	16	10	16	60	76	42
Stoke City	42	16	9	17	66	68	41
Liverpool	42	13	14	15	53	43	40
Chelsea	42	12	14	16	69	68	38
Bolton Wanderers	42	14	10	18	59	68	38
Burnley	42	12	14	16	43	50	38
Blackpool	42	11	16	15	54	67	38
Birmingham City	42	11	15	16	36	38	37
Everton	42	13	11	18	41	63	37
Middlesbrough	42	11	12	19	46	57	34
Huddersfield Town	42	12	10	20	40	69	34
Preston North End	42	11	11	20	62	75	33
Sheffield United	42	11	11	20	57	78	33

DIVISION 3N 1948-49

Hull City	42	27	11	4	93	28	65
Rotherham United	42	28	6	8	90	46	62
Doncaster Rovers	42	20	10	12	53	40	50
Darlington	42	20	6	16	83	74	46
Gateshead	42	16	13	13	69	58	45
Oldham Athletic	42	18	9	15	75	67	45
Rochdale	42	18	9	15	55	53	45
Stockport County	42	16	11	15	61	56	43
Wrexham	42	17	9	16	56	62	43
Mansfield Town	42	14	14	14	52	48	42
Tranmere Rovers	42	13	15	14	46	57	41
Crewe Alexandra	42	16	9	17	52	74	41
Barrow	42	14	12	16	41	48	40
York City	42	15	9	18	74	74	39
Carlisle United	42	14	11	17	60	77	39
Hartlepools United	42	14	10	18	45	58	38
New Brighton	42	14	8	20	46	58	36
Chester	42	11	13	18	57	56	35
Halifax Town	42	12	11	19	45	62	35
Accrington Stanley	42	12	10	20	55	64	34
Southport	42	11	9	22	45	64	31
Bradford City	42	10	9	23	48	77	29

DIVISION 2 1948-49

Fulham	42	24	9	9	77	37	57
West Bromwich Albion	42	24	8	10	69	39	56
Southampton	42	23	9	10	69	36	55
Cardiff City	42	19	13	10	62	47	51
Tottenham Hotspur	42	17	16	9	72	44	50
Chesterfield	42	15	17	10	51	45	47
West Ham United	42	18	10	14	56	58	46
Sheffield Wednesday	42	15	13	14	63	56	43
Barnsley	42	14	12	16	62	61	40
Luton Town	42	14	12	16	55	57	40
Grimsby Town	42	15	10	17	72	76	40
Bury	42	17	6	19	67	76	40
Queen's Park Rangers	42	14	11	17	44	62	39
Blackburn Rovers	42	15	8	19	53	63	38
Leeds United	42	12	13	17	55	63	37
Coventry City	42	15	7	20	55	64	37
Bradford Park Avenue	42	13	11	18	65	78	37
Brentford	42	11	14	17	42	53	36
Leicester City	42	10	16	16	62	79	36
Plymouth Argyle	42	12	12	18	49	64	36
Nottingham Forest	42	14	7	21	50	54	35
Lincoln City	42	8	12	22	53	91	28

DIVISION 3S 1948-49

Swansea Town	42	27	8	7	87	34	62
Reading	42	25	5	12	77	50	55
Bournemouth & Boscombe Ath.	42	22	8	12	69	48	52
Swindon Town	42	18	15	9	64	56	51
Bristol Rovers	42	19	10	13	61	51	48
Brighton & Hove Albion	42	15	18	9	55	55	48
Ipswich Town	42	18	9	15	78	77	45
Millwall	42	17	11	14	63	64	45
Torquay United	42	17	11	14	65	70	45
Norwich City	42	16	12	14	67	49	44
Notts County	42	19	5	18	102	68	43
Exeter City	42	15	10	17	63	76	40
Port Vale	42	14	11	17	51	54	39
Walsall	42	15	8	19	56	64	38
Newport County	42	14	9	19	68	92	37
Bristol City	42	11	14	17	44	62	36
Watford	42	10	15	17	41	54	35
Southend United	42	9	16	17	41	46	34
Leyton Orient	42	11	12	19	58	80	34
Northampton Town	42	12	9	21	51	62	33
Aldershot	42	11	11	20	48	59	33
Crystal Palace	42	8	11	23	38	76	27

1949 F.A. Cup

Semi-finals

Manchester Utd. vs Wolverhampton Wanderers	1-1, 0-1
Leicester City vs Portsmouth	3-1

Final

Wembley, 30th April 1949

Wolverhampton Wanderers 3 (Pye 2, Smyth)
Leicester City 1 (Griffiths)

Attendance 99,500

DIVISION 1 1949-50

Portsmouth	42	22	9	11	74	38	53
Wolverhampton Wanderers	42	20	13	9	76	49	53
Sunderland	42	21	10	11	83	62	52
Manchester United	42	18	14	10	69	44	50
Newcastle United	42	19	12	11	77	55	50
Arsenal	42	19	11	12	79	55	49
Blackpool	42	17	15	10	46	35	49
Liverpool	42	17	14	11	64	54	48
Middlesbrough	42	20	7	15	59	48	47
Burnley	42	16	13	13	40	40	45
Derby County	42	17	10	15	69	61	44
Aston Villa	42	15	12	15	61	61	42
Chelsea	42	12	16	14	58	65	40
West Bromwich Albion	42	14	12	16	47	53	40
Huddersfield Town	42	14	9	19	52	73	37
Bolton Wanderers	42	10	14	18	45	59	34
Fulham	42	10	14	18	41	54	34
Everton	42	10	14	18	42	66	34
Stoke City	42	11	12	19	45	75	34
Charlton Athletic	42	13	6	23	53	65	32
Manchester City	42	8	13	21	36	68	29
Birmingham City	42	7	14	21	31	67	28

DIVISION 3N 1949-50

Doncaster Rovers	42	19	17	6	66	38	55
Gateshead	42	23	7	12	87	54	53
Rochdale	42	21	9	12	68	41	51
Lincoln City	42	21	9	12	60	39	51
Tranmere Rovers	42	19	11	12	51	48	49
Rotherham United	42	19	10	13	80	59	48
Crewe Alexandra	42	17	14	11	68	55	48
Mansfield Town	42	18	12	12	66	54	48
Carlisle United	42	16	15	11	68	51	47
Stockport County	42	19	7	16	55	52	45
Oldham Athletic	42	16	11	15	58	63	43
Chester	42	17	6	19	70	79	40
Accrington Stanley	42	16	7	19	57	62	39
New Brighton	42	14	10	18	45	63	38
Barrow	42	14	9	19	47	53	37
Southport	42	12	13	17	51	71	37
Darlington	42	11	13	18	56	69	35
Hartlepools United	42	14	5	23	52	79	33
Bradford City	42	12	8	22	61	76	32
Wrexham	42	10	12	20	39	54	32
Halifax Town	42	12	8	22	58	85	32
York City	42	9	13	20	52	70	31

DIVISION 2 1949-50

Tottenham Hotspur	42	27	7	8	81	35	61
Sheffield Wednesday	42	18	16	8	67	48	52
Sheffield United	42	19	14	9	68	49	52
Southampton	42	19	14	9	64	48	52
Leeds United	42	17	13	12	54	45	47
Preston North End	42	18	9	15	60	49	45
Hull City	42	17	11	14	64	72	45
Swansea Town	42	17	9	16	53	49	43
Brentford	42	15	13	14	44	49	43
Cardiff City	42	16	10	16	41	44	42
Grimsby Town	42	16	8	18	74	73	40
Coventry City	42	13	13	16	55	55	39
Barnsley	42	13	13	16	64	67	39
Chesterfield	42	15	9	18	43	47	39
Leicester City	42	12	15	15	55	65	39
Blackburn Rovers	42	14	10	18	55	60	38
Luton Town	42	10	18	14	41	51	38
Bury	42	14	9	19	60	65	37
West Ham United	42	12	12	18	53	61	36
Queen's Park Rangers	42	11	12	19	40	57	34
Plymouth Argyle	42	8	16	18	44	65	32
Bradford Park Avenue	42	10	11	21	51	77	31

DIVISION 3S 1949-50

Notts County	42	25	8	9	95	50	58
Northampton Town	42	20	11	11	72	50	51
Southend United	42	19	13	10	66	48	51
Nottingham Forest	42	20	9	13	67	39	49
Torquay United	42	19	10	13	66	63	48
Watford	42	16	13	13	45	35	45
Crystal Palace	42	15	14	13	55	54	44
Brighton & Hove Albion	42	16	12	14	57	69	44
Bristol Rovers	42	19	5	18	51	51	43
Reading	42	17	8	17	70	64	42
Norwich City	42	16	10	16	65	63	42
Bournemouth & Boscombe Ath.	42	16	10	16	57	56	42
Port Vale	42	15	11	16	47	42	41
Swindon Town	42	15	11	16	59	62	41
Bristol City	42	15	10	17	60	61	40
Exeter City	42	14	11	17	63	75	39
Ipswich Town	42	12	11	19	57	86	35
Leyton Orient	42	12	11	19	53	85	35
Walsall	42	9	16	17	61	62	34
Aldershot	42	13	8	21	48	60	34
Newport County	42	13	8	21	67	98	34
Millwall	42	14	4	24	55	63	32

1950 F.A. Cup

Semi-final

Arsenal vs Chelsea	2-2, 1-0
Liverpool vs Everton	2-0

Final

Wembley, 29th April 1950

Arsenal 2   (Lewis 2)

Liverpool 0

Attendance 100,000

DIVISION 1 1950-51

Tottenham Hotspur	42	25	10	7	82	44	60
Manchester United	42	24	8	10	74	40	56
Blackpool	42	20	10	12	79	53	50
Newcastle United	42	18	13	11	62	53	49
Arsenal	42	19	9	14	73	56	47
Middlesbrough	42	18	11	13	76	65	47
Portsmouth	42	16	15	11	71	68	47
Bolton Wanderers	42	19	7	16	64	61	45
Liverpool	42	16	11	15	53	59	43
Burnley	42	14	14	14	48	43	42
Derby County	42	16	8	18	81	75	40
Sunderland	42	12	16	14	63	73	40
Stoke City	42	13	14	15	50	59	40
Wolverhampton Wanderers	42	15	8	19	74	61	38
Aston Villa	42	12	13	17	66	68	37
West Bromwich Albion	42	13	11	18	53	61	37
Charlton Athletic	42	14	9	19	63	80	37
Fulham	42	13	11	18	52	68	37
Huddersfield Town	42	15	6	21	64	92	36
Chelsea	42	12	8	22	53	65	32
Sheffield Wednesday	42	12	8	22	64	83	32
Everton	42	12	8	22	48	86	32

DIVISION 3N 1950-51

Rotherham United	46	31	9	6	103	41	71
Mansfield Town	46	26	12	8	78	48	64
Carlisle United	46	25	12	9	79	50	62
Tranmere Rovers	46	24	11	11	83	62	59
Lincoln City	46	25	8	13	89	58	58
Bradford Park Avenue	46	23	8	15	90	72	54
Bradford City	46	21	10	15	90	63	52
Gateshead	46	21	8	17	84	62	50
Crewe Alexandra	46	19	10	17	61	60	48
Stockport County	46	20	8	18	63	63	48
Rochdale	46	17	11	18	69	62	45
Scunthorpe United	46	13	18	15	58	57	44
Chester	46	17	9	20	62	64	43
Wrexham	46	15	12	19	55	71	42
Oldham Athletic	46	16	8	22	73	73	40
Hartlepools United	46	16	7	23	64	66	39
York City	46	12	15	19	66	77	39
Darlington	46	13	13	20	59	77	39
Barrow	46	16	6	24	51	76	38
Shrewsbury Town	46	15	7	24	43	74	37
Southport	46	13	10	23	56	72	36
Halifax Town	46	11	12	23	50	69	34
Accrington Stanley	46	11	10	25	42	101	32
New Brighton	46	11	8	27	40	90	30

DIVISION 2 1950-51

Preston North End	42	26	5	11	91	49	57
Manchester City	42	19	14	9	89	61	52
Cardiff City	42	17	16	9	53	45	50
Birmingham City	42	20	9	13	64	53	49
Leeds United	42	20	8	14	63	55	48
Blackburn Rovers	42	19	8	15	65	66	46
Coventry City	42	19	7	16	75	59	45
Sheffield United	42	16	12	14	72	62	44
Brentford	42	18	8	16	75	74	44
Hull City	42	16	11	15	74	70	43
Doncaster Rovers	42	15	13	14	64	68	43
Southampton	42	15	13	14	66	73	43
West Ham United	42	16	10	16	68	69	42
Leicester City	42	15	11	16	68	58	41
Barnsley	42	15	10	17	74	68	40
Queen's Park Rangers	42	15	10	17	71	82	40
Notts County	42	13	13	16	61	60	39
Swansea Town	42	16	4	22	54	77	36
Luton Town	42	9	14	19	57	70	32
Bury	42	12	8	22	60	86	32
Chesterfield	42	9	12	21	44	69	30
Grimsby Town	42	8	12	22	61	95	28

DIVISION 3S 1950-51

Nottingham Forest	46	30	10	6	110	40	70
Norwich City	46	25	14	7	82	45	64
Reading	46	21	15	10	88	53	57
Plymouth Argyle	46	24	9	13	85	55	57
Millwall	46	23	10	13	80	57	56
Bristol Rovers	46	20	15	11	64	42	55
Southend United	46	21	10	15	92	69	52
Ipswich Town	46	23	6	17	69	58	52
Bournemouth & Boscombe Ath.	46	22	7	17	65	57	51
Bristol City	46	20	11	15	64	59	51
Newport County	46	19	9	18	77	70	47
Port Vale	46	16	13	17	60	65	45
Brighton & Hove Albion	46	13	17	16	71	79	43
Exeter City	46	18	6	22	62	85	42
Walsall	46	15	10	21	52	62	40
Colchester United	46	14	12	20	63	76	40
Swindon Town	46	18	4	24	55	67	40
Aldershot	46	15	10	21	56	88	40
Leyton Orient	46	15	8	23	53	75	38
Torquay United	46	14	9	23	64	81	37
Northampton Town	46	10	16	20	55	67	36
Gillingham	46	13	9	24	69	101	35
Watford	46	9	11	26	54	88	29
Crystal Palace	46	8	11	27	33	84	27

1951 F.A. Cup

Semi-final

Newcastle Utd. vs Wolverhampton Wanderers	0-0, 2-1
Blackpool vs Birmingham City	0-0, 2-1

Final

Wembley, 28th April 1951

Newcastle United 2 (Milburn 2)

Blackpool 0

Attendance 100,000

DIVISION 1 1951-52

Manchester United	42	23	11	8	95	52	57
Tottenham Hotspur	42	22	9	11	76	51	53
Arsenal	42	21	11	10	80	61	53
Portsmouth	42	20	8	14	68	58	48
Bolton Wanderers	42	19	10	13	65	61	48
Aston Villa	42	19	9	14	79	70	47
Preston North End	42	17	12	13	74	54	46
Newcastle United	42	18	9	15	98	73	45
Blackpool	42	18	9	15	64	64	45
Charlton Athletic	42	17	10	15	68	63	44
Liverpool	42	12	19	11	57	61	43
Sunderland	42	15	12	15	70	61	42
West Bromwich Albion	42	14	13	15	74	77	41
Burnley	42	15	10	17	56	63	40
Manchester City	42	13	13	16	58	61	39
Wolverhampton Wanderers	42	12	14	16	73	73	38
Derby County	42	15	7	20	63	80	37
Middlesbrough	42	15	6	21	64	88	36
Chelsea	42	14	8	20	52	72	36
Stoke City	42	12	7	23	49	88	31
Huddersfield Town	42	10	8	24	49	82	28
Fulham	42	8	11	23	58	77	27

DIVISION 3N 1951-52

Lincoln City	46	30	9	7	121	52	69
Grimsby Town	46	29	8	9	96	45	66
Stockport County	46	23	13	10	74	40	59
Oldham Athletic	46	24	9	13	90	61	57
Gateshead	46	21	11	14	66	49	53
Mansfield Town	46	22	8	16	73	60	52
Carlisle United	46	19	13	14	62	57	51
Bradford Park Avenue	46	19	12	15	74	64	50
Hartlepools United	46	21	8	17	71	65	50
York City	46	18	13	15	73	52	49
Tranmere Rovers	46	21	6	19	76	71	48
Barrow	46	17	12	17	57	61	46
Chesterfield	46	17	11	18	65	66	45
Scunthorpe United	46	14	16	16	65	74	44
Bradford City	46	16	10	20	61	68	42
Crewe Alexandra	46	17	8	21	63	82	42
Southport	46	15	11	20	53	71	41
Wrexham	46	15	9	22	63	73	39
Chester	46	15	9	22	72	85	39
Halifax Town	46	14	7	25	61	97	35
Rochdale	46	11	13	22	47	79	35
Accrington Stanley	46	10	12	24	61	92	32
Darlington	46	11	9	26	64	103	31
Workington	46	11	7	28	50	91	29

DIVISION 2 1951-52

Sheffield Wednesday	42	21	11	10	100	66	53
Cardiff City	42	20	11	11	72	54	51
Birmingham City	42	21	9	12	67	56	51
Nottingham Forest	42	18	13	11	77	62	49
Leicester City	42	19	9	14	78	64	47
Leeds United	42	18	11	13	59	57	47
Everton	42	17	10	15	64	58	44
Luton Town	42	16	12	14	77	78	44
Rotherham United	42	17	8	17	73	71	42
Brentford	42	15	12	15	54	55	42
Sheffield United	42	18	5	19	90	76	41
West Ham United	42	15	11	16	67	77	41
Southampton	42	15	11	16	61	73	41
Blackburn Rovers	42	17	6	19	54	63	40
Notts County	42	16	7	19	71	68	39
Doncaster Rovers	42	13	12	17	55	60	38
Bury	42	15	7	20	67	69	37
Hull City	42	13	11	18	60	70	37
Swansea Town	42	12	12	18	72	76	36
Barnsley	42	11	14	17	59	72	36
Coventry City	42	14	6	22	59	82	34
Queen's Park Rangers	42	11	12	19	52	81	34

DIVISION 3S 1951-52

Plymouth Argyle	46	29	8	9	107	53	66
Reading	46	29	3	14	112	60	61
Norwich City	46	26	9	11	89	50	61
Millwall	46	23	12	11	74	53	58
Brighton & Hove Albion	46	24	10	12	87	63	58
Newport County	46	21	12	13	77	76	54
Bristol Rovers	46	20	12	14	89	53	52
Northampton Town	46	22	5	19	93	74	49
Southend United	46	19	10	17	75	66	48
Colchester United	46	17	12	17	56	77	46
Torquay United	46	17	10	19	86	98	44
Aldershot	46	18	8	20	78	89	44
Port Vale	46	14	15	17	50	66	43
Bournemouth & Boscombe Ath.	46	16	10	20	69	75	42
Bristol City	46	15	12	19	58	69	42
Swindon Town	46	14	14	18	51	68	42
Ipswich Town	46	16	9	21	63	74	41
Leyton Orient	46	16	9	21	55	68	41
Crystal Palace	46	15	9	22	61	80	39
Shrewsbury Town	46	13	10	23	62	86	36
Watford	46	13	10	23	57	81	36
Gillingham	46	11	13	22	71	81	35
Exeter City	46	13	9	24	65	86	35
Walsall	46	13	5	28	55	94	31

1952 F.A. Cup

Semi-finals

Newcastle United vs Blackburn Rovers	0-0, 2-1
Arsenal vs Chelsea	1-1, 3-0

Final

Wembley, 3rd May 1952

Newcastle United 1 (G. Robledo)

Arsenal 0

Attendance 100,000

DIVISION 1 1952-53

Arsenal	42	21	12	9	97	64	54
Preston North End	42	21	12	9	85	60	54
Wolverhampton Wanderers	42	19	13	10	86	63	51
West Bromwich Albion	42	21	8	13	66	60	50
Charlton Athletic	42	19	11	12	77	63	49
Burnley	42	18	12	12	67	52	48
Blackpool	42	19	9	14	71	70	47
Manchester United	42	18	10	14	69	72	46
Sunderland	42	15	13	14	68	82	43
Tottenham Hotspur	42	15	11	16	78	69	41
Aston Villa	42	14	13	15	63	61	41
Cardiff City	42	14	12	16	54	46	40
Middlesbrough	42	14	11	17	70	77	39
Bolton Wanderers	42	15	9	18	61	69	39
Portsmouth	42	14	10	18	74	83	38
Newcastle United	42	14	9	19	59	70	37
Liverpool	42	14	8	20	61	82	36
Sheffield Wednesday	42	12	11	19	62	72	35
Chelsea	42	12	11	19	56	66	35
Manchester City	42	14	7	21	72	87	35
Stoke City	42	12	10	20	53	66	34
Derby County	42	11	10	21	59	74	32

DIVISION 2 1952-53

Sheffield United	42	25	10	7	97	55	60
Huddersfield Town	42	24	10	8	84	33	58
Luton Town	42	22	8	12	84	49	52
Plymouth Argyle	42	20	9	13	65	60	49
Leicester City	42	18	12	12	89	74	48
Birmingham City	42	19	10	13	71	66	48
Nottingham Forest	42	18	8	16	77	67	44
Fulham	42	17	10	15	81	71	44
Blackburn Rovers	42	18	8	16	68	65	44
Leeds United	42	14	15	13	71	63	43
Swansea Town	42	15	12	15	78	81	42
Rotherham United	42	16	9	17	75	74	41
Doncaster Rovers	42	12	16	14	58	64	40
West Ham United	42	13	13	16	58	60	39
Lincoln City	42	11	17	14	64	71	39
Everton	42	12	14	16	71	75	38
Brentford	42	13	11	18	59	76	37
Hull City	42	14	8	20	57	69	36
Notts County	42	14	8	20	60	88	36
Bury	42	13	9	20	53	81	35
Southampton	42	10	13	19	68	85	33
Barnsley	42	5	8	29	47	108	18

DIVISION 3N 1952-53

Oldham Athletic	46	22	15	9	77	45	59
Port Vale	46	20	18	8	67	35	58
Wrexham	46	24	8	14	86	66	56
York City	46	20	13	13	60	45	53
Grimsby Town	46	21	10	15	75	59	52
Southport	46	20	11	15	63	60	51
Bradford Park Avenue	46	19	12	15	75	61	50
Gateshead	46	17	15	14	76	60	49
Carlisle United	46	18	13	15	82	68	49
Crewe Alexandra	46	20	8	18	70	68	48
Stockport County	46	17	13	16	82	69	47
Chesterfield	46	18	11	17	65	63	47
Tranmere Rovers	46	21	5	20	65	63	47
Halifax Town	46	16	15	15	68	68	47
Scunthorpe United	46	16	14	16	62	56	46
Bradford City	46	14	18	14	75	80	46
Hartlepools United	46	16	14	16	57	61	46
Mansfield Town	46	16	14	16	55	62	46
Barrow	46	16	12	18	66	71	44
Chester	46	11	15	20	64	85	37
Darlington	46	14	6	26	58	96	34
Rochdale	46	14	5	27	62	83	33
Workington	46	11	10	25	55	91	32
Accrington Stanley	46	8	11	27	39	89	27

DIVISION 3S 1952-53

Bristol Rovers	46	26	12	8	92	46	64
Millwall	46	24	14	8	82	44	62
Northampton Town	46	26	10	10	109	70	62
Norwich City	46	25	10	11	99	55	60
Bristol City	46	22	15	9	95	61	59
Coventry City	46	19	12	15	77	62	50
Brighton & Hove Albion	46	19	12	15	81	75	50
Southend United	46	18	13	15	69	74	49
Bournemouth & Boscombe Ath.	46	19	9	18	74	69	47
Watford	46	15	17	14	62	63	47
Reading	46	19	8	19	69	64	46
Torquay United	46	18	9	19	87	88	45
Crystal Palace	46	15	13	18	66	82	43
Leyton Orient	46	16	10	20	68	73	42
Newport County	46	16	10	20	70	82	42
Ipswich Town	46	13	15	18	60	69	41
Exeter City	46	13	14	19	61	71	40
Swindon Town	46	14	12	20	64	79	40
Aldershot	46	12	15	19	61	77	39
Queen's Park Rangers	46	12	15	19	61	82	39
Gillingham	46	12	15	19	55	74	39
Colchester United	46	12	14	20	59	76	38
Shrewsbury Town	46	12	12	22	68	91	36
Walsall	46	7	10	29	56	118	24

1953 F.A. Cup

Semi-finals

Blackpool vs Tottenham Hotspur	2-1
Bolton Wanderers vs Everton	4-3

Final

Wembley, 2nd May 1953

Blackpool 4   (Mortensen 3, Perry)

Bolton Wanderers 3   (Lofthouse, Moir, Bell)

Attendance 100,000

DIVISION 1 1953-54

Wolverhampton Wanderers	42	25	7	10	96	56	57
West Bromwich Albion	42	22	9	11	86	63	53
Huddersfield Town	42	20	11	11	78	61	51
Manchester United	42	18	12	12	73	58	48
Bolton Wanderers	42	18	12	12	75	60	48
Blackpool	42	19	10	13	80	69	48
Burnley	42	21	4	17	78	67	46
Chelsea	42	16	12	14	74	68	44
Charlton Athletic	42	19	6	17	75	77	44
Cardiff City	42	18	8	16	51	71	44
Preston North End	42	19	5	18	87	58	43
Arsenal	42	15	13	14	75	73	43
Aston Villa	42	16	9	17	70	68	41
Portsmouth	42	14	11	17	81	89	39
Newcastle United	42	14	10	18	72	77	38
Tottenham Hotspur	42	16	5	21	65	76	37
Manchester City	42	14	9	19	62	77	37
Sunderland	42	14	8	20	81	89	36
Sheffield Wednesday	42	15	6	21	70	91	36
Sheffield United	42	11	10	20	69	90	33
Middlesbrough	42	10	10	22	60	91	30
Liverpool	42	9	10	23	68	97	28

DIVISION 3N 1953-54

Port Vale	46	26	17	3	74	21	69
Barnsley	46	24	10	12	77	57	58
Scunthorpe United	46	21	15	10	77	56	57
Gateshead	46	21	13	12	74	55	55
Bradford City	46	22	9	15	60	55	53
Chesterfield	46	19	14	13	76	64	52
Mansfield Town	46	20	11	15	88	67	51
Wrexham	46	21	9	16	81	68	51
Bradford Park Avenue	46	18	14	14	77	68	50
Stockport County	46	18	11	17	77	67	47
Southport	46	17	12	17	63	60	46
Barrow	46	16	12	18	72	71	44
Carlisle United	46	14	15	17	83	71	43
Tranmere Rovers	46	18	7	21	59	70	43
Accrington Stanley	46	16	10	20	66	74	42
Crewe Alexandra	46	14	13	19	49	67	41
Grimsby Town	46	16	9	21	51	77	41
Hartlepools United	46	13	14	19	59	65	40
Rochdale	46	15	10	21	59	77	40
Workington	46	13	14	19	59	80	40
Darlington	46	12	14	20	50	71	38
York City	46	12	13	21	64	86	37
Halifax Town	46	12	10	24	44	73	34
Chester	46	11	10	25	48	67	32

DIVISION 2 1953-54

Leicester City	42	23	10	9	97	60	56
Everton	42	20	16	6	92	58	56
Blackburn Rovers	42	23	9	10	86	50	55
Nottingham Forest	42	20	12	10	86	59	52
Rotherham United	42	21	7	14	80	67	49
Luton Town	42	18	12	12	64	59	48
Birmingham City	42	18	11	13	78	58	47
Fulham	42	17	10	15	98	85	44
Bristol Rovers	42	14	16	12	64	58	44
Leeds United	42	15	13	14	89	81	43
Stoke City	42	12	17	13	71	60	41
Doncaster Rovers	42	16	9	17	59	63	41
West Ham United	42	15	9	18	67	69	39
Notts County	42	13	13	16	54	74	39
Hull City	42	16	6	20	64	66	38
Lincoln City	42	14	9	19	65	83	37
Bury	42	11	14	17	54	72	36
Derby County	42	12	11	19	64	82	35
Plymouth Argyle	42	9	16	17	65	82	34
Swansea Town	42	13	8	21	58	82	34
Brentford	42	10	11	21	40	78	31
Oldham Athletic	42	8	9	25	40	89	25

DIVISION 3S 1953-54

Ipswich Town	46	27	10	9	82	51	64
Brighton & Hove Albion	46	26	9	11	86	61	61
Bristol City	46	25	6	15	88	66	56
Watford	46	21	10	15	85	69	52
Northampton Town	46	20	11	15	82	55	51
Southampton	46	22	7	17	76	63	51
Norwich City	46	20	11	15	73	66	51
Reading	46	20	9	17	86	73	49
Exeter City	46	20	8	18	68	58	48
Gillingham	46	19	10	17	61	66	48
Leyton Orient	46	18	11	17	79	73	47
Millwall	46	19	9	18	74	77	47
Torquay United	46	17	12	17	81	88	46
Coventry City	46	18	9	19	61	56	45
Newport County	46	19	6	21	61	81	44
Southend United	46	18	7	21	69	71	43
Aldershot	46	17	9	20	74	86	43
Queen's Park Rangers	46	16	10	20	60	68	42
Bournemouth & Boscombe Ath.	46	16	8	22	67	70	40
Swindon Town	46	15	10	21	67	70	40
Shrewsbury Town	46	14	12	20	65	76	40
Crystal Palace	46	14	12	20	60	86	40
Colchester United	46	10	10	26	50	78	30
Walsall	46	9	8	29	40	87	26

1954 F.A. Cup

Semi-finals

West Bromwich Albion vs Port Vale	2-1
Sheffield Wednesday vs Preston North End	0-2

Final

Wembley, 1st May 1954

West Bromwich Albion 3 (Allen 2 (1 pen), Griffin)

Preston North End 2 (Morrison, Wayman)

Attendance 100,000

DIVISION 1 1954-55

Chelsea	42	20	12	10	81	57	52
Wolverhampton Wanderers	42	19	10	13	89	70	48
Portsmouth	42	18	12	12	74	62	48
Sunderland	42	15	18	9	64	54	48
Manchester United	42	20	7	15	84	74	47
Aston Villa	42	20	7	15	72	73	47
Manchester City	42	18	10	14	76	69	46
Newcastle United	42	17	9	16	89	77	43
Arsenal	42	17	9	16	69	63	43
Burnley	42	17	9	16	51	48	43
Everton	42	16	10	16	62	68	42
Huddersfield Town	42	14	13	15	63	68	41
Sheffield United	42	17	7	18	70	86	41
Preston North End	42	16	8	18	83	64	40
Charlton Athletic	42	15	10	17	76	75	40
Tottenham Hotspur	42	16	8	18	72	73	40
West Bromwich Albion	42	16	8	18	76	96	40
Bolton Wanderers	42	13	13	16	62	69	39
Blackpool	42	14	10	18	60	64	38
Cardiff City	42	13	11	18	62	76	37
Leicester City	42	12	11	19	74	86	35
Sheffield Wednesday	42	8	10	24	63	100	26

DIVISION 2 1954-55

Birmingham City	42	22	10	10	92	47	54
Luton Town	42	23	8	11	88	53	54
Rotherham United	42	25	4	13	94	64	54
Leeds United	42	23	7	12	70	53	53
Stoke City	42	21	10	11	69	46	52
Blackburn Rovers	42	22	6	14	114	79	50
Notts County	42	21	6	15	74	71	48
West Ham United	42	18	10	14	74	70	46
Bristol Rovers	42	19	7	16	75	70	45
Swansea Town	42	17	9	16	86	83	43
Liverpool	42	16	10	16	92	96	42
Middlesbrough	42	18	6	18	73	82	42
Bury	42	15	11	16	77	72	41
Fulham	42	14	11	17	76	79	39
Nottingham Forest	42	16	7	19	58	62	39
Lincoln City	42	13	10	19	68	79	36
Port Vale	42	12	11	19	48	71	35
Doncaster Rovers	42	14	7	21	58	95	35
Hull City	42	12	10	20	44	69	34
Plymouth Argyle	42	12	7	23	57	82	31
Ipswich Town	42	11	6	25	57	92	28
Derby County	42	7	9	26	53	82	23

DIVISION 3N 1954-55

Barnsley	46	30	5	11	86	46	65
Accrington Stanley	46	25	11	10	96	67	61
Scunthorpe United	46	23	12	11	81	53	58
York City	46	24	10	12	92	63	58
Hartlepools United	46	25	5	16	64	49	55
Chesterfield	46	24	6	16	81	70	54
Gateshead	46	20	12	14	65	69	52
Workington	46	18	14	14	68	55	50
Stockport County	46	18	12	16	84	70	48
Oldham Athletic	46	19	10	17	74	68	48
Southport	46	16	16	14	47	44	48
Rochdale	46	17	14	15	69	66	48
Mansfield Town	46	18	9	19	65	71	45
Halifax Town	46	15	13	18	63	67	43
Darlington	46	14	14	18	62	73	42
Bradford Park Avenue	46	15	11	20	56	70	41
Barrow	46	17	6	23	70	89	40
Wrexham	46	13	12	21	65	77	38
Tranmere Rovers	46	13	11	22	55	70	37
Carlisle United	46	15	6	25	78	89	36
Bradford City	46	13	10	23	47	55	36
Crewe Alexandra	46	10	14	22	68	91	34
Grimsby Town	46	13	8	25	47	78	34
Chester	46	12	9	25	44	77	33

DIVISION 3S 1954-55

Bristol City	46	30	10	6	101	47	70
Leyton Orient	46	26	9	11	89	47	61
Southampton	46	24	11	11	75	51	59
Gillingham	46	20	15	11	77	66	55
Millwall	46	20	11	15	72	68	51
Brighton & Hove Albion	46	20	10	16	76	63	50
Watford	46	18	14	14	71	62	50
Torquay United	46	18	12	16	82	82	48
Coventry City	46	18	11	17	67	59	47
Southend United	46	17	12	17	83	80	46
Brentford	46	16	14	16	82	82	46
Norwich City	46	18	10	18	60	60	46
Northampton Town	46	19	8	19	73	81	46
Aldershot	46	16	13	17	75	71	45
Queen's Park Rangers	46	15	14	17	69	75	44
Shrewsbury Town	46	16	10	20	70	78	42
Bournemouth & Boscombe Ath.	46	12	18	16	57	65	42
Reading	46	13	15	18	65	73	41
Newport County	46	11	16	19	60	73	38
Crystal Palace	46	11	16	19	52	80	38
Swindon Town	46	11	15	20	46	64	37
Exeter City	46	11	15	20	47	73	37
Walsall	46	10	14	22	75	86	34
Colchester United	46	9	13	24	53	91	31

1955 F.A. Cup

Semi-finals

Newcastle United vs York City	1-1, 2-0
Sunderland vs Manchester City	0-1

Final

Wembley, 7th May 1955

Newcastle United 3 (Milburn, Mitchell, Hannah)
Manchester City 1 (Johnstone)

Attendance 100,000

DIVISION 1 1955-56

Manchester United	42	25	10	7	83	51	60
Blackpool	42	20	9	13	86	62	49
Wolverhampton Wanderers	42	20	9	13	89	65	49
Manchester City	42	18	10	14	82	69	46
Arsenal	42	18	10	14	60	61	46
Birmingham City	42	18	9	15	75	57	45
Burnley	42	18	8	16	64	54	44
Bolton Wanderers	42	18	7	17	71	58	43
Sunderland	42	17	9	16	80	95	43
Luton Town	42	17	8	17	66	64	42
Newcastle United	42	17	7	18	85	70	41
Portsmouth	42	16	9	17	78	85	41
West Bromwich Albion	42	18	5	19	58	70	41
Charlton Athletic	42	17	6	19	75	81	40
Everton	42	15	10	17	55	69	40
Chelsea	42	14	11	17	64	77	39
Cardiff City	42	15	9	18	55	69	39
Tottenham Hotspur	42	15	7	20	61	71	37
Preston North End	42	14	8	20	73	72	36
Aston Villa	42	11	13	18	52	69	35
Huddersfield Town	42	14	7	21	54	83	35
Sheffield United	42	12	9	21	63	77	33

DIVISION 2 1955-56

Sheffield Wednesday	42	21	13	8	101	62	55
Leeds United	42	23	6	13	80	60	52
Liverpool	42	21	6	15	85	63	48
Blackburn Rovers	42	21	6	15	84	65	48
Leicester City	42	21	6	15	94	78	48
Bristol Rovers	42	21	6	15	84	70	48
Nottingham Forest	42	19	9	14	68	63	47
Lincoln City	42	18	10	14	79	65	46
Fulham	42	20	6	16	89	79	46
Swansea Town	42	20	6	16	83	81	46
Bristol City	42	19	7	16	80	64	45
Port Vale	42	16	13	13	60	58	45
Stoke City	42	20	4	18	71	62	44
Middlesbrough	42	16	8	18	76	78	40
Bury	42	16	8	18	86	90	40
West Ham United	42	14	11	17	74	69	39
Doncaster Rovers	42	12	11	19	69	96	35
Barnsley	42	11	12	19	47	84	34
Rotherham United	42	12	9	21	56	75	33
Notts County	42	11	9	22	55	82	31
Plymouth Argyle	42	10	8	24	54	87	28
Hull City	42	10	6	26	53	97	26

DIVISION 3N 1955-56

Grimsby Town	46	31	6	9	76	29	68
Derby County	46	28	7	11	110	55	63
Accrington Stanley	46	25	9	12	92	57	59
Hartlepools United	46	26	5	15	81	60	57
Southport	46	23	11	12	66	53	57
Chesterfield	46	25	4	17	94	66	54
Stockport County	46	21	9	16	90	61	51
Bradford City	46	18	13	15	78	64	49
Scunthorpe United	46	20	8	18	75	63	48
Workington	46	19	9	18	75	63	47
York City	46	19	9	18	85	72	47
Rochdale	46	17	13	16	66	84	47
Gateshead	46	17	11	18	77	84	45
Wrexham	46	16	10	20	66	73	42
Darlington	46	16	9	21	60	73	41
Tranmere Rovers	46	16	9	21	59	84	41
Chester	46	13	14	19	52	82	40
Mansfield Town	46	14	11	21	84	81	39
Halifax Town	46	14	11	21	66	76	39
Oldham Athletic	46	10	18	18	76	86	38
Carlisle United	46	15	8	23	71	95	38
Barrow	46	12	9	25	61	83	33
Bradford Park Avenue	46	13	7	26	61	122	33
Crewe Alexandra	46	9	10	27	50	105	28

DIVISION 3S 1955-56

Leyton Orient	46	29	8	9	106	49	66
Brighton & Hove Albion	46	29	7	10	112	50	65
Ipswich Town	46	25	14	7	106	60	64
Southend United	46	21	11	14	88	80	53
Torquay United	46	20	12	14	86	63	52
Brentford	46	19	14	13	69	66	52
Norwich City	46	19	13	14	86	82	51
Coventry City	46	20	9	17	73	60	49
Bournemouth & Boscombe Ath.	46	19	10	17	63	51	48
Gillingham	46	19	10	17	69	71	48
Northampton Town	46	20	7	19	67	71	47
Colchester United	46	18	11	17	76	81	47
Shrewsbury Town	46	17	12	17	69	66	46
Southampton	46	18	8	20	91	81	44
Aldershot	46	12	16	18	70	90	40
Exeter City	46	15	10	21	58	77	40
Reading	46	15	9	22	70	79	39
Queen's Park Rangers	46	14	11	21	64	86	39
Newport County	46	15	9	22	58	79	39
Walsall	46	15	8	23	68	84	38
Watford	46	13	11	22	52	85	37
Millwall	46	15	6	25	83	100	36
Crystal Palace	46	12	10	24	54	83	34
Swindon Town	46	8	14	24	34	78	30

1956 F.A. Cup

Semi-finals

Tottenham Hotspur vs Manchester City	0-1
Birmingham City vs Sunderland	3-0

Final

Wembley, 5th May 1956

Manchester City 3 (Hayes, Dyson, Johnstone)

Birmingham City 1 (Kinsey)

Attendance 100,000

DIVISION 1 1956-57

Manchester United	42	28	8	6	103	54	64
Tottenham Hotspur	42	22	12	8	104	56	56
Preston North End	42	23	10	9	84	56	56
Blackpool	42	22	9	11	93	65	53
Arsenal	42	21	8	13	85	69	50
Wolverhampton Wanderers	42	20	8	14	94	70	48
Burnley	42	18	10	14	56	50	46
Leeds United	42	15	14	13	72	63	44
Bolton Wanderers	42	16	12	14	65	65	44
Aston Villa	42	14	15	13	65	55	43
West Bromwich Albion	42	14	14	14	59	61	42
Birmingham City	42	15	9	18	69	69	39
Chelsea	42	13	13	16	73	73	39
Sheffield Wednesday	42	16	6	20	82	88	38
Everton	42	14	10	18	61	79	38
Luton Town	42	14	9	19	58	76	37
Newcastle United	42	14	8	20	67	87	36
Manchester City	42	13	9	20	78	88	35
Portsmouth	42	10	13	19	62	92	33
Sunderland	42	12	8	22	67	88	32
Cardiff City	42	10	9	23	53	88	29
Charlton Athletic	42	9	4	29	62	120	22

DIVISION 2 1956-57

Leicester City	42	25	11	6	109	67	61
Nottingham Forest	42	22	10	10	94	55	54
Liverpool	42	21	11	10	82	54	53
Blackburn Rovers	42	21	10	11	83	75	52
Stoke City	42	20	8	14	83	58	48
Middlesbrough	42	19	10	13	84	60	48
Sheffield United	42	19	8	15	87	76	46
West Ham United	42	19	8	15	59	63	46
Bristol Rovers	42	18	9	15	81	67	45
Swansea Town	42	19	7	16	90	90	45
Fulham	42	19	4	19	84	76	42
Huddersfield Town	42	18	6	18	68	74	42
Bristol City	42	16	9	17	74	79	41
Doncaster Rovers	42	15	10	17	77	77	40
Leyton Orient	42	15	10	17	66	84	40
Grimsby Town	42	17	5	20	61	62	39
Rotherham United	42	13	11	18	74	75	37
Lincoln City	42	14	6	22	54	80	34
Barnsley	42	12	10	20	59	89	34
Notts County	42	9	12	21	58	86	30
Bury	42	8	9	25	60	96	25
Port Vale	42	8	6	28	57	101	22

DIVISION 3N 1956-57

Derby County	46	26	11	9	111	53	63
Hartlepools United	46	25	9	12	90	63	59
Accrington Stanley	46	25	8	13	95	64	58
Workington	46	24	10	12	93	63	58
Stockport County	46	23	8	15	91	75	54
Chesterfield	46	22	9	15	96	79	53
York City	46	21	10	15	75	61	52
Hull City	46	21	10	15	84	69	52
Bradford City	46	22	8	16	78	68	52
Barrow	46	21	9	16	76	62	51
Halifax Town	46	21	7	18	65	70	49
Wrexham	46	19	10	17	97	74	48
Rochdale	46	18	12	16	65	65	48
Scunthorpe United	46	15	15	16	71	69	45
Carlisle United	46	16	13	17	76	85	45
Mansfield Town	46	17	10	19	91	90	44
Gateshead	46	17	10	19	72	90	44
Darlington	46	17	8	21	82	95	42
Oldham Athletic	46	12	15	19	66	74	39
Bradford Park Avenue	46	16	3	27	66	93	35
Chester	46	10	13	23	55	84	33
Southport	46	10	12	24	52	94	32
Tranmere Rovers	46	7	13	26	51	91	27
Crewe Alexandra	46	6	9	31	43	110	21

DIVISION 3S 1956-57

Ipswich Town	46	25	9	12	101	54	59
Torquay United	46	24	11	11	89	64	59
Colchester United	46	22	14	10	84	56	58
Southampton	46	22	10	14	76	52	54
Bournemouth & Boscombe Ath.	46	19	14	13	88	62	52
Brighton & Hove Albion	46	19	14	13	86	65	52
Southend United	46	18	12	16	73	65	48
Brentford	46	16	16	14	78	76	48
Shrewsbury Town	46	15	18	13	72	79	48
Queen's Park Rangers	46	18	11	17	61	60	47
Watford	46	18	10	18	72	75	46
Newport County	46	16	13	17	65	62	45
Reading	46	18	9	19	80	81	45
Northampton Town	46	18	9	19	66	73	45
Walsall	46	16	12	18	80	74	44
Coventry City	46	16	12	18	74	84	44
Millwall	46	16	12	18	64	84	44
Plymouth Argyle	46	16	11	19	68	73	43
Aldershot	46	15	12	19	79	92	42
Crystal Palace	46	11	18	17	62	75	40
Exeter City	46	12	13	21	61	79	37
Gillingham	46	12	13	21	54	85	37
Swindon Town	46	15	6	25	66	96	36
Norwich City	46	8	15	23	61	94	31

1957 F.A. Cup

Semi-finals

Aston Villa vs West Bromwich Albion	2-2, 1-0
Manchester United vs Birmingham City	2-0

Final

Wembley, 4th May 1957

Aston Villa 2 (McParland 2)

Manchester United 1 (Taylor)

Attendance 100,000

DIVISION 1 1957-58

Wolverhampton Wanderers	42	28	8	6	103	47	64
Preston North End	42	26	7	9	100	51	59
Tottenham Hotspur	42	21	9	12	93	77	51
West Bromwich Albion	42	18	14	10	92	70	50
Manchester City	42	22	5	15	104	100	49
Burnley	42	21	5	16	80	74	47
Blackpool	42	19	6	17	80	67	44
Luton Town	42	19	6	17	69	63	44
Manchester United	42	16	11	15	85	75	43
Nottingham Forest	42	16	10	16	69	63	42
Chelsea	42	15	12	15	83	79	42
Arsenal	42	16	7	19	73	85	39
Birmingham City	42	14	11	17	76	89	39
Aston Villa	42	16	7	19	73	86	39
Bolton Wanderers	42	14	10	18	65	87	38
Everton	42	13	11	18	65	75	37
Leeds United	42	14	9	19	51	63	37
Leicester City	42	14	5	23	91	112	33
Newcastle United	42	12	8	22	73	81	32
Portsmouth	42	12	8	22	73	88	32
Sunderland	42	10	12	20	54	97	32
Sheffield Wednesday	42	12	7	23	69	92	31

DIVISION 2 1957-58

West Ham United	42	23	11	8	101	54	57
Blackburn Rovers	42	22	12	8	93	57	56
Charlton Athletic	42	24	7	11	107	69	55
Liverpool	42	22	10	10	79	54	54
Fulham	42	20	12	10	97	59	52
Sheffield United	42	21	10	11	75	50	52
Middlesbrough	42	19	7	16	83	74	45
Ipswich Town	42	16	12	14	68	69	44
Huddersfield Town	42	14	16	12	63	66	44
Bristol Rovers	42	17	8	17	85	80	42
Stoke City	42	18	6	18	75	73	42
Leyton Orient	42	18	5	19	77	79	41
Grimsby Town	42	17	6	19	86	83	40
Barnsley	42	14	12	16	70	74	40
Cardiff City	42	14	9	19	63	77	37
Derby County	42	14	8	20	60	81	36
Bristol City	42	13	9	20	63	88	35
Rotherham United	42	14	5	23	65	101	33
Swansea Town	42	11	9	22	72	99	31
Lincoln City	42	11	9	22	55	82	31
Notts County	42	12	6	24	44	80	30
Doncaster Rovers	42	8	11	23	56	88	27

DIVISION 3N 1957-58

Scunthorpe United	46	29	8	9	88	50	66
Accrington Stanley	46	25	9	12	83	61	59
Bradford City	46	21	15	10	73	49	57
Bury	46	23	10	13	94	62	56
Hull City	46	19	15	12	78	67	53
Mansfield Town	46	22	8	16	100	92	52
Halifax Town	46	20	11	15	83	69	51
Chesterfield	46	18	15	13	71	69	51
Stockport County	46	18	11	17	74	67	47
Rochdale	46	19	8	19	79	67	46
Tranmere Rovers	46	18	10	18	82	76	46
Wrexham	46	17	12	17	61	63	46
York City	46	17	12	17	68	76	46
Gateshead	46	15	15	16	68	76	45
Oldham Athletic	46	14	17	15	72	84	45
Carlisle United	46	19	6	21	80	78	44
Hartlepools United	46	16	12	18	73	76	44
Barrow	46	13	15	18	66	74	41
Workington	46	14	13	19	72	81	41
Darlington	46	17	7	22	78	89	41
Chester	46	13	13	20	73	81	39
Bradford Park Avenue	46	13	11	22	68	95	37
Southport	46	11	6	29	52	88	28
Crewe Alexandra	46	8	7	31	47	93	23

DIVISION 3S 1957-58

Brighton & Hove Albion	46	24	12	10	88	64	60
Brentford	46	24	10	12	82	56	58
Plymouth Argyle	46	25	8	13	67	48	58
Swindon Town	46	21	15	10	79	50	57
Reading	46	21	13	12	79	51	55
Southampton	46	22	10	14	112	72	54
Southend United	46	21	12	13	90	58	54
Norwich City	46	19	15	12	75	70	53
Bournemouth & Boscombe Ath.	46	21	9	16	81	74	51
Queen's Park Rangers	46	18	14	14	64	65	50
Newport County	46	17	14	15	73	67	48
Colchester United	46	17	13	16	77	79	47
Northampton Town	46	19	6	21	87	79	44
Crystal Palace	46	15	13	18	70	72	43
Port Vale	46	16	10	20	67	58	42
Watford	46	13	16	17	59	77	42
Shrewsbury Town	46	15	10	21	49	71	40
Aldershot	46	12	16	18	59	89	40
Coventry City	46	13	13	20	61	81	39
Walsall	46	14	9	23	61	75	37
Torquay United	46	11	13	22	49	74	35
Gillingham	46	13	9	24	52	81	35
Millwall	46	11	9	26	63	91	31
Exeter City	46	11	9	26	57	99	31

1958 F.A. Cup

Semi-finals

Blackburn Rovers vs Bolton Wanderers	1-2
Manchester United vs Fulham	2-2, 5-3

Final

Wembley, 3rd May 1958

Bolton Wanderers 2   (Lofthouse 2)

Manchester United 0

Attendance 100,000

DIVISION 1 1958-59

Wolverhampton Wanderers	42	28	5	9	110	49	61
Manchester United	42	24	7	11	103	66	55
Arsenal	42	21	8	13	88	68	50
Bolton Wanderers	42	20	10	12	79	66	50
West Bromwich Albion	42	18	13	11	88	68	49
West Ham United	42	21	6	15	85	70	48
Burnley	42	19	10	13	81	70	48
Blackpool	42	18	11	13	66	49	47
Birmingham City	42	20	6	16	84	68	46
Blackburn Rovers	42	17	10	15	76	70	44
Newcastle United	42	17	7	18	80	80	41
Preston North End	42	17	7	18	70	77	41
Nottingham Forest	42	17	6	19	71	74	40
Chelsea	42	18	4	20	77	98	40
Leeds United	42	15	9	18	57	74	39
Everton	42	17	4	21	71	87	38
Luton Town	42	12	13	17	68	71	37
Tottenham Hotspur	42	13	10	19	85	95	36
Leicester City	42	11	10	21	67	98	32
Manchester City	42	11	9	22	64	95	31
Aston Villa	42	11	8	23	58	87	30
Portsmouth	42	6	9	27	64	112	21

DIVSION 2 1958-59

Sheffield Wednesday	42	28	6	8	106	48	62
Fulham	42	27	6	9	96	61	60
Sheffield United	42	23	7	12	82	48	53
Liverpool	42	24	5	13	87	62	53
Stoke City	42	21	7	14	72	58	49
Bristol Rovers	42	18	12	12	80	64	48
Derby County	42	20	8	14	74	71	48
Charlton Athletic	42	18	7	17	92	90	43
Cardiff City	42	18	7	17	65	65	43
Bristol City	42	17	7	18	74	70	41
Swansea Town	42	16	9	17	79	81	41
Brighton & Hove Albion	42	15	11	16	74	90	41
Middlesbrough	42	15	10	17	87	71	40
Huddersfield Town	42	16	8	18	62	55	40
Sunderland	42	16	8	18	64	75	40
Ipswich Town	42	17	6	19	62	77	40
Leyton Orient	42	14	8	20	71	78	36
Scunthorpe United	42	12	9	21	55	84	33
Lincoln City	42	11	7	24	63	93	29
Rotherham United	42	10	9	23	42	82	29
Grimsby Town	42	9	10	23	62	90	28
Barnsley	42	10	7	25	55	91	27

DIVISION 3 1958-59

Plymouth Argyle	46	23	16	7	89	59	62
Hull City	46	26	9	11	90	55	61
Brentford	46	21	15	10	76	49	57
Norwich City	46	22	13	11	89	62	57
Colchester United	46	21	10	15	71	67	52
Reading	46	21	8	17	78	63	50
Tranmere Rovers	46	21	8	17	82	67	50
Southend United	46	21	8	17	85	80	50
Halifax Town	46	21	8	17	80	77	50
Bury	46	17	14	15	69	58	48
Bradford City	46	18	11	17	84	76	47
Bournemouth & Boscombe Ath.	46	17	12	17	69	69	46
Queen's Park Rangers	46	19	8	19	74	77	46
Southampton	46	17	11	18	88	80	45
Swindon Town	46	16	13	17	59	57	45
Chesterfield	46	17	10	19	67	64	44
Newport County	46	17	9	20	69	68	43
Wrexham	46	14	14	18	63	77	42
Accrington Stanley	46	15	12	19	71	87	42
Mansfield Town	46	14	13	19	73	98	41
Stockport County	46	13	10	23	65	78	36
Doncaster Rovers	46	14	5	27	50	90	33
Notts County	46	8	13	25	55	96	29
Rochdale	46	8	12	26	37	79	28

DIVISION 4 1958-59

Port Vale	46	26	12	81	110	58	64
Coventry City	46	24	12	10	84	47	60
York City	46	21	18	7	73	52	60
Shrewsbury Town	46	24	10	12	101	63	58
Exeter City	46	23	11	12	87	61	57
Walsall	46	21	10	15	95	64	52
Crystal Palace	46	20	12	14	90	71	52
Northampton Town	46	21	9	16	85	78	51
Millwall	46	20	10	16	76	69	50
Carlisle United	46	19	12	15	62	65	50
Gillingham	46	20	9	17	82	77	49
Torquay United	46	16	12	18	78	77	44
Chester	46	16	12	18	72	84	44
Bradford Park Avenue	46	18	7	21	75	77	43
Watford	46	16	10	20	81	79	42
Darlington	46	13	16	17	66	68	42
Workington	46	12	17	17	63	78	41
Crewe Alexandra	46	15	10	21	70	82	40
Hartlepools United	46	15	10	21	74	88	40
Gateshead	46	16	8	22	56	85	40
Oldham Athletic	46	16	4	26	59	84	36
Aldershot	46	14	7	25	63	97	35
Barrow	46	9	10	27	51	104	28
Southport	46	7	12	27	41	86	26

1959 F.A. Cup

Semi-finals

Nottingham Forest vs Aston Villa	1-0
Norwich City vs Luton Town	1-1, 0-1

Final

Wembley, 2nd May 1959

Nottingham Forest 2   (Dwight, Wilson)

Luton Town 1   (Pacey)

Attendance 100,000

DIVISION 1 1959-60

Burnley	42	24	7	11	85	61	55
Wolverhampton Wanderers	42	24	6	12	106	67	54
Tottenham Hotspur	42	21	11	10	86	50	53
West Bromwich Albion	42	19	11	12	83	57	49
Sheffield Wednesday	42	19	11	12	80	59	49
Bolton Wanderers	42	20	8	14	59	51	48
Manchester United	42	19	7	16	102	80	45
Newcastle United	42	18	8	16	82	78	44
Preston North End	42	16	12	14	79	76	44
Fulham	42	17	10	15	73	80	44
Blackpool	42	15	10	17	59	71	40
Leicester City	42	13	13	16	66	75	39
Arsenal	42	15	9	18	68	80	39
West Ham United	42	16	6	20	75	91	38
Everton	42	13	11	18	73	78	37
Manchester City	42	17	3	22	78	84	37
Blackburn Rovers	42	16	5	21	60	70	37
Chelsea	42	14	9	19	76	91	37
Birmingham City	42	13	10	19	63	80	36
Nottingham Forest	42	13	9	20	50	74	35
Leeds United	42	12	10	20	65	92	34
Luton Town	42	9	12	21	50	73	30

DIVISION 2 1959-60

Aston Villa	42	25	9	8	89	43	59
Cardiff City	42	23	12	7	90	62	58
Liverpool	42	20	10	12	90	66	50
Sheffield United	42	19	12	11	68	51	50
Middlesbrough	42	19	10	13	90	64	48
Huddersfield Town	42	19	9	14	73	52	47
Charlton Athletic	42	17	13	12	90	87	47
Rotherham United	42	17	13	12	61	60	47
Bristol Rovers	42	18	11	13	72	78	47
Leyton Orient	42	15	14	13	76	61	44
Ipswich Town	42	19	6	17	78	68	44
Swansea Town	42	15	10	17	82	84	40
Lincoln City	42	16	7	19	75	78	39
Brighton & Hove Albion	42	13	12	17	67	76	38
Scunthorpe United	42	13	10	19	57	71	36
Sunderland	42	12	12	18	52	65	36
Stoke City	42	14	7	21	66	83	35
Derby County	42	14	7	21	61	77	35
Plymouth Argyle	42	13	9	20	61	89	35
Portsmouth	42	10	12	20	59	77	32
Hull City	42	10	10	22	48	76	30
Bristol City	42	11	5	26	60	97	27

DIVISION 3 1959-60

Southampton	46	26	9	11	106	75	61
Norwich City	46	24	11	11	82	54	59
Shrewsbury Town	46	18	16	12	97	75	52
Grimsby Town	46	18	16	12	87	70	52
Coventry City	46	21	10	15	78	63	52
Brentford	46	21	9	16	78	61	51
Bury	46	21	9	16	64	51	51
Queen's Park Rangers	46	18	13	15	73	54	49
Colchester United	46	18	11	17	83	74	47
Bournemouth & Boscombe Ath.	46	17	13	16	72	72	47
Reading	46	18	10	18	84	77	46
Southend United	46	19	8	19	76	74	46
Newport County	46	20	6	20	80	79	46
Port Vale	46	19	8	19	80	79	46
Halifax Town	46	18	10	18	70	72	46
Swindon Town	46	19	8	19	69	78	46
Barnsley	46	15	14	17	65	66	44
Chesterfield	46	18	7	21	71	84	43
Bradford City	46	15	12	19	66	74	42
Tranmere Rovers	46	14	13	19	72	75	41
York City	46	13	12	21	57	73	38
Mansfield Town	46	15	6	25	81	112	36
Wrexham	46	14	8	24	68	101	36
Accrington Stanley	46	11	5	30	57	123	27

DIVISION 4 1959-60

Walsall	46	28	9	9	102	60	65
Notts County	46	26	8	12	107	69	60
Torquay United	46	26	8	12	84	58	60
Watford	46	24	9	13	92	67	57
Millwall	46	18	17	11	84	61	53
Northampton Town	46	22	9	15	85	63	53
Gillingham	46	21	10	15	74	69	52
Crystal Palace	46	19	12	15	84	64	50
Exeter City	46	19	11	16	80	70	49
Stockport County	46	19	11	16	58	54	49
Bradford Park Avenue	46	17	15	14	70	68	49
Rochdale	46	18	10	18	65	60	46
Aldershot	46	18	9	19	77	74	45
Crewe Alexandra	46	18	9	19	79	88	45
Darlington	46	17	9	20	63	73	43
Workington	46	14	14	18	68	60	42
Doncaster Rovers	46	16	10	20	69	76	42
Barrow	46	15	11	20	77	84	41
Carlisle United	46	15	11	20	51	66	41
Chester	46	14	12	20	59	77	40
Southport	46	10	14	22	48	92	34
Gateshead	46	12	9	25	58	86	33
Oldham Athletic	46	8	12	26	41	83	28
Hartlepools United	46	10	7	29	59	109	27

1960 F.A. Cup

Semi-finals

Wolverhampton Wanderers vs Aston Villa	1-0
Sheffield Wednesday vs Blackburn Rovers	1-2

Final

Wembley, 7th May 1960

Wolverhampton Wands. 3   (McGrath (og), Deeley 2)

Blackburn Rovers 0

Attendance 100,000

DIVISION 1 1960-61

Tottenham Hotspur	42	31	4	7	115	55	66
Sheffield Wednesday	42	23	12	7	78	47	58
Wolverhampton Wanderers	42	25	7	10	103	75	57
Burnley	42	22	7	13	102	77	51
Everton	42	22	6	14	87	69	50
Leicester City	42	18	9	15	87	70	45
Manchester United	42	18	9	15	88	76	45
Blackburn Rovers	42	15	13	14	77	76	43
Aston Villa	42	17	9	16	78	77	43
West Bromwich Albion	42	18	5	19	67	71	41
Arsenal	42	15	11	16	77	85	41
Chelsea	42	15	7	20	98	100	37
Manchester City	42	13	11	18	79	90	37
Nottingham Forest	42	14	9	19	62	78	37
Cardiff City	42	13	11	18	60	85	37
West Ham United	42	13	10	19	77	88	36
Fulham	42	14	8	20	72	95	36
Bolton Wanderers	42	12	11	19	58	73	35
Birmingham City	42	14	6	22	62	84	34
Blackpool	42	12	9	21	68	73	33
Newcastle United	42	11	10	21	86	109	32
Preston North End	42	10	10	22	43	71	30

DIVISION 2 1960-61

Ipswich Town	42	26	7	9	100	55	59
Sheffield United	42	26	6	10	81	51	58
Liverpool	42	21	10	11	87	58	52
Norwich City	42	20	9	13	70	53	49
Middlesbrough	42	18	12	12	83	74	48
Sunderland	42	17	13	12	75	60	47
Swansea Town	42	18	11	13	77	73	47
Southampton	42	18	8	16	84	81	44
Scunthorpe United	42	14	15	13	69	64	43
Charlton Athletic	42	16	11	15	97	91	43
Plymouth Argyle	42	17	8	17	81	82	42
Derby County	42	15	10	17	80	80	40
Luton Town	42	15	9	18	71	79	39
Leeds United	42	14	10	18	75	83	38
Rotherham United	42	12	13	17	65	64	37
Brighton & Hove Albion	42	14	9	19	61	75	37
Bristol Rovers	42	15	7	20	73	92	37
Stoke City	42	12	12	18	51	59	36
Leyton Orient	42	14	8	20	55	78	36
Huddersfield Town	42	13	9	20	62	71	35
Portsmouth	42	11	11	20	64	91	33
Lincoln City	42	8	8	26	48	95	24

DIVISION 3 1960-61

Bury	46	30	8	8	108	45	68
Walsall	46	28	6	12	98	60	62
Queen's Park Rangers	46	25	10	11	93	60	60
Watford	46	20	12	14	85	72	52
Notts County	46	21	9	16	82	77	51
Grimsby Town	46	20	10	16	77	69	50
Port Vale	46	17	15	14	96	79	49
Barnsley	46	21	7	18	83	80	49
Halifax Town	46	16	17	13	71	78	49
Shrewsbury Town	46	15	16	15	83	75	46
Hull City	46	17	12	17	73	73	46
Torquay United	46	14	17	15	75	83	45
Newport County	46	17	11	18	81	90	45
Bristol City	46	17	10	19	70	68	44
Coventry City	46	16	12	18	80	83	44
Swindon Town	46	14	15	17	62	55	43
Brentford	46	13	17	16	56	70	43
Reading	46	14	12	20	72	83	40
Bournemouth & Boscombe Ath.	46	15	10	21	58	76	40
Southend United	46	14	11	21	60	76	39
Tranmere Rovers	46	15	8	23	79	115	38
Bradford City	46	11	14	21	65	87	36
Colchester United	46	11	11	24	68	101	33
Chesterfield	46	10	12	24	67	87	32

DIVISION 4 1960-61

Peterborough United	46	28	10	8	134	65	66
Crystal Palace	46	29	6	11	110	69	64
Northampton Town	46	25	10	11	90	62	60
Bradford Park Avenue	46	26	8	12	84	74	60
York City	46	21	9	16	80	60	51
Millwall	46	21	8	17	97	86	50
Darlington	46	18	13	15	78	70	49
Workington	46	21	7	18	74	76	49
Crewe Alexandra	46	20	9	17	61	67	49
Aldershot	46	18	9	19	79	69	45
Doncaster Rovers	46	19	7	20	76	78	45
Oldham Athletic	46	19	7	20	79	88	45
Stockport County	46	18	9	19	57	66	45
Southport	46	19	6	21	69	67	44
Gillingham	46	15	13	18	64	66	43
Wrexham	46	17	8	21	62	56	42
Rochdale	46	17	8	21	60	66	42
Accrington Stanley	46	16	8	22	74	88	40
Carlisle United	46	13	13	20	61	79	39
Mansfield Town	46	16	6	24	71	78	38
Exeter City	46	14	10	22	66	94	38
Barrow	46	13	11	22	52	79	37
Hartlepools United	46	12	8	26	71	103	32
Chester	46	11	9	26	61	104	31

1961 F.A. Cup

Semi-finals

Burnley vs Tottenham Hotspur	0-3
Leicester City vs Sheffield United	0-0, 0-0, 2-0

Final

Wembley, 6th May 1961

Tottenham Hotspur 2 (Smith, Dyson)
Leicester City 0

Attendance 100,000

1961 Football League Cup

Semi-finals

Rotherham United vs Shrewsbury Town (3-2, 1-1)	4-3
Burnley vs Aston Villa (1-1, 2-2)	3-3

Play-off

Burnley vs Aston Villa	2-1

Final (1st leg)

Rotherham, 22nd August 1961

Rotherham United 2   (Webster, Kirkman)
Aston Villa 0

Attendance 12,226

Final (2nd leg)

Villa Park, 5th September 1961

Aston Villa 3   (O'Neill, Burrows, McParland)
Rotherham United 0 (aet.)

Attendance 27,000

Aston Villa won 3-2 on aggregate

DIVISION 1 1961-62

Ipswich Town	42	24	8	10	93	67	56
Burnley	42	21	11	10	101	67	53
Tottenham Hotspur	42	21	10	11	88	69	52
Everton	42	20	11	11	88	54	51
Sheffield United	42	19	9	14	61	69	47
Sheffield Wednesday	42	20	6	16	72	58	46
Aston Villa	42	18	8	16	65	56	44
West Ham United	42	17	10	15	76	82	44
West Bromwich Albion	42	15	13	14	83	67	43
Arsenal	42	16	11	15	71	72	43
Bolton Wanderers	42	16	10	16	62	66	42
Manchester City	42	17	7	18	78	81	41
Blackpool	42	15	11	16	70	75	41
Leicester City	42	17	6	19	72	71	40
Manchester United	42	15	9	18	72	75	39
Blackburn Rovers	42	14	11	17	50	58	39
Birmingham City	42	14	10	18	65	81	38
Wolverhampton Wanderers	42	13	10	19	73	86	36
Nottingham Forest	42	13	10	19	63	79	36
Fulham	42	13	7	22	66	74	33
Cardiff City	42	9	14	19	50	81	32
Chelsea	42	9	10	23	63	94	28

DIVISION 2 1961-62

Liverpool	42	27	8	7	99	43	62
Leyton Orient	42	22	10	10	69	40	54
Sunderland	42	22	9	11	85	50	53
Scunthorpe United	42	21	7	14	86	71	49
Plymouth Argyle	42	19	8	15	75	75	46
Southampton	42	18	9	15	77	62	45
Huddersfield Town	42	16	12	14	67	59	44
Stoke City	42	17	8	17	55	57	42
Rotherham United	42	16	9	17	70	76	41
Preston North End	42	15	10	17	55	57	40
Newcastle United	42	15	9	18	64	58	39
Middlesbrough	42	16	7	19	76	72	39
Luton Town	42	17	5	20	69	71	39
Walsall	42	14	11	17	70	75	39
Charlton Athletic	42	15	9	18	69	75	39
Derby County	42	14	11	17	68	75	39
Norwich City	42	14	11	17	61	70	39
Bury	42	17	5	20	52	76	39
Leeds United	42	12	12	18	50	61	36
Swansea Town	42	12	12	18	61	83	36
Bristol Rovers	42	13	7	22	53	81	33
Brighton & Hove Albion	42	10	11	21	42	86	31

DIVISION 3 1961-62

Portsmouth	46	27	11	8	87	47	65
Grimsby Town	46	28	6	12	80	56	62
Bournemouth & Boscombe Ath.	46	21	17	8	69	45	59
Queen's Park Rangers	46	24	11	11	111	73	59
Peterborough United	46	26	6	14	107	82	58
Bristol City	46	23	8	15	94	72	54
Reading	46	22	9	15	77	66	53
Northampton Town	46	20	11	15	85	57	51
Swindon Town	46	17	15	14	78	71	49
Hull City	46	20	8	18	67	54	48
Bradford Park Avenue	46	20	7	19	80	78	47
Port Vale	46	17	11	18	65	58	45
Notts County	46	17	9	20	67	74	43
Coventry City	46	16	11	19	64	71	43
Crystal Palace	46	14	14	18	83	80	42
Southend United	46	13	16	17	57	69	42
Watford	46	14	13	19	63	74	41
Halifax Town	46	15	10	21	62	84	40
Shrewsbury Town	46	13	12	21	73	84	38
Barnsley	46	13	12	21	71	95	38
Torquay United	46	15	6	25	76	100	36
Lincoln City	46	9	17	20	57	87	35
Brentford	46	13	8	25	53	93	34
Newport County	46	7	8	31	46	102	22

DIVISION 4 1961-62

Millwall	44	23	10	11	87	62	56
Colchester United	44	23	9	12	104	71	55
Wrexham	44	22	9	13	96	56	53
Carlisle United	44	22	8	14	64	63	52
Bradford City	44	21	9	14	94	86	51
York City	44	20	10	14	84	53	50
Aldershot	44	22	5	17	81	60	49
Workington	44	19	11	14	69	70	49
Barrow	44	17	14	13	74	58	48
Crewe Alexandra	44	20	6	18	79	70	46
Oldham Athletic	44	17	12	15	77	70	46
Rochdale	44	19	7	18	71	71	45
Darlington	44	18	9	17	61	73	45
Mansfield Town	44	19	6	19	77	66	44
Tranmere Rovers	44	20	4	20	70	81	44
Stockport County	44	17	9	18	70	69	43
Southport	44	17	9	18	61	71	43
Exeter City	44	13	11	20	62	77	37
Chesterfield	44	14	9	21	70	87	37
Gillingham	44	13	11	20	73	94	37
Doncaster Rovers	44	11	7	26	60	85	29
Hartlepools United	44	8	11	25	52	101	27
Chester	44	7	12	25	54	96	26

Accrington Stanley resigned from the League after 33 matches

1962 F.A. Cup

Semi-finals

Manchester United vs Tottenham Hotspur	1-3
Burnley vs Fulham	1-1, 2-1

Final

Wembley, 5th May 1962

Tottenham Hotspur 3   (Greaves, Smith, Blanchflower (pen))

Burnley 1   (Robson)

Attendance 100,000

1962 Football League Cup

Semi-finals

Norwich City vs Blackpool (4-1, 0-2)	4-3
Rochdale vs Blackburn Rovers (3-1, 1-2)	4-3

Final (1st leg)

Rochdale, 26th April 1962

Rochdale 0

Norwich City 3   (Lythgoe 2, Punton)

Attendance 11,123

Final (2nd leg)

Norwich, 1st May 1962

Norwich City 1   (Hill)

Rochdale 0

Attendance 19,708

Norwich City won 4-0 on aggregate

DIVISION 1 1962-63

Everton	42	25	11	6	84	42	61
Tottenham Hotspur	42	23	9	10	111	62	55
Burnley	42	22	10	10	78	57	54
Leicester City	42	20	12	10	79	53	52
Wolverhampton Wanderers	42	20	10	12	93	65	50
Sheffield Wednesday	42	19	10	13	77	63	48
Arsenal	42	18	10	14	86	77	46
Liverpool	42	17	10	15	71	59	44
Nottingham Forest	42	17	10	15	67	69	44
Sheffield United	42	16	12	14	58	60	44
Blackburn Rovers	42	15	12	15	79	71	42
West Ham United	42	14	12	16	73	69	40
Blackpool	42	13	14	15	58	64	40
West Bromwich Albion	42	16	7	19	71	79	39
Aston Villa	42	15	8	19	62	68	38
Fulham	42	14	10	18	50	71	38
Ipswich Town	42	12	11	19	59	78	35
Bolton Wanderers	42	15	5	22	55	75	35
Manchester United	42	12	10	20	67	81	34
Birmingham City	42	10	13	19	63	90	33
Manchester City	42	10	11	21	58	102	31
Leyton Orient	42	6	9	27	37	81	21

DIVISION 3 1962-63

Northampton Town	46	26	10	10	109	60	62
Swindon Town	46	22	14	10	87	56	58
Port Vale	46	23	8	15	72	58	54
Coventry City	46	18	17	11	83	69	53
Bournemouth & Boscombe Ath.	46	18	16	12	63	46	52
Peterborough United	46	20	11	15	93	75	51
Notts County	46	19	13	14	73	74	51
Southend United	46	19	12	15	75	77	50
Wrexham	46	20	9	17	84	83	49
Hull City	46	19	10	17	74	69	48
Crystal Palace	46	17	13	16	68	58	47
Colchester United	46	18	11	17	73	93	47
Queen's Park Rangers	46	17	11	18	85	76	45
Bristol City	46	16	13	17	100	92	45
Shrewsbury Town	46	16	12	18	83	81	44
Millwall	46	15	13	18	82	87	43
Watford	46	17	8	21	82	85	42
Barnsley	46	15	11	20	63	74	41
Bristol Rovers	46	15	11	20	70	88	41
Reading	46	16	8	22	74	78	40
Bradford Park Avenue	46	14	12	20	79	97	40
Brighton & Hove Albion	46	12	12	22	58	84	36
Carlisle United	46	13	9	24	61	89	35
Halifax Town	46	9	12	25	64	106	30

DIVISION 2 1962-63

Stoke City	42	20	13	9	73	50	53
Chelsea	42	24	4	14	81	42	52
Sunderland	42	20	12	10	84	55	52
Middlesbrough	42	20	9	13	86	85	49
Leeds United	42	19	10	13	79	53	48
Huddersfield Town	42	17	14	11	63	50	48
Newcastle United	42	18	11	13	79	59	47
Bury	42	18	11	13	51	47	47
Scunthorpe United	42	16	12	14	57	59	44
Cardiff City	42	18	7	17	83	73	43
Southampton	42	17	8	17	72	67	42
Plymouth Argyle	42	15	12	15	76	73	42
Norwich City	42	17	8	17	80	79	42
Rotherham United	42	17	6	19	67	74	40
Swansea Town	42	15	9	18	51	72	39
Portsmouth	42	13	11	18	63	79	37
Preston North End	42	13	11	18	59	74	37
Derby County	42	12	12	18	61	72	36
Grimsby Town	42	11	13	18	55	66	35
Charlton Athletic	42	13	5	24	62	94	31
Walsall	42	11	9	22	53	89	31
Luton Town	42	11	7	24	61	84	29

DIVISION 4 1962-63

Brentford	46	27	8	11	98	64	62
Oldham Athletic	46	24	11	11	95	60	59
Crewe Alexandra	46	24	11	11	86	58	59
Mansfield Town	46	24	9	13	108	69	57
Gillingham	46	22	13	11	71	49	57
Torquay United	46	20	16	10	75	56	56
Rochdale	46	20	11	15	67	59	51
Tranmere Rovers	46	20	10	16	81	67	50
Barrow	46	19	12	15	82	80	50
Workington	46	17	13	16	76	68	47
Aldershot	46	15	17	14	73	69	47
Darlington	46	19	6	21	72	87	44
Southport	46	15	14	17	72	106	44
York City	46	16	11	19	67	62	43
Chesterfield	46	13	16	17	70	64	42
Doncaster Rovers	46	14	14	18	64	77	42
Exeter City	46	16	10	20	57	77	42
Oxford United	46	13	15	18	70	71	41
Stockport County	46	15	11	20	56	70	41
Newport County	46	14	11	21	76	90	39
Chester	46	15	9	22	51	66	39
Lincoln City	46	13	9	24	68	89	35
Bradford City	46	11	10	25	64	93	32
Hartlepools United	46	7	11	28	56	104	25

1963 F.A. Cup

Semi-finals

Leicester City vs Liverpool	1-0
Southampton vs Manchester United	0-1

Final

Wembley, 25th May 1963

Manchester United 3　(Law, Herd 2)
Leicester City 1　(Keyworth)

Attendance 100,000

1963 Football League Cup

Semi-finals

Birmingham City vs Bury (3-2, 1-1)	4-3
Sunderland vs Aston Villa (1-3, 0-0)	1-3

Final (1st leg)

St. Andrews, 23rd May 1963

Birmingham City 3　(Leek 2, Bloomfield)
Aston Villa 1　(Thomson)

Attendance 31,850

Final (2nd leg)

Villa Park, 27th May 1963

Aston Villa 0
Birmingham City 0

Attendance 37,920

Birmingham City won 3-1 on aggregate

DIVISION 1 1963-64

Liverpool	42	26	5	11	92	45	57
Manchester United	42	23	7	12	90	62	53
Everton	42	21	10	11	84	64	52
Tottenham Hotspur	42	22	7	13	97	81	51
Chelsea	42	20	10	12	72	56	50
Sheffield Wednesday	42	19	11	12	84	67	49
Blackburn Rovers	42	18	10	14	89	65	46
Arsenal	42	17	11	14	90	82	45
Burnley	42	17	10	15	71	64	44
West Bromwich Albion	42	16	11	15	70	61	43
Leicester City	42	16	11	15	61	58	43
Sheffield United	42	16	11	15	61	64	43
Nottingham Forest	42	16	9	17	64	68	41
West Ham United	42	14	12	16	69	74	40
Fulham	42	13	13	16	58	65	39
Wolverhampton Wanderers	42	12	15	15	70	80	39
Stoke City	42	14	10	18	77	78	38
Blackpool	42	13	9	20	52	73	35
Aston Villa	42	11	12	19	62	71	34
Birmingham City	42	11	7	24	54	92	29
Bolton Wanderers	42	10	8	24	48	80	28
Ipswich Town	42	9	7	26	56	121	25

DIVISION 2 1963-64

Leeds United	42	24	15	3	71	34	63
Sunderland	42	25	11	6	81	37	61
Preston North End	42	23	10	9	79	54	56
Charlton Athletic	42	19	10	13	76	70	48
Southampton	42	19	9	14	100	73	47
Manchester City	42	18	10	14	84	66	46
Rotherham United	42	19	7	16	90	78	45
Newcastle United	42	20	5	17	74	69	45
Portsmouth	42	16	11	15	79	70	43
Middlesbrough	42	15	11	16	67	52	41
Northampton Town	42	16	9	17	58	60	41
Huddersfield Town	42	15	10	17	57	64	40
Derby County	42	14	11	17	56	67	39
Swindon Town	42	14	10	18	57	69	38
Cardiff City	42	14	10	18	56	81	38
Leyton Orient	42	13	10	19	54	72	36
Norwich City	42	11	13	18	64	80	35
Bury	42	13	9	20	57	73	35
Swansea Town	42	12	9	21	63	74	33
Plymouth Argyle	42	8	16	18	45	67	32
Grimsby Town	42	9	14	19	47	75	32
Scunthorpe United	42	10	10	22	52	82	30

DIVISION 3 1963-64

Coventry City	46	22	16	8	98	61	60
Crystal Palace	46	23	14	9	73	51	60
Watford	46	23	12	11	79	59	58
Bournemouth & Boscombe Ath.	46	24	8	14	79	58	56
Bristol City	46	20	15	11	84	64	55
Reading	46	21	10	15	79	62	52
Mansfield Town	46	20	11	15	76	62	51
Hull City	46	16	17	13	73	68	49
Oldham Athletic	46	20	8	18	73	70	48
Peterborough United	46	18	11	17	75	70	47
Shrewsbury Town	46	18	11	17	73	80	47
Bristol Rovers	46	19	8	19	91	79	46
Port Vale	46	16	14	16	53	49	46
Southend United	46	15	15	16	77	78	45
Queen's Park Rangers	46	18	9	19	76	78	45
Brentford	46	15	14	17	87	80	44
Colchester United	46	12	19	15	70	68	43
Luton Town	46	16	10	20	64	80	42
Walsall	46	13	14	19	59	76	40
Barnsley	46	12	15	19	68	94	39
Millwall	46	14	10	22	53	67	38
Crewe Alexandra	46	11	12	23	50	77	34
Wrexham	46	13	6	27	75	107	32
Notts County	46	9	9	28	45	92	27

DIVISION 4 1963-64

Gillingham	46	23	14	9	59	30	60
Carlisle United	46	25	10	11	113	58	60
Workington	46	24	11	11	76	52	59
Exeter City	46	20	18	8	62	37	58
Bradford City	46	25	6	15	76	62	56
Torquay United	46	20	11	15	80	54	51
Tranmere Rovers	46	20	11	15	85	73	51
Brighton & Hove Albion	46	19	12	15	71	52	50
Aldershot	46	19	10	17	83	78	48
Halifax Town	46	17	14	15	77	77	48
Lincoln City	46	19	9	18	67	75	47
Chester	46	19	8	19	65	60	46
Bradford Park Avenue	46	18	9	19	75	81	45
Doncaster Rovers	46	15	12	19	70	75	42
Newport County	46	17	8	21	64	73	42
Chesterfield	46	15	12	19	57	71	42
Stockport County	46	15	12	19	50	68	42
Oxford United	46	14	13	19	59	63	41
Darlington	46	14	12	20	66	93	40
Rochdale	46	12	15	19	56	59	39
Southport	46	15	9	22	63	88	39
York City	46	14	7	25	52	66	35
Hartlepools United	46	12	9	25	54	93	33
Barrow	46	6	18	22	51	93	30

1964 F.A. Cup

Semi-finals

West Ham United vs Manchester United	3-1
Swansea Town vs Preston North End	1-2

Final

Wembley, 2nd May 1964

West Ham United 3 (Sissons, Hurst, Boyce)
Preston North End 2 (Holden, Dawson)

Attendance 100,000

1964 Football League Cup

Semi-finals

Leicester City vs West Ham United (4-3, 2-0)	6-3
Stoke City vs Manchester City (2-0, 0-1)	2-1

Final (1st leg)

Stoke, 15th April 1964

Stoke City 1 (Bebbington)
Leicester City 1 (Gibson)

Attendance 22,309

Final (2nd leg)

Leicester, 22nd April 1964

Leicester City 3 (Stringfellow, Gibson, Riley)
Stoke City 2 (Viollet, Kinnell)

Attendance 25,372

Leicester City won 4-3 on aggregate

DIVISION 1 1964-65

Manchester United	42	26	9	7	89	39	61
Leeds United	42	26	9	7	83	52	61
Chelsea	42	24	8	10	89	54	56
Everton	42	17	15	10	69	60	49
Nottingham Forest	42	17	13	12	71	67	47
Tottenham Hotspur	42	19	7	16	87	71	45
Liverpool	42	17	10	15	67	73	44
Sheffield Wednesday	42	16	11	15	57	55	43
West Ham United	42	19	4	19	82	71	42
Blackburn Rovers	42	16	10	16	83	79	42
Stoke City	42	16	10	16	67	66	42
Burnley	42	16	10	16	70	70	42
Arsenal	42	17	7	18	69	75	41
West Bromwich Albion	42	13	13	16	70	65	39
Sunderland	42	14	9	19	64	74	37
Aston Villa	42	16	5	21	57	82	37
Blackpool	42	12	11	19	67	78	35
Leicester City	42	11	13	18	69	85	35
Sheffield United	42	12	11	19	50	64	35
Fulham	42	11	12	19	60	78	34
Wolverhampton Wanderers	42	13	4	25	59	89	30
Birmingham City	42	8	11	23	64	96	27

DIVISION 2 1964-65

Newcastle United	42	24	9	9	81	45	57
Northampton Town	42	20	16	6	66	50	56
Bolton Wanderers	42	20	10	12	80	58	50
Southampton	42	17	14	11	83	63	48
Ipswich Town	42	15	17	10	74	67	47
Norwich City	42	20	7	15	61	57	47
Crystal Palace	42	16	13	13	55	51	45
Huddersfield Town	42	17	10	15	53	51	44
Derby County	42	16	11	15	84	79	43
Coventry City	42	17	9	16	72	70	43
Manchester City	42	16	9	17	63	62	41
Preston North End	42	14	13	15	76	81	41
Cardiff City	42	13	14	15	64	57	40
Rotherham United	42	14	12	16	70	69	40
Plymouth Argyle	42	16	8	18	63	79	40
Bury	42	14	10	18	60	66	38
Middlesbrough	42	13	9	20	70	76	35
Charlton Athletic	42	13	9	20	64	75	35
Leyton Orient	42	12	11	19	50	72	35
Portsmouth	42	12	10	20	56	77	34
Swindon Town	42	14	5	23	63	81	33
Swansea Town	42	11	10	21	62	84	32

DIVISION 3 1964-65

Carlisle United	46	25	10	11	76	53	60
Bristol City	46	24	11	11	92	55	59
Mansfield Town	46	24	11	11	95	61	59
Hull City	46	23	12	11	91	57	58
Brentford	46	24	9	13	83	55	57
Bristol Rovers	46	20	15	11	82	58	55
Gillingham	46	23	9	14	70	50	55
Peterborough United	46	22	7	17	85	74	51
Watford	46	17	16	13	71	64	50
Grimsby Town	46	16	17	13	68	67	49
Bournemouth & Boscombe Ath.	46	18	11	17	72	63	47
Southend United	46	19	8	19	78	71	46
Reading	46	16	14	16	70	70	46
Queen's Park Rangers	46	17	12	17	72	80	46
Workington	46	17	12	17	58	69	46
Shrewsbury Town	46	15	12	19	76	84	42
Exeter City	46	12	17	17	51	52	41
Scunthorpe United	46	14	12	20	65	72	40
Walsall	46	15	7	24	55	80	37
Oldham Athletic	46	13	10	23	61	83	36
Luton Town	46	11	11	24	51	94	33
Port Vale	46	9	14	23	41	76	32
Colchester United	46	10	10	26	50	89	30
Barnsley	46	9	11	26	54	90	29

DIVISION 4 1964-65

Brighton & Hove Albion	46	26	11	9	102	57	63
Millwall	46	23	16	7	78	45	62
York City	46	28	6	12	91	56	62
Oxford United	46	23	15	8	87	44	61
Tranmere Rovers	46	27	6	13	99	56	60
Rochdale	46	22	14	10	74	53	58
Bradford Park Avenue	46	20	17	9	86	62	57
Chester	46	25	6	15	119	81	56
Doncaster Rovers	46	20	11	15	84	72	51
Crewe Alexandra	46	18	13	15	90	81	49
Torquay United	46	21	7	18	70	70	49
Chesterfield	46	20	8	18	58	70	48
Notts County	46	15	14	17	61	73	44
Wrexham	46	17	9	20	84	92	43
Hartlepools United	46	15	13	18	61	85	43
Newport County	46	17	8	21	85	81	42
Darlington	46	18	6	22	84	87	42
Aldershot	46	15	7	24	64	84	37
Bradford City	46	12	8	26	70	88	32
Southport	46	8	16	22	58	89	32
Barrow	46	12	6	28	59	105	30
Lincoln City	46	11	6	29	58	99	28
Halifax	46	11	6	29	54	103	28
Stockport County	46	10	7	29	44	87	27

1965 F.A. Cup

Semi-finals

Liverpool vs Chelsea	2-0
Manchester United vs Leeds United	0-0, 0-1

Final

Wembley, 1st May 1965

Liverpool 2 (Hunt, St. John)

Leeds United 1 (aet.) (Bremner)

Attendance 100,000

1965 Football League Cup

Semi-finals

Aston Villa vs Chelsea (2-3, 1-1)	3-4
Leicester City vs Plymouth Argyle (3-2, 1-0)	4-2

Final (1st leg)

Stamford Bridge, 15th March 1965

Chelsea 3 (Tambling, Venables (pen), McCreadie)

Leicester City 2 (Appleton, Goodfellow)

Attendance 20,690

Final (2nd leg)

Leicester, 5th April 1965

Leicester City 0

Chelsea 0

Attendance 26,958

Chelsea won 3-2 on aggregate

DIVISION 1 1965-66

Liverpool	42	26	9	7	79	34	61
Leeds United	42	23	9	10	79	38	55
Burnley	42	24	7	11	79	47	55
Manchester United	42	18	15	9	84	59	51
Chelsea	42	22	7	13	65	53	51
West Bromwich Albion	42	19	12	11	91	69	50
Leicester City	42	21	7	14	80	65	49
Tottenham Hotspur	42	16	12	14	75	66	44
Sheffield United	42	16	11	15	56	59	43
Stoke City	42	15	12	15	65	64	42
Everton	42	15	11	16	56	62	41
West Ham United	42	15	9	18	70	83	39
Blackpool	42	14	9	19	55	65	37
Arsenal	42	12	13	17	62	75	37
Newcastle United	42	14	9	19	50	63	37
Aston Villa	42	15	6	21	69	80	36
Sheffield Wednesday	42	14	8	20	56	66	36
Nottingham Forest	42	14	8	20	56	72	36
Sunderland	42	14	8	20	51	72	36
Fulham	42	14	7	21	67	85	35
Northampton Town	42	10	13	19	55	92	33
Blackburn Rovers	42	8	4	30	57	88	20

DIVISION 2 1965-66

Manchester City	42	22	15	5	76	44	59
Southampton	42	22	10	10	85	56	54
Coventry City	42	20	13	9	73	53	53
Huddersfield Town	42	19	13	10	62	36	51
Bristol City	42	17	17	8	63	48	51
Wolverhampton Wanderers	42	20	10	12	87	61	50
Rotherham United	42	16	14	12	75	74	46
Derby County	42	16	11	15	71	68	43
Bolton Wanderers	42	16	9	17	62	59	41
Birmingham City	42	16	9	17	70	75	41
Crystal Palace	42	14	13	15	47	52	41
Portsmouth	42	16	8	18	74	78	40
Norwich City	42	12	15	15	52	52	39
Carlisle United	42	17	5	20	60	63	39
Ipswich Town	42	15	9	18	58	66	39
Charlton Athletic	42	12	14	16	61	70	38
Preston North End	42	11	15	16	62	70	37
Plymouth Argyle	42	12	13	17	54	63	37
Bury	42	14	7	21	62	76	35
Cardiff City	42	12	10	20	71	91	34
Middlesbrough	42	10	13	19	58	86	33
Leyton Orient	42	5	13	24	38	80	23

DIVISION 3 1965-66

Hull City	46	31	7	8	109	62	69
Millwall	46	27	11	8	76	43	65
Queen's Park Rangers	46	24	9	13	95	65	57
Scunthorpe United	46	21	11	14	80	67	53
Workington	46	19	14	13	67	57	52
Gillingham	46	22	8	16	62	54	52
Swindon Town	46	19	13	14	74	48	51
Reading	46	19	13	14	70	63	51
Walsall	46	20	10	16	77	64	50
Shrewsbury Town	46	19	11	16	73	64	49
Grimsby Town	46	17	13	16	68	62	47
Watford	46	17	13	16	55	51	47
Peterborough United	46	17	12	17	80	66	46
Oxford United	46	19	8	19	70	74	46
Brighton & Hove Albion	46	16	11	19	67	65	43
Bristol Rovers	46	14	14	18	64	64	42
Swansea Town	46	15	11	20	81	96	41
Bournemouth & Boscombe Ath.	46	13	12	21	38	56	38
Mansfield Town	46	15	8	23	59	89	38
Oldham Athletic	46	12	13	21	55	81	37
Southend United	46	16	4	26	54	83	36
Exeter City	46	12	11	23	53	79	35
Brentford	46	10	12	24	48	69	32
York City	46	9	9	28	53	106	27

DIVISION 4 1965-66

Doncaster Rovers	46	24	11	11	85	54	59
Darlington	46	25	9	12	72	53	59
Torquay United	46	24	10	12	72	49	58
Colchester United	46	23	10	13	70	47	56
Tranmere Rovers	46	24	8	14	93	66	56
Luton Town	46	24	8	14	90	70	56
Chester	46	20	12	14	79	70	52
Notts County	46	19	12	15	61	53	50
Newport County	46	18	12	16	75	75	48
Southport	46	18	12	16	68	69	48
Bradford Park Avenue	46	21	5	20	102	92	47
Barrow	46	16	15	15	72	76	47
Stockport County	46	18	6	22	71	70	42
Crewe Alexandra	46	16	9	21	61	63	41
Halifax Town	46	15	11	20	67	75	41
Barnsley	46	15	10	21	74	78	40
Aldershot	46	15	10	21	75	84	40
Hartlepools United	46	16	8	22	63	75	40
Port Vale	46	15	9	22	48	59	39
Chesterfield	46	13	13	20	62	78	39
Rochdale	46	16	5	25	71	87	37
Lincoln City	46	13	11	22	57	82	37
Bradford City	46	12	13	21	63	94	37
Wrexham	46	13	9	24	72	104	35

1966 F.A. Cup

Semi-finals

Everton vs Manchester United	1-0
Sheffield Wednesday vs Chelsea	2-0

Final

Wembley, 14th May 1966

Everton 3 (Trebilcock 2, Temple)
Sheffield Wednesday 2 (McCalliog, Ford)

Attendance 100,000

1966 Football League Cup

Semi-finals

West Brom. Albion vs Peterborough Utd. (2-1, 4-2)	6-3
West Ham United vs Cardiff City (5-2, 5-1)	10-3

Final (1st leg)

Upton Park, 9th March 1966

West Ham United 2 (Moore, Byrne)
West Bromwich Albion 1 (Astle)

Attendance 28,341

Final (2nd leg)

The Hawthorns, 23rd March 1966

West Bromwich Albion 4 (Kaye, Brown, Clark, Williams)
West Ham United 1 (Peters)

Attendance 31,925

West Bromwich Albion won 5-3 on aggregate

DIVISION 1 1966-67

Manchester United	42	24	12	6	84	45	60
Nottingham Forest	42	23	10	9	64	41	56
Tottenham Hotspur	42	24	8	10	71	48	56
Leeds United	42	22	11	9	62	42	55
Liverpool	42	19	13	10	64	47	51
Everton	42	19	10	13	65	46	48
Arsenal	42	16	14	12	58	47	46
Leicester City	42	18	8	16	78	71	44
Chelsea	42	15	14	13	67	62	44
Sheffield United	42	16	10	16	52	59	42
Sheffield Wednesday	42	14	13	15	56	47	41
Stoke City	42	17	7	18	63	58	41
West Bromwich Albion	42	16	7	19	77	73	39
Burnley	42	15	9	18	66	76	39
Manchester City	42	12	15	15	43	52	39
West Ham United	42	14	8	20	80	84	36
Sunderland	42	14	8	20	58	72	36
Fulham	42	11	12	19	71	83	34
Southampton	42	14	6	22	74	92	34
Newcastle United	42	12	9	21	39	81	33
Aston Villa	42	11	7	24	54	85	29
Blackpool	42	6	9	27	41	76	21

DIVISION 2 1966-67

Coventry City	42	23	13	6	74	43	59
Wolverhampton Wanderers	42	25	8	9	88	48	58
Carlisle United	42	23	6	13	71	54	52
Blackburn Rovers	42	19	13	10	56	46	51
Ipswich Town	42	17	16	9	70	54	50
Huddersfield Town	42	20	9	13	58	46	49
Crystal Palace	42	19	10	13	61	55	48
Millwall	42	18	9	15	49	58	45
Bolton Wanderers	42	14	14	14	64	58	42
Birmingham City	42	16	8	18	70	66	40
Norwich City	42	13	14	15	49	55	40
Hull City	42	16	7	19	77	72	39
Preston North End	42	16	7	19	65	67	39
Portsmouth	42	13	13	16	59	70	39
Bristol City	42	12	14	16	56	62	38
Plymouth Argyle	42	14	9	19	59	58	37
Derby County	42	12	12	18	68	72	36
Rotherham United	42	13	10	19	61	70	36
Charlton Athletic	42	13	9	20	49	53	35
Cardiff City	42	12	9	21	61	87	33
Northampton Town	42	12	6	24	47	84	30
Bury	42	11	6	25	49	83	28

DIVISION 3 1966-67

Queen's Park Rangers	46	26	15	5	103	38	67
Middlesbrough	46	23	9	14	87	64	55
Watford	46	20	14	12	61	46	54
Reading	46	22	9	15	76	57	53
Bristol Rovers	46	20	13	13	76	67	53
Shrewsbury Town	46	20	12	14	77	62	52
Torquay United	46	21	9	16	73	54	51
Swindon Town	46	20	10	16	81	59	50
Mansfield Town	46	20	9	17	84	79	49
Oldham Athletic	46	19	10	17	80	63	48
Gillingham	46	15	16	15	58	62	46
Walsall	46	18	10	18	65	72	46
Colchester United	46	17	10	19	76	73	44
Leyton Orient	46	13	18	15	58	68	44
Peterborough United	46	14	15	17	66	71	43
Oxford United	46	15	13	18	61	66	43
Grimsby Town	46	17	9	20	61	68	43
Scunthorpe United	46	17	8	21	58	73	42
Brighton & Hove Albion	46	13	15	18	61	71	41
Bournemouth & Boscombe Ath.	46	12	17	17	39	57	41
Swansea Town	46	12	15	19	85	89	39
Darlington	46	13	11	22	47	81	37
Doncaster Rovers	46	12	8	26	58	117	32
Workington	46	12	7	27	55	89	31

DIVISION 4 1966-67

Stockport County	46	26	12	8	69	42	64
Southport	46	23	13	10	69	42	59
Barrow	46	24	11	11	76	54	59
Tranmere Rovers	46	22	14	10	66	43	58
Crewe Alexandra	46	21	12	13	70	55	54
Southend United	46	22	9	15	70	49	53
Wrexham	46	16	20	10	76	62	52
Hartlepools United	46	22	7	17	66	64	51
Brentford	46	18	13	15	58	56	49
Aldershot	46	18	12	16	72	57	48
Bradford City	46	19	10	17	74	62	48
Halifax Town	46	15	14	17	59	68	44
Port Vale	46	14	15	17	55	58	43
Exeter City	46	14	15	17	50	60	43
Chesterfield	46	17	8	21	60	63	42
Barnsley	46	13	15	18	60	64	41
Luton Town	46	16	9	21	59	73	41
Newport County	46	12	16	18	56	63	40
Chester	46	15	10	21	54	78	40
Notts County	46	13	11	22	53	72	37
Rochdale	46	13	11	22	53	75	37
York City	46	12	11	23	65	79	35
Bradford Park Avenue	46	11	13	22	52	79	35
Lincoln City	46	9	13	24	58	82	31

1967 F.A. Cup

Semi-finals

Tottenham Hotspur vs Nottingham Forest	2-1
Chelsea vs Leeds United	1-0

Final

Wembley, 20th May 1967

Tottenham Hotspur 2 (Robertson, Saul)

Chelsea 1 (Tambling)

Attendance 100,000

1967 Football League Cup

Semi-finals

Birmingham City vs Queen's Pk. Rangers (1-4, 1-3)	2-7
West Bromwich Albion vs West Ham Utd. (4-0, 2-2)	6-2

Final

Wembley, 4th March 1967

Queen's Park Rangers 3 (R. Morgan, Marsh, Lazarus)

West Bromwich Albion 2 (Clark 2)

Attendance 97,952

DIVISION 1 1967-68

	P	W	D	L	F	A	Pts
Manchester City	42	26	6	10	86	43	58
Manchester United	42	24	8	10	89	55	56
Liverpool	42	22	11	9	71	40	55
Leeds United	42	22	9	11	71	41	53
Everton	42	23	6	13	67	40	52
Chelsea	42	18	12	12	62	68	48
Tottenham Hotspur	42	19	9	14	70	59	47
West Bromwich Albion	42	17	12	13	75	62	46
Arsenal	42	17	10	15	60	56	44
Newcastle United	42	13	15	14	54	67	41
Nottingham Forest	42	14	11	17	52	64	39
West Ham United	42	14	10	18	73	69	38
Leicester City	42	13	12	17	64	69	38
Burnley	42	14	10	18	64	71	38
Sunderland	42	13	11	18	51	61	37
Southampton	42	13	11	18	66	83	37
Wolverhampton Wanderers	42	14	8	20	66	75	36
Stoke City	42	14	7	21	50	73	35
Sheffield Wednesday	42	11	12	19	51	63	34
Coventry City	42	9	15	18	51	71	33
Sheffield United	42	11	10	21	49	70	32
Fulham	42	10	7	25	56	98	27

DIVISION 3 1967-68

	P	W	D	L	F	A	Pts
Oxford United	46	22	13	11	69	47	57
Bury	46	24	8	14	91	66	56
Shrewsbury Town	46	20	15	11	61	49	55
Torquay United	46	21	11	14	60	56	53
Reading	46	21	9	16	70	60	51
Watford	46	21	8	17	74	50	50
Walsall	46	19	12	15	74	61	50
Barrow	46	21	8	17	65	54	50
Swindon Town	46	16	17	13	74	51	49
Brighton & Hove Albion	46	16	16	14	57	55	48
Gillingham	46	18	12	16	59	63	48
Bournemouth & Boscombe Ath.	46	16	15	15	56	51	47
Stockport County	46	19	9	18	70	75	47
Southport	46	17	12	17	65	65	46
Bristol Rovers	46	17	9	20	72	78	43
Oldham Athletic	46	18	7	21	60	65	43
Northampton Town	46	14	13	19	58	72	41
Orient	46	12	17	17	46	62	41
Tranmere Rovers	46	14	12	20	62	74	40
Mansfield Town	46	12	13	21	51	67	37
Grimsby Town	46	14	9	23	52	69	37
Colchester United	46	9	15	22	50	87	33
Scunthorpe United	46	10	12	24	56	87	32
Peterborough United	46	20	10	16	79	67	31†

† Peterborough United were 'fined' 19 points and relegated for offering illegal bonuses.

DIVISION 2 1967-68

	P	W	D	L	F	A	Pts
Ipswich Town	42	22	15	5	79	44	59
Queen's Park Rangers	42	25	8	9	67	36	58
Blackpool	42	24	10	8	71	43	58
Birmingham City	42	19	14	9	83	51	52
Portsmouth	42	18	13	11	68	55	49
Middlesbrough	42	17	12	13	60	54	46
Millwall	42	14	17	11	62	50	45
Blackburn Rovers	42	16	11	15	56	49	43
Norwich City	42	16	11	15	60	65	43
Carlisle United	42	14	13	15	58	52	41
Crystal Palace	42	14	11	17	56	56	39
Bolton Wanderers	42	13	13	16	60	63	39
Cardiff City	42	13	12	17	60	66	38
Huddersfield Town	42	13	12	17	46	61	38
Charlton Athletic	42	12	13	17	63	68	37
Aston Villa	42	15	7	20	54	64	37
Hull City	42	12	13	17	58	73	37
Derby County	42	13	10	19	71	78	36
Bristol City	42	13	10	19	48	62	36
Preston North End	42	12	11	19	43	65	35
Rotherham United	42	10	11	21	42	76	31
Plymouth Argyle	42	9	9	24	38	72	27

DIVISION 4 1967-68

	P	W	D	L	F	A	Pts
Luton Town	46	27	12	7	87	44	66
Barnsley	46	24	13	9	68	46	61
Hartlepools United	46	25	10	11	60	46	60
Crewe Alexandra	46	20	18	8	74	49	58
Bradford City	46	23	11	12	72	51	57
Southend United	46	20	14	12	77	58	54
Chesterfield	46	21	11	14	71	50	53
Wrexham	46	20	13	13	72	53	53
Aldershot	46	18	17	11	70	55	53
Doncaster Rovers	46	18	15	13	66	56	51
Halifax Town	46	15	16	15	52	49	46
Newport County	46	16	13	17	58	63	45
Lincoln City	46	17	9	20	71	68	43
Brentford	46	18	7	21	61	64	43
Swansea Town	46	16	10	20	63	77	42
Darlington	46	12	17	17	47	53	41
Notts County	46	15	11	20	53	79	41
Port Vale	46	12	15	19	61	72	39
Rochdale	46	12	14	20	51	72	38
Exeter City	46	11	16	19	45	65	38
York City	46	11	14	21	65	68	36
Chester	46	9	14	23	57	78	32
Workington	46	10	11	25	54	87	31
Bradford Park Avenue	46	4	15	27	30	82	23

Port Vale was expelled from the League for financial irregularities but successfully applied for re-election for the 1968/69 season.

1968 F.A. Cup

Semi-finals

West Bromwich Albion vs Birmingham City	2-0
Everton vs Leeds United	1-0

Final

Wembley, 18th May 1968

West Bromwich Albion 1   (Astle)

Everton 0   (aet.)

Attendance 100,000

1968 Football League Cup

Semi-finals

Derby County vs Leeds United (0-1, 2-3)	2-4
Arsenal vs Huddersfield Town (3-2, 3-1)	6-3

Final

Wembley, 2nd March 1968

Leeds United 1   (Cooper)

Arsenal 0

Attendance 97,887

DIVISION 1 1968-69

Leeds United	42	27	13	2	66	26	67
Liverpool	42	25	11	6	63	24	61
Everton	42	21	15	6	77	36	57
Arsenal	42	22	12	8	56	27	56
Chelsea	42	20	10	12	73	53	50
Tottenham Hotspur	42	14	17	11	61	51	45
Southampton	42	16	13	13	57	48	45
West Ham United	42	13	18	11	66	50	44
Newcastle United	42	15	14	13	61	55	44
West Bromwich Albion	42	16	11	15	64	67	43
Manchester United	42	15	12	15	57	53	42
Ipswich Town	42	15	11	16	59	60	41
Manchester City	42	15	10	17	64	55	40
Burnley	42	15	9	18	55	82	39
Sheffield Wednesday	42	10	16	16	41	54	36
Wolverhampton Wanderers	42	10	15	17	41	58	35
Sunderland	42	11	12	19	43	67	34
Nottingham Forest	42	10	13	19	45	57	33
Stoke City	42	9	15	18	40	63	33
Coventry City	42	10	11	21	46	64	31
Leicester City	42	9	12	21	39	68	30
Queen's Park Rangers	42	4	10	28	39	95	18

DIVISION 3 1968-69

Watford	46	27	10	9	74	34	64
Swindon Town	46	27	10	9	71	35	64
Luton Town	46	25	11	10	74	38	61
Bournemouth & Boscombe Ath.	46	21	9	16	60	45	51
Plymouth Argyle	46	17	15	14	53	49	49
Torquay United	46	18	12	16	54	46	48
Tranmere Rovers	46	19	10	17	70	68	48
Southport	46	17	13	16	71	64	47
Stockport County	46	16	14	16	67	68	46
Barnsley	46	16	14	16	58	63	46
Rotherham United	46	16	13	17	56	50	45
Brighton & Hove Albion	46	16	13	17	72	65	45
Walsall	46	14	16	16	50	49	44
Reading	46	15	13	18	67	66	43
Mansfield Town	46	16	11	19	58	62	43
Bristol Rovers	46	16	11	19	63	71	43
Shrewsbury Town	46	16	11	19	51	67	43
Orient	46	14	14	18	51	58	42
Barrow	46	17	8	21	56	75	42
Gillingham	46	13	15	18	54	63	41
Northampton Town	46	14	12	20	54	61	40
Hartlepool	46	10	19	17	40	70	39
Crewe Alexandra	46	13	9	24	52	76	35
Oldham Athletic	46	13	9	24	50	83	35

DIVISION 2 1968-69

Derby County	42	26	11	5	65	32	63
Crystal Palace	42	22	12	8	70	47	56
Charlton Athletic	42	18	14	10	61	52	50
Middlesbrough	42	19	11	12	58	49	49
Cardiff City	42	20	7	15	67	54	47
Huddersfield Town	42	17	12	13	53	46	46
Birmingham City	42	18	8	16	73	59	44
Blackpool	42	14	15	13	51	41	43
Sheffield United	42	16	11	15	61	50	43
Millwall	42	17	9	16	57	49	43
Hull City	42	13	16	13	59	52	42
Carlisle United	42	16	10	16	46	49	42
Norwich City	42	15	10	17	53	56	40
Preston North End	42	12	15	15	38	44	39
Portsmouth	42	12	14	16	58	58	38
Bristol City	42	11	16	15	46	53	38
Bolton Wanderers	42	12	14	16	55	67	38
Aston Villa	42	12	14	16	37	48	38
Blackburn Rovers	42	13	11	18	52	63	37
Oxford United	42	12	9	21	34	55	33
Bury	42	11	8	23	51	80	30
Fulham	42	7	11	24	40	81	25

DIVISION 4 1968-69

Doncaster Rovers	46	21	17	8	65	38	59
Halifax Town	46	20	17	9	53	37	57
Rochdale	46	18	20	8	68	35	56
Bradford City	46	18	20	8	65	46	56
Darlington	46	17	18	11	62	45	52
Colchester United	46	20	12	14	57	53	52
Southend United	46	19	13	14	78	61	51
Lincoln City	46	17	17	12	54	52	51
Wrexham	46	18	14	14	61	52	50
Swansea Town	46	19	11	16	58	54	49
Brentford	46	18	12	16	64	65	48
Workington	46	15	17	14	40	43	47
Port Vale	46	16	14	16	46	46	46
Chester	46	16	13	17	76	66	45
Aldershot	46	19	7	20	66	66	45
Scunthorpe United	46	18	8	20	61	60	44
Exeter City	46	16	11	19	66	65	43
Peterborough United	46	13	16	17	60	57	42
Notts County	46	12	18	16	48	57	42
Chesterfield	46	13	15	18	43	50	41
York City	46	14	11	21	53	75	39
Newport County	46	11	14	21	49	74	36
Grimsby Town	46	9	15	22	47	69	33
Bradford Park Avenue	46	5	10	31	32	106	20

1969 F.A. Cup

Semi-finals

Manchester City vs Everton	1-0
West Bromwich Albion vs Leicester City	0-1

Final

Wembley, 26th April 1969

Manchester City 1 (Young)

Leicester City 0

Attendance 100,000

1969 Football League Cup

Semi-finals

Arsenal vs Tottenham Hotspur (1-0, 1-1)	2-1
Burnley vs Swindon Town (1-2, 2-1)	3-3

Play-off

Burnley vs Swindon Town	2-3

Final

Wembley, 15th March 1969

Swindon Town 3 (Smart, Rogers 2)

Arsenal 1 (Gould)

Attendance 98,189

DIVISION 1 1969-70

Everton	42	29	8	5	72	34	66
Leeds United	42	21	15	6	84	49	57
Chelsea	42	21	13	8	70	50	55
Derby County	42	22	9	11	64	37	53
Liverpool	42	20	11	11	65	42	51
Coventry City	42	19	11	12	58	48	49
Newcastle United	42	17	13	12	57	35	47
Manchester United	42	14	17	11	66	61	45
Stoke City	42	15	15	12	56	52	45
Manchester City	42	16	11	15	55	48	43
Tottenham Hotspur	42	17	9	16	54	55	43
Arsenal	42	12	18	12	51	49	42
Wolverhampton Wanderers	42	12	16	14	55	57	40
Burnley	42	12	15	15	56	61	39
Nottingham Forest	42	10	18	14	50	71	38
West Bromwich Albion	42	14	9	19	58	66	37
West Ham United	42	12	12	18	51	60	36
Ipswich Town	42	10	11	21	40	63	31
Southampton	42	6	17	19	46	67	29
Crystal Palace	42	6	15	21	34	68	27
Sunderland	42	6	14	22	30	68	26
Sheffield Wednesday	42	8	9	25	40	71	25

DIVISION 3 1969-70

Orient	46	25	12	9	67	36	62
Luton Town	46	23	14	9	77	43	60
Bristol Rovers	46	20	16	10	80	59	56
Fulham	46	20	15	11	81	55	55
Brighton & Hove Albion	46	23	9	14	57	43	55
Mansfield Town	46	21	11	14	70	49	53
Barnsley	46	19	15	12	68	59	53
Reading	46	21	11	14	87	77	53
Rochdale	46	18	10	18	69	60	46
Bradford City	46	17	12	17	57	50	46
Doncaster Rovers	46	17	12	17	52	54	46
Walsall	46	17	12	17	54	67	46
Torquay United	46	14	17	15	62	59	45
Rotherham United	46	15	14	17	62	54	44
Shrewsbury Town	46	13	18	15	62	63	44
Tranmere Rovers	46	14	16	16	56	72	44
Plymouth Argyle	46	16	11	19	56	64	43
Halifax Town	46	14	15	17	47	63	43
Bury	46	15	11	20	75	80	41
Gillingham	46	13	13	20	52	64	39
Bournemouth & Boscombe Ath.	46	12	15	19	48	71	39
Southport	46	14	10	22	48	66	38
Barrow	46	8	14	24	46	81	30
Stockport County	46	6	11	29	27	71	23

DIVISION 2 1969-70

Huddersfield Town	42	24	12	6	68	37	60
Blackpool	42	20	13	9	56	45	53
Leicester City	42	19	13	10	64	50	51
Middlesbrough	42	20	10	12	55	45	50
Swindon Town	42	17	16	9	57	47	50
Sheffield United	42	22	5	15	73	38	49
Cardiff City	42	18	13	11	61	41	49
Blackburn Rovers	42	20	7	15	54	50	47
Queen's Park Rangers	42	17	11	14	66	57	45
Millwall	42	15	14	13	56	56	44
Norwich City	42	16	11	15	49	46	43
Carlisle United	42	14	13	15	58	56	41
Hull City	42	15	11	16	72	70	41
Bristol City	42	13	13	16	54	50	39
Oxford United	42	12	15	15	35	42	39
Bolton Wanderers	42	12	12	18	54	61	36
Portsmouth	42	13	9	20	66	80	35
Birmingham City	42	11	11	20	51	78	33
Watford	42	9	13	20	44	57	31
Charlton Athletic	42	7	17	18	35	76	31
Aston Villa	42	8	13	21	36	62	29
Preston North End	42	8	12	22	43	63	28

DIVISION 4 1969-70

Chesterfield	46	27	10	9	77	32	64
Wrexham	46	26	9	11	84	49	61
Swansea City	46	21	18	7	66	45	60
Port Vale	46	20	19	7	61	33	59
Brentford	46	20	16	10	58	39	56
Aldershot	46	20	13	13	78	65	53
Notts County	46	22	8	16	73	62	52
Lincoln City	46	17	16	13	66	52	50
Peterborough United	46	17	14	15	77	69	48
Colchester United	46	17	14	15	64	63	48
Chester	46	21	6	19	58	66	48
Scunthorpe United	46	18	10	18	67	65	46
York City	46	16	14	16	55	62	46
Northampton Town	46	16	12	18	64	55	44
Crewe Alexandra	46	16	12	18	51	51	44
Grimsby Town	46	14	15	17	54	58	43
Southend United	46	15	10	21	59	85	40
Exeter City	46	14	11	21	57	59	39
Oldham Athletic	46	13	13	20	60	65	39
Workington	46	12	14	20	46	64	38
Newport County	46	13	11	22	53	74	37
Darlington	46	13	10	23	53	73	36
Hartlepool	46	10	10	26	42	82	30
Bradford Park Avenue	46	6	11	29	41	96	23

1970 F.A. Cup

Semi-finals

Chelsea vs Watford	5-1
Manchester United vs Leeds United	0-0, 0-0, 0-1

Final

Wembley, 11th April 1970

Chelsea 2 (Houseman, Hutchinson)
Leeds United 2 (aet.) (Charlton, Jones)

Attendance 100,000

Replay

Old Trafford, 29th April 1970

Chelsea 2 (Osgood, Webb)
Leeds United 1 (aet.) (Jones)

Attendance 62,000

1970 Football League Cup

Semi-finals

Manchester City vs Manchester United	(2-1, 2-2)	4-3
Carlisle United vs West Bromwich Albion	(1-0, 1-4)	2-4

Final

Wembley, 7th March 1970

Manchester City 2 (Doyle, Pardoe)
West Bromwich Albion 1 (Astle)

Attendance 97,963

DIVISION 1 1970-71

Arsenal	42	29	7	6	71	29	65
Leeds United	42	27	10	5	72	30	64
Tottenham Hotspur	42	19	14	9	54	33	52
Wolverhampton Wanderers	42	22	8	12	64	54	52
Liverpool	42	17	17	8	42	24	51
Chelsea	42	18	15	9	52	42	51
Southampton	42	17	12	13	56	44	46
Manchester United	42	16	11	15	65	66	43
Derby County	42	16	10	16	56	54	42
Coventry City	42	16	10	16	37	38	42
Manchester City	42	12	17	13	47	42	41
Newcastle United	42	14	13	15	44	46	41
Stoke City	42	12	13	17	44	48	37
Everton	42	12	13	17	54	60	37
Huddersfield Town	42	11	14	17	40	49	36
Nottingham Forest	42	14	8	20	42	61	36
West Bromwich Albion	42	10	15	17	58	75	35
Crystal Palace	42	12	11	19	39	57	35
Ipswich Town	42	12	10	20	42	48	34
West Ham United	42	10	14	18	47	60	34
Burnley	42	7	13	22	29	63	27
Blackpool	42	4	15	23	34	66	23

DIVISION 2 1970-71

Leicester City	42	23	13	6	57	30	59
Sheffield United	42	21	14	7	73	39	56
Cardiff City	42	20	13	9	64	41	53
Carlisle United	42	20	13	9	65	43	53
Hull City	42	19	13	10	54	41	51
Luton Town	42	18	13	11	62	43	49
Middlesbrough	42	17	14	11	60	43	48
Millwall	42	19	9	14	59	42	47
Birmingham City	42	17	12	13	58	48	46
Norwich City	42	15	14	13	54	52	44
Queen's Park Rangers	42	16	11	15	58	53	43
Swindon Town	42	15	12	15	61	51	42
Sunderland	42	15	12	15	52	54	42
Oxford United	42	14	14	14	41	48	42
Sheffield Wednesday	42	12	12	18	51	69	36
Portsmouth	42	10	14	18	46	61	34
Orient	42	9	16	17	29	51	34
Watford	42	10	13	19	38	60	33
Bristol City	42	10	11	21	46	64	31
Charlton Athletic	42	8	14	20	41	65	30
Blackburn Rovers	42	6	15	21	37	69	27
Bolton Wanderers	42	7	10	25	35	74	24

DIVISION 3 1970-71

Preston North End	46	22	17	7	63	39	61
Fulham	46	24	12	10	68	41	60
Halifax Town	46	22	12	12	74	55	56
Aston Villa	46	19	15	12	54	46	53
Chesterfield	46	17	17	12	66	38	51
Bristol Rovers	46	19	13	14	69	50	51
Mansfield Town	46	18	15	13	64	62	51
Rotherham United	46	17	16	13	64	60	50
Wrexham	46	18	13	15	72	65	49
Torquay United	46	19	11	16	54	57	49
Swansea City	46	15	16	15	59	56	46
Barnsley	46	17	11	18	49	52	45
Shrewsbury Town	46	16	13	17	58	62	45
Brighton & Hove Albion	46	14	16	16	50	47	44
Plymouth Argyle	46	12	19	15	63	63	43
Rochdale	46	14	15	17	61	68	43
Port Vale	46	15	12	19	52	59	42
Tranmere Rovers	46	10	22	14	45	55	42
Bradford City	46	13	14	19	49	62	40
Walsall	46	14	11	21	51	57	39
Reading	46	14	11	21	48	85	39
Bury	46	12	13	21	52	60	37
Doncaster Rovers	46	13	9	24	45	66	35
Gillingham	46	10	13	23	42	67	33

DIVISION 4 1970-71

Notts County	46	30	9	7	89	36	69
Bournemouth & Boscombe Ath.	46	24	12	10	81	46	60
Oldham Athletic	46	24	11	11	88	63	59
York City	46	23	10	13	78	54	56
Chester	46	24	7	15	69	55	55
Colchester United	46	21	12	13	70	54	54
Northampton Town	46	19	13	14	63	59	51
Southport	46	21	6	19	63	57	48
Exeter City	46	17	14	15	67	68	48
Workington	46	18	12	16	48	49	48
Stockport County	46	16	14	16	49	65	46
Darlington	46	17	11	18	58	57	45
Aldershot	46	14	17	15	66	71	45
Brentford	46	18	8	20	66	62	44
Crewe Alexandra	46	18	8	20	75	76	44
Peterborough United	46	18	7	21	70	71	43
Scunthorpe United	46	15	13	18	56	61	43
Southend United	46	14	15	17	53	66	43
Grimsby Town	46	18	7	21	57	71	43
Cambridge United	46	15	13	18	51	66	43
Lincoln City	46	13	13	20	70	71	39
Newport County	46	10	8	28	55	85	28
Hartlepool	46	8	12	26	34	74	28
Barrow	46	7	8	31	51	90	22

1971 F.A. Cup

Semi-finals

Stoke City vs Arsenal	2-2, 0-2
Liverpool vs Everton	2-1

Final

Wembley, 8th May 1971

Arsenal 2 (Kelly, George)

Liverpool 1 (aet.) (Heighway)

Attendance 100,000

1971 Football League Cup

Semi-finals

Bristol City vs Tottenham Hotspur (1-1, 0-2)		1-3
Manchester United vs Aston Villa (1-1, 1-2)		2-3

Final

Wembley, 27th February 1971

Tottenham Hotspur 2 (Chivers 2)

Aston Villa 0

Attendance 100,000

DIVISION 1 1971-72

Derby County	42	24	10	8	69	33	58
Leeds United	42	24	9	9	73	31	57
Liverpool	42	24	9	9	64	30	57
Manchester City	42	23	11	8	77	45	57
Arsenal	42	22	8	12	58	40	52
Tottenham Hotspur	42	19	13	10	63	42	51
Chelsea	42	18	12	12	58	49	48
Manchester United	42	19	10	13	69	61	48
Wolverhampton Wanderers	42	18	11	13	65	57	47
Sheffield United	42	17	12	13	61	60	46
Newcastle United	42	15	11	16	49	52	41
Leicester City	42	13	13	16	41	46	39
Ipswich Town	42	11	16	15	39	53	38
West Ham United	42	12	12	18	47	51	36
Everton	42	9	18	15	37	48	36
West Bromwich Albion	42	12	11	19	42	54	35
Stoke City	42	10	15	17	39	56	35
Coventry City	42	9	15	18	44	67	33
Southampton	42	12	7	23	52	80	31
Crystal Palace	42	8	13	21	39	65	29
Nottingham Forest	42	8	9	25	47	81	25
Huddersfield Town	42	6	13	23	27	59	25

DIVISION 2 1971-72

Norwich City	42	21	15	6	60	36	57
Birmingham City	42	19	18	5	60	31	56
Millwall	42	19	17	6	64	46	55
Queen's Park Rangers	42	20	14	8	57	28	54
Sunderland	42	17	16	9	67	57	50
Blackpool	42	20	7	15	70	50	47
Burnley	42	20	6	16	70	55	46
Bristol City	42	18	10	14	61	49	46
Middlesbrough	42	19	8	15	50	48	46
Carlisle United	42	17	9	16	61	57	43
Swindon Town	42	15	12	15	47	47	42
Hull City	42	14	10	18	49	53	38
Luton Town	42	10	18	14	43	48	38
Sheffield Wednesday	42	13	12	17	51	58	38
Oxford United	42	12	14	16	43	55	38
Portsmouth	42	12	13	17	59	68	37
Orient	42	14	9	19	50	61	37
Preston North End	42	12	12	18	52	58	36
Cardiff City	42	10	14	18	56	69	34
Fulham	42	12	10	20	45	68	34
Charlton Athletic	42	12	9	21	55	77	33
Watford	42	5	9	28	24	75	19

DIVISION 3 1971-72

Aston Villa	46	32	6	8	85	32	70
Brighton & Hove Albion	46	27	11	8	82	47	65
Bournemouth & Boscombe Ath.	46	23	16	7	73	37	62
Notts County	46	25	12	9	74	44	62
Rotherham United	46	20	15	11	69	52	55
Bristol Rovers	46	21	12	13	75	56	54
Bolton Wanderers	46	17	16	13	51	41	50
Plymouth Argyle	46	20	10	16	74	64	50
Walsall	46	15	18	13	62	57	48
Blackburn Rovers	46	19	9	18	54	57	47
Oldham Athletic	46	17	11	18	59	63	45
Shrewsbury Town	46	17	10	19	73	65	44
Chesterfield	46	18	8	20	57	57	44
Swansea City	46	17	10	19	46	59	44
Port Vale	46	13	15	18	43	59	41
Wrexham	46	16	8	22	59	63	40
Halifax Town	46	13	12	21	48	61	38
Rochdale	46	12	13	21	57	83	37
York City	46	12	12	22	57	66	36
Tranmere Rovers	46	10	16	20	50	71	36
Mansfield Town	46	8	20	18	41	63	36
Barnsley	46	9	18	19	32	64	36
Torquay United	46	10	12	24	41	69	32
Bradford City	46	11	10	25	45	77	32

DIVISION 4 1971-72

Grimsby Town	46	28	7	11	88	56	63
Southend United	46	24	12	10	81	55	60
Brentford	46	24	11	11	76	44	59
Scunthorpe United	46	22	13	11	56	37	57
Lincoln City	46	21	14	11	77	59	56
Workington	46	16	19	11	50	34	51
Southport	46	18	14	14	66	46	50
Peterborough United	46	17	16	13	82	64	50
Bury	46	19	12	15	73	59	50
Cambridge United	46	17	14	15	62	60	48
Colchester United	46	19	10	17	70	69	48
Doncaster Rovers	46	16	14	16	56	63	46
Gillingham	46	16	13	17	61	67	45
Newport County	46	18	8	20	60	72	44
Exeter City	46	16	11	19	61	68	43
Reading	46	17	8	21	56	76	42
Aldershot	46	9	22	15	48	54	40
Hartlepool	46	17	6	23	58	69	40
Darlington	46	14	11	21	64	82	39
Chester	46	10	18	18	47	56	38
Northampton Town	46	12	13	21	66	79	37
Barrow	46	13	11	22	40	71	37
Stockport County	46	9	14	23	55	87	32
Crewe Alexandra	46	10	9	27	43	69	29

1972 F.A. Cup

Semi-finals

Leeds United vs Birmingham City	3-0
Arsenal vs Stoke City	1-1, 2-1

Final

Wembley, 6th May 1972

Leeds United 1   (Clarke)

Arsenal 0

Attendance 100,000

1972 Football League Cup

Semi-finals

Stoke City vs West Ham Utd. (1-2, 1-0, 0-0*, 3-2†)	5-4
Chelsea vs Tottenham Hotspur (3-2, 2-2)	5-4

* 1st play-off at Hillsborough; † 2nd play-off at Old Trafford

Final

Wembley, 4th March 1972

Stoke City 2   (Conroy, Eastham)

Chelsea 1   (Osgood)

Attendance 100,000

DIVISION 1 1972-73

Liverpool	42	25	10	7	72	42	60
Arsenal	42	23	11	8	57	43	57
Leeds United	42	21	11	10	71	45	53
Ipswich Town	42	17	14	11	55	45	48
Wolverhampton Wanderers	42	18	11	13	66	54	47
West Ham United	42	17	12	13	67	53	46
Derby County	42	19	8	15	56	54	46
Tottenham Hotspur	42	16	13	13	58	48	45
Newcastle United	42	16	13	13	60	51	45
Birmingham City	42	15	12	15	53	54	42
Manchester City	42	15	11	16	57	60	41
Chelsea	42	13	14	15	49	51	40
Southampton	42	11	18	13	47	52	40
Sheffield United	42	15	10	17	51	59	40
Stoke City	42	14	10	18	61	56	38
Leicester City	42	10	17	15	40	46	37
Everton	42	13	11	18	41	49	37
Manchester United	42	12	13	17	44	60	37
Coventry City	42	13	9	20	40	55	35
Norwich City	42	11	10	21	36	63	32
Crystal Palace	42	9	12	21	41	58	30
West Bromwich Albion	42	9	10	23	38	62	28

DIVISION 3 1972-73

Bolton Wanderers	46	25	11	10	73	39	61
Notts County	46	23	11	12	67	47	57
Blackburn Rovers	46	20	15	11	57	47	55
Oldham Athletic	46	19	16	11	72	54	54
Bristol Rovers	46	20	13	13	77	56	53
Port Vale	46	21	11	14	56	69	53
Bournemouth	46	17	16	13	66	44	50
Plymouth Argyle	46	20	10	16	74	66	50
Grimsby Town	46	20	8	18	67	61	48
Tranmere Rovers	46	15	16	15	56	52	46
Charlton Athletic	46	17	11	18	69	67	45
Wrexham	46	14	17	15	55	54	45
Rochdale	46	14	17	15	48	54	45
Southend United	46	17	10	19	61	54	44
Shrewsbury Town	46	15	14	17	46	54	44
Chesterfield	46	17	9	20	57	61	43
Walsall	46	18	7	21	56	66	43
York City	46	13	15	18	42	46	41
Watford	46	12	17	17	43	48	41
Halifax Town	46	13	15	18	43	53	41
Rotherham United	46	17	7	22	51	65	41
Brentford	46	15	7	24	51	69	37
Swansea City	46	14	9	23	51	73	37
Scunthorpe United	46	10	10	26	33	72	30

DIVISION 2 1972-73

Burnley	42	24	14	4	72	35	62
Queen's Park Rangers	42	24	13	5	81	37	61
Aston Villa	42	18	14	10	51	47	50
Middlesbrough	42	17	13	12	46	43	47
Bristol City	42	17	12	13	63	51	46
Sunderland	42	17	12	13	59	49	46
Blackpool	42	18	10	14	56	51	46
Oxford United	42	19	7	16	52	43	45
Fulham	42	16	12	14	58	49	44
Sheffield Wednesday	42	17	10	15	59	55	44
Millwall	42	16	10	16	55	47	42
Luton Town	42	15	11	16	44	53	41
Hull City	42	14	12	16	64	59	40
Nottingham Forest	42	14	12	16	47	52	40
Orient	42	12	12	18	49	53	36
Swindon Town	42	10	16	16	46	60	36
Portsmouth	42	12	11	19	42	59	35
Carlisle United	42	11	12	19	50	52	34
Preston North End	42	11	12	19	37	64	34
Cardiff City	42	11	11	20	43	58	33
Huddersfield Town	42	8	17	17	36	56	33
Brighton & Hove Albion	42	8	13	21	46	83	29

DIVISION 4 1972-73

Southport	46	26	10	10	71	48	62
Hereford United	46	23	12	11	56	38	58
Cambridge United	46	20	17	9	67	57	57
Aldershot	46	22	12	12	60	38	56
Newport County	46	22	12	12	64	44	56
Mansfield Town	46	20	14	12	78	51	54
Reading	46	17	18	11	51	38	52
Exeter City	46	18	14	14	57	51	50
Gillingham	46	19	11	16	63	58	49
Lincoln City	46	16	16	14	64	57	48
Stockport County	46	18	12	16	53	53	48
Bury	46	14	18	14	58	51	46
Workington	46	17	12	17	59	61	46
Barnsley	46	14	16	16	58	60	44
Chester	46	14	15	17	61	52	43
Bradford City	46	16	11	19	61	65	43
Doncaster Rovers	46	15	12	19	49	58	42
Torquay United	46	12	17	17	44	47	41
Peterborough United	46	14	13	19	71	76	41
Hartlepool	46	12	17	17	34	49	41
Crewe Alexandra	46	9	18	19	38	61	36
Colchester United	46	10	11	25	48	76	31
Northampton Town	46	10	11	25	40	73	31
Darlington	46	7	15	24	42	85	29

1973 F.A. Cup

Semi-finals

Arsenal vs Sunderland	1-2
Leeds United vs Wolverhampton Wanderers	1-0

Final

Wembley, 5th May 1973

Sunderland 1 (Porterfield)

Leeds United 0

Attendance 100,000

1973 Football League Cup

Semi-finals

Wolverhampton Wands. vs Tottenham H. (1-2, 2-2)	3-4
Chelsea vs Norwich City (0-2, 0-1)	0-3

Final

Wembley, 3rd March 1973

Tottenham Hotspur 1 (Coates)

Norwich City 0

Attendance 100,000

DIVISION 1 1973-74

Leeds United	42	24	14	4	66	31	62
Liverpool	42	22	13	7	52	31	57
Derby County	42	17	14	11	52	42	48
Ipswich Town	42	18	11	13	67	58	47
Stoke City	42	15	16	11	54	42	46
Burnley	42	16	14	12	56	53	46
Everton	42	16	12	14	50	48	44
Queen's Park Rangers	42	13	17	12	56	52	43
Leicester City	42	13	16	13	51	41	42
Arsenal	42	14	14	14	49	51	42
Tottenham Hotspur	42	14	14	14	45	50	42
Wolverhampton Wanderers	42	13	15	14	49	49	41
Sheffield United	42	14	12	16	44	49	40
Manchester City	42	14	12	16	39	46	40
Newcastle United	42	13	12	17	49	48	38
Coventry City	42	14	10	18	43	54	38
Chelsea	42	12	13	17	56	60	37
West Ham United	42	11	15	16	55	60	37
Birmingham City	42	12	13	17	52	64	37
Southampton	42	11	14	17	47	68	36
Manchester United	42	10	12	20	38	48	32
Norwich City	42	7	15	20	37	62	29

DIVISION 3 1973-74

Oldham Athletic	46	25	12	9	83	47	62
Bristol Rovers	46	22	17	7	65	33	61
York City	46	21	19	6	67	38	61
Wrexham	46	22	12	12	63	43	56
Chesterfield	46	21	14	11	55	42	56
Grimsby Town	46	18	15	13	67	50	51
Watford	46	19	12	15	64	56	50
Aldershot	46	19	11	16	65	52	49
Halifax Town	46	14	21	11	48	51	49
Huddersfield Town	46	17	13	16	56	55	47
Bournemouth	46	16	15	15	54	58	47
Southend United	46	16	14	16	62	62	46
Blackburn Rovers	46	18	10	18	62	64	46
Charlton Athletic	46	19	8	19	66	73	46
Walsall	46	16	13	17	57	48	45
Tranmere Rovers	46	15	15	16	50	44	45
Plymouth Argyle	46	17	10	19	59	54	44
Hereford United	46	14	15	17	53	57	43
Brighton & Hove Albion	46	16	11	19	52	58	43
Port Vale	46	14	14	18	52	58	42
Cambridge United	46	13	9	24	48	81	35
Shrewsbury Town	46	10	11	25	41	62	31
Southport	46	6	16	24	35	82	28
Rochdale	46	2	17	27	38	94	21

DIVISION 2 1973-74

Middlesbrough	42	27	11	4	77	30	65
Luton Town	42	19	12	11	64	51	50
Carlisle United	42	20	9	13	61	48	49
Orient	42	15	18	9	55	42	48
Blackpool	42	17	13	12	57	40	47
Sunderland	42	19	9	14	58	44	47
Nottingham Forest	42	15	15	12	57	43	45
West Bromwich Albion	42	14	16	12	48	45	44
Hull City	42	13	17	12	46	47	43
Notts County	42	15	13	14	55	60	43
Bolton Wanderers	42	15	12	15	44	40	42
Millwall	42	14	14	14	51	51	42
Fulham	42	16	10	16	39	43	42
Aston Villa	42	13	15	14	48	45	41
Portsmouth	42	14	12	16	45	62	40
Bristol City	42	14	10	18	47	54	38
Cardiff City	42	10	16	16	49	62	36
Oxford United	42	10	16	16	35	46	36
Sheffield Wednesday	42	12	11	19	51	63	35
Crystal Palace	42	11	12	19	43	56	34
Preston North End	42	9	14	19	40	62	31
Swindon Town	42	7	11	24	36	72	25

Preston North End had one point deducted

DIVISION 4 1973-74

Peterborough United	46	27	11	8	75	38	65
Gillingham	46	25	12	9	90	49	62
Colchester United	46	24	12	10	73	36	60
Bury	46	24	11	11	81	49	59
Northampton Town	46	20	13	13	63	48	53
Reading	46	16	19	11	58	37	51
Chester	46	17	15	14	54	55	49
Bradford City	46	17	14	15	58	52	48
Newport County	46	16	14	16	56	65	45
Exeter City	45	18	8	19	58	55	44
Hartlepool	46	16	12	18	48	47	44
Lincoln City	46	16	12	18	63	67	44
Barnsley	46	17	10	19	58	64	44
Swansea City	46	16	11	19	45	46	43
Rotherham United	46	15	13	18	56	58	43
Torquay United	46	13	17	16	52	57	43
Mansfield Town	46	13	17	16	62	69	43
Scunthorpe United	45	14	12	19	47	64	42
Brentford	46	12	16	18	48	50	40
Darlington	46	13	13	20	40	62	39
Crewe Alexandra	46	14	10	22	43	71	38
Doncaster Rovers	46	12	11	23	47	80	35
Workington	46	11	13	22	43	74	35
Stockport County	46	7	20	19	44	69	34

Newport County had one point deducted
Scunthorpe United vs Exeter City match not played
Scunthorpe United awarded two points

1974 F.A. Cup

Semi-finals

Burnley vs Newcastle United	0-2
Leicester City vs Liverpool	0-0, 1-3

Final

Wembley, 4th May 1974

Liverpool 3 (Keegan 2, Heighway)
Newcastle United 0

Attendance 100,000

1974 Football League Cup

Semi-finals

Norwich City vs Wolverhampton Wanderers	(1-1, 0-1)	1-2
Plymouth Argyle vs Manchester City	(1-1, 0-2)	1-3

Final

Wembley, 2nd March 1974

Wolverhampton Wanderers 2 (Hibbitt, Richards)
Manchester City 1 (Bell)

Attendance 100,000

DIVISION 1 1974-75

Derby County	42	21	11	10	67	49	53
Liverpool	42	20	11	11	60	39	51
Ipswich Town	42	23	5	14	66	44	51
Everton	42	16	18	8	56	42	50
Stoke City	42	17	15	10	64	48	49
Sheffield United	42	18	13	11	58	51	49
Middlesbrough	42	18	12	12	54	40	48
Manchester City	42	18	10	14	54	54	46
Leeds United	42	16	13	13	57	49	45
Burnley	42	17	11	14	68	67	45
Queen's Park Rangers	42	16	10	16	54	54	42
Wolverhampton Wanderers	42	14	11	17	57	54	39
West Ham United	42	13	13	16	58	59	39
Coventry City	42	12	15	15	51	62	39
Newcastle United	42	15	9	18	59	72	39
Arsenal	42	13	11	18	47	49	37
Birmingham City	42	14	9	19	53	61	37
Leicester City	42	12	12	18	46	60	36
Tottenham Hotspur	42	13	8	21	52	63	34
Luton Town	42	11	11	20	47	65	33
Chelsea	42	9	15	18	42	72	33
Carlisle United	42	12	5	25	43	59	29

DIVISION 2 1974-75

Manchester United	42	26	9	7	66	30	61
Aston Villa	42	25	8	9	79	32	58
Norwich City	42	20	13	9	58	37	53
Sunderland	42	19	13	10	65	35	51
Bristol City	42	21	8	13	47	33	50
West Bromwich Albion	42	18	9	15	54	42	45
Blackpool	42	14	17	11	38	33	45
Hull City	42	15	14	13	40	53	44
Fulham	42	13	16	13	44	39	42
Bolton Wanderers	42	15	12	15	45	41	42
Oxford United	42	15	12	15	41	51	42
Orient	42	11	20	11	28	39	42
Southampton	42	15	11	16	53	54	41
Notts County	42	12	16	14	49	59	40
York City	42	14	10	18	51	55	38
Nottingham Forest	42	12	14	16	43	55	38
Portsmouth	42	12	13	17	44	54	37
Oldham Athletic	42	10	15	17	40	48	35
Bristol Rovers	42	12	11	19	42	64	35
Millwall	42	10	12	20	44	56	32
Cardiff City	42	9	14	19	36	62	32
Sheffield Wednesday	42	5	11	26	29	64	21

DIVISION 3 1974-75

Blackburn Rovers	46	22	16	8	68	45	60
Plymouth Argyle	46	24	11	11	79	58	59
Charlton Athletic	46	22	11	13	76	61	55
Swindon Town	46	21	11	14	64	58	53
Crystal Palace	46	18	15	13	66	57	51
Port Vale	46	18	15	13	61	54	51
Peterborough United	46	19	12	15	47	53	50
Walsall	46	18	13	15	67	52	49
Preston North End	46	19	11	16	63	56	49
Gillingham	46	17	14	15	65	60	48
Colchester United	46	17	13	16	70	63	47
Hereford United	46	16	14	16	64	66	46
Wrexham	46	15	15	16	65	55	45
Bury	46	16	12	18	53	50	44
Chesterfield	46	16	12	18	62	66	44
Grimsby Town	46	15	13	18	55	64	43
Halifax Town	46	13	17	16	49	65	43
Southend United	46	13	16	17	46	51	42
Brighton & Hove Albion	46	16	10	20	56	64	42
Aldershot	46	14	11	21	53	63	38
Bournemouth	46	13	12	21	44	58	38
Tranmere Rovers	46	14	9	23	55	57	37
Watford	46	10	17	19	52	75	37
Huddersfield Town	46	11	10	25	47	76	32

Aldershot had one point deducted

DIVISION 4 1974-75

Mansfield Town	46	28	12	6	90	40	68
Shrewsbury Town	46	26	10	10	80	43	62
Rotherham United	46	22	15	9	71	41	59
Chester	46	23	11	12	64	38	57
Lincoln City	46	21	15	10	79	48	57
Cambridge United	46	20	14	12	62	44	54
Reading	46	21	10	15	63	47	52
Brentford	46	18	13	15	53	45	49
Exeter City	46	19	11	16	60	63	49
Bradford City	46	17	13	16	56	51	47
Southport	46	15	17	14	56	56	47
Newport County	46	19	9	18	68	75	47
Hartlepool	46	16	11	19	52	62	43
Torquay United	46	14	14	18	46	61	42
Barnsley	46	15	11	20	62	65	41
Northampton Town	46	15	11	20	67	73	41
Doncaster Rovers	46	14	12	20	65	79	40
Crewe Alexandra	46	11	18	17	34	47	40
Rochdale	46	13	13	20	59	75	39
Stockport County	46	12	14	20	43	70	38
Darlington	46	13	10	23	54	67	36
Swansea City	46	15	6	25	46	73	36
Workington	46	10	11	25	36	66	31
Scunthorpe United	46	7	15	24	41	78	29

1975 F.A. Cup

Semi-finals

West Ham United vs Ipswich Town	0-0, 2-1
Fulham vs Birmingham City	1-1, 1-0

Final

Wembley, 2nd May 1975

West Ham United 2　(A. Taylor 2)
Fulham 0

Attendance 100,000

1975 Football League Cup

Semi-finals

Chester vs Aston Villa (2-2, 2-3)	4-5
Manchester United vs Norwich City (2-2, 0-1)	2-3

Final

Wembley, 1st March 1975

Aston Villa 1　(Graydon)
Norwich City 0

Attendance 100,000

DIVISION 1 1975-76

Team	P	W	D	L	F	A	Pts
Liverpool	42	23	14	5	66	31	60
Queen's Park Rangers	42	24	11	7	67	33	59
Manchester United	42	23	10	9	68	42	56
Derby County	42	21	11	10	75	58	53
Leeds United	42	21	9	12	65	46	51
Ipswich Town	42	16	14	12	54	48	46
Leicester City	42	13	19	10	48	51	45
Manchester City	42	16	11	15	64	46	43
Tottenham Hotspur	42	14	15	13	63	63	43
Norwich City	42	16	10	16	58	58	42
Everton	42	15	12	15	60	66	42
Stoke City	42	15	11	16	48	50	41
Middlesbrough	42	15	10	17	46	45	40
Coventry City	42	13	14	15	47	57	40
Newcastle United	42	15	9	18	71	62	39
Aston Villa	42	11	17	14	51	59	39
Arsenal	42	13	10	19	47	53	36
West Ham United	42	13	10	19	48	71	36
Birmingham City	42	13	7	22	57	75	33
Wolverhampton Wanderers	42	10	10	22	51	68	30
Burnley	42	9	10	23	43	66	28
Sheffield United	42	6	10	26	33	82	22

DIVISION 3 1975-76

Team	P	W	D	L	F	A	Pts
Hereford United	46	26	11	9	86	55	63
Cardiff City	46	22	13	11	69	48	57
Millwall	46	20	16	10	54	43	56
Brighton & Hove Albion	46	22	9	15	78	53	53
Crystal Palace	46	18	17	11	61	46	53
Wrexham	46	20	12	14	66	55	52
Walsall	46	18	14	14	74	61	50
Preston North End	46	19	10	17	62	57	48
Shrewsbury Town	46	19	10	17	61	59	48
Peterborough United	46	15	18	13	63	63	48
Mansfield Town	46	16	15	15	58	52	47
Port Vale	46	15	16	15	55	54	46
Bury	46	14	16	16	51	46	44
Chesterfield	46	17	9	20	69	69	43
Gillingham	46	12	19	15	58	68	43
Rotherham United	46	15	12	19	54	65	42
Chester	46	15	12	19	43	62	42
Grimsby Town	46	15	10	21	62	74	40
Swindon Town	46	16	8	22	62	75	40
Sheffield Wednesday	46	12	16	18	48	59	40
Aldershot	46	13	13	20	59	75	39
Colchester United	46	12	14	20	41	65	38
Southend United	46	12	13	21	65	75	37
Halifax Town	46	11	13	22	41	61	35

DIVISION 2 1975-76

Team	P	W	D	L	F	A	Pts
Sunderland	42	24	8	10	67	36	56
Bristol City	42	19	15	8	59	35	53
West Bromwich Albion	42	20	13	9	50	33	53
Bolton Wanderers	42	20	12	10	64	38	52
Notts County	42	19	11	12	60	41	49
Southampton	42	21	7	14	66	50	49
Luton Town	42	19	10	13	61	51	48
Nottingham Forest	42	17	12	13	55	40	46
Charlton Athletic	42	15	12	15	61	72	42
Blackpool	42	14	14	14	40	49	42
Chelsea	42	12	16	14	53	54	40
Fulham	42	13	14	15	45	47	40
Orient	42	13	14	15	37	39	40
Hull City	42	14	11	17	45	49	39
Blackburn Rovers	42	12	14	16	45	50	38
Plymouth Argyle	42	13	12	17	48	54	38
Oldham Athletic	42	13	12	17	57	68	38
Bristol Rovers	42	11	16	15	38	50	38
Carlisle United	42	12	13	17	45	59	37
Oxford United	42	11	11	20	39	59	33
York City	42	10	8	24	39	71	28
Portsmouth	42	9	7	26	32	61	25

DIVISION 4 1975-76

Team	P	W	D	L	F	A	Pts
Lincoln City	46	32	10	4	111	39	74
Northampton Town	46	29	10	7	87	40	68
Reading	46	24	12	10	70	51	60
Tranmere Rovers	46	24	10	12	89	55	58
Huddersfield Town	46	21	14	11	56	41	56
Bournemouth	46	20	12	14	57	48	52
Exeter City	46	18	14	14	56	47	50
Watford	46	22	6	18	62	62	50
Torquay United	46	18	14	14	55	63	50
Doncaster Rovers	46	19	11	16	75	69	49
Swansea City	46	16	15	15	66	57	47
Barnsley	46	14	16	16	52	48	44
Cambridge United	46	14	15	17	58	62	43
Hartlepool	46	16	10	20	62	78	42
Rochdale	46	12	18	16	40	54	42
Crewe Alexandra	46	13	15	18	58	57	41
Bradford City	46	12	17	17	63	65	41
Brentford	46	14	13	19	56	60	41
Scunthorpe United	46	14	10	22	50	59	38
Darlington	46	14	10	22	48	57	38
Stockport County	46	13	12	21	43	76	38
Newport County	46	13	9	24	57	90	35
Southport	46	8	10	28	41	77	26
Workington	46	7	7	32	30	87	21

1976 F.A. Cup

Semi-finals

Southampton vs Crystal Palace	2-0
Manchester United vs Derby County	2-0

Final

Wembley, 1st May 1976

Southampton 1 (Stokes)

Manchester United 0

Attendance 100,000

1976 Football League Cup

Semi-finals

Middlesbrough vs Manchester City (1-0, 0-4)	1-4
Tottenham Hotspur vs Newcastle United (1-0, 1-3)	2-3

Final

Wembley, 28th February 1976

Manchester City 2 (Barnes, Tueart)

Newcastle United 1 (Gowling)

Attendance 100,000

DIVISION 1 1976-77

Liverpool	42	23	11	8	62	33	57
Manchester City	42	21	14	7	60	34	56
Ipswich Town	42	22	8	12	66	39	52
Aston Villa	42	22	7	13	76	50	51
Newcastle United	42	18	13	11	64	49	49
Manchester United	42	18	11	13	71	62	47
West Bromwich Albion	42	16	13	13	62	56	45
Arsenal	42	16	11	15	64	59	43
Everton	42	14	14	14	62	64	42
Leeds United	42	15	12	15	48	51	42
Leicester City	42	12	18	12	47	60	42
Middlesbrough	42	14	13	15	40	45	41
Birmingham City	42	13	12	17	63	61	38
Queen's Park Rangers	42	13	12	17	47	52	38
Derby County	42	9	19	14	50	55	37
Norwich City	42	14	9	19	47	64	37
West Ham United	42	11	14	17	46	65	36
Bristol City	42	11	13	18	38	48	35
Coventry City	42	10	15	17	48	59	35
Sunderland	42	11	12	19	46	54	34
Stoke City	42	10	14	18	28	51	34
Tottenham Hotspur	42	12	9	21	48	72	33

DIVISION 3 1976-77

Mansfield Town	46	28	8	10	78	33	64
Brighton & Hove Albion	46	25	11	10	83	39	61
Crystal Palace	46	23	13	10	68	40	59
Rotherham United	46	22	15	9	69	44	59
Wrexham	46	24	10	12	80	54	58
Preston North End	46	21	12	13	64	43	54
Bury	46	23	8	15	64	59	54
Sheffield Wednesday	46	22	9	15	65	55	53
Lincoln City	46	19	14	13	77	70	52
Shrewsbury Town	46	18	11	17	65	59	47
Swindon Town	46	15	15	16	68	75	45
Gillingham	46	16	12	18	55	64	44
Chester	46	18	8	20	48	58	44
Tranmere Rovers	46	13	17	16	51	53	43
Walsall	46	13	15	18	57	65	41
Peterborough United	46	13	15	18	55	65	41
Oxford United	46	12	15	19	55	65	39
Chesterfield	46	14	10	22	56	64	38
Port Vale	46	11	16	19	47	71	38
Portsmouth	46	11	14	21	43	70	36
Reading	46	13	9	24	49	73	35
Northampton Town	46	13	8	25	60	75	34
Grimsby Town	46	12	9	25	45	69	33
York City	46	10	12	24	50	89	32

DIVISION 2 1976-77

Wolverhampton Wanderers	42	22	13	7	84	45	57
Chelsea	42	21	13	8	73	53	55
Nottingham Forest	42	21	10	11	77	43	52
Bolton Wanderers	42	20	11	11	74	54	51
Blackpool	42	17	17	8	58	42	51
Luton Town	42	21	6	15	67	48	48
Charlton Athletic	42	16	16	10	71	58	48
Notts County	42	19	10	13	65	60	48
Southampton	42	17	10	15	72	67	44
Millwall	42	15	13	14	57	53	43
Sheffield United	42	14	12	16	54	63	40
Blackburn Rovers	42	15	9	18	42	54	39
Oldham Athletic	42	14	10	18	52	64	38
Hull City	42	10	17	15	45	53	37
Bristol Rovers	42	12	13	17	53	68	37
Burnley	42	11	14	17	46	64	36
Fulham	42	11	13	18	54	61	35
Cardiff City	42	12	10	20	56	67	34
Orient	42	9	16	17	37	55	34
Carlisle United	42	11	12	19	49	75	34
Plymouth Argyle	42	8	16	18	46	65	32
Hereford United	42	8	15	19	57	78	31

DIVISION 4 1976-77

Cambridge United	46	26	13	7	87	40	65
Exeter City	46	25	12	9	70	46	62
Colchester United	46	25	9	12	77	43	59
Bradford City	46	23	13	10	78	51	59
Swansea City	46	25	8	13	92	68	58
Barnsley	46	23	9	14	62	39	55
Watford	46	18	15	13	67	50	51
Doncaster Rovers	46	21	9	16	71	65	51
Huddersfield Town	46	19	12	15	60	49	50
Southend United	46	15	19	12	52	45	49
Darlington	46	18	13	15	59	64	49
Crewe Alexandra	46	19	11	16	47	60	49
Bournemouth	46	15	18	13	54	44	48
Stockport County	46	13	19	14	53	57	45
Brentford	46	18	7	21	77	76	43
Torquay United	46	17	9	20	59	67	43
Aldershot	46	16	11	19	49	59	43
Rochdale	46	13	12	21	50	59	38
Newport County	46	14	10	22	42	58	38
Scunthorpe United	46	13	11	22	49	73	37
Halifax Town	46	11	14	21	47	58	36
Hartlepool	46	10	12	24	47	73	32
Southport	46	3	19	24	33	77	25
Workington	46	4	11	31	41	102	19

1977 Football League Cup

Semi-finals

Queen's Park Rangers vs Aston Villa (0-0, 2-2, 0-3*)   2-5
Everton vs Bolton Wanderers (1-1, 1-0)   2-1
* Play-off at Highbury

Final

Wembley, 12th March 1977

Aston Villa 0
Everton 0

Attendance 100,000

Replay

Hillsborough, 16th March 1977

Aston Villa 1   (Kenyon (og))
Everton 1 (aet.)   (Latchford)

Attendance 55,000

2nd Replay
* Old Trafford, 13th April 1977

Aston Villa 3   (Little 2, Nicholl)
Everton 2 (aet.)   (Latchford, Lyons)

Attendance 54,749

1977 F.A. Cup

Semi-finals

Leeds United vs Manchester United   1-2
Everton vs Liverpool   2-2, 0-3

Final

Wembley, 21st May 1977

Manchester United 2   (Pearson, J. Greenhoff)
Liverpool 1   (Case)

Attendance 100,000

DIVISION 1 1977-78

Nottingham Forest	42	25	14	3	69	24	64
Liverpool	42	24	9	9	65	34	57
Everton	42	22	11	9	76	45	55
Manchester City	42	20	12	10	74	51	52
Arsenal	42	21	10	11	60	37	52
West Bromwich Albion	42	18	14	10	62	53	50
Coventry City	42	18	12	12	75	62	48
Aston Villa	42	18	10	14	57	42	46
Leeds United	42	18	10	14	63	53	46
Manchester United	42	16	10	16	67	63	42
Birmingham City	42	16	9	17	55	60	41
Derby County	42	14	13	15	54	59	41
Norwich City	42	11	18	13	52	66	40
Middlesbrough	42	12	15	15	42	54	39
Wolverhampton Wanderers	42	12	12	18	51	64	36
Chelsea	42	11	14	17	46	69	36
Bristol City	42	11	13	18	49	53	35
Ipswich Town	42	11	13	18	47	61	35
Queen's Park Rangers	42	9	15	18	47	64	33
West Ham United	42	12	8	22	52	69	32
Newcastle United	42	6	10	26	42	78	22
Leicester City	42	5	12	25	26	70	22

DIVISION 3 1977-78

Wrexham	46	23	15	8	78	45	61
Cambridge United	46	23	12	11	72	51	58
Preston North End	46	20	16	10	63	38	56
Peterborough United	46	20	16	10	47	33	56
Chester	46	16	22	8	59	56	54
Walsall	46	18	17	11	61	50	53
Gillingham	46	15	20	11	67	60	50
Colchester United	46	15	18	13	55	44	48
Chesterfield	46	17	14	15	58	49	48
Swindon Town	46	16	16	14	67	60	48
Shrewsbury Town	46	16	15	15	63	57	47
Tranmere Rovers	46	16	15	15	57	52	47
Carlisle United	46	14	19	13	59	59	47
Sheffield Wednesday	46	15	16	15	50	52	46
Bury	46	13	19	14	62	56	45
Lincoln City	46	15	15	16	53	61	45
Exeter City	46	15	14	17	49	59	44
Oxford United	46	13	14	19	64	67	40
Plymouth Argyle	46	11	17	18	61	68	39
Rotherham United	46	13	13	20	51	68	39
Port Vale	46	8	20	18	46	67	36
Bradford City	46	12	10	24	56	86	34
Hereford United	46	9	14	23	34	60	32
Portsmouth	46	7	17	22	41	75	31

DIVISION 2 1977-78

Bolton Wanderers	42	24	10	8	63	33	58
Southampton	42	22	13	7	70	39	57
Tottenham Hotspur	42	20	16	6	83	49	56
Brighton & Hove Albion	42	22	12	8	63	38	56
Blackburn Rovers	42	16	13	13	56	60	45
Sunderland	42	14	16	12	67	59	44
Stoke City	42	16	10	16	53	49	42
Oldham Athletic	42	13	16	13	54	58	42
Crystal Palace	42	13	15	14	50	47	41
Fulham	42	14	13	15	49	49	41
Burnley	42	15	10	17	56	64	40
Sheffield United	42	16	8	18	62	73	40
Luton Town	42	14	10	18	54	52	38
Orient	42	10	18	14	43	49	38
Notts County	42	11	16	15	54	62	38
Millwall	42	12	14	16	49	57	38
Charlton Athletic	42	13	12	17	55	68	38
Bristol Rovers	42	13	12	17	61	77	38
Cardiff City	42	13	12	17	51	71	38
Blackpool	42	12	13	17	59	60	37
Mansfield Town	42	10	11	21	49	69	31
Hull City	42	8	12	22	34	52	28

DIVISION 4 1977-78

Watford	46	30	11	5	85	38	71
Southend United	46	25	10	11	66	39	60
Swansea City	46	23	10	13	87	47	56
Brentford	46	21	14	11	86	54	56
Aldershot	46	19	16	11	67	47	54
Grimsby Town	46	21	11	14	57	51	53
Barnsley	46	18	14	14	61	49	50
Reading	46	18	14	14	55	52	50
Torquay United	46	16	15	15	57	56	47
Northampton Town	46	17	13	16	63	68	47
Huddersfield Town	46	15	15	16	63	55	45
Doncaster Rovers	46	14	17	15	52	65	45
Wimbledon	46	14	16	16	66	67	44
Scunthorpe United	46	14	16	16	50	55	44
Crewe Alexandra	46	15	14	17	50	69	44
Newport County	46	16	11	19	65	73	43
Bournemouth	46	14	15	17	41	51	43
Stockport County	46	16	10	20	56	56	42
Darlington	46	14	13	19	52	59	41
Halifax Town	46	10	21	15	52	62	41
Hartlepool United	46	15	7	24	51	84	37
York City	46	12	12	22	50	69	36
Southport	46	6	19	21	52	76	31
Rochdale	46	8	8	30	43	85	24

1978 F.A. Cup

Semi-finals

Ipswich Town vs West Bromwich Albion	3-1
Arsenal vs Orient	3-0

Final

Wembley, 6th May 1978

Ipswich Town 1 (Osborne)
Arsenal 0

Attendance 100,000

1978 Football League Cup

Semi-finals

Leeds United vs Nottingham Forest (1-3, 2-4)	3-7
Liverpool vs Arsenal (2-1, 0-0)	2-1

Final

Wembley, 18th March 1978

Nottingham Forest 0
Liverpool 0 (aet.)

Attendance 100,000

Replay

Old Trafford, 22nd March 1978

Nottingham Forest 1 (Robertson (penalty))
Liverpool 0

Attendance 54,375

DIVISION 1 1978-79

Liverpool	42	30	8	4	85	16	68
Nottingham Forest	42	21	18	3	61	26	60
West Bromwich Albion	42	24	11	7	72	35	59
Everton	42	17	17	8	52	40	51
Leeds United	42	18	14	10	70	52	50
Ipswich Town	42	20	9	13	63	49	49
Arsenal	42	17	14	11	61	48	48
Aston Villa	42	15	16	11	59	49	46
Manchester United	42	15	15	12	60	63	45
Coventry City	42	14	16	12	58	68	44
Tottenham Hotspur	42	13	15	14	48	61	41
Middlesbrough	42	15	10	17	57	50	40
Bristol City	42	15	10	17	47	51	40
Southampton	42	12	16	14	47	53	40
Manchester City	42	13	13	16	58	56	39
Norwich City	42	7	23	12	51	57	37
Bolton Wanderers	42	12	11	19	54	75	35
Wolverhampton Wanderers	42	13	8	21	44	68	34
Derby County	42	10	11	21	44	71	31
Queen's Park Rangers	42	6	13	23	45	73	25
Birmingham City	42	6	10	26	37	64	22
Chelsea	42	5	10	27	44	92	20

DIVISION 3 1978-79

Shrewsbury Town	46	21	19	6	61	41	61
Watford	46	24	12	10	83	52	60
Swansea City	46	24	12	10	83	61	60
Gillingham	46	21	17	8	65	42	59
Swindon Town	46	25	7	14	74	52	57
Carlisle United	46	15	22	9	53	42	52
Colchester United	46	17	17	12	60	55	51
Hull City	46	19	11	16	66	61	49
Exeter City	46	17	15	14	61	56	49
Brentford	46	19	9	18	53	49	47
Oxford United	46	14	18	14	44	50	46
Blackpool	46	18	9	19	61	59	45
Southend United	46	15	15	16	51	49	45
Sheffield Wednesday	46	13	19	14	53	53	45
Plymouth Argyle	46	15	14	17	67	68	44
Chester	46	14	16	16	57	61	44
Rotherham United	46	17	10	19	49	55	44
Mansfield Town	46	12	19	15	51	52	43
Bury	46	11	20	15	59	65	42
Chesterfield	46	13	14	19	51	65	40
Peterborough United	46	11	14	21	44	63	36
Walsall	46	10	12	24	56	71	32
Tranmere Rovers	46	6	16	24	45	78	28
Lincoln City	46	7	11	28	41	88	25

DIVISION 2 1978-79

Crystal Palace	42	19	19	4	51	24	57
Brighton & Hove Albion	42	23	10	9	72	39	56
Stoke City	42	20	16	6	58	31	56
Sunderland	42	22	11	9	70	44	55
West Ham United	42	18	14	10	70	39	50
Notts County	42	14	16	12	48	60	44
Preston North End	42	12	18	12	59	57	42
Newcastle United	42	17	8	17	51	55	42
Cardiff City	42	16	10	16	56	70	42
Fulham	42	13	15	14	50	47	41
Orient	42	15	10	17	51	51	40
Cambridge United	42	12	16	14	44	52	40
Burnley	42	14	12	16	51	62	40
Oldham Athletic	42	13	13	16	52	61	39
Wrexham	42	12	14	16	45	42	38
Bristol Rovers	42	14	10	18	48	60	38
Leicester City	42	10	17	15	43	52	37
Luton Town	42	13	10	19	60	57	36
Charlton Athletic	42	11	13	18	60	69	35
Sheffield United	42	11	12	19	52	69	34
Millwall	42	11	10	21	42	61	32
Blackburn Rovers	42	10	10	22	41	72	30

DIVISION 4 1978-79

Reading	46	26	13	7	76	35	65
Grimsby Town	46	26	9	11	82	49	61
Wimbledon	46	25	11	10	78	46	61
Barnsley	46	24	13	9	73	42	61
Aldershot	46	20	17	9	63	47	57
Wigan Athletic	46	21	13	12	63	48	55
Portsmouth	46	20	12	14	62	48	52
Newport County	46	21	10	15	66	55	52
Huddersfield Town	46	18	11	17	57	53	47
York City	46	18	11	17	51	55	47
Torquay United	46	19	8	19	58	65	46
Scunthorpe United	46	17	11	18	54	60	45
Hartlepool United	46	13	18	15	57	66	44
Hereford United	46	15	13	18	53	53	43
Bradford City	46	17	9	20	62	68	43
Port Vale	46	14	14	18	57	70	42
Stockport County	46	14	12	20	58	60	40
Bournemouth	46	14	11	21	47	48	39
Northampton Town	46	15	9	22	64	76	39
Rochdale	46	15	9	22	47	64	39
Darlington	46	11	15	20	49	66	37
Doncaster Rovers	46	13	11	22	50	73	37
Halifax Town	46	9	8	29	39	72	26
Crewe Alexandra	46	6	14	26	43	90	26

1979 F.A. Cup

Semi-finals

Arsenal vs Wolverhampton Wanderers 2-0
Manchester United vs Liverpool 2-2, 1-0

Final

Wembley, 12th May 1979

Arsenal 3 (Talbot, Stapleton, Sunderland)
Manchester United 2 (McQueen, McIlroy)

Attendance 100,000

1979 Football League Cup

Semi-finals

Nottingham Forest vs Watford (3-1, 0-0) 3-1
Leeds United vs Southampton (2-2, 0-1) 2-3

Final

Wembley, 17th March 1979

Nottingham Forest 3 (Birtles 2, Woodcock)
Southampton 2 (Peach, Holmes)

Attendance 100,000

DIVISION 1 1979-80

Liverpool	42	25	10	7	81	30	60
Manchester United	42	24	10	8	65	35	58
Ispwich	42	22	9	11	68	39	53
Arsenal	42	18	16	8	52	36	52
Nottingham Forest	42	20	8	14	63	43	48
Wolverhampton Wanderers	42	19	9	14	58	47	47
Aston Villa	42	16	14	12	51	50	46
Southampton	42	18	9	15	65	53	45
Middlesbrough	42	16	12	14	50	44	44
West Bromwich Albion	42	11	19	12	54	50	41
Leeds United	42	13	14	15	46	50	40
Norwich City	42	13	14	15	58	66	40
Crystal Palace	42	12	16	14	41	50	40
Tottenham Hotspur	42	15	10	17	52	62	40
Coventry City	42	16	7	19	56	66	39
Brighton & Hove Albion	42	11	15	16	47	57	37
Manchester City	42	12	13	17	43	66	37
Stoke City	42	13	10	19	44	58	36
Everton	42	9	17	16	43	51	35
Bristol City	42	9	13	20	37	66	31
Derby County	42	11	8	23	47	67	30
Bolton Wanderers	42	5	15	22	38	73	25

DIVISION 2 1979-80

Leicester City	42	21	13	8	58	38	55
Sunderland	42	21	12	9	69	42	54
Birmingham City	42	21	11	10	58	38	53
Chelsea	42	23	7	12	66	52	53
Queen's Park Rangers	42	18	13	11	75	53	49
Luton Town	42	16	17	9	66	45	49
West Ham United	42	20	7	15	54	43	47
Cambridge United	42	14	16	12	61	53	44
Newcastle United	42	15	14	13	53	49	44
Preston North End	42	12	19	11	56	52	43
Oldham Athletic	42	16	11	15	49	53	43
Swansea City	42	17	9	16	48	53	43
Shrewsbury Town	42	18	5	19	60	53	41
Orient	42	12	17	13	48	54	41
Cardiff City	42	16	8	18	41	48	40
Wrexham	42	16	6	20	40	49	38
Notts County	42	11	15	16	51	52	37
Watford	42	12	13	17	39	46	37
Bristol Rovers	42	11	13	18	50	64	35
Fulham	42	11	7	24	42	74	29
Burnley	42	6	15	21	39	73	27
Charlton Athletic	42	6	10	26	39	78	22

DIVISION 3 1979-80

Grimsby Town	46	26	10	10	73	42	62
Blackburn Rovers	46	25	9	12	58	36	59
Sheffield Wednesday	46	21	16	9	81	47	58
Chesterfield	46	23	11	12	71	46	57
Colchester United	46	20	12	14	64	56	52
Carlisle United	46	18	12	16	66	56	48
Reading	46	16	16	14	66	65	48
Exeter City	46	19	10	17	60	68	48
Chester	46	17	13	16	49	57	47
Swindon Town	46	19	8	19	71	63	46
Barnsley	46	16	14	16	53	56	46
Sheffield United	46	18	10	18	60	66	46
Rotherham United	46	18	10	18	58	66	46
Millwall	46	16	13	17	65	59	45
Plymouth Argyle	46	16	12	18	59	55	44
Gillingham	46	14	14	18	49	51	42
Oxford United	46	14	13	19	57	62	41
Blackpool	46	15	11	20	62	74	41
Brentford	46	15	11	20	59	73	41
Hull City	46	12	16	18	51	69	40
Bury	46	16	7	23	45	59	39
Southend United	46	14	10	22	47	58	38
Mansfield Town	46	10	16	20	47	58	36
Wimbledon	46	10	14	22	52	81	34

DIVISION 4 1979-80

Huddersfield Town	46	27	12	7	101	48	66
Walsall	46	23	18	5	75	47	64
Newport County	46	27	7	12	83	50	61
Portsmouth	46	24	12	10	91	49	60
Bradford City	46	24	12	10	77	50	60
Wigan Athletic	46	21	13	12	76	61	55
Lincoln City	46	18	17	11	64	42	53
Peterborough United	46	21	10	15	58	47	52
Torquay United	46	15	17	14	70	69	47
Aldershot	46	16	13	17	62	53	45
Bournemouth	46	13	18	15	52	51	44
Doncaster Rovers	46	15	14	17	62	63	44
Northampton Town	46	16	12	18	51	66	44
Scunthorpe United	46	14	15	17	58	75	43
Tranmere Rovers	46	14	13	19	50	56	41
Stockport County	46	14	12	20	48	72	40
York City	46	14	11	21	65	82	39
Halifax Town	46	13	13	20	46	72	39
Hartlepool United	46	14	10	22	59	64	38
Port Vale	46	12	12	22	56	70	36
Hereford United	46	11	14	21	38	52	36
Darlington	46	9	17	20	50	74	35
Crewe Alexandra	46	11	13	22	35	68	35
Rochdale	46	7	13	26	33	79	27

1980 F.A. Cup

Semi-finals

West Ham United vs Everton	1-1, 2-1
Arsenal vs Liverpool	0-0, 1-1, 1-1, 1-0

Final

Wembley, 10th May 1980

West Ham United 1   (Brooking)

Arsenal 0

Attendance 100,000

1980 Football League Cup

Semi-finals

Swindon Town vs Wolverhampton Wands. (2-1, 1-3)	3-4
Nottingham Forest vs Liverpool (1-0, 1-1)	2-1

Final

Wembley, 15th March 1980

Wolverhampton Wanderers 1   (Gray)

Nottingham Forest 0

Attendance 100,000

DIVISION 1 1980-81

Aston Villa	42	26	8	8	72	40	60
Ipswich Town	42	23	10	9	77	43	56
Arsenal	42	19	15	8	61	45	53
West Bromwich Albion	42	20	12	10	60	42	52
Liverpool	42	17	17	8	62	42	51
Southampton	42	20	10	12	76	56	50
Nottingham Forest	42	19	12	11	62	44	50
Manchester United	42	15	18	9	51	36	48
Leeds United	42	17	10	15	39	47	44
Tottenham Hotspur	42	14	15	13	70	68	43
Stoke City	42	12	18	12	51	60	42
Manchester City	42	14	11	17	56	59	39
Birmingham City	42	13	12	17	50	61	38
Middlesbrough	42	16	5	21	53	61	37
Everton	42	13	10	19	55	58	36
Coventry City	42	13	10	19	48	68	36
Sunderland	42	14	7	21	52	53	35
Wolverhampton Wanderers	42	13	9	20	43	55	35
Brighton & Hove Albion	42	14	7	21	54	67	35
Norwich City	42	13	7	22	49	73	33
Leicester City	42	13	6	23	40	67	32
Crystal Palace	42	6	7	29	47	83	19

DIVISION 3 1980-81

Rotherham United	46	24	13	9	62	32	61
Barnsley	46	21	17	8	72	45	59
Charlton Athletic	46	25	9	12	63	44	59
Huddersfield Town	46	21	14	11	71	40	56
Chesterfield	46	23	10	13	72	48	56
Portsmouth	46	22	9	15	55	47	53
Plymouth Argyle	46	19	14	13	56	44	52
Burnley	46	18	14	14	60	48	50
Brentford	46	14	19	13	52	49	47
Reading	46	18	10	18	62	62	46
Exeter City	46	16	13	17	62	66	45
Newport County	46	15	13	18	64	61	43
Fulham	46	15	13	18	57	64	43
Oxford United	46	13	17	16	39	47	43
Gillingham	46	12	18	16	48	58	42
Millwall	46	14	14	18	43	60	42
Swindon Town	46	13	15	18	51	56	41
Chester	46	15	11	20	38	48	41
Carlisle United	46	14	13	19	56	70	41
Walsall	46	13	15	18	59	74	41
Sheffield United	46	14	12	20	65	63	40
Colchester United	46	14	11	21	45	65	39
Blackpool	46	9	14	23	45	75	32
Hull City	46	8	16	22	40	71	32

DIVISION 2 1980-81

West Ham United	42	28	10	4	79	29	66
Notts County	42	18	17	7	49	38	53
Swansea City	42	18	14	10	64	44	50
Blackburn Rovers	42	16	18	8	42	29	50
Luton Town	42	18	12	12	61	46	48
Derby County	42	15	15	12	57	52	45
Grimsby Town	42	15	15	12	44	42	45
Queen's Park Rangers	42	15	13	14	56	46	43
Watford	42	16	11	15	50	45	43
Sheffield Wednesday	42	17	8	17	53	51	42
Newcastle United	42	14	14	14	30	45	42
Chelsea	42	14	12	16	46	41	40
Cambridge United	42	17	6	19	53	65	40
Shrewsbury Town	42	11	17	14	46	47	39
Oldham Athletic	42	12	15	15	39	48	39
Wrexham	42	12	14	16	43	45	38
Orient	42	13	12	17	52	56	38
Bolton Wanderers	42	14	10	18	61	66	38
Cardiff City	42	12	12	18	44	60	36
Preston North End	42	11	14	17	41	62	36
Bristol City	42	7	16	19	29	51	30
Bristol Rovers	42	5	13	24	34	65	23

DIVISION 4 1980-81

Southend United	46	30	7	9	79	31	67
Lincoln City	46	25	15	6	66	25	65
Doncaster Rovers	46	22	12	12	59	49	56
Wimbledon	46	23	9	14	64	46	55
Peterborough United	46	17	18	11	68	54	52
Aldershot	46	18	14	14	43	41	50
Mansfield Town	46	20	9	17	58	44	49
Darlington	46	19	11	16	65	59	49
Hartlepool United	46	20	9	17	64	61	49
Northampton Town	46	18	13	15	65	67	49
Wigan Athletic	46	18	11	17	51	55	47
Bury	46	17	11	18	70	62	45
Bournemouth	46	16	13	17	47	48	45
Bradford City	46	14	16	16	53	60	44
Rochdale	46	14	15	17	60	70	43
Scunthorpe United	46	11	20	15	60	69	42
Torquay United	46	18	5	23	55	63	41
Crewe Alexandra	46	13	14	19	48	61	40
Port Vale	46	12	15	19	57	70	39
Stockport County	46	16	7	23	44	57	39
Tranmere Rovers	46	13	10	23	59	73	36
Hereford United	46	11	13	22	38	62	35
Halifax Town	46	11	12	23	44	71	34
York City	46	12	9	25	47	66	33

1981 F.A. Cup

Semi-finals

Tottenham Hotspur vs Wolverhampton Wanderers 2-2, 3-0
Ipswich Town vs Manchester City 0-1

Final

Wembley, 9th May 1981

Tottenham Hotspur 1 (Hutchinson (og))
Manchester City 1 (Hutchinson)

Attendance 100,000

Replay

Wembley, 14th May 1981

Tottenham Hotspur 3 (Villa 2, Crooks)
Manchester City 2 (MacKenzie, Reeves (pen))

Attendance 92,000

1981 Football League Cup

Semi-finals

Manchester City vs Liverpool (0-1, 1-1) 1-2
Coventry City vs West Ham United (3-2, 0-2) 3-4

Final

Wembley, 14th March 1981

Liverpool 1 (A. Kennedy)
West Ham United 1 (aet.) (Stewart)

Attendance 100,000

Replay

Villa Park, 1st April 1981

Liverpool 2 (Dalglish, R. Kennedy)
West Ham United 1 (Goddard)

Attendance 36,693

DIVISION 1 1981-82

Liverpool	42	26	9	7	80	32	87
Ipswich Town	42	26	5	11	75	53	83
Manchester United	42	22	12	8	59	29	78
Tottenham Hotspur	42	20	11	11	67	48	71
Arsenal	42	20	11	11	48	37	71
Swansea City	42	21	6	15	58	51	69
Southampton	42	19	9	14	72	67	66
Everton	42	17	13	12	56	50	64
West Ham United	42	14	16	12	66	57	58
Manchester City	42	15	13	14	49	50	58
Aston Villa	42	15	12	15	55	53	57
Nottingham Forest	42	15	12	15	42	48	57
Brighton & Hove Albion	42	13	13	16	43	52	52
Coventry City	42	13	11	18	56	62	50
Notts County	42	13	8	21	61	69	47
Birmingham City	42	10	14	18	53	61	44
West Bromwich Albion	42	11	11	20	46	57	44
Stoke City	42	12	8	22	44	63	44
Sunderland	42	11	11	20	38	58	44
Leeds United	42	10	12	20	39	61	42
Wolverhampton Wanderers	42	10	10	22	32	63	40
Middlesbrough	42	8	15	19	34	52	39

DIVISION 2 1981-82

Luton Town	42	25	13	4	86	46	88
Watford	42	23	11	8	76	42	80
Norwich City	42	22	5	15	64	50	71
Sheffield Wednesday	42	20	10	12	55	51	70
Queen's Park Rangers	42	21	6	15	65	43	69
Barnsley	42	19	10	13	59	41	67
Rotherham United	42	20	7	15	66	54	67
Leicester City	42	18	12	12	56	48	66
Newcastle United	42	18	8	16	52	50	62
Blackburn Rovers	42	16	11	15	47	43	59
Oldham Athletic	42	15	14	13	50	51	59
Chelsea	42	15	12	15	60	60	57
Charlton Athletic	42	13	12	17	50	65	51
Cambridge United	42	13	9	20	48	53	48
Crystal Palace	42	13	9	20	34	45	48
Derby County	42	12	12	18	53	68	48
Grimsby Town	42	11	13	18	53	65	46
Shrewsbury Town	42	11	13	18	37	57	46
Bolton Wanderers	42	13	7	22	39	61	46
Cardiff City	42	12	8	22	45	61	44
Wrexham	42	11	11	20	40	56	44
Orient	42	10	9	23	39	61	39

DIVISION 3 1981-82

Burnley	46	21	17	8	66	45	80
Carlisle United	46	23	11	12	65	50	80
Fulham	46	21	15	10	77	51	78
Lincoln City	46	21	14	11	66	40	77
Oxford United	46	19	14	13	63	49	71
Gillingham	46	20	11	15	64	56	71
Southend United	46	18	15	13	63	51	69
Brentford	46	19	11	16	56	47	68
Millwall	46	18	13	15	62	62	67
Plymouth Argyle	46	18	11	17	64	56	65
Chesterfield	46	18	10	18	57	58	64
Reading	46	17	11	18	67	75	62
Portsmouth	46	14	19	13	56	51	61
Preston North End	46	16	13	17	50	56	61
Bristol Rovers	46	18	9	19	58	65	61
Newport County	46	14	16	16	54	54	58
Huddersfield Town	46	15	12	19	64	59	57
Exeter City	46	16	9	21	71	84	57
Doncaster Rovers	46	13	17	16	55	68	56
Walsall	46	13	14	19	51	55	53
Wimbledon	46	14	11	21	61	75	53
Swindon Town	46	13	13	20	55	71	52
Bristol City	46	11	13	22	40	65	46
Chester	46	7	11	28	36	78	32

Bristol Rovers had two points deducted

DIVISION 4 1981-82

Sheffield United	46	27	15	4	94	41	96
Bradford City	46	26	13	7	88	45	91
Wigan Athletic	46	26	13	7	80	46	91
Bournemouth	46	23	19	4	62	30	88
Peterborough United	46	24	10	12	71	57	82
Colchester United	46	20	12	14	82	57	72
Port Vale	46	18	16	12	56	49	70
Hull City	46	19	12	15	70	61	69
Bury	46	17	17	12	80	59	68
Hereford United	46	16	19	11	64	58	67
Tranmere Rovers	46	14	18	14	51	56	60
Blackpool	46	15	13	18	66	60	58
Darlington	46	15	13	18	61	62	58
Hartlepool United	46	13	16	17	73	84	55
Torquay United	46	14	13	19	47	59	55
Aldershot	46	13	15	18	57	68	54
York City	46	14	8	24	69	91	50
Stockport County	46	12	13	21	48	67	49
Halifax Town	46	9	22	15	51	72	49
Mansfield Town	46	13	10	23	63	81	47
Rochdale	46	10	16	20	50	62	46
Northampton Town	46	11	9	26	57	84	42
Scunthorpe United	46	9	15	22	43	79	42
Crewe Alexandra	46	6	9	31	29	84	27

Mansfield Town had two points deducted

1982 F.A. Cup

Semi-finals
Tottenham Hotspur vs Leicester City	2-0
West Bromwich Albion vs Queen's Park Rangers	0-1

Final
Wembley, 22nd May 1982

Tottenham Hotspur 1   (Hoddle)

Queen's Park Rangers 1 (aet.)

Attendance 100,000

Replay
Wembley, 27th May 1982

Tottenham Hotspur 1   (Hoddle (pen))
Queen's Park Rangers 0

Attendance 90,000

1982 Football League Cup

Semi-finals
Ipswich Town vs Liverpool (0-2, 2-2)	2-4
West Brom. Albion vs Tottenham Hotspur (0-0, 0-1)	0-1

Final
Wembley, 13th March 1982

Liverpool 3   (Whelan 2, Rush)
Tottenham Hotspur 1 (aet.)   (Archibald)

Attendance 100,000

DIVISION 1 1982-83

Liverpool	42	24	10	8	87	37	82
Watford	42	22	5	15	74	57	71
Manchester United	42	19	13	10	56	38	70
Tottenham Hotspur	42	20	9	13	65	50	69
Nottingham Forest	42	20	9	13	62	50	69
Aston Villa	42	21	5	16	62	50	68
Everton	42	18	10	14	66	48	64
West Ham United	42	20	4	18	68	62	64
Ipswich Town	42	15	13	14	64	50	58
Arsenal	42	16	10	16	58	56	58
West Bromwich Albion	42	15	12	15	51	49	57
Southampton	42	15	12	15	54	58	57
Stoke City	42	16	9	17	53	64	57
Norwich City	42	14	12	16	52	58	54
Notts County	42	15	7	20	55	71	52
Sunderland	42	12	14	16	48	61	50
Birmingham City	42	12	14	16	40	55	50
Luton Town	42	12	13	17	65	84	49
Coventry City	42	13	9	20	48	59	48
Manchester City	42	13	8	21	47	70	47
Swansea City	42	10	11	21	51	69	41
Brighton & Hove Albion	42	9	13	20	38	68	40

DIVISION 2 1982-83

Queen's Park Rangers	42	26	7	9	77	36	85
Wolverhampton Wanderers	42	20	15	7	68	44	75
Leicester City	42	20	10	12	72	44	70
Fulham	42	20	9	13	64	47	69
Newcastle United	42	18	13	11	75	53	67
Sheffield Wednesday	42	16	15	11	60	47	63
Oldham Athletic	42	14	19	9	64	47	61
Leeds United	42	13	21	8	51	46	60
Shrewsbury Town	42	15	14	13	48	48	59
Barnsley	42	14	15	13	57	55	57
Blackburn Rovers	42	15	12	15	58	58	57
Cambridge United	42	13	12	17	42	60	51
Derby County	42	10	19	13	49	58	49
Carlisle United	42	12	12	18	68	70	48
Crystal Palace	42	12	12	18	43	52	48
Middlesbrough	42	11	15	16	46	67	48
Charlton Athletic	42	13	9	20	63	86	48
Chelsea	42	11	14	17	51	61	47
Grimsby Town	42	12	11	19	45	70	47
Rotherham United	42	10	15	17	45	68	45
Burnley	42	12	8	22	56	66	44
Bolton Wanderers	42	11	11	20	42	61	44

DIVISION 3 1982-83

Portsmouth	46	27	10	9	74	41	91
Cardiff City	46	25	11	10	76	50	86
Huddersfield Town	46	23	13	10	84	49	82
Newport County	46	23	9	14	76	54	78
Oxford United	46	22	12	12	74	53	78
Lincoln City	46	23	7	16	77	51	76
Bristol Rovers	46	22	9	15	84	57	75
Plymouth Argyle	46	19	8	19	61	66	65
Brentford	46	18	10	18	88	77	64
Walsall	46	17	13	16	64	63	64
Sheffield United	46	19	7	20	62	64	64
Bradford City	46	16	13	17	68	69	61
Gillingham	46	16	13	17	58	59	61
Bournemouth	46	16	13	17	59	68	61
Southend United	46	15	14	17	66	65	59
Preston North End	46	15	13	18	60	69	58
Millwall	46	14	13	19	64	78	55
Wigan Athletic	46	15	9	22	60	72	54
Exeter City	46	14	12	20	81	104	54
Orient	46	15	9	22	64	88	54
Reading	46	12	17	17	63	80	53
Wrexham	46	12	15	19	57	76	51
Doncaster Rovers	46	9	11	26	57	97	38
Chesterfield	46	8	13	25	44	68	37

DIVISION 4 1982-83

Wimbledon	46	29	11	6	96	45	98
Hull City	46	25	15	6	75	34	90
Port Vale	46	26	10	10	67	34	88
Scunthorpe United	46	23	14	9	71	42	83
Bury	46	23	12	11	74	46	81
Colchester United	46	24	9	13	75	55	81
York City	46	22	13	11	88	58	79
Swindon Town	46	19	11	16	61	54	68
Peterborough United	46	17	13	16	58	52	64
Mansfield Town	46	16	13	17	61	70	61
Halifax Town	46	16	12	18	59	66	60
Torquay United	46	17	7	22	56	65	58
Chester	46	15	11	20	55	60	56
Bristol City	46	13	17	16	59	70	56
Northampton Town	46	14	12	20	65	75	54
Stockport County	46	14	12	20	60	79	54
Darlington	46	13	13	20	61	71	52
Aldershot	46	12	15	19	61	82	51
Tranmere Rovers	46	13	11	22	49	71	50
Rochdale	46	11	16	19	55	73	49
Blackpool	46	13	12	21	55	74	49
Hartlepool United	46	13	9	24	46	76	48
Crewe Alexandra	46	11	8	27	53	71	41
Hereford United	46	11	8	27	42	79	41

Blackpool had two point deducted

1983 F.A. Cup

Semi-finals

Manchester United vs Arsenal	2-1
Brighton & Hove Albion vs Sheffield Wednesday	2-1

Final

Wembley, 21st May 1983

Manchester United 2 (Stapleton, Wilkins)
Brighton & Hove Albion 2 (Smith, Stevens)

Attendance 100,000

Replay

Wembley, 26th May 1983

Manchester United 4 (Robson 2, Whiteside, Muhren (pen))
Brighton & Hove Albion 0

Attendance 100,000

1983 Football League Cup

Semi-finals

Liverpool vs Burnley (3-0, 0-1)	3-1
Arsenal vs Manchester United (2-4, 1-2)	3-6

Final

Wembley, 26th March 1983

Liverpool 2 (Kennedy, Whelan)
Manchester United 1 (aet.) (Whiteside)

Attendance 100,000

DIVISION 1 1983-84

Liverpool	42	22	14	6	73	32	80
Southampton	42	22	11	9	66	38	77
Nottingham Forest	42	22	8	12	76	45	74
Manchester United	42	20	14	8	71	41	74
Queen's Park Rangers	42	22	7	13	67	37	73
Arsenal	42	18	9	15	74	60	63
Everton	42	16	14	12	44	42	62
Tottenham Hotspur	42	17	10	15	64	65	61
West Ham United	42	17	9	16	60	55	60
Aston Villa	42	17	9	16	59	61	60
Watford	42	16	9	17	68	77	57
Ipswich Town	42	15	8	19	55	57	53
Sunderland	42	13	13	16	42	53	52
Norwich City	42	12	15	15	48	49	51
Leicester City	42	13	12	17	65	68	51
Luton Town	42	14	9	19	53	66	51
West Bromwich Albion	42	14	9	19	48	62	51
Stoke City	42	13	11	18	44	63	50
Coventry City	42	13	11	18	57	77	50
Birmingham City	42	12	12	18	39	50	48
Notts County	42	10	11	21	50	72	41
Wolverhampton Wanderers	42	6	11	25	27	80	29

DIVISION 2 1983-84

Chelsea	42	25	13	4	90	40	88
Sheffield Wednesday	42	26	10	6	72	34	88
Newcastle United	42	24	8	10	85	53	80
Manchester City	42	20	10	12	66	48	70
Grimsby Town	42	19	13	10	60	47	70
Blackburn Rovers	42	17	16	9	57	46	67
Carlisle United	42	16	16	10	48	41	64
Shrewsbury Town	42	17	10	15	49	53	61
Brighton & Hove Albion	42	17	9	16	69	60	60
Leeds United	42	16	12	14	55	56	60
Fulham	42	15	12	15	60	53	57
Huddersfield Town	42	14	15	13	56	49	57
Charlton Athletic	42	16	9	17	53	64	57
Barnsley	42	15	7	20	57	53	52
Cardiff City	42	15	6	21	53	66	51
Portsmouth	42	14	7	21	73	64	49
Middlesbrough	42	12	13	17	41	47	49
Crystal Palace	42	12	11	19	42	52	47
Oldham Athletic	42	13	8	21	47	73	47
Derby County	42	11	9	22	36	72	42
Swansea City	42	7	8	27	36	85	29
Cambridge United	42	4	12	26	28	77	24

DIVISION 3 1983-84

Oxford United	46	28	11	7	91	50	95
Wimbledon	46	26	9	11	97	76	87
Sheffield United	46	24	11	11	86	53	83
Hull City	46	23	14	9	71	38	83
Bristol Rovers	46	22	13	11	68	54	79
Walsall	46	22	9	15	68	61	75
Bradford City	46	20	11	15	73	65	71
Gillingham	46	20	10	16	74	69	70
Millwall	46	18	13	15	71	65	67
Bolton Wanderers	46	18	10	18	56	60	64
Orient	46	18	9	19	71	81	63
Burnley	46	16	14	16	76	61	62
Newport County	46	16	14	16	58	75	62
Lincoln City	46	17	10	19	59	62	61
Wigan Athletic	46	16	13	17	46	56	61
Preston North End	46	15	11	20	66	66	56
Bournemouth	46	16	7	23	63	73	55
Rotherham United	46	15	9	22	57	64	54
Plymouth Argyle	46	13	12	21	56	62	51
Brentford	46	11	16	19	69	79	49
Scunthorpe United	46	9	19	18	54	73	46
Southend United	46	10	14	22	55	76	44
Port Vale	46	11	10	25	51	83	43
Exeter City	46	6	15	25	50	84	33

DIVISION 4 1983-84

York City	46	31	8	7	96	39	101
Doncaster Rovers	46	24	13	9	82	54	85
Reading	46	22	16	8	84	56	82
Bristol City	46	24	10	12	70	44	82
Aldershot	46	22	9	15	76	69	75
Blackpool	46	21	9	16	70	52	72
Peterborough United	46	18	14	14	72	48	68
Colchester United	46	17	16	13	69	53	67
Torquay United	46	18	13	15	59	64	67
Tranmere Rovers	46	17	15	14	53	53	66
Hereford United	46	16	15	15	54	53	63
Stockport County	46	17	11	18	60	64	62
Chesterfield	46	15	15	16	59	61	60
Darlington	46	17	8	21	49	50	59
Bury	46	15	14	17	61	64	59
Crewe Alexandra	46	16	11	19	56	67	59
Swindon Town	46	15	13	18	58	56	58
Northampton Town	46	13	14	19	53	78	53
Mansfield Town	46	13	13	20	66	70	52
Wrexham	46	11	15	20	59	74	48
Halifax Town	46	12	12	22	55	89	48
Rochdale	46	11	13	22	52	80	46
Hartlepool United	46	10	10	26	47	85	40
Chester City	46	7	13	26	45	82	34

1984 F.A. Cup

Semi-finals

Everton vs Southampton	1-0
Watford vs Plymouth Argyle	1-0

Final

Wembley, 19th May 1984

Everton 2　(Sharp, Gray)
Watford 0

Attendance 100,000

1984 Football League Cup

Semi-finals

Liverpool vs Walsall (2-2, 2-0)	4-2
Everton vs Aston Villa (2-0, 0-1)	2-1

Final

Wembley, 25th March 1984

Liverpool 0
Everton 0 (aet.)

Attendance 100,000

Replay

Maine Road, 28th March 1984

Liverpool 1　(Souness)
Everton 0

Attendance 52,089

DIVISION 1 1984-85

Team	P	W	D	L	F	A	Pts
Everton	42	28	6	8	88	43	90
Liverpool	42	22	11	9	68	35	77
Tottenham Hotspur	42	23	8	11	78	51	77
Manchester United	42	22	10	10	77	47	76
Southampton	42	19	11	12	56	47	68
Chelsea	42	18	12	12	63	48	66
Arsenal	42	19	9	14	61	49	66
Sheffield Wednesday	42	17	14	11	58	45	65
Nottingham Forest	42	19	7	16	56	48	64
Aston Villa	42	15	11	16	60	60	56
Watford	42	14	13	15	81	71	55
West Bromwich Albion	42	16	7	19	58	62	55
Luton Town	42	15	9	18	57	61	54
Newcastle United	42	13	13	16	55	70	52
Leicester City	42	15	6	21	65	73	51
West Ham United	42	13	12	17	51	68	51
Ipswich Town	42	13	11	18	46	57	50
Coventry City	42	15	5	22	47	64	50
Queen's Park Rangers	42	13	11	18	53	72	50
Norwich City	42	13	10	19	46	64	49
Sunderland	42	10	10	22	40	62	40
Stoke City	42	3	8	31	24	91	17

DIVISION 3 1984-85

Team	P	W	D	L	F	A	Pts
Bradford City	46	28	10	8	77	45	94
Millwall	46	26	12	8	73	42	90
Hull City	46	25	12	9	78	49	87
Gillingham	46	25	8	13	80	62	83
Bristol City	46	24	9	13	74	47	81
Bristol Rovers	46	21	12	13	66	48	75
Derby County	46	19	13	14	65	54	70
York City	46	20	9	17	70	57	69
Reading	46	19	12	15	68	62	69
Bournemouth	46	19	11	16	57	46	68
Walsall	46	18	13	15	58	52	67
Rotherham United	46	18	11	17	55	55	65
Brentford	46	16	14	16	62	64	62
Doncaster Rovers	46	17	8	21	72	74	59
Plymouth Argyle	46	15	14	17	62	65	59
Wigan Athletic	46	15	14	17	60	64	59
Bolton Wanderers	46	16	6	24	69	75	54
Newport County	46	13	13	20	55	67	52
Lincoln City	46	11	18	17	50	51	51
Swansea City	46	12	11	23	53	80	47
Burnley	46	11	13	22	60	73	46
Orient	46	11	13	22	51	76	46
Preston North End	46	13	7	26	51	100	46
Cambridge United	46	4	9	33	37	95	21

DIVISION 2 1984-85

Team	P	W	D	L	F	A	Pts
Oxford United	42	25	9	8	84	36	84
Birmingham City	42	25	7	10	59	33	82
Manchester City	42	21	11	10	66	40	74
Portsmouth	42	20	14	8	69	50	74
Blackburn Rovers	42	21	10	11	66	41	73
Brighton & Hove Albion	42	20	12	10	54	34	72
Leeds United	42	19	12	11	66	43	69
Shrewsbury Town	42	18	11	13	66	53	65
Fulham	42	19	8	15	68	64	65
Grimsby Town	42	18	8	16	72	64	62
Barnsley	42	14	16	12	42	42	58
Wimbledon	42	16	10	16	71	75	58
Huddersfield Town	42	15	10	17	52	64	55
Oldham Athletic	42	15	8	19	49	67	53
Crystal Palace	42	12	12	18	46	65	48
Carlisle United	42	13	8	21	50	67	47
Charlton Athletic	42	11	12	19	51	63	45
Sheffield United	42	10	14	18	54	66	44
Middlesbrough	42	10	10	22	41	57	40
Notts County	42	10	7	25	45	73	37
Cardiff City	42	9	8	25	47	79	35
Wolverhampton Wanderers	42	8	9	25	37	79	33

DIVISION 4 1984-85

Team	P	W	D	L	F	A	Pts
Chesterfield	46	26	13	7	64	35	91
Blackpool	46	24	14	8	73	39	86
Darlington	46	24	13	9	66	49	85
Bury	46	24	12	10	76	50	84
Hereford United	46	22	11	13	65	47	77
Tranmere Rovers	46	24	3	19	83	66	75
Colchester United	46	20	14	12	87	65	74
Swindon Town	46	21	9	16	62	58	72
Scunthorpe United	46	19	14	13	83	62	71
Crewe Alexandra	46	18	12	16	65	69	66
Peterborough United	46	16	14	16	54	53	62
Port Vale	46	14	18	14	61	59	60
Aldershot	46	17	8	21	56	63	59
Mansfield Town	46	13	18	15	41	38	57
Wrexham	46	15	9	22	67	70	54
Chester City	46	15	9	22	60	72	54
Rochdale	46	13	14	19	55	69	53
Exeter City	46	13	14	19	57	79	53
Hartlepool United	46	14	10	22	54	67	52
Southend United	46	13	11	22	58	53	50
Halifax Town	46	15	5	26	42	69	50
Stockport County	46	13	8	25	58	79	47
Northampton Town	46	14	5	27	53	74	47
Torquay United	46	9	14	23	38	63	41

1985 F.A.Cup

Semi-finals

Luton Town vs Everton	1-2
Manchester United vs Liverpool	2-2, 2-1

Final

Wembley, 18 May 1985

Everton 0
Manchester United 1 (Whiteside)

Attendance 100,000

1985 Football League Cup

Semi-finals

Sunderland vs Chelsea (1-0, 3-2)	4-2
Ipswich Town vs Norwich City (1-0, 0-2)	1-2

Final

Wembley, 24th March 1985

Norwich City 1 (Chisholm (og))
Sunderland 0

Attendance 100,000

DIVISION 1 1985-86

Liverpool	42	26	10	6	89	37	88
Everton	42	26	8	8	87	41	86
West Ham United	42	26	6	10	74	40	84
Manchester United	42	22	10	10	70	36	76
Sheffield Wednesday	42	21	10	11	63	54	73
Chelsea	42	20	11	11	57	56	71
Arsenal	42	20	9	13	49	47	69
Nottingham Forest	42	19	11	12	69	53	68
Luton Town	42	18	12	12	61	44	66
Tottenham Hotspur	42	19	8	15	74	52	65
Newcastle United	42	17	12	13	67	72	63
Watford	42	16	11	15	69	62	59
Queen's Park Rangers	42	15	7	20	53	64	52
Southampton	42	12	10	20	51	62	46
Manchester City	42	11	12	19	43	57	45
Aston Villa	42	10	14	18	51	67	44
Coventry City	42	11	10	21	48	71	43
Oxford United	42	10	12	20	62	80	42
Leicester City	42	10	12	20	54	76	42
Ipswich Town	42	11	8	23	32	55	41
Birmingham City	42	8	5	29	30	73	29
West Bromwich Albion	42	4	12	26	35	89	24

DIVISION 3 1985-86

Reading	46	29	7	10	67	51	94
Plymouth Argyle	46	26	9	11	88	53	87
Derby County	46	23	15	8	80	41	84
Wigan Athletic	46	23	14	9	82	48	83
Gillingham	46	22	13	11	81	54	79
Walsall	46	22	9	15	90	64	75
York City	46	20	11	15	77	58	71
Notts County	46	19	14	13	71	60	71
Bristol City	46	18	14	14	69	60	68
Brentford	46	18	12	16	58	61	66
Doncaster Rovers	46	16	16	14	45	52	64
Blackpool	46	17	12	17	66	55	63
Darlington	46	15	13	18	61	78	58
Rotherham United	46	15	12	19	61	59	57
Bournemouth	46	15	9	22	65	72	54
Bristol Rovers	46	14	12	20	51	75	54
Chesterfield	46	13	14	19	61	64	53
Bolton Wanderers	46	15	8	23	54	68	53
Newport County	46	11	18	17	52	65	51
Bury	46	12	13	21	63	67	49
Lincoln City	46	10	16	20	55	77	46
Cardiff City	46	12	9	25	53	83	45
Wolverhampton Wanderers	46	11	10	25	57	98	43
Swansea City	46	11	10	25	43	87	43

DIVISION 2 1985-86

Norwich City	42	25	9	8	84	39	84
Charlton Athletic	42	22	11	9	78	45	77
Wimbledon	42	21	13	8	58	37	76
Portsmouth	42	22	7	13	69	41	73
Crystal Palace	42	19	9	14	57	52	66
Hull City	42	17	13	12	65	55	64
Sheffield United	42	17	11	14	64	63	62
Oldham Athletic	42	17	9	16	62	61	60
Millwall	42	17	8	17	64	65	59
Stoke City	42	14	15	13	48	50	57
Brighton & Hove Albion	42	16	8	18	64	64	56
Barnsley	42	14	14	14	47	50	56
Bradford City	42	16	6	20	51	63	54
Leeds United	42	15	8	19	56	72	53
Grimsby Town	42	14	10	18	58	62	52
Huddersfield Town	42	14	10	18	51	67	52
Shrewsbury Town	42	14	9	19	52	64	51
Sunderland	42	13	11	18	47	61	50
Blackburn Rovers	42	12	13	17	53	62	49
Carlisle United	42	13	7	22	47	71	46
Middlesbrough	42	12	9	21	44	53	45
Fulham	42	10	6	26	45	69	36

DIVISION 4 1985-86

Swindon Town	46	32	6	8	82	43	102
Chester City	46	23	15	8	83	50	84
Mansfield Town	46	23	12	11	74	47	81
Port Vale	46	21	16	9	67	37	79
Orient	46	20	12	14	79	64	72
Colchester United	46	19	13	14	88	63	70
Hartlepool United	46	20	10	16	68	67	70
Northampton Town	46	18	10	18	79	58	64
Southend United	46	18	10	18	69	67	64
Hereford United	46	18	10	18	74	73	64
Stockport County	46	17	13	16	63	71	64
Crewe Alexandra	46	18	9	19	54	61	63
Wrexham	46	17	9	20	68	80	60
Burnley	46	16	11	19	60	65	59
Scunthorpe United	46	15	14	17	50	55	59
Aldershot	46	17	7	22	66	74	58
Peterborough United	46	13	17	16	52	64	56
Rochdale	46	14	13	19	57	77	55
Tranmere Rovers	46	15	9	22	74	73	54
Halifax Town	46	14	12	20	60	71	54
Exeter City	46	13	15	18	47	59	54
Cambridge United	46	15	9	22	65	80	54
Preston North End	46	11	10	25	54	89	43
Torquay United	46	9	10	27	43	88	37

1986 F.A. Cup

Semi-finals

Everton vs Sheffield Wednesday	2-1
Liverpool vs Southampton	2-0

Final

Wembley, 10th May 1986

Everton 1   (Lineker)
Liverpool 3   (Rush 2, Johnston)

Attendance 98,000

1986 Football League Cup

Semi-finals

Queen's Park Rangers vs Liverpool (1-0, 2-2)	3-2
Aston Villa vs Oxford United (2-2, 1-2)	3-4

Final

Wembley, 20 April 1985

Oxford United 3   (Hebberd, Houghton, Charles)
Queen's Park Rangers 0

Attendance 90,396

DIVISION 1 1986-87

Everton	42	26	8	8	76	31	86
Liverpool	42	23	8	11	72	42	77
Tottenham Hotspur	42	21	8	13	68	43	71
Arsenal	42	20	10	12	58	35	70
Norwich City	42	17	17	8	53	51	68
Wimbledon	42	19	9	14	57	50	66
Luton Town	42	18	12	12	47	45	66
Nottingham Forest	42	18	11	13	64	51	65
Watford	42	18	9	15	67	54	63
Coventry City	42	17	12	13	50	45	63
Manchester United	42	14	14	14	52	45	56
Southampton	42	14	10	18	69	68	52
Sheffield Wednesday	42	13	13	16	58	59	52
Chelsea	42	13	13	16	53	64	52
West Ham United	42	14	10	18	52	67	52
Queen's Park Rangers	42	13	11	18	48	64	50
Newcastle United	42	12	11	19	47	65	47
Oxford United	42	11	13	18	44	69	46
Charlton Athletic	42	11	11	20	45	55	44
Leicester City	42	11	9	22	54	76	42
Manchester City	42	8	15	19	36	57	39
Aston Villa	42	8	12	22	45	79	36

DIVISION 3 1986-87

Bournemouth	46	29	10	7	76	40	97
Middlesbrough	46	28	10	8	67	30	94
Swindon Town	46	25	12	9	77	47	87
Wigan Athletic	46	25	10	11	83	60	85
Gillingham	46	23	9	14	65	48	78
Bristol City	46	21	14	11	63	36	77
Notts County	46	21	13	12	77	56	76
Walsall	46	22	9	15	80	67	75
Blackpool	46	16	16	14	74	59	64
Mansfield Town	46	15	16	15	52	55	61
Brentford	46	15	15	16	64	66	60
Port Vale	46	15	12	19	76	70	57
Doncaster Rovers	46	14	15	17	56	62	57
Rotherham United	46	15	12	19	48	57	57
Chester City	46	13	17	16	61	59	56
Bury	46	14	13	19	54	60	55
Chesterfield	46	13	15	18	56	69	54
Fulham	46	12	17	17	59	77	53
Bristol Rovers	46	13	12	21	49	75	51
York City	46	12	13	21	55	79	49
Bolton Wanderers	46	10	15	21	46	58	45
Carlisle United	46	10	8	28	39	78	38
Darlington	46	7	16	23	45	77	37
Newport County	46	8	13	25	49	86	37

DIVISION 2 1986-87

Derby County	42	25	9	8	64	38	84
Portsmouth	42	23	9	10	53	28	78
Oldham Athletic	42	22	9	11	65	44	75
Leeds United	42	19	11	12	58	44	68
Ipswich Town	42	17	13	12	59	43	64
Crystal Palace	42	19	5	18	51	53	62
Plymouth Argyle	42	16	13	13	62	57	61
Stoke City	42	16	10	16	63	53	58
Sheffield United	42	15	13	14	50	49	58
Bradford City	42	15	10	17	62	62	55
Barnsley	42	14	13	15	49	52	55
Blackburn Rovers	42	15	10	17	45	55	55
Reading	42	14	11	17	52	59	53
Hull City	42	13	14	15	41	55	53
West Bromwich Albion	42	13	12	17	51	49	51
Millwall	42	14	9	19	39	45	51
Huddersfield Town	42	13	12	17	54	61	51
Shrewsbury Town	42	15	6	21	41	53	51
Birmingham City	42	11	17	14	47	59	50
Sunderland	42	12	12	18	49	59	48
Grimsby Town	42	10	14	18	39	59	44
Brighton & Hove Albion	42	9	12	21	37	54	39

DIVISION 4 1986-87

Northampton Town	46	30	9	7	103	53	99
Preston North End	46	26	12	8	72	47	90
Southend United	46	25	5	16	68	55	80
Wolverhampton Wanderers	46	24	7	15	69	50	79
Colchester United	46	21	7	18	64	56	70
Aldershot	46	20	10	16	64	57	70
Orient	46	20	9	17	64	61	69
Scunthorpe United	46	18	12	16	73	57	66
Wrexham	46	15	20	11	70	51	65
Peterborough United	46	17	14	15	57	50	65
Cambridge United	46	17	11	18	60	62	62
Swansea City	46	17	11	18	56	61	62
Cardiff City	46	15	16	15	48	50	61
Exeter City	46	11	23	12	53	49	56
Halifax Town	46	15	10	21	59	74	55
Hereford United	46	14	11	21	60	61	53
Crewe Alexandra	46	13	14	19	70	72	53
Hartlepool United	46	11	18	17	44	65	51
Stockport County	46	13	12	21	40	69	51
Tranmere Rovers	46	11	17	18	54	72	50
Rochdale	46	11	17	18	54	73	50
Burnley	46	12	13	21	53	74	49
Torquay United	46	10	18	18	56	72	48
Lincoln City	46	12	12	22	45	65	48

1987 F.A. Cup

Semi-finals

Tottenham Hotspur vs Watford	4-1
Coventry City vs Leeds United	3-2

Final

Wembley, 16th May 1987

Coventry City 3 (Bennett, Houchen, Mabbutt (og))
Tottenham Hotspur 2 (C. Allen, Mabbutt)

Attendance 98,000

1987 Football League Cup

Semi-finals

Arsenal vs Tottenham Hotspur (0-1, 2-1, 2-1*)	4-3
Southampton vs Liverpool (0-0, 0-3)	0-3
* Play-off	

Final

Wembley, 5th April 1987

Arsenal 2 (Nicholas 2)
Liverpool 1 (Rush)

Attendance 96,000

DIVISION 1 1987-88

Liverpool	40	26	12	2	87	24	90
Manchester United	40	23	12	5	71	38	81
Nottingham Forest	40	20	13	7	67	39	73
Everton	40	19	13	8	53	27	70
Queen's Park Rangers	40	19	10	11	48	38	67
Arsenal	40	18	12	10	58	39	66
Wimbledon	40	14	15	11	58	47	57
Newcastle United	40	14	14	12	55	53	56
Luton Town	40	14	11	15	57	58	53
Coventry City	40	13	14	13	46	53	53
Sheffield Wednesday	40	15	8	17	52	66	53
Southampton	40	12	14	14	49	53	50
Tottenham Hotspur	40	12	11	17	38	48	47
Norwich City	40	12	9	19	40	52	45
Derby County	40	10	13	17	35	45	43
West Ham United	40	9	15	16	40	52	42
Charlton Athletic	40	9	15	16	38	52	42
Chelsea	40	9	15	16	50	68	42
Portsmouth	40	7	14	19	36	66	35
Watford	40	7	11	22	27	51	32
Oxford United	40	6	13	21	44	80	31

DIVISION 2 1987-88

Millwall	44	25	7	12	72	52	82
Aston Villa	44	22	12	10	68	41	78
Middlesbrough	44	22	12	10	63	36	78
Bradford City	44	22	11	11	74	54	77
Blackburn Rovers	44	21	14	9	68	52	77
Crystal Palace	44	22	9	13	86	59	75
Leeds United	44	19	12	13	61	51	69
Ipswich Town	44	19	9	16	61	52	66
Manchester City	44	19	8	17	80	60	65
Oldham Athletic	44	18	11	15	72	64	65
Stoke City	44	17	11	16	50	57	62
Swindon Town	44	16	11	17	73	60	59
Leicester City	44	16	11	17	62	61	59
Barnsley	44	15	12	17	61	62	57
Hull City	44	14	15	15	54	60	57
Plymouth Argyle	44	16	8	20	65	67	56
Bournemouth	44	13	10	21	56	68	49
Shrewsbury Town	44	11	16	17	42	54	49
Birmingham City	44	11	15	18	41	66	48
West Bromwich Albion	44	12	11	21	50	69	47
Sheffield United	44	13	7	24	45	74	46
Reading	44	10	12	22	44	70	42
Huddersfield Town	44	6	10	28	41	100	28

DIVISION 3 1987-88

Sunderland	46	27	12	7	92	48	93
Brighton & Hove Albion	46	23	15	8	69	47	84
Walsall	46	23	13	10	68	50	82
Notts County	46	23	12	11	82	49	81
Bristol City	46	21	12	13	77	62	75
Northampton Town	46	18	19	9	70	51	73
Wigan Athletic	46	20	12	14	70	61	72
Bristol Rovers	46	18	12	16	68	56	66
Fulham	46	19	9	18	69	60	66
Blackpool	46	17	14	15	71	62	65
Port Vale	46	18	11	17	58	56	65
Brentford	46	16	14	16	53	59	62
Gillingham	46	14	17	15	77	61	59
Bury	46	15	14	17	58	57	59
Chester City	46	14	16	16	51	62	58
Preston North End	46	15	13	18	48	59	58
Southend United	46	14	13	19	65	83	55
Chesterfield	46	15	10	21	41	70	55
Mansfield Town	46	14	12	20	48	59	54
Aldershot	46	15	8	23	64	74	53
Rotherham United	46	12	16	18	50	66	52
Grimsby Town	46	12	14	20	48	58	50
York City	46	8	9	29	48	91	33
Doncaster Rovers	46	8	9	29	40	84	33

DIVISION 4 1987-88

Wolverhampton Wanderers	46	27	9	10	82	43	90
Cardiff City	46	24	13	9	66	41	85
Bolton Wanderers	46	22	12	12	66	42	78
Scunthorpe United	46	20	17	9	76	51	77
Torquay United	46	21	14	11	66	41	77
Swansea City	46	20	10	16	62	56	70
Peterborough United	46	20	10	16	52	53	70
Leyton Orient	46	19	12	15	85	63	69
Colchester United	46	19	10	17	47	51	67
Burnley	46	20	7	19	57	62	67
Wrexham	46	20	6	20	69	58	66
Scarborough	46	17	14	15	56	48	65
Darlington	46	18	11	17	71	69	65
Tranmere Rovers	46	19	9	18	61	53	64
Cambridge United	46	16	13	17	50	52	61
Hartlepool United	46	15	14	17	50	57	59
Crewe Alexandra	46	13	19	14	57	53	58
Halifax Town	46	14	14	18	54	59	55
Hereford United	46	14	12	20	41	59	54
Stockport County	46	12	15	19	44	58	51
Rochdale	46	11	15	20	47	76	48
Exeter City	46	11	13	22	53	68	46
Carlisle United	46	12	8	26	57	86	44
Newport County	46	6	7	33	35	105	25

Tranmere Rovers 2 points deducted
Halifax Town 1 point deducted

1988 F.A. Cup

Semi-finals

Liverpool vs Nottingham Forest	2-1
Luton Town vs Wimbledon	1-2

Final

Wembley, 14th May 1988

Wimbledon 1   (Sanchez)

Liverpool 0

Attendance 98,203

1988 Football League Cup

Semi-finals

Oxford United vs Luton Town (1-1, 0-2)	1-3
Everton vs Arsenal (0-1, 1-3)	1-4

Final

Wembley, 24th April 1988

Luton Town 3   (B. Stein 2, Wilson)

Arsenal 2   (Hayes, Smith)

Attendance 95,732

DIVISION 1 1988-89

Arsenal	38	22	10	6	73	36	76
Liverpool	38	22	10	6	65	28	76
Nottingham Forest	38	17	13	8	64	43	64
Norwich City	38	17	11	10	48	45	62
Derby County	38	17	7	14	40	38	58
Tottenham Hotspur	38	15	12	11	60	46	57
Coventry City	38	14	13	11	47	42	55
Everton	38	14	12	12	50	45	54
Queen's Park Rangers	38	14	11	13	43	37	53
Millwall	38	14	11	13	47	52	53
Manchester United	38	13	12	13	45	35	51
Wimbledon	38	14	9	15	50	46	51
Southampton	38	10	15	13	52	66	45
Charlton Athletic	38	10	12	16	44	58	42
Sheffield Wednesday	38	10	12	16	34	51	42
Luton Town	38	10	11	17	42	52	41
Aston Villa	38	9	13	16	45	56	40
Middlesbrough	38	9	12	17	44	61	39
West Ham United	38	10	8	20	37	62	38
Newcastle United	38	7	10	21	32	63	31

DIVISION 3 1988-89

Wolverhampton Wanderers	46	26	14	6	96	49	92
Sheffield United	46	25	9	12	93	54	84
Port Vale	46	24	12	10	78	48	84
Fulham	46	22	9	15	69	67	75
Bristol Rovers	46	19	17	10	67	51	74
Preston North End	46	19	15	12	79	60	72
Brentford	46	18	14	14	66	61	68
Chester City	46	19	11	16	64	61	68
Notts County	46	18	13	15	64	54	67
Bolton Wanderers	46	16	16	14	58	54	64
Bristol City	46	18	9	19	53	55	63
Swansea City	46	15	16	15	51	53	61
Bury	46	16	13	17	55	67	61
Huddersfield Town	46	17	9	20	63	73	60
Mansfield Town	46	14	17	15	48	52	59
Cardiff City	46	14	15	17	44	56	57
Wigan Athletic	46	14	14	18	55	53	56
Reading	46	15	11	20	68	72	56
Blackpool	46	14	13	19	56	59	55
Northampton Town	46	16	6	24	66	76	54
Southend United	46	13	15	18	56	75	54
Chesterfield	46	14	7	25	51	86	49
Gillingham	46	12	4	30	47	81	40
Aldershot	46	8	13	25	48	78	37

DIVISION 2 1988-89

Chelsea	46	29	12	5	96	50	99
Manchester City	46	23	13	10	77	53	82
Crystal Palace	46	23	12	11	71	49	81
Watford	46	22	12	12	74	48	78
Blackburn Rovers	46	22	11	13	74	59	77
Swindon Town	46	20	16	10	68	53	76
Barnsley	46	20	14	12	66	58	74
Ipswich Town	46	22	7	17	71	61	73
West Bromwich Albion	46	18	18	10	65	41	72
Leeds United	46	17	16	13	59	50	67
Sunderland	46	16	15	15	60	60	63
Bournemouth	46	18	8	20	53	62	62
Stoke City	46	15	14	17	57	72	59
Bradford City	46	13	17	16	52	59	56
Leicester City	46	13	16	17	56	63	55
Oldham Athletic	46	11	21	14	75	72	54
Oxford United	46	14	12	20	62	70	54
Plymouth Argyle	46	14	12	20	55	66	54
Brighton & Hove Albion	46	14	9	23	57	66	51
Portsmouth	46	13	12	21	53	62	51
Hull City	46	11	14	21	52	68	47
Shrewsbury Town	46	8	18	20	40	67	42
Birmingham City	46	8	11	27	31	76	35
Walsall	46	5	16	25	41	80	31

DIVISION 4 1988-89

Rotherham United	46	22	16	8	76	35	82
Tranmere Rovers	46	21	17	8	62	43	80
Crewe Alexandra	46	21	15	10	67	48	78
Scunthorpe United	46	21	14	11	77	57	77
Scarborough	46	21	14	11	67	52	77
Leyton Orient	46	21	12	13	86	50	75
Wrexham	46	19	14	13	77	63	71
Cambridge United	46	18	14	14	71	62	68
Grimsby Town	46	17	15	14	65	59	66
Lincoln City	46	18	10	18	64	60	64
York City	46	17	13	16	62	63	64
Carlisle United	46	15	15	16	53	52	60
Exeter City	46	18	6	22	65	68	60
Torquay United	46	17	8	21	45	60	59
Hereford United	46	14	16	16	66	72	58
Burnley	46	14	13	19	52	61	55
Peterborough United	46	14	12	20	52	74	54
Rochdale	46	13	14	19	56	82	53
Hartlepool United	46	14	10	22	50	78	52
Stockport County	46	10	21	15	54	52	51
Halifax Town	46	13	11	22	69	75	50
Colchester United	46	12	14	20	60	78	50
Doncaster Rovers	46	13	10	23	49	78	49
Darlington	46	8	18	20	53	76	42

1989 F.A. Cup

Semi-finals

Liverpool vs Nottingham Forest
(abandoned after 6 minutes)   0-0
Everton vs Norwich City   1-0

Replay

Liverpool vs Nottingham Forest   3-1

Final

Wembley, 20 May 1989

Liverpool 3 (aet.) (Aldridge, Rush 2)
Everton 2 (McCall 2)

Attendance 82,800

1989 Football League Cup

Semi-finals

West Ham United vs Luton Town (0-3, 0-2)   0-5
Nottingham Forest vs Bristol City (1-1, 1-0)   2-1

Final

Wembley, 9th April 1989

Nottingham Forest 3 (Clough 2 (1 pen), Webb)
Luton Town 1 (Harford)

Attendance 76,130

DIVISION 1 1989-90

Liverpool	38	23	10	5	78	37	79
Aston Villa	38	21	7	10	57	38	70
Tottenham Hotspur	38	19	6	13	59	47	63
Arsenal	38	18	8	12	54	38	62
Chelsea	38	16	12	10	58	50	60
Everton	38	17	8	13	57	46	59
Southampton	38	15	10	13	71	63	55
Wimbledon	38	13	16	9	47	40	55
Nottingham Forest	38	15	9	14	55	47	54
Norwich City	38	13	14	11	44	42	53
Queen's Park Rangers	38	13	11	14	45	44	50
Coventry City	38	14	7	17	39	59	49
Manchester United	38	13	9	16	46	47	48
Manchester City	38	12	12	14	43	52	48
Crystal Palace	38	13	9	16	42	66	48
Derby County	38	13	7	18	43	40	46
Luton Town	38	10	13	15	43	57	43
Sheffield Wednesday	38	11	10	17	35	51	43
Charlton Athletic	38	7	9	22	31	57	30
Millwall	38	5	11	22	39	65	26

DIVISION 2 1989-90

Leeds United	46	24	13	9	79	52	85
Sheffield United	46	24	13	9	78	58	85
Newcastle United	46	22	14	10	80	55	80
Swindon Town	46	20	14	12	79	59	74
Blackburn Rovers	46	19	17	10	74	59	74
Sunderland	46	20	14	12	70	64	74
West Ham United	46	20	12	14	80	57	72
Oldham Athletic	46	19	14	13	70	57	71
Ipswich Town	46	19	12	15	67	66	69
Wolverhampton Wanderers	46	18	13	15	67	60	67
Port Vale	46	15	16	15	62	57	61
Portsmouth	46	15	16	15	62	65	61
Leicester City	46	15	14	17	67	79	59
Hull City	46	14	16	16	58	65	58
Watford	46	14	15	17	58	60	57
Plymouth Argyle	46	14	13	19	58	63	55
Oxford United	46	15	9	22	57	66	54
Brighton & Hove Albion	46	15	9	22	56	72	54
Barnsley	46	13	15	18	49	71	54
West Bromwich Albion	46	12	15	19	67	71	51
Middlesbrough	46	13	11	22	52	63	50
Bournemouth	46	12	12	22	57	76	48
Bradford City	46	9	14	23	44	68	41
Stoke City	46	6	19	21	35	63	37

Swindon Town were promoted through the play-offs. However, they were then immediately relegated for financial irregularities and their promotion place was taken by Sunderland.

DIVISION 3 1989-90

Bristol Rovers	46	26	15	5	71	35	93
Bristol City	46	27	10	9	76	40	91
Notts County	46	25	12	9	73	53	87
Tranmere Rovers	46	23	11	12	86	49	80
Bury	46	21	11	14	70	49	74
Bolton Wanderers	46	18	15	13	59	48	69
Birmingham City	46	18	12	16	60	59	66
Huddersfield Town	46	17	14	15	61	62	65
Rotherham United	46	17	13	16	71	62	64
Reading	46	15	19	12	57	53	64
Shrewsbury Town	46	16	15	15	59	54	63
Crewe Alexandra	46	15	17	14	56	53	62
Brentford	46	18	7	21	66	66	61
Leyton Orient	46	16	10	20	52	56	58
Mansfield Town	46	16	7	23	50	65	55
Chester City	46	13	15	18	43	55	54
Swansea City	46	14	12	20	45	63	54
Wigan Athletic	46	13	14	19	48	64	53
Preston North End	46	14	10	22	65	79	52
Fulham	46	12	15	19	55	66	51
Cardiff City	46	12	14	20	51	70	50
Northampton Town	46	11	14	21	51	68	47
Blackpool	46	10	16	20	49	73	46
Walsall	46	9	14	23	40	72	41

DIVISION 4 1989-90

Exeter City	46	28	5	13	83	48	89
Grimsby Town	46	22	13	11	70	47	79
Southend United	46	22	9	15	61	48	75
Stockport County	46	21	11	14	68	62	74
Maidstone United	46	22	7	17	77	61	73
Cambridge United	46	21	10	15	76	66	73
Chesterfield	46	19	14	13	63	50	71
Carlisle United	46	21	8	17	61	60	71
Peterborough United	46	17	17	12	59	46	68
Lincoln City	46	18	14	14	48	48	68
Scunthorpe United	46	17	15	14	69	54	66
Rochdale	46	20	6	20	52	55	66
York City	46	16	16	14	55	53	64
Gillingham	46	17	11	18	46	48	62
Torquay United	46	15	12	19	53	66	57
Burnley	46	14	14	18	45	55	56
Hereford United	46	15	10	21	56	62	55
Scarborough	46	15	10	21	60	73	55
Hartlepool United	46	15	10	21	66	88	55
Doncaster Rovers	46	14	9	23	53	60	51
Wrexham	46	13	12	21	51	67	51
Aldershot	46	12	14	20	49	69	50
Halifax Town	46	12	13	21	57	65	49
Colchester United	46	11	10	25	48	75	43

1990 F.A. Cup

Semi-finals

Crystal Palace vs Liverpool	4-3
Manchester United vs Oldham Athletic	3-3, 2-1

Final

Wembley, 12th May 1990

Manchester United 3   (Robson, Hughes 2)
Crystal Palace 3 (aet.)   (O'Reilly, Wright 2)

Attendance 80,000

Replay

Wembley, 17th May 1990

Manchester United 1   (Martin)
Crystal Palace 0

Attendance 80,000

1990 Football League Cup

Semi-finals

Nottingham Forest vs Coventry City (2-1, 0-0)	2-1
Oldham Athletic vs West Ham United (6-0, 0-3)	6-3

Final

Wembley, 29th April 1990

Nottingham Forest 1   (Jemson)
Oldham Athletic 0

Attendance 74,343

DIVISION 1 1990-91

Arsenal	38	24	13	1	74	18	83
Liverpool	38	23	7	8	77	40	76
Crystal Palace	38	20	9	9	50	41	69
Leeds United	38	19	7	12	65	47	64
Manchester City	38	17	11	10	64	53	62
Manchester United	38	16	12	10	58	45	60
Wimbledon	38	14	14	10	53	46	56
Nottingham Forest	38	14	12	12	65	50	54
Everton	38	13	12	13	50	46	51
Tottenham Hotspur	38	11	16	11	51	50	49
Chelsea	38	13	10	15	58	69	49
Queen's Park Rangers	38	12	10	16	44	53	46
Sheffield United	38	13	7	18	36	55	46
Southampton	38	12	9	17	58	69	45
Norwich City	38	13	6	19	41	64	45
Coventry City	38	11	11	16	42	49	44
Aston Villa	38	9	14	15	46	58	41
Luton Town	38	10	7	21	42	61	37
Sunderland	38	8	10	20	38	60	34
Derby County	38	5	9	24	37	75	24

Arsenal 2 points deducted
Manchester United 1 point deducted

DIVISION 2 1990-91

Oldham Athletic	46	25	13	8	83	53	88
West Ham United	46	24	15	7	60	34	87
Sheffield Wednesday	46	22	16	8	80	51	82
Notts County	46	23	11	12	76	55	80
Millwall	46	20	13	13	70	51	73
Brighton & Hove Albion	46	21	7	18	63	69	70
Middlesbrough	46	20	9	17	66	47	69
Barnsley	46	19	12	15	63	48	69
Bristol City	46	20	7	19	68	71	67
Oxford United	46	14	19	13	69	66	61
Newcastle United	46	14	17	15	49	56	59
Wolverhampton Wanderers	46	13	19	14	63	63	58
Bristol Rovers	46	15	13	18	56	59	58
Ipswich Town	46	13	18	15	60	68	57
Port Vale	46	15	12	19	56	64	57
Charlton Athletic	46	13	17	16	57	61	56
Portsmouth	46	14	11	21	58	70	53
Plymouth Argyle	46	12	17	17	54	68	53
Blackburn Rovers	46	14	10	22	51	66	52
Watford	46	12	15	19	45	59	51
Swindon Town	46	12	14	20	65	73	50
Leicester City	46	14	8	24	60	83	50
West Bromwich Albion	46	10	18	18	52	61	48
Hull City	46	10	15	21	57	85	45

DIVISION 3 1990-91

Cambridge United	46	25	11	10	75	45	86
Southend United	46	26	7	13	67	51	85
Grimsby Town	46	24	11	11	66	34	83
Bolton Wanderers	46	24	11	11	64	50	83
Tranmere Rovers	46	23	9	14	64	46	78
Brentford	46	21	13	12	59	47	76
Bury	46	20	13	13	67	56	73
Bradford City	46	20	10	16	62	54	70
Bournemouth	46	19	13	14	58	58	70
Wigan Athletic	46	20	9	17	71	54	69
Huddersfield Town	46	18	13	15	57	51	67
Birmingham City	46	16	17	13	45	49	65
Leyton Orient	46	18	10	18	55	58	64
Stoke City	46	16	12	18	55	59	60
Reading	46	17	8	21	53	66	59
Exeter City	46	16	9	21	58	52	57
Preston North End	46	15	11	20	54	67	56
Shrewsbury Town	46	14	10	22	61	68	52
Chester City	46	14	9	23	46	58	51
Swansea City	46	13	9	24	49	72	48
Fulham	46	10	16	20	41	56	46
Crewe Alexandra	46	11	11	24	62	80	44
Rotherham United	46	10	12	24	50	87	42
Mansfield Town	46	8	14	24	42	63	38

DIVISION 4 1990-91

Darlington	46	22	17	7	68	38	83
Stockport County	46	23	13	10	84	47	82
Hartlepool United	46	24	10	12	67	48	82
Peterborough United	46	21	17	8	67	45	80
Blackpool	46	23	10	13	78	47	79
Burnley	46	23	10	13	70	51	79
Torquay United	46	18	18	10	64	47	72
Scunthorpe United	46	20	11	15	71	62	71
Scarborough	46	19	12	15	59	56	69
Northampton Town	46	18	13	15	57	58	67
Doncaster Rovers	46	17	14	15	56	46	65
Rochdale	46	15	17	14	50	53	62
Cardiff City	46	15	15	16	43	54	60
Lincoln City	46	14	17	15	50	61	59
Gillingham	46	12	18	16	57	60	54
Walsall	46	12	17	17	48	51	53
Hereford United	46	13	14	19	53	58	53
Chesterfield	46	13	14	19	47	62	53
Maidstone United	46	13	12	21	66	71	51
Carlisle United	46	13	9	24	47	89	48
York City	46	11	13	22	45	57	46
Halifax Town	46	12	10	24	59	79	46
Aldershot	46	10	11	25	61	101	41
Wrexham	46	10	10	26	48	74	40

1991 F.A. Cup

Semi-finals

Arsenal vs Tottenham Hotspur	1-3
Nottingham Forest vs West Ham United	4-0

Final

Wembley, 18th May 1991

Tottenham Hotspur 2   (Stewart, Walker (og))
Nottingham Forest 1   (Pearce)

Attendance 80,000

1991 Football League Cup

Semi-finals

Manchester United vs Leeds United	(2-1, 1-0)	3-1
Chelsea vs Sheffield Wednesday	(0-2, 1-3)	1-5

Final

Wembley, 21st April 1991

Sheffield Wednesday 1   (Sheridan)
Manchester United 0

Attendance 80,000

DIVISION 1 1991-92

Leeds United	42	22	16	4	74	37	82
Manchester United	42	21	15	6	63	33	78
Sheffield Wednesday	42	21	12	9	62	49	75
Arsenal	42	19	15	8	81	46	72
Manchester City	42	20	10	12	61	48	70
Liverpool	42	16	16	10	47	40	64
Aston Villa	42	17	9	16	48	44	60
Nottingham Forest	42	16	11	15	60	58	59
Sheffield United	42	16	9	17	65	63	57
Crystal Palace	42	14	15	13	53	61	57
Queen's Park Rangers	42	12	18	12	48	47	54
Everton	42	13	14	15	52	51	53
Wimbledon	42	13	14	15	53	53	53
Chelsea	42	13	14	15	50	60	53
Tottenham Hotspur	42	15	7	20	58	63	52
Southampton	42	14	10	18	39	55	52
Oldham Athletic	42	14	9	19	63	67	51
Norwich City	42	11	12	19	47	63	45
Coventry City	42	11	11	20	35	44	44
Luton Town	42	10	12	20	38	71	42
Notts County	42	10	10	22	40	62	40
West Ham United	42	9	11	22	37	59	38

DIVISION 3 1991-92

Brentford	46	25	7	14	81	55	82
Birmingham City	46	23	12	11	69	52	81
Huddersfield Town	46	22	12	12	59	38	78
Stoke City	46	21	14	11	69	49	77
Stockport County	46	22	10	14	75	51	76
Peterborough United	46	20	14	12	65	58	74
West Bromwich Albion	46	19	14	13	64	49	71
Bournemouth	46	20	11	15	52	48	71
Fulham	46	19	13	14	57	53	70
Leyton Orient	46	18	11	17	62	52	65
Hartlepool United	46	18	11	17	57	57	65
Reading	46	16	13	17	59	62	61
Bolton Wanderers	46	14	17	15	57	56	59
Hull City	46	16	11	19	54	54	59
Wigan Athletic	46	15	14	17	58	64	59
Bradford City	46	13	19	14	62	61	58
Preston North End	46	15	12	19	61	72	57
Chester City	46	14	14	18	56	59	56
Swansea City	46	14	14	18	55	65	56
Exeter City	46	14	11	21	57	80	53
Bury	46	13	12	21	55	74	51
Shrewsbury Town	46	12	11	23	53	68	47
Torquay United	46	13	8	25	42	68	47
Darlington	46	10	7	29	56	90	37

DIVISION 2 1991-92

Ipswich Town	46	24	12	10	70	50	84
Middlesbrough	46	23	11	12	58	41	80
Derby County	46	23	9	14	69	51	78
Leicester City	46	23	8	15	62	55	77
Cambridge United	46	19	17	10	65	47	74
Blackburn Rovers	46	21	11	14	70	53	74
Charlton Athletic	46	20	11	15	54	48	71
Swindon Town	46	18	15	13	69	55	69
Portsmouth	46	19	12	15	65	51	69
Watford	46	18	11	17	51	48	65
Wolverhampton Wanderers	46	18	10	18	61	54	64
Southend United	46	17	11	18	63	63	62
Bristol Rovers	46	16	14	16	60	63	62
Tranmere Rovers	46	14	19	13	56	56	61
Millwall	46	17	10	19	64	71	61
Barnsley	46	16	11	19	46	57	59
Bristol City	46	13	15	18	55	71	54
Sunderland	46	14	11	21	61	65	53
Grimsby Town	46	14	11	21	47	62	53
Newcastle United	46	13	13	20	66	84	52
Oxford United	46	13	11	22	66	73	50
Plymouth Argyle	46	13	9	24	42	64	48
Brighton & Hove Albion	46	12	11	23	56	77	47
Port Vale	46	10	15	21	42	59	45

DIVISION 4 1991-92

Burnley	42	25	8	9	79	43	83
Rotherham United	42	22	11	9	70	37	77
Mansfield Town	42	23	8	11	75	53	77
Blackpool	42	22	10	10	71	45	76
Scunthorpe United	42	21	9	12	64	59	72
Crewe Alexandra	42	20	10	12	66	51	70
Barnet	42	21	6	15	81	61	69
Rochdale	42	18	13	11	57	53	67
Cardiff City	42	17	15	10	66	53	66
Lincoln City	42	17	11	14	50	44	62
Gillingham	42	15	12	15	63	53	57
Scarborough	42	15	12	15	64	68	57
Chesterfield	42	14	11	17	49	61	53
Wrexham	42	14	9	19	52	73	51
Walsall	42	12	13	17	48	58	49
Northampton Town	42	11	13	18	46	57	46
Hereford United	42	12	8	22	44	57	44
Maidstone United	42	8	18	16	45	56	42
York City	42	8	16	18	42	58	40
Halifax Town	42	10	8	24	34	75	38
Doncaster Rovers	42	9	8	25	40	65	35
Carlisle United	42	7	13	22	41	67	34

Aldershot were declared bankrupt and obliged to resign from the League after playing 36 matches, results of which were declared void.

1992 F.A. Cup

Semi-finals

Liverpool vs Portsmouth	1-1, 0-0
Liverpool won 3-1 on penalties	
Sunderland vs Norwich	1-0

Final

Wembley, 9th May 1992

Liverpool 2   (Thomas, I. Rush)
Sunderland 0

Attendance 79,544

1992 Football League Cup

Semi-finals

Nottingham Forest vs Tottenham Hotspur (1-1, 2-1)	3-2
Middlesbrough vs Manchester United (0-0, 1-2)	1-2

Final

Wembley, 12th April 1992

Manchester United 1   (McClair)
Nottingham Forest 0

Attendance 76,810

F.A. PREMIER LEAGUE 1992-93

Manchester United	42	24	12	6	67	31	84
Aston Villa	42	21	11	10	57	40	74
Norwich City	42	21	9	12	61	65	72
Blackburn Rovers	42	20	11	11	68	46	71
Queen's Park Rangers	42	17	12	13	63	55	63
Liverpool	42	16	11	15	62	55	59
Sheffield Wednesday	42	15	14	13	55	51	59
Tottenham Hotspur	42	16	11	15	60	66	59
Manchester City	42	15	12	15	56	51	57
Arsenal	42	15	11	16	40	38	56
Chelsea	42	14	14	14	51	54	56
Wimbledon	42	14	12	16	56	55	54
Everton	42	15	8	19	53	55	53
Sheffield United	42	14	10	18	54	53	52
Coventry City	42	13	13	16	52	57	52
Ipswich Town	42	12	16	14	50	55	52
Leeds United	42	12	15	15	57	62	51
Southampton	42	13	11	18	54	61	50
Oldham Athletic	42	13	10	19	63	74	49
Crystal Palace	42	11	16	15	48	61	49
Middlesbrough	42	11	11	20	54	75	44
Nottingham Forest	42	10	10	22	41	62	40

DIVISION 2 1992-93

Stoke City	46	27	12	7	73	34	93
Bolton Wanderers	46	27	9	10	80	41	90
Port Vale	46	26	11	9	79	44	89
West Bromwich Albion	46	25	10	11	88	54	85
Swansea City	46	20	13	13	65	47	73
Stockport County	46	19	15	12	81	57	72
Leyton Orient	46	21	9	16	69	53	72
Reading	46	18	15	13	66	51	69
Brighton & Hove Albion	46	20	9	17	63	59	69
Bradford City	46	18	14	14	69	67	68
Rotherham United	46	17	14	15	60	60	65
Fulham	46	16	17	13	57	55	65
Burnley	46	15	16	15	57	59	61
Plymouth Argyle	46	16	12	18	59	64	60
Huddersfield Town	46	17	9	20	54	61	60
Hartlepool United	46	14	12	20	42	60	54
Bournemouth	46	12	17	17	45	52	53
Blackpool	46	12	15	19	63	75	51
Exeter City	46	11	17	18	54	69	50
Hull City	46	13	11	22	46	69	50
Preston North End	46	13	8	25	65	94	47
Mansfield Town	46	11	11	24	52	80	44
Wigan Athletic	46	10	11	25	43	72	41
Chester City	46	8	5	33	49	102	29

DIVISION 1 1992-93

Newcastle United	46	29	9	8	92	38	96
West Ham United	46	26	10	10	81	41	88
Portsmouth	46	26	10	10	80	46	88
Tranmere Rovers	46	23	10	13	72	56	79
Swindon Town	46	21	13	12	74	59	76
Leicester City	46	22	10	14	71	64	76
Millwall	46	18	16	12	65	53	70
Derby County	46	19	9	18	68	57	66
Grimsby Town	46	19	7	20	58	57	64
Peterborough United	46	16	14	16	55	63	62
Wolverhampton Wanderers	46	16	13	17	57	56	61
Charlton Athletic	46	16	13	17	49	46	61
Barnsley	46	17	9	20	56	60	60
Oxford United	46	14	14	18	53	56	56
Bristol City	46	14	14	18	49	67	56
Watford	46	14	13	19	57	71	55
Notts County	46	12	16	18	55	70	52
Southend United	46	13	13	20	54	64	52
Birmingham City	46	13	12	21	50	72	51
Luton Town	46	10	21	15	48	62	51
Sunderland	46	13	11	22	50	64	50
Brentford	46	13	10	23	52	71	49
Cambridge United	46	11	16	19	48	69	49
Bristol Rovers	46	10	11	25	55	87	41

DIVISION 3 1992-93

Cardiff City	42	25	8	9	77	47	83
Wrexham	42	23	11	8	75	52	80
Barnet	42	23	10	9	66	48	79
York City	42	21	12	9	72	45	75
Walsall	42	22	7	13	76	61	73
Crewe Alexandra	42	21	7	14	75	56	70
Bury	42	18	9	15	63	55	63
Lincoln City	42	18	9	15	57	53	63
Shrewsbury Town	42	17	11	14	57	52	62
Colchester United	42	18	5	19	67	76	59
Rochdale	42	16	10	16	70	70	58
Chesterfield	42	15	11	16	59	63	56
Scarborough	42	15	9	18	66	71	54
Scunthorpe United	42	14	12	16	57	54	54
Darlington	42	12	14	16	48	53	50
Doncaster Rovers	42	11	14	17	42	57	47
Hereford United	42	10	15	17	47	60	45
Carlisle United	42	11	11	20	51	65	44
Torquay United	42	12	7	23	45	67	43
Northampton Town	42	11	8	23	48	74	41
Gillingham	42	9	13	20	48	64	40
Halifax Town	42	9	9	24	45	68	36

Maidstone United were declared bankrupt

1993 F.A. Cup

Semi-finals

Sheffield United vs Sheffield Wednesday	1-2
Arsenal vs Tottenham Hotspur	1-0

Final

Wembley, 15th May 1993

Arsenal 1 (Wright)
Sheffield Wednesday 1 (aet.) (Hirst)

Attendance 79,347

Replay

Wembley, 20th May 1993

Arsenal 2 (Wright, Linighan)
Sheffield Wednesday 1 (aet.) (Waddle)

Attendance 62,267

1993 Football League Cup

Semi-finals

Crystal Palace vs Arsenal (1-3, 0-2)	1-5
Blackburn Rovers vs Sheffield Wednesday (2-4, 1-2)	3-6

Final

Wembley, 18th April 1993

Arsenal 2 (Merson, Morrow)
Sheffield Wednesday 1 (Harkes)

Attendance 74,007

F.A. PREMIER LEAGUE 1993-94

Manchester United	42	27	11	4	80	38	92
Blackburn Rovers	42	25	9	8	63	36	84
Newcastle United	42	23	8	11	82	41	77
Arsenal	42	18	17	7	53	28	71
Leeds United	42	18	16	8	65	39	70
Wimbledon	42	18	11	13	56	53	65
Sheffield Wednesday	42	16	16	10	76	54	64
Liverpool	42	17	9	16	59	55	60
Queen's Park Rangers	42	16	12	14	62	61	60
Aston Villa	42	15	12	15	46	50	57
Coventry City	42	14	14	14	43	45	56
Norwich City	42	12	17	13	65	61	53
West Ham United	42	13	13	16	47	58	52
Chelsea	42	13	12	17	49	53	51
Tottenham Hotspur	42	11	12	19	54	59	45
Manchester City	42	9	18	15	38	49	45
Everton	42	12	8	22	42	63	44
Southampton	42	12	7	23	49	66	43
Ipswich Town	42	9	16	17	35	58	43
Sheffield United	42	8	18	16	42	60	42
Oldham Athletic	42	9	13	20	42	68	40
Swindon Town	42	5	15	22	47	100	30

DIVISION 2 1993-94

Reading	46	26	11	9	81	44	89
Port Vale	46	26	10	10	79	46	88
Plymouth Argyle	46	25	10	11	88	56	85
Stockport County	46	24	13	9	74	44	85
York City	46	21	12	13	64	40	75
Burnley	46	21	10	15	79	58	73
Bradford City	46	19	13	14	61	53	70
Bristol Rovers	46	20	10	16	60	59	70
Hull City	46	18	14	14	62	54	68
Cambridge United	46	19	9	18	79	73	66
Huddersfield Town	46	17	14	15	58	61	65
Wrexham	46	17	11	18	66	77	62
Swansea City	46	16	12	18	56	58	60
Brighton & Hove Albion	46	15	14	17	60	67	59
Rotherham United	46	15	13	18	63	60	58
Brentford	46	13	19	14	57	55	58
Bournemouth	46	14	15	17	51	59	57
Leyton Orient	46	14	14	18	57	71	56
Cardiff City	46	13	15	18	66	79	54
Blackpool	46	16	5	25	63	75	53
Fulham	46	14	10	22	50	63	52
Exeter City	46	11	12	23	52	83	45
Hartlepool United	46	9	9	28	41	87	36
Barnet	46	5	13	28	41	86	28

DIVISION 1 1993-94

Crystal Palace	46	27	9	10	73	46	90
Nottingham Forest	46	23	14	9	74	49	83
Millwall	46	19	17	10	58	49	74
Leicester City	46	19	16	11	72	59	73
Tranmere Rovers	46	21	9	16	69	53	72
Derby County	46	20	11	15	73	68	71
Notts County	46	20	8	18	65	69	68
Wolverhampton Wanderers	46	17	17	12	60	47	68
Middlesbrough	46	18	13	15	66	54	67
Stoke City	46	18	13	15	57	59	67
Charlton Athletic	46	19	8	19	61	58	65
Sunderland	46	19	8	19	54	57	65
Bristol City	46	16	16	14	47	50	64
Bolton Wanderers	46	15	14	17	63	64	59
Southend United	46	17	8	21	63	67	59
Grimsby Town	46	13	20	13	52	47	59
Portsmouth	46	15	13	18	52	58	58
Barnsley	46	16	7	23	55	67	55
Watford	46	15	9	22	66	80	54
Luton Town	46	14	11	21	56	60	53
West Bromwich Albion	46	13	12	21	60	69	51
Birmingham City	46	13	12	21	42	69	51
Oxford United	46	13	10	23	54	75	49
Peterborough United	46	8	13	25	48	76	37

DIVISION 3 1993-94

Shrewsbury Town	42	22	13	7	63	39	79
Chester City	42	21	11	10	69	46	74
Crewe Alexandra	42	21	10	11	80	61	73
Wycombe Wanderers	42	19	13	10	67	53	70
Preston North End	42	18	13	11	79	60	67
Torquay United	42	17	16	9	64	56	67
Carlisle United	42	18	10	14	57	42	64
Chesterfield	42	16	14	12	55	48	62
Rochdale	42	16	12	14	63	51	60
Walsall	42	17	9	16	48	53	60
Scunthorpe United	42	15	14	13	64	56	59
Mansfield Town	42	15	10	17	53	62	55
Bury	42	14	11	17	55	56	53
Scarborough	42	15	8	19	55	61	53
Doncaster Rovers	42	14	10	18	44	57	52
Gillingham	42	12	15	15	44	51	51
Colchester United	42	13	10	19	56	71	49
Lincoln City	42	12	11	19	52	63	47
Wigan Athletic	42	11	12	19	51	70	45
Hereford United	42	12	6	24	60	79	42
Darlington	42	10	11	21	42	64	41
Northampton Town	42	9	11	22	44	66	38

1994 F.A. Cup

Semi-finals

Chelsea vs Luton Town	2-0
Manchester United vs Oldham Athletic	1-1, 4-1

Final

Wembley, 14th May 1994

Manchester United 4 (Cantona 2 (2 pens), Hughes, McClair)

Chelsea 0

Attendance 79,634

1994 Football League Cup

Semi-finals

Manchester Utd. vs Sheffield Wednesday	(1-0, 4-1)	5-1
Tranmere Rovers vs Aston Villa	(3-1, 1-3)	4-4

Aston Villa won 5-4 on penalties

Final

Wembley, 27th March 1994

Aston Villa 3 (Atkinson, Saunders 2 (1 pen))

Manchester United 1 (Hughes)

Attendance 77,231

F.A. PREMIER LEAGUE 1994-95

Blackburn Rovers	42	27	8	7	80	39	89
Manchester United	42	26	10	6	77	28	88
Nottingham Forest	42	22	11	9	72	43	77
Liverpool	42	21	11	10	65	37	74
Leeds United	42	20	13	9	59	38	73
Newcastle United	42	20	12	10	67	47	72
Tottenham Hotspur	42	16	14	12	66	58	62
Queen's Park Rangers	42	17	9	16	61	59	60
Wimbledon	42	15	11	16	48	65	56
Southampton	42	12	18	12	61	63	54
Chelsea	42	13	15	14	50	55	54
Arsenal	42	13	12	17	52	49	51
Sheffield Wednesday	42	13	12	17	49	57	51
West Ham United	42	13	11	18	44	48	50
Everton	42	11	17	14	44	51	50
Coventry City	42	12	14	16	44	62	50
Manchester City	42	12	13	17	53	64	49
Aston Villa	42	11	15	16	51	56	48
Crystal Palace	42	11	12	19	34	49	45
Norwich City	42	10	13	19	37	54	43
Leicester City	42	6	11	25	45	80	29
Ipswich Town	42	7	6	29	36	93	27

DIVISION 2 1994-95

Birmingham City	46	25	14	7	84	37	89
Brentford	46	25	10	11	81	39	85
Crewe Alexandra	46	25	8	13	80	68	84
Bristol Rovers	46	22	16	8	70	40	82
Huddersfield Town	46	22	15	9	79	49	81
Wycombe Wanderers	46	21	15	10	60	46	78
Oxford United	46	21	12	13	66	52	75
Hull City	46	21	11	14	70	57	74
York City	46	21	9	16	67	51	72
Swansea City	46	19	14	13	57	45	71
Stockport County	46	19	8	19	63	60	65
Blackpool	46	18	10	18	64	70	64
Wrexham	46	16	15	15	65	64	63
Bradford City	46	16	12	18	57	64	60
Peterborough United	46	14	18	14	54	69	60
Brighton & Hove Albion	46	14	17	15	54	53	59
Rotherham United	46	14	14	18	57	61	56
Shrewsbury Town	46	13	14	19	54	62	53
Bournemouth	46	13	11	22	49	69	50
Cambridge United	46	11	15	20	52	69	48
Plymouth Argyle	46	12	10	24	45	83	46
Cardiff City	46	9	11	26	46	74	38
Chester City	46	6	11	29	37	84	29
Leyton Orient	46	6	8	32	30	75	26

DIVISION 1 1994-95

Middlesbrough	46	23	13	10	67	40	82
Reading	46	23	10	13	58	44	79
Bolton Wanderers	46	21	14	11	67	45	76
Wolverhampton Wanderers	46	21	13	12	77	61	76
Tranmere Rovers	46	22	10	14	67	58	76
Barnsley	46	20	12	14	63	52	72
Watford	46	19	13	14	52	46	70
Sheffield United	46	17	17	12	74	55	68
Derby County	46	18	12	16	66	51	66
Grimsby Town	46	17	14	15	62	56	65
Stoke City	46	16	15	15	50	53	63
Millwall	46	16	14	16	60	60	62
Southend United	46	18	8	20	54	73	62
Oldham Athletic	46	16	13	17	60	60	61
Charlton Athletic	46	16	11	19	58	66	59
Luton Town	46	15	13	18	61	64	58
Port Vale	46	15	13	18	58	64	58
Portsmouth	46	15	13	18	53	63	58
West Bromwich Albion	46	16	10	20	51	57	58
Sunderland	46	12	18	16	41	45	54
Swindon Town	46	12	12	22	54	73	48
Burnley	46	11	13	22	49	74	46
Bristol City	46	11	12	23	42	63	45
Notts County	46	9	13	24	45	66	40

DIVISION 3 1994-95

Carlisle United	42	27	10	5	67	31	91
Walsall	42	24	11	7	75	40	83
Chesterfield	42	23	12	7	62	37	81
Bury	42	23	11	8	73	36	80
Preston North End	42	19	10	13	58	41	67
Mansfield Town	42	18	11	13	84	59	65
Scunthorpe United	42	18	8	16	68	63	62
Fulham	42	16	14	12	60	54	62
Doncaster Rovers	42	17	10	15	58	43	61
Colchester United	42	16	10	16	56	64	58
Barnet	42	15	11	16	56	63	56
Lincoln City	42	15	11	16	54	55	56
Torquay United	42	14	13	15	54	57	55
Wigan Athletic	42	14	10	18	53	60	52
Rochdale	42	12	14	16	44	67	50
Hereford United	42	12	13	17	45	62	49
Northampton Town	42	10	14	18	45	67	44
Hartlepool United	42	11	10	21	43	69	43
Gillingham	42	10	11	21	46	64	41
Darlington	42	11	8	23	43	57	41
Scarborough	42	8	10	24	49	70	34
Exeter City	42	8	10	24	36	70	34

1995 F.A. Cup

Semi-finals

Crystal Palace vs Manchester United	2-2, 0-2
Everton vs Tottenham Hotspur	4-1

Final

Wembley, 20th May 1995

Everton 1 (Rideout)

Manchester United 0

Attendance 79,592

1995 Football League Cup

Semi-finals

Liverpool vs Crystal Palace (1-0, 1-0)	2-0
Swindon Town vs Bolton Wanderers (2-1, 1-3)	3-4

Final

Wembley, 2nd April 1995

Liverpool 2 (McManaman 2)

Bolton Wanderers 1 (Thompson)

Attendance 75,595

F.A. PREMIER LEAGUE 1995-96

Manchester United	38	25	7	6	73	35	82
Newcastle United	38	24	6	8	66	37	78
Liverpool	38	20	11	7	70	34	71
Aston Villa	38	18	9	11	52	35	63
Arsenal	38	17	12	9	49	32	63
Everton	38	17	10	11	64	44	61
Blackburn Rovers	38	18	7	13	61	47	61
Tottenham Hotspur	38	16	13	9	50	38	61
Nottingham Forest	38	15	13	10	50	54	58
West Ham United	38	14	9	15	43	52	51
Chelsea	38	12	14	12	46	44	50
Middlesbrough	38	11	10	17	35	50	43
Leeds United	38	12	7	19	40	57	43
Wimbledon	38	10	11	17	55	70	41
Sheffield Wednesday	38	10	10	18	48	61	40
Coventry City	38	8	14	16	42	60	38
Southampton	38	9	11	18	34	52	38
Manchester City	38	9	11	18	33	58	38
Queen's Park Rangers	38	9	6	23	38	57	33
Bolton Wanderers	38	8	5	25	39	71	29

DIVISION 2 1995-96

Swindon Town	46	25	17	4	71	34	92
Oxford United	46	24	11	11	76	39	83
Blackpool	46	23	13	10	67	40	82
Notts County	46	21	15	10	63	39	78
Crewe Alexandra	46	22	7	17	77	60	73
Bradford City	46	22	7	17	71	69	73
Chesterfield	46	20	12	14	56	51	72
Wrexham	46	18	16	12	76	55	70
Stockport County	46	19	13	14	61	47	70
Bristol Rovers	46	20	10	16	57	60	70
Walsall	46	19	12	15	60	45	69
Wycombe Wanderers	46	15	15	16	63	59	60
Bristol City	46	15	15	16	55	60	60
Bournemouth	46	16	10	20	51	70	58
Brentford	46	15	13	18	43	49	58
Rotherham United	46	14	14	18	54	62	56
Burnley	46	14	13	19	56	68	55
Shrewsbury Town	46	13	14	19	58	70	53
Peterborough United	46	13	13	20	59	66	52
York City	46	13	13	20	58	73	52
Carlisle United	46	12	13	21	57	72	49
Swansea City	46	11	14	21	43	79	47
Brighton & Hove Albion	46	10	10	26	46	69	40
Hull City	46	5	16	25	36	78	31

DIVISION 1 1995-96

Sunderland	46	22	17	7	59	33	83
Derby County	46	21	16	9	71	51	79
Crystal Palace	46	20	15	11	67	48	75
Stoke City	46	20	13	13	60	49	73
Leicester City	46	19	14	13	66	60	71
Charlton Athletic	46	17	20	9	57	45	71
Ipswich Town	46	19	12	15	79	69	69
Huddersfield Town	46	17	12	17	61	58	63
Sheffield United	46	16	14	16	57	54	62
Barnsley	46	14	18	14	60	66	60
West Bromwich Albion	46	16	12	18	60	68	60
Port Vale	46	15	15	16	59	66	60
Tranmere Rovers	46	14	17	15	64	60	59
Southend United	46	15	14	17	52	61	59
Birmingham City	46	15	13	18	61	64	58
Norwich City	46	14	15	17	59	55	57
Grimsby Town	46	14	14	18	55	69	56
Oldham Athletic	46	14	14	18	54	50	56
Reading	46	13	17	16	54	63	56
Wolverhampton Wanderers	46	13	16	17	56	62	55
Portsmouth	46	13	13	20	61	69	52
Millwall	46	13	13	20	43	63	52
Watford	46	10	18	18	62	70	48
Luton Town	46	11	12	23	40	64	45

DIVISION 3 1995-96

Preston North End	46	23	17	6	78	38	86
Gillingham	46	22	17	7	49	20	83
Bury	46	22	13	11	66	48	79
Plymouth Argyle	46	22	12	12	68	49	78
Darlington	46	20	18	8	60	42	78
Hereford United	46	20	14	12	65	47	74
Colchester United	46	18	18	10	61	51	72
Chester City	46	18	16	12	72	53	70
Barnet	46	18	16	12	65	45	70
Wigan Athletic	46	20	10	16	62	56	70
Northampton Town	46	18	13	15	51	44	67
Scunthorpe United	46	15	15	16	67	61	60
Doncaster Rovers	46	16	11	19	49	60	59
Exeter City	46	13	18	15	46	53	57
Rochdale	46	14	13	19	57	61	55
Cambridge United	46	14	12	20	61	71	54
Fulham	46	12	17	17	57	63	53
Lincoln City	46	13	14	19	57	73	53
Mansfield Town	46	11	20	15	54	64	53
Hartlepool United	46	12	13	21	47	67	49
Leyton Orient	46	12	11	23	44	63	47
Cardiff City	46	11	12	23	41	64	45
Scarborough	46	8	16	22	39	69	40
Torquay United	46	5	14	27	30	84	29

1996 F.A. Cup

Semi-finals

Chelsea vs Manchester United	1-2
Aston Villa vs Liverpool	0-3

Final

Wembley, 11th May 1996

Manchester United 1   (Cantona)
Liverpool 0

Attendance 79,007

1996 Football League Cup

Semi-finals

Birmingham City vs Leeds United (1-2, 0-3)	1-5
Arsenal vs Aston Villa (2-2, 0-0)	2-2

Aston Villa won on the away goals rule

Final

Wembley, 24th March 1996

Aston Villa 3   (Milosevic, Taylor, Yorke)
Leeds United 0

Attendance 77,056

F.A. PREMIER LEAGUE 1996-97

Manchester United	38	21	12	5	76	44	75
Newcastle United	38	19	11	8	73	40	68
Arsenal	38	19	11	8	62	32	68
Liverpool	38	19	11	8	62	37	68
Aston Villa	38	17	10	11	47	34	61
Chelsea	38	16	11	11	58	55	59
Sheffield Wednesday	38	14	15	9	50	51	57
Wimbledon	38	15	11	12	49	46	56
Leicester City	38	12	11	15	46	54	47
Tottenham Hotspur	38	13	7	18	44	51	46
Leeds United	38	11	13	14	28	38	46
Derby County	38	11	13	14	45	58	46
Blackburn Rovers	38	9	15	14	42	43	42
West Ham United	38	10	12	16	39	48	42
Everton	38	10	12	16	44	57	42
Southampton	38	10	11	17	50	56	41
Coventry City	38	9	14	15	38	54	41
Sunderland	38	10	10	18	35	53	40
Middlesbrough	38	10	12	16	51	60	39
Nottingham Forest	38	6	16	16	31	59	34

Middlesbrough had 3 points deducted

DIVISION 2 1996-97

Bury	46	24	12	10	62	38	84
Stockport County	46	23	13	10	59	41	82
Luton Town	46	21	15	10	71	45	78
Brentford	46	20	14	12	56	43	74
Bristol City	46	21	10	15	69	51	73
Crewe Alexandra	46	22	7	17	56	47	73
Blackpool	46	18	15	13	60	47	69
Wrexham	46	17	18	11	54	50	69
Burnley	46	19	11	16	71	55	68
Chesterfield	46	18	14	14	42	39	68
Gillingham	46	19	10	17	60	59	67
Walsall	46	19	10	17	54	53	67
Watford	46	16	19	11	45	38	67
Millwall	46	16	13	17	50	55	61
Preston North End	46	18	7	21	49	55	61
Bournemouth	46	15	15	16	43	45	60
Bristol Rovers	46	15	11	20	47	50	56
Wycombe Wanderers	46	15	10	21	51	56	55
Plymouth Argyle	46	12	18	16	47	58	54
York City	46	13	13	20	47	68	52
Peterborough United	46	11	14	21	55	73	47
Shrewsbury Town	46	11	13	22	49	74	46
Rotherham United	46	7	14	25	39	70	35
Notts County	46	7	14	25	33	59	35

DIVISION 1 1996-97

Bolton Wanderers	46	28	14	4	100	53	98
Barnsley	46	22	14	10	76	55	80
Wolverhampton Wanderers	46	22	10	14	68	51	76
Ipswich Town	46	20	14	12	68	50	74
Sheffield United	46	20	13	13	75	52	73
Crystal Palace	46	19	14	13	78	48	71
Portsmouth	46	20	8	18	59	53	68
Port Vale	46	17	16	13	58	55	67
Queen's Park Rangers	46	18	12	16	64	60	66
Birmingham City	46	17	15	14	52	48	66
Tranmere Rovers	46	17	14	15	63	56	65
Stoke City	46	18	10	18	51	57	64
Norwich City	46	17	12	17	63	68	63
Manchester City	46	17	10	19	59	60	61
Charlton Athletic	46	16	11	19	52	66	59
West Bromwich Albion	46	14	15	17	68	72	57
Oxford United	46	16	9	21	64	68	57
Reading	46	15	12	19	58	67	57
Swindon Town	46	15	9	22	52	71	54
Huddersfield Town	46	13	15	18	48	61	54
Bradford City	46	12	12	22	47	72	48
Grimsby Town	46	11	13	22	60	81	46
Oldham Athletic	46	10	13	23	51	66	43
Southend United	46	8	15	23	42	86	39

DIVISION 3 1996-97

Wigan Athletic	46	26	9	11	84	51	87
Fulham	46	25	12	9	72	38	87
Carlisle United	46	24	12	10	67	44	84
Northampton Town	46	20	12	14	67	44	72
Swansea City	46	21	8	17	62	58	71
Chester City	46	18	16	12	55	43	70
Cardiff City	46	20	9	17	56	54	69
Colchester United	46	17	17	12	62	51	68
Lincoln City	46	18	12	16	70	69	66
Cambridge United	46	18	11	17	53	59	65
Mansfield Town	46	16	16	14	47	45	64
Scarborough	46	16	15	15	65	68	63
Scunthorpe United	46	18	9	19	59	62	63
Rochdale	46	14	16	16	58	58	58
Barnet	46	14	16	16	46	51	58
Leyton Orient	46	15	12	19	50	58	57
Hull City	46	13	18	15	44	50	57
Darlington	46	14	10	22	64	78	52
Doncaster Rovers	46	14	10	22	52	66	52
Hartlepool United	46	14	9	23	53	66	51
Torquay United	46	13	11	22	46	62	50
Exeter City	46	12	12	22	48	73	48
Brighton & Hove Albion	46	13	10	23	53	70	47
Hereford United	46	11	14	21	50	65	47

Brighton & Hove Albion had two points deducted

1997 F.A. Cup

Semi-finals

Middlesbrough vs Chesterfield	3-3, 3-0
Wimbledon vs Chelsea	0-3

Final

Wembley, 17th May 1997

Chelsea 2   (Di Matteo, Newton)

Middlesbrough 0

Attendance 79,160

1997 Football League Cup

Semi-finals

Leicester City vs Wimbledon (0-0, 1-1)	1-1

Leicester City won on the away goals rule

Stockport County vs Middlesbrough (0-2, 1-0)	1-2

Final

Wembley, 6th April 1997

Leicester City 1   (Heskey)

Middlesbrough 1 (aet.)   (Ravanelli)

Attendance 76,757

Replay

Hillsborough, 16th April 1997

Leicester City 1   (Claridge)

Middlesbrough 0

Attendance 39,428

F.A. PREMIER LEAGUE 1997-98

Arsenal	38	23	9	6	68	33	78
Manchester United	38	23	8	7	73	26	77
Liverpool	38	18	11	9	68	42	65
Chelsea	38	20	3	15	71	43	63
Leeds United	38	17	8	13	57	46	59
Blackburn Rovers	38	16	10	12	57	52	58
Aston Villa	38	17	6	15	49	48	57
West Ham United	38	16	8	14	56	57	56
Derby County	38	16	7	15	52	49	55
Leicester City	38	13	14	11	51	41	53
Coventry City	38	12	16	10	46	44	52
Southampton	38	14	6	18	50	55	48
Newcastle United	38	11	11	16	35	44	44
Tottenham Hotspur	38	11	11	16	44	56	44
Wimbledon	38	10	14	14	34	46	44
Sheffield Wednesday	38	12	8	18	52	67	44
Everton	38	9	13	16	41	56	40
Bolton Wanderers	38	9	13	16	41	61	40
Barnsley	38	10	5	23	37	82	35
Crystal Palace	38	8	9	21	37	71	33

DIVISION 2 1997-98

Watford	46	24	16	6	67	41	88
Bristol City	46	25	10	11	69	39	85
Grimsby Town	46	19	15	12	55	37	72
Northampton Town	46	18	17	11	52	37	71
Bristol Rovers	46	20	10	16	70	64	70
Fulham	46	20	10	16	60	43	70
Wrexham	46	18	16	12	55	51	70
Gillingham	46	19	13	14	52	47	70
Bournemouth	46	18	12	16	57	52	66
Chesterfield	46	16	17	13	46	44	65
Wigan Athletic	46	17	11	18	64	66	62
Blackpool	46	17	11	18	59	67	62
Oldham Athletic	46	15	16	15	62	54	61
Wycombe Wanderers	46	14	18	14	51	53	60
Preston North End	46	15	14	17	56	56	59
York City	46	14	17	15	52	58	59
Luton Town	46	14	15	17	60	64	57
Millwall	46	14	13	19	43	54	55
Walsall	46	14	12	20	43	52	54
Burnley	46	13	13	20	55	65	52
Brentford	46	11	17	18	50	71	50
Plymouth Argyle	46	12	13	21	55	70	49
Carlisle United	46	12	8	26	57	73	44
Southend United	46	11	10	25	47	79	43

DIVISION 1 1997-98

Nottingham Forest	46	28	10	8	82	42	94
Middlesbrough	46	27	10	9	77	41	91
Sunderland	46	26	12	8	86	50	90
Charlton Athletic	46	26	10	10	80	49	88
Ipswich Town	46	23	14	9	77	43	83
Sheffield United	46	19	17	10	69	54	74
Birmingham City	46	19	17	10	60	35	74
Stockport County	46	19	8	19	71	69	65
Wolverhampton Wanderers	46	18	11	17	57	53	65
West Bromwich Albion	46	16	13	17	50	56	61
Crewe Alexandra	46	18	5	23	58	65	59
Oxford United	46	16	10	20	60	64	58
Bradford City	46	14	15	17	46	59	57
Tranmere Rovers	46	14	14	18	54	57	56
Norwich City	46	14	13	19	52	69	55
Huddersfield Town	46	14	11	21	50	72	53
Bury	46	11	19	16	42	58	52
Swindon Town	46	14	10	22	42	73	52
Port Vale	46	13	10	23	56	66	49
Portsmouth	46	13	10	23	51	63	49
Queen's Park Rangers	46	10	19	17	51	63	49
Manchester City	46	12	12	22	56	57	48
Stoke City	46	11	13	22	44	74	46
Reading	46	11	9	26	39	78	42

DIVISION 3 1997-98

Notts County	46	29	12	5	82	43	99
Macclesfield Town	46	23	13	10	63	44	82
Lincoln City	46	20	15	11	60	51	75
Colchester United	46	21	11	14	72	60	74
Torquay United	46	21	11	14	68	59	74
Scarborough	46	19	15	12	67	58	72
Barnet	46	19	13	14	61	51	70
Scunthorpe United	46	19	12	15	56	52	69
Rotherham United	46	16	19	11	67	61	67
Peterborough United	46	18	13	15	63	51	67
Leyton Orient	46	19	12	15	62	47	66
Mansfield Town	46	16	16	17	13	64	55	64
Shrewsbury Town	46	16	13	17	61	62	61
Chester City	46	17	10	19	60	61	61
Exeter City	46	15	15	16	68	63	60
Cambridge United	46	14	18	14	63	57	60
Hartlepool United	46	12	23	11	61	53	59
Rochdale	46	17	7	22	56	55	58
Darlington	46	14	12	20	56	72	54
Swansea City	46	13	11	22	49	62	50
Cardiff City	46	9	23	14	48	52	50
Hull City	46	11	8	27	56	83	41
Brighton & Hove Albion	46	6	17	23	38	66	35
Doncaster Rovers	46	4	8	34	30	113	20

Leyton Orient had 3 points deducted

1998 F.A. Cup

Semi-finals

Sheffield United vs Newcastle United	0-1
Wolverhampton Wanderers vs Arsenal	0-1

Final

Wembley, 16th May 1998

Arsenal 2 (Overmars, Anelka)
Newcastle United 0

Attendance 79,183

1998 Football League Cup

Semi-finals

Liverpool vs Middlesbrough (2-1, 0-2)	2-3
Arsenal vs Chelsea (2-1, 1-3)	3-4

Final

Wembley, 29th March 1998

Chelsea 2 (Sinclair, Di Matteo)
Middlesbrough 0 (aet.)

Attendance 77,698

F.A. PREMIER LEAGUE 1998-99

Manchester United	38	22	13	3	80	37	79
Arsenal	38	22	12	4	59	17	78
Chelsea	38	20	15	3	57	30	75
Leeds United	38	18	13	7	62	34	67
West Ham United	38	16	9	13	46	53	57
Aston Villa	38	15	10	13	51	46	55
Liverpool	38	15	9	14	68	49	54
Derby County	38	13	13	12	40	45	52
Middlesbrough	38	12	15	11	48	54	51
Leicester City	38	12	13	13	40	46	49
Tottenham Hotspur	38	11	14	13	47	50	47
Sheffield Wednesday	38	13	7	18	41	42	46
Newcastle United	38	11	13	14	48	54	46
Everton	38	11	10	17	42	47	43
Coventry City	38	11	9	18	39	51	42
Wimbledon	38	10	12	16	40	63	42
Southampton	38	11	8	19	37	64	41
Charlton Athletic	38	8	12	18	41	56	36
Blackburn Rovers	38	7	14	17	38	52	35
Nottingham Forest	38	7	9	22	35	69	30

DIVISION 2 1998-99

Fulham	46	31	8	7	79	32	101
Walsall	46	26	9	11	63	47	87
Manchester City	46	22	16	8	69	33	82
Gillingham	46	22	14	10	75	44	80
Preston North End	46	22	13	11	78	50	79
Wigan Athletic	46	22	10	14	75	48	76
Bournemouth	46	21	13	12	63	41	76
Stoke City	46	21	6	19	59	63	69
Chesterfield	46	17	13	16	46	44	64
Millwall	46	17	11	18	52	59	62
Reading	46	16	13	17	54	63	61
Luton Town	46	16	10	20	51	60	58
Bristol Rovers	46	13	17	16	65	56	56
Blackpool	46	14	14	18	44	54	56
Burnley	46	13	16	17	54	73	55
Notts County	46	14	12	20	52	61	54
Wrexham	46	13	14	19	43	62	53
Colchester United	46	12	16	18	52	70	52
Wycombe Wanderers	46	13	12	21	52	58	51
Oldham Athletic	46	14	9	23	48	66	51
York City	46	13	11	22	56	80	50
Northampton Town	46	10	18	18	43	57	48
Lincoln City	46	13	7	26	42	74	46
Macclesfield Town	46	11	10	25	43	63	43

DIVISION 1 1998-99

Sunderland	46	31	12	3	91	28	105
Bradford City	46	26	9	11	82	47	87
Ipswich Town	46	26	8	12	69	32	86
Birmingham City	46	23	12	11	66	37	81
Watford	46	21	14	11	65	56	77
Bolton Wanderers	46	20	16	10	78	59	76
Wolverhampton Wanderers	46	19	16	11	64	43	73
Sheffield United	46	18	13	15	71	66	67
Norwich City	46	15	17	14	62	61	62
Huddersfield Town	46	15	16	15	62	71	61
Grimsby Town	46	17	10	19	40	52	61
West Bromwich Albion	46	16	11	19	69	76	59
Barnsley	46	14	17	15	59	56	59
Crystal Palace	46	14	16	16	58	71	58
Tranmere Rovers	46	12	20	14	63	61	56
Stockport County	46	12	17	17	49	60	53
Swindon Town	46	13	11	22	59	81	50
Crewe Alexandra	46	12	12	22	54	78	48
Portsmouth	46	11	14	21	57	73	47
Queen's Park Rangers	46	12	12	13	52	61	47
Port Vale	46	13	8	25	45	75	47
Bury	46	10	17	19	35	60	47
Oxford United	46	10	14	22	48	71	44
Bristol City	46	9	15	22	57	80	42

DIVISION 3 1998-99

Brentford	46	26	7	13	79	56	85
Cambridge United	46	23	12	11	78	48	81
Cardiff City	46	22	14	10	60	39	80
Scunthorpe United	46	22	8	16	69	58	74
Rotherham United	46	20	13	13	79	61	73
Leyton Orient	46	19	15	12	68	59	72
Swansea City	46	19	14	13	56	48	71
Mansfield Town	46	19	10	17	60	58	67
Peterborough United	46	18	12	16	72	56	66
Halifax Town	46	17	15	14	58	56	66
Darlington	46	18	11	17	69	58	65
Exeter City	46	17	12	17	47	50	63
Plymouth Argyle	46	17	10	19	58	54	61
Chester City	46	13	18	15	57	66	57
Shrewsbury Town	46	14	14	18	52	63	56
Barnet	46	14	13	19	54	71	55
Brighton & Hove Albion	46	16	7	23	49	66	55
Southend United	46	14	12	20	52	58	54
Rochdale	46	13	15	18	42	55	54
Torquay United	46	12	17	17	47	58	53
Hull City	46	14	11	21	44	62	53
Hartlepool United	46	13	12	21	52	65	51
Carlisle United	46	11	16	19	43	53	49
Scarborough	46	14	6	26	50	77	48

1999 F.A. Cup

Semi-finals

Newcastle United vs Tottenham Hotspur	2-0 (aet)
Manchester United vs Arsenal	0-0, 2-1 (aet)

Final

Wembley, 22nd May 1999

Manchester United 2　(Sheringham, Scholes)
Newcastle United 0

Attendance 79,101

1999 Football League Cup

Semi-finals

Sunderland vs Leicester City　(1-2, 1-1)	2-3
Tottenham Hotspur vs Wimbledon　(0-0, 1-0)	1-0

Final

Wembley, 21st March 1999

Tottenham Hotspur 1　(Nielsen)
Leicester City 0

Attendance 77,892

F.A. PREMIER LEAGUE 1999-2000

Manchester United	38	28	7	3	97	45	91
Arsenal	38	22	7	9	73	43	73
Leeds United	38	21	6	11	58	43	69
Liverpool	38	19	10	9	51	30	67
Chelsea	38	18	11	9	53	34	65
Aston Villa	38	15	13	10	46	35	58
Sunderland	38	16	10	12	57	56	58
Leicester City	38	16	7	15	55	55	55
West Ham United	38	15	10	13	52	53	55
Tottenham Hotspur	38	15	8	15	57	49	53
Newcastle United	38	14	10	14	63	54	52
Middlesbrough	38	14	10	14	46	52	52
Everton	38	12	14	12	59	49	50
Coventry City	38	12	8	18	47	54	44
Southampton	38	12	8	18	45	62	44
Derby County	38	9	11	18	44	57	38
Bradford City	38	9	9	20	38	68	36
Wimbledon	38	7	12	19	46	74	33
Sheffield Wednesday	38	8	7	23	38	70	31
Watford	38	6	6	26	35	77	24

DIVISION 2 1999-2000

Preston North End	46	28	11	7	74	37	95
Burnley	46	25	13	8	69	47	88
Gillingham	46	25	10	11	79	48	85
Wigan Athletic	46	22	17	7	72	38	83
Millwall	46	23	13	10	76	50	82
Stoke City	46	23	13	10	68	42	82
Bristol Rovers	46	23	11	12	69	45	80
Notts County	46	18	11	17	61	55	65
Bristol City	46	15	19	12	59	57	64
Reading	46	16	14	16	57	63	62
Wrexham	46	17	11	18	52	61	62
Wycombe Wanderers	46	16	13	17	56	53	61
Luton Town	46	17	10	19	61	65	61
Oldham Athletic	46	16	12	18	50	55	60
Bury	46	13	18	15	61	64	57
Bournemouth	46	16	9	21	59	62	57
Brentford	46	13	13	20	47	61	52
Colchester United	46	14	10	22	59	82	52
Cambridge United	46	12	12	22	64	65	48
Oxford United	46	12	9	25	43	73	45
Cardiff City	46	9	17	20	45	67	44
Blackpool	46	8	17	21	49	77	41
Scunthorpe United	46	9	12	25	40	74	39
Chesterfield	46	7	15	24	34	63	36

DIVISION 1 1999-2000

Charlton Athletic	46	27	10	9	79	45	91
Manchester City	46	26	11	9	78	40	89
Ipswich Town	46	25	12	9	71	42	87
Barnsley	46	24	10	12	88	67	82
Birmingham City	46	22	11	13	65	44	77
Bolton Wanderers	46	21	13	12	69	50	76
Wolverhampton Wanderers	46	21	11	14	64	48	74
Huddersfield Town	46	21	11	14	62	49	74
Fulham	46	17	16	13	49	41	67
Queen's Park Rangers	46	16	18	12	62	53	66
Blackburn Rovers	46	15	17	14	55	51	62
Norwich City	46	14	15	17	45	50	57
Tranmere Rovers	46	15	12	19	57	68	57
Nottingham Forest	46	14	14	18	53	55	56
Crystal Palace	46	13	15	18	57	67	54
Sheffield United	46	13	15	18	59	71	54
Stockport County	46	13	15	18	55	67	54
Portsmouth	46	13	12	21	55	66	51
Crewe Alexandra	46	14	9	23	46	67	51
Grimsby Town	46	13	12	21	41	67	51
West Bromwich Albion	46	10	19	17	43	60	49
Walsall	46	11	13	22	52	77	46
Port Vale	46	7	15	24	48	69	36
Swindon Town	46	8	12	26	38	77	36

DIVISION 3 1999-2000

Swansea City	46	24	13	9	51	30	85
Rotherham United	46	24	12	10	72	36	84
Northampton Town	46	25	7	14	63	45	82
Darlington	46	21	16	9	66	36	79
Peterborough United	46	22	12	12	63	54	78
Barnet	46	21	12	13	59	53	75
Hartlepool United	46	21	9	16	60	49	72
Cheltenham Town	46	20	10	16	50	42	70
Torquay United	46	19	12	15	62	52	69
Rochdale	46	18	14	14	57	54	68
Brighton & Hove Albion	46	17	16	13	64	46	67
Plymouth Argyle	46	16	18	12	55	51	66
Macclesfield Town	46	18	11	17	66	61	65
Hull City	46	15	14	17	43	43	59
Lincoln City	46	15	14	17	67	69	59
Southend United	46	15	11	20	53	61	56
Mansfield Town	46	16	8	22	50	65	56
Halifax Town	46	15	9	22	44	58	54
Leyton Orient	46	13	13	20	47	52	52
York City	46	12	16	18	39	53	52
Exeter City	46	11	11	24	46	72	44
Shrewsbury Town	46	9	13	24	40	67	40
Carlisle United	46	9	12	25	42	75	39
Chester City	46	10	9	27	44	79	39

2000 F.A. Cup

Semi-finals

Bolton Wanderers vs Aston Villa	0-0
Aston Villa won 4-1 on penalties	
Newcastle United vs Chelsea	1-2

Final

Wembley, 20th May 2000

Chelsea 1 (Di Matteo)

Aston Villa 0

Attendance 78,217

2000 Football League Cup

Semi-finals

Bolton Wanderers vs Tranmere Rovers (0-1, 0-3)	0-4
Aston Villa vs Leicester City (0-0, 0-1)	0-1

Final

Wembley, 27th February 2000

Leicester City 2 (Elliott 2)

Tranmere Rovers 1 (Kelly)

Attendance 74,313

F.A. PREMIER LEAGUE 2000-2001

	P	W	D	L	F	A	Pts
Manchester United	38	24	8	6	79	31	80
Arsenal	38	20	10	8	63	38	70
Liverpool	38	20	9	9	71	39	69
Leeds United	38	20	8	10	64	43	68
Ipswich Town	38	20	6	12	57	42	66
Chelsea	38	17	10	11	68	45	61
Sunderland	38	15	12	11	46	41	57
Aston Villa	38	13	15	10	46	43	54
Charlton Athletic	38	14	10	14	50	57	52
Southampton	38	14	10	14	40	48	52
Newcastle United	38	14	9	15	44	50	51
Tottenham Hotspur	38	13	10	15	47	54	49
Leicester City	38	14	6	18	39	51	48
Middlesbrough	38	9	15	14	44	44	42
West Ham United	38	10	12	16	45	50	42
Everton	38	11	9	18	45	59	42
Derby County	38	10	12	16	37	59	42
Manchester City	38	8	10	20	41	65	34
Coventry City	38	8	10	20	36	63	34
Bradford City	38	5	11	22	30	70	26

DIVISION 2 2000-2001

	P	W	D	L	F	A	Pts
Millwall	46	28	9	9	89	38	93
Rotherham United	46	27	10	9	79	55	91
Reading	46	25	11	10	86	52	86
Walsall	46	23	12	11	79	50	81
Stoke City	46	21	14	11	74	49	77
Wigan Athletic	46	19	18	9	53	42	75
Bournemouth	46	20	13	13	79	55	73
Notts County	46	19	12	15	62	66	69
Bristol City	46	18	14	14	70	56	68
Wrexham	46	17	12	17	65	71	63
Port Vale	46	16	14	16	55	49	62
Peterborough United	46	15	14	17	61	66	59
Wycombe Wanderers	46	15	14	17	46	53	59
Brentford	46	14	17	15	56	70	59
Oldham Athletic	46	15	13	18	53	65	58
Bury	46	16	10	20	45	59	58
Colchester United	46	15	12	19	55	59	57
Northampton Town	46	15	12	19	46	59	57
Cambridge United	46	14	11	21	61	77	53
Swindon Town	46	13	13	20	47	65	52
Bristol Rovers	46	12	15	19	53	57	51
Luton Town	46	9	13	24	52	80	40
Swansea City	46	8	13	25	47	73	37
Oxford United	46	7	6	33	53	100	27

DIVISION 1 2000-2001

	P	W	D	L	F	A	Pts
Fulham	46	30	11	5	90	32	101
Blackburn Rovers	46	26	13	7	76	39	91
Bolton Wanderers	46	24	15	7	76	45	87
Preston North End	46	23	9	14	64	52	78
Birmingham City	46	23	9	14	59	48	78
West Bromwich Albion	46	21	11	14	60	52	74
Burnley	46	21	9	16	50	54	72
Wimbledon	46	17	18	11	71	50	69
Watford	46	20	9	17	76	67	69
Sheffield United	46	19	11	16	52	49	68
Nottingham Forest	46	20	8	18	55	53	68
Wolverhampton Wanderers	46	14	13	19	45	48	55
Gillingham	46	13	16	17	61	66	55
Crewe Alexandra	46	15	10	21	47	62	55
Norwich City	46	14	12	20	46	58	54
Barnsley	46	15	9	22	49	62	54
Sheffield Wednesday	46	15	8	23	52	71	53
Grimsby Town	46	14	10	22	43	62	52
Stockport County	46	11	18	17	58	65	51
Portsmouth	46	10	19	17	47	59	49
Crystal Palace	46	12	13	21	57	70	49
Huddersfield Town	46	11	15	20	48	57	48
Queen's Park Rangers	46	7	19	20	45	75	40
Tranmere Rovers	46	9	11	26	46	77	38

DIVISION 3 2000-2001

	P	W	D	L	F	A	Pts
Brighton & Hove Albion	46	28	8	10	73	35	92
Cardiff City	46	23	13	10	95	58	82
Chesterfield	46	25	14	7	79	42	80
Hartlepool United	46	21	14	11	71	54	77
Leyton Orient	46	20	15	11	59	51	75
Hull City	46	19	17	10	47	39	74
Blackpool	46	22	6	18	74	58	72
Rochdale	46	18	17	11	59	48	71
Cheltenham Town	46	18	14	14	59	52	68
Scunthorpe United	46	18	11	17	62	52	65
Southend United	46	15	18	13	55	53	63
Mansfield Town	46	18	13	17	64	72	58
Plymouth Argyle	46	15	13	18	54	61	58
Macclesfield Town	46	14	14	18	51	62	56
Shrewsbury Town	46	15	10	21	49	65	55
Kidderminster Harriers	46	13	14	19	47	61	53
York City	46	13	13	20	42	63	52
Lincoln City	46	12	15	19	58	66	51
Exeter City	46	12	14	20	40	58	50
Darlington	46	12	13	21	44	56	49
Torquay United	46	12	13	21	52	77	49
Carlisle United	46	11	15	20	42	65	48
Halifax Town	46	12	11	23	54	68	47
Barnet	46	12	9	25	67	81	45

Chesterfield had 9 points deducted

2001 F.A. Cup

Semi-finals

Arsenal vs Tottenham Hotspur	2-1
Wycombe Wanderers vs Liverpool	1-2

Final

The Millennium Stadium, Cardiff, 12th May 2001

Arsenal 1 (Ljungberg)
Liverpool 2 (Owen 2)

Attendance 72,500

2001 Football League Cup

Semi-finals

Ipswich Town vs Birmingham City	(1-0, 1-4)	2-4
Crystal Palace vs Liverpool	(2-1, 0-5)	2-6

Final

The Millennium Stadium, Cardiff, 25th February 2001

Birmingham City 1 (Purse (pen))
Liverpool 1 (aet.) (Fowler)

Attendance 73,500

Liverpool won on 5-4 on penalties.

F.A. PREMIER LEAGUE 2001-2002

Arsenal	38	26	9	3	79	36	87
Liverpool	38	24	8	6	67	30	80
Manchester United	38	24	5	9	87	45	77
Newcastle United	38	21	8	9	74	52	71
Leeds United	38	18	12	8	53	37	66
Chelsea	38	17	13	8	66	38	64
West Ham United	38	15	8	15	48	57	53
Aston Villa	38	12	14	12	46	47	50
Tottenham Hotspur	38	14	8	16	49	53	50
Blackburn Rovers	38	12	10	16	55	51	46
Southampton	38	12	9	17	46	54	45
Middlesbrough	38	12	9	17	35	47	45
Fulham	38	10	14	14	36	44	44
Charlton Athletic	38	10	14	14	38	49	44
Everton	38	11	10	17	45	57	43
Bolton Wanderers	38	9	13	16	44	62	40
Sunderland	38	10	10	18	29	51	40
Ipswich Town	38	9	9	20	41	64	36
Derby County	38	8	6	24	33	63	30
Leicester City	38	5	13	20	30	64	28

DIVISION 2 2001-2002

Brighton & Hove Albion	46	25	15	6	66	42	90
Reading	46	23	15	8	70	43	84
Brentford	46	24	11	11	77	43	83
Cardiff City	46	23	14	9	75	50	83
Stoke City	46	23	11	12	67	40	80
Huddersfield Town	46	21	15	10	65	47	78
Bristol City	46	21	10	15	68	53	73
Queen's Park Rangers	46	19	14	13	60	49	71
Oldham Athletic	46	18	16	12	77	65	70
Wigan Athletic	46	16	16	14	66	51	64
Wycombe Wanderers	46	17	13	16	58	64	64
Tranmere Rovers	46	16	15	15	63	60	63
Swindon Town	46	15	14	17	46	56	59
Port Vale	46	16	10	20	51	62	58
Colchester United	46	15	12	19	65	76	57
Blackpool	46	14	14	18	66	69	56
Peterborough United	46	15	10	21	64	59	55
Chesterfield	46	13	13	20	53	65	52
Notts County	46	13	11	22	59	71	50
Northampton Town	46	14	7	25	54	79	49
Bournemouth	46	10	14	22	56	71	44
Bury	46	11	11	24	43	75	44
Wrexham	46	11	10	25	56	89	43
Cambridge United	46	7	13	26	47	93	34

DIVISION 1 2001-2002

Manchester City	46	31	6	9	108	52	99
West Bromwich Albion	46	27	8	11	61	29	89
Wolverhampton Wanderers	46	25	11	10	76	43	86
Millwall	46	22	11	13	69	48	77
Birmingham City	46	21	13	12	70	49	76
Norwich City	46	22	9	15	60	51	75
Burnley	46	21	12	13	70	62	75
Preston North End	46	20	12	14	71	59	72
Wimbledon	46	18	13	15	63	57	67
Crystal Palace	46	20	6	20	70	62	66
Coventry City	46	20	6	20	59	53	66
Gillingham	46	18	10	18	64	67	64
Sheffield United	46	15	15	16	53	54	60
Watford	46	16	11	19	62	56	59
Bradford City	46	15	10	21	69	76	55
Nottingham Forest	46	12	18	16	50	51	54
Portsmouth	46	13	14	19	60	72	53
Walsall	46	13	12	21	51	71	51
Grimsby Town	46	12	14	20	50	72	50
Sheffield Wednesday	46	12	14	20	49	71	50
Rotherham United	46	10	19	17	52	66	49
Crewe Alexandra	46	12	13	21	47	76	49
Barnsley	46	11	15	20	59	86	48
Stockport County	46	6	8	32	42	102	26

DIVISION 3 2001-2002

Plymouth Argyle	46	31	9	6	71	28	102
Luton Town	46	30	7	9	96	48	97
Mansfield Town	46	24	7	15	72	60	79
Cheltenham Town	46	21	15	10	66	49	78
Rochdale	46	21	15	10	65	52	78
Rushden & Diamonds	46	20	13	13	69	53	73
Hartlepool United	46	20	11	15	74	48	71
Scunthorpe United	46	19	14	13	74	56	71
Shrewsbury Town	46	20	10	16	64	53	70
Kidderminster Harriers	46	19	9	18	56	47	66
Hull City	46	16	13	17	57	51	61
Southend United	46	15	13	18	51	54	58
Macclesfield Town	46	15	13	18	41	52	58
York City	46	16	9	21	54	67	57
Darlington	46	15	11	20	60	71	56
Exeter City	46	14	13	19	48	73	55
Carlisle United	46	12	16	18	49	56	52
Leyton Orient	46	13	13	20	55	71	52
Torquay United	46	12	15	19	46	63	51
Swansea City	46	13	12	21	53	77	51
Oxford United	46	11	14	21	53	62	47
Lincoln City	46	10	16	20	44	62	46
Bristol Rovers	46	11	12	23	40	60	45
Halifax Town	46	8	12	26	39	84	36

2002 F.A. Cup

Semi-finals

Fulham vs Chelsea	0-1
Newcastle United vs Arsenal	1-1, 0-3

Final

The Millennium Stadium, Cardiff, 4th May 2002

Arsenal 2   (Parlour, Ljungberg)

Chelsea 0

Attendance 73,963

2002 Football League Cup

Semi-finals

Chelsea vs Tottenham Hotspur (2-1, 1-5)	3-6
Sheffield Wednesday vs Blackburn Rovers (1-2, 2-4)	3-6

Final

The Millennium Stadium, Cardiff, 24th February 2002

Blackburn Rovers 2   (Jansen, Cole)

Tottenham Hotspur 1   (Ziege)

Attendance 72,500

F.A. PREMIER LEAGUE 2002-2003

Manchester United	38	25	8	5	74	34	83
Arsenal	38	23	9	6	85	42	78
Newcastle United	38	21	6	11	63	48	69
Chelsea	38	19	10	9	68	38	67
Liverpool	38	18	10	10	61	41	64
Blackburn Rovers	38	16	12	10	52	43	60
Everton	38	17	8	13	48	49	59
Southampton	38	13	13	12	43	46	52
Manchester City	38	15	6	17	47	54	51
Tottenham Hotspur	38	14	8	16	51	62	50
Middlesbrough	38	13	10	15	48	44	49
Charlton Athletic	38	14	7	17	45	56	49
Birmingham City	38	13	9	16	41	49	48
Fulham	38	13	9	16	41	50	48
Leeds United	38	14	5	19	58	57	47
Aston Villa	38	12	9	17	42	47	45
Bolton Wanderers	38	10	14	14	41	51	44
West Ham United	38	10	12	16	42	59	42
West Bromwich Albion	38	6	8	24	29	65	26
Sunderland	38	4	7	27	21	65	19

DIVISION 2 2002-2003

Wigan Athletic	46	29	13	4	68	25	100
Crewe Alexandra	46	25	11	10	76	40	86
Bristol City	46	24	11	11	79	48	83
Queenís Park Rangers	46	24	11	11	69	45	83
Oldham Athletic	46	22	16	8	68	38	82
Cardiff City	46	23	12	11	68	43	81
Tranmere Rovers	46	23	11	12	66	57	80
Plymouth Argyle	46	17	14	15	63	52	65
Luton Town	46	17	14	15	67	62	65
Swindon Town	46	16	12	18	59	63	60
Peterborough United	46	14	16	16	51	54	58
Colchester United	46	14	16	16	52	56	58
Blackpool	46	15	13	18	56	64	58
Stockport County	46	15	10	21	65	70	55
Notts County	46	13	16	17	62	70	55
Brentford	46	14	12	20	47	56	54
Port Vale	46	14	11	21	54	70	53
Wycombe Wanderers	46	13	13	20	59	66	52
Barnsley	46	13	13	20	51	64	52
Chesterfield	46	14	8	24	43	73	50
Cheltenham Town	46	10	18	18	53	68	48
Huddersfield Town	46	11	12	23	39	61	45
Mansfield Town	46	12	8	26	66	97	44
Northampton Town	46	10	9	27	40	79	39

DIVISION 1 2002-2003

Portsmouth	46	29	11	6	97	45	98
Leicester City	46	26	14	6	73	40	92
Sheffield United	46	23	11	12	72	52	80
Reading	46	25	4	17	61	46	79
Wolverhampton Wanderers	46	20	16	10	81	44	76
Nottingham Forest	46	20	14	12	82	50	74
Ipswich Town	46	19	13	14	80	64	70
Norwich City	46	19	12	15	60	49	69
Millwall	46	19	9	18	59	69	66
Wimbledon	46	18	11	17	76	73	65
Gillingham	46	16	14	16	56	65	62
Preston North End	46	16	13	17	68	70	61
Watford	46	17	9	20	54	70	60
Crystal Palace	46	14	17	15	59	52	59
Rotherham United	46	15	14	17	62	62	59
Burnley	46	15	10	21	65	89	55
Walsall	46	15	9	22	57	69	54
Derby County	46	15	7	24	55	74	52
Bradford City	46	14	10	22	51	73	52
Coventry City	46	12	14	20	46	62	50
Stoke City	46	12	14	20	45	69	50
Sheffield Wednesday	46	10	16	20	56	73	46
Brighton & Hove Albion	46	11	12	23	49	67	45
Grimsby Town	46	9	12	25	48	85	39

DIVISION 3 2002-2003

Rushden & Diamonds	46	24	15	7	73	47	87
Hartlepool United	46	24	13	9	71	51	85
Wrexham	46	23	15	8	84	50	84
Bournemouth	46	20	14	12	60	48	74
Scunthorpe United	46	19	15	12	68	49	72
Lincoln City	46	18	16	12	46	37	70
Bury	46	18	16	12	57	56	70
Oxford United	46	19	12	15	57	47	69
Torquay United	46	16	18	12	71	71	66
York City	46	17	15	14	52	53	66
Kidderminster Harriers	46	16	15	15	62	63	63
Cambridge United	46	16	13	17	67	70	61
Hull City	46	14	17	15	58	53	59
Darlington	46	12	18	16	58	59	54
* Boston United	46	15	13	18	55	56	54
Macclesfield Town	46	14	12	20	57	63	54
Southend United	46	17	3	26	47	59	54
Leyton Orient	46	14	11	21	51	61	53
Rochdale	46	12	16	18	63	70	52
Bristol Rovers	46	12	15	19	50	57	51
Swansea City	46	12	13	21	48	65	49
Carlisle United	46	13	10	23	52	78	49
Exeter City	46	11	15	20	50	64	48
Shrewsbury Town	46	9	14	23	62	92	41

* Boston United had 4 points deducted

2003 F.A. Cup

Semi-finals

Arsenal vs Sheffield United	1-0
Southampton vs Watford	2-1

Final

The Millennium Stadium, Cardiff, 17th May 2003

Arsenal 1 (Pires)

Southampton 0

Attendance 73,726

2003 Football League Cup

Semi-finals

Manchester United vs Blackburn Rovers (1-1, 3-1)	4-2
Sheffield United vs Liverpool (2-1, 0-2 aet)	2-3

Final

The Millennium Stadium, Cardiff, 2nd March 2003

Liverpool 2 (Gerrard, Owen)

Manchester United 0

Attendance 74,500

F.A. PREMIER LEAGUE 2003-2004

Arsenal	38	26	12	0	73	26	90
Chelsea	38	24	7	7	67	30	79
Manchester United	38	23	6	9	64	35	75
Liverpool	38	16	12	10	55	37	60
Newcastle United	38	13	17	8	52	40	56
Aston Villa	38	15	11	12	48	44	56
Charlton Athletic	38	14	11	13	51	51	53
Bolton Wanderers	38	14	11	13	48	56	53
Fulham	38	14	10	14	52	46	52
Birmingham City	38	12	14	12	43	48	50
Middlesbrough	38	13	9	16	44	52	48
Southampton	38	12	11	15	44	45	47
Portsmouth	38	12	9	17	47	54	45
Tottenham Hotspur	38	13	6	19	47	57	45
Blackburn Rovers	38	12	8	18	51	59	44
Manchester City	38	9	14	15	55	54	41
Everton	38	9	12	17	45	57	39
Leicester City	38	6	15	17	48	65	33
Leeds United	38	8	9	21	40	79	33
Wolverhampton Wanderers	38	7	12	19	38	77	33

DIVISION 2 2003-2004

Plymouth Argyle	46	26	12	8	85	41	90
Queen's Park Rangers	46	22	17	7	80	45	83
Bristol City	46	23	13	10	58	37	82
Brighton & Hove Albion	46	22	11	13	64	43	77
Swindon Town	46	20	13	13	76	58	73
Hartlepool United	46	20	13	13	76	61	73
Port Vale	46	21	10	15	73	63	73
Tranmere Rovers	46	17	16	13	59	56	67
AFC Bournemouth	46	17	15	14	56	51	66
Luton Town	46	17	15	14	69	66	66
Colchester United	46	17	13	16	52	56	64
Barnsley	46	15	17	14	54	58	62
Wrexham	46	17	9	20	50	60	60
Blackpool	46	16	11	19	58	65	59
Oldham Athletic	46	12	21	13	66	60	57
Sheffield Wednesday	46	13	14	19	48	64	53
Brentford	46	14	11	21	52	69	53
Peterborough United	46	12	16	18	58	58	52
Stockport County	46	11	19	16	62	70	52
Chesterfield	46	12	15	19	49	71	51
Grimsby Town	46	13	11	22	55	81	50
Rushden & Diamonds	46	13	9	24	60	74	48
Notts County	46	10	12	24	50	78	42
Wycombe Wanderers	46	6	19	21	50	75	37

DIVISION 1 2003-2004

Norwich City	46	28	10	8	79	39	94
West Bromwich Albion	46	25	11	10	64	42	86
Sunderland	46	22	13	11	62	45	79
West Ham United	46	19	17	10	67	45	74
Ipswich Town	46	21	10	15	84	72	73
Crystal Palace	46	21	10	15	72	61	73
Wigan Athletic	46	18	17	11	60	45	71
Sheffield United	46	20	11	15	65	56	71
Reading	46	20	10	16	55	57	70
Millwall	46	18	15	13	55	48	69
Stoke City	46	18	12	16	58	55	66
Coventry City	46	17	14	15	67	54	65
Cardiff City	46	17	14	15	68	58	65
Nottingham Forest	46	15	15	16	61	58	60
Preston North End	46	15	14	17	69	71	59
Watford	46	15	12	19	54	68	57
Rotherham United	46	13	15	18	53	61	54
Crewe Alexandra	46	14	11	21	57	66	53
Burnley	46	13	14	19	60	77	53
Derby County	46	13	13	20	53	67	52
Gillingham	46	14	9	23	48	67	51
Walsall	46	13	12	21	45	65	51
Bradford City	46	10	6	30	38	69	36
Wimbledon	46	8	5	33	41	89	29

DIVISION 3 2003-2004

Doncaster Rovers	46	27	11	8	79	37	92
Hull City	46	25	13	8	82	44	88
Torquay United	46	23	12	11	68	44	81
Huddersfield Town	46	23	12	11	68	52	81
Mansfield Town	46	22	9	15	76	62	75
Northampton Town	46	22	9	15	58	51	75
Lincoln City	46	19	17	10	68	47	74
Yeovil Town	46	23	5	18	70	57	74
Oxford United	46	18	17	11	55	44	71
Swansea City	46	15	14	17	58	61	59
Boston United	46	16	11	19	50	54	59
Bury	46	15	11	20	54	64	56
Cambridge United	46	14	14	18	55	67	56
Cheltenham Town	46	14	14	18	57	71	56
Bristol Rovers	46	14	13	19	50	61	55
Kidderminster Harriers	46	14	13	19	45	59	55
Southend United	46	14	12	20	51	63	54
Darlington	46	14	11	21	53	61	53
Leyton Orient	46	13	14	19	48	65	53
Macclesfield Town	46	13	13	20	53	69	52
Rochdale	46	12	14	20	49	58	50
Scunthorpe United	46	11	16	19	69	72	49
Carlisle United	46	12	9	25	46	69	45
York City	46	10	14	22	35	66	44

2004 F.A. Cup

Semi-finals

Arsenal vs Manchester United	0-1
Sunderland vs Millwall	0-1

Final

The Millennium Stadium, Cardiff, 22nd May 2004

Manchester United 3 (Ronaldo, Van Nistelrooy 2)
Millwall 0

Attendance 71,350

2004 Football League Cup

Semi-finals

Arsenal vs Middlesbrough (0-1, 1-2)	1-3
Bolton vs Aston Villa (5-2, 0-2)	5-4

Final

The Millennium Stadium, Cardiff, 29th February 2004

Bolton Wanderers 1 (Davies)
Middlesbrough 2 (Job, Zenden)

Attendance 72,634

F.A. PREMIER LEAGUE 2004-2005

Chelsea	38	29	8	1	72	15	95
Arsenal	38	25	8	5	87	36	83
Manchester United	38	22	11	5	58	26	77
Everton	38	18	7	13	45	46	61
Liverpool	38	17	7	14	52	41	58
Bolton Wanderers	38	16	10	12	49	44	58
Middlesbrough	38	14	13	11	53	46	55
Manchester City	38	13	13	12	47	39	52
Tottenham Hotspur	38	14	10	14	47	41	52
Aston Villa	38	12	11	15	45	52	47
Charlton Athletic	38	12	10	16	42	58	46
Birmingham City	38	11	12	15	40	46	45
Fulham	38	12	8	18	52	60	44
Newcastle United	38	10	14	14	47	57	44
Blackburn Rovers	38	9	15	14	32	43	42
Portsmouth	38	10	9	19	43	59	39
West Bromwich Albion	38	6	16	16	36	61	34
Crystal Palace	38	7	12	19	41	62	33
Norwich City	38	7	12	19	42	77	33
Southampton	38	6	14	18	45	66	32

LEAGUE ONE 2004-2005

Luton Town	46	29	11	6	87	48	98
Hull City	46	26	8	12	80	53	86
Tranmere Rovers	46	22	13	11	73	55	79
Brentford	46	22	9	15	57	60	75
Sheffield Wednesday	46	19	15	12	77	59	72
Hartlepool United	46	21	8	17	76	66	71
Bristol City	46	18	16	12	74	57	70
AFC Bournemouth	46	20	10	16	77	64	70
Huddersfield Town	46	20	10	16	74	65	70
Doncaster Rovers	46	16	18	12	65	60	66
Bradford City	46	17	14	15	64	62	65
Swindon Town	46	17	12	17	66	68	63
Barnsley	46	14	19	13	69	64	61
Walsall	46	16	12	18	65	69	60
Colchester United	46	14	17	15	60	50	59
Blackpool	46	15	12	19	54	59	57
Chesterfield	46	14	15	17	55	62	57
Port Vale	46	17	5	24	49	59	56
Oldham Athletic	46	14	10	22	60	73	52
Milton Keynes Dons	46	12	15	19	54	68	51
Torquay United	46	12	15	19	55	79	51
Wrexham	46	13	14	19	62	80	43
Peterborough United	46	9	12	25	49	73	39
Stockport County	46	6	8	32	49	98	26

Wrexham had 10 points deducted

THE CHAMPIONSHIP 2004-2005

Sunderland	46	29	7	10	76	41	94
Wigan Athletic	46	25	12	9	79	35	87
Ipswich Town	46	24	13	9	85	56	85
Derby County	46	22	10	14	71	60	76
Preston North End	46	21	12	13	67	58	75
West Ham United	46	21	10	15	66	56	73
Reading	46	19	13	14	51	44	70
Sheffield United	46	18	13	15	57	56	67
Wolverhampton Wndrs	46	15	21	10	72	59	66
Millwall	46	18	12	16	51	45	66
Queens Park Rangers	46	17	11	18	54	58	62
Stoke City	46	17	10	19	36	38	61
Burnley	46	15	15	16	38	39	60
Leeds United	46	14	18	14	49	52	60
Leicester City	46	12	21	13	49	46	57
Cardiff City	46	13	15	18	48	51	54
Plymouth Argyle	46	14	11	21	52	64	53
Watford	46	12	16	18	52	59	52
Coventry City	46	13	13	20	61	73	52
Brighton & Hove Albion	46	13	12	21	40	65	51
Crewe Alexandra	46	12	14	20	66	86	50
Gillingham	46	12	14	20	45	66	50
Nottingham Forest	46	9	17	20	42	66	44
Rotherham United	46	5	14	27	35	69	29

LEAGUE TWO 2004-2005

Yeovil Town	46	25	8	13	90	65	83
Scunthorpe United	46	22	14	10	69	42	80
Swansea City	46	24	8	14	62	43	80
Southend United	46	22	12	12	65	46	78
Macclesfield Town	46	22	9	15	60	49	75
Lincoln City	46	20	12	14	64	47	72
Northampton Town	46	20	12	14	62	51	72
Darlington	46	20	12	14	57	49	72
Rochdale	46	16	18	12	54	48	66
Wycombe Wanderers	46	17	14	15	58	52	65
Leyton Orient	46	16	15	15	65	67	63
Bristol Rovers	46	13	21	12	60	57	60
Mansfield Town	46	15	15	16	56	56	60
Cheltenham Town	46	16	12	18	51	54	60
Oxford United	46	16	11	19	50	63	59
Boston United	46	14	16	16	62	58	58
Bury	46	14	16	16	54	54	58
Grimsby Town	46	13	17	16	47	51	56
Notts County	46	13	13	20	46	62	52
Chester City	46	12	16	18	43	69	52
Shrewsbury Town	46	11	16	19	48	53	49
Rushden & Diamonds	46	10	14	22	42	63	44
Kidderminster Harriers	46	10	9	27	38	81	39
Cambridge United	46	8	16	22	39	62	30

Cambridge United had 10 points deducted

2005 F.A. Cup

Semi-finals

Arsenal vs Blackburn Rovers	3-0
Manchester United vs Newcastle United	4-1

Final

The Millennium Stadium, Cardiff, 21st May 2005

Arsenal 0
Manchester United 0   (aet.)

Attendance 71,876

Arsenal won 5-4 on penalties

2005 Football League Cup

Semi-finals

Chelsea vs Manchester United (0-0, 2-1)		2-1
Liverpool vs Watford (1-0, 1-0)		2-0

Final

The Millennium Stadium, Cardiff, 27th February 2005

Chelsea 3   (Gerrard (og), Drogba, Kezman)
Liverpool 2   (aet.)   (Riise, Nunez)

Attendance 78,000

THE SCOTTISH LEAGUE – AN OUTLINE HISTORY

1890-91 SEASON   The League was formed with the 10 Original Founding Clubs in one Division.

1891-92 SEASON   The League was enlarged to 12 Clubs in a single Division.

1892-93 SEASON   The League was reduced to 10 Clubs in a single Division.

1893-94 SEASON   The League was enlarged to 20 Clubs, comprised of First Division of 10 Clubs and a new Second Division also of 10 Clubs.

1900-01 SEASON   The League was enlarged to 21 Clubs by increasing First Division to 11 Clubs.

1901-02 SEASON   The League was enlarged to 22 Clubs – a First Division of 10 Clubs and a Second Division of 12 Clubs.

1902-03 SEASON   The League was enlarged to 24 Clubs – a First Division of 12 Clubs and a Second Division of 12 Clubs.

1903-04 SEASONS   The League was enlarged to 26 Clubs – a First Division of 14 Clubs and a Second Division of 12 Clubs.

1905-06 SEASON   The League was enlarged to 28 Clubs – a First Division of 16 Clubs and a Second Division of 12 Clubs.

1906-07 SEASON   The League was enlarged to 30 Clubs – a First Division of 18 Clubs and a Second Division of 12 Clubs.

1912-13 SEASON   The League was enlarged to 32 Clubs – a First Division of 18 Clubs and a Second Division of 14 Clubs.

1913-14 SEASON   The League was altered to a First Division of 20 Clubs and a Second Division of 12 Clubs.

1914-15 SEASON   The League was enlarged to 34 Clubs in two Divisions – Division 'A' of 20 Clubs and Division 'B' of 14 Clubs.

1915-16 SEASON   The League was reduced to 20 Clubs by eliminating the entire Division 'B'.

1917-18 SEASON   The League was further reduced to 18 Clubs.

1919-20 SEASON   The League was enlarged to 22 Clubs in a single Division

1921-22 SEASON   The League was enlarged to 42 Clubs – a First Division of 22 Clubs and a Second Division of 20 Clubs.

1922-23 SEASON   The League was reduced to 40 Clubs in two Divisions of 20 Clubs each.

1928-29 SEASON   The League was reduced to 39 Clubs by excluding one Second Division Club.

1929-30 SEASON   The League was enlarged back to 40 Clubs in two Divisions of 20 Clubs each.

1932-33 SEASON   The League was reduced to 38 Clubs by reducing Second Division to 18 Clubs.

1939-46 SEASONS   The League was suspended for the duration of the Second World War.

1946-47 SEASON   The League was reformed with 30 Clubs comprising Division 'A' of 16 Clubs and Division 'B' of 14 Clubs.

1947-48 SEASON   The League was enlarged to 32 Clubs by adding two Clubs to Division 'B'.

1955-56 SEASON   The League was enlarged to 37 Clubs – Division 'A' of 18 Clubs and Division 'B' of 19 Clubs.

1956-57 SEASON   Division 'A' and Division 'B' were redesignated as First and Second Divisions.

1966-67 SEASON   The League was enlarged to 38 Clubs by admission of an additional Second Division Club.

1967-68 SEASON   The League reduced to 37 Clubs by the resignation of a Second Division club

1974-75 SEASON   The League was enlarged to 38 Clubs by admission of an additional Second Division Club.

1976-77 SEASON   The League was restructured into a Premier Division of 10 Clubs, a First Division of 14 Clubs and a Second Division of 14 Clubs.

1986-87 SEASON   Premier Division was increased to 12 Clubs & the First Division reduced to 12.

1988-89 SEASON   The Premier Division reverted to 10 Clubs and the First Division to 14 Clubs.

1991-92 SEASON   Premier Division was increased to 12 Clubs & the First Division reduced to 12.

1994-95 SEASON   The League was increased to 40 clubs and restructured to comprise Premier, First, Second and Third Divisions each containing 10 Clubs.

1998-99 SEASON   A 10 Club Scottish Premier League, backed by the Scottish F.A., was formed. The Scottish Football League now consists of 3 Divisions of 10 Clubs each.

1874 Scottish F.A. Cup

Semi-finals

Queen's Park vs Renton   2-0
Clydesdale vs Blythwood   4-0

Final

First Hampden Park, 21st March 1874

Queen's Park 2 (McKinnon, Leckie)
Clydesdale 0

Attendance 3,000

1875 Scottish F.A. Cup

Semi-finals

Queen's Park vs Clydesdale   0-0, 2-2, 0-0
Renton vs Dumbarton   0-0, 1-0

Final

First Hampden Park, 10th April 1875

Queen's Park 3 (Weir, Highet, McKinnon)
Renton 0

Attendance 7,000

1876 Scottish F.A. Cup

Semi-finals

Queen's Park vs Vale of Leven   3-1
3rd Lanark Rifle Volunteers vs Dumbarton   3-0

Final

Hamilton Crescent, 11th March 1876

Queen's Park 1 (Highet)
3rd Lanark Rifle Volunteers 1 (Drinnan)

Attendance 10,000

Replay

Hamilton Crescent, 18th March 1876

Queen's Park 2 (Highet 2)
3rd Lanark Rifle Volunteers 0

Attendance 8,000

1877 Scottish F.A. Cup

Semi-finals

Vale of Leven vs Ayr Thistle   9-0
Rangers received a bye

Final

First Hampden Park, 17th March 1877

Vale of Leven 1 (Paton)
Rangers 1 (McDougall (og))

Attendance 12,000

Replay

First Hampden Park, 7th April 1877

Vale of Leven 0
Rangers 0

Attendance 14,000

2nd Replay

First Hampden Park, 13th April 1877

Vale of Leven 3 (Baird, Paton, Watt (og))
Rangers 2 (M. McNiel, W. McNiel)

Attendance 15,000

1878 Scottish F.A. Cup

Semi-final

3rd Lanark Rifle Volunteers vs Renton   1-1, 1-0
Vale of Leven received a bye

Final

First Hampden Park, 30th March 1878

Vale of Leven 1 (Hunter (og))
3rd Lanark Rifle Volunteers 0

Attendance 6,000

1879 Scottish F.A. Cup

Semi-finals

Vale of Leven vs Helensburgh   3-0
Rangers received a bye

Final

First Hampden Park, 19th April 1879

Vale of Leven 1 (McFarlane)
Rangers 1 (Struthers)

Attendance 6,000

Vale of Leven were awarded the trophy after Rangers refused
to play in the replay on 26th April 1879. Rangers declined to
appear after the Scottish F.A. had turned down a protest that
they had scored a legitimate second goal in the first game.

1880 Scottish F.A. Cup

Semi-finals

Queen's Park vs Dumbarton   1-0
Thornliebank vs Pollockshields Athletic   2-1

Final

First Cathkin Park, 21st February 1880

Queen's Park 3 (Highet 2, Ker)
Thornliebank 0

Attendance 7,000

1881 Scottish F.A. Cup

Semi-finals

Dumbarton vs Vale of Leven   2-0
Queen's Park received a bye

Final

Kinning Park, 26th March 1881

Queen's Park 2 (Kay 2)
Dumbarton 1 (Brown)

Attendance 20,000

A replay was ordered after Dumbarton's protest about
spectators on the pitch was upheld.

Replay

Kinning Park, 9th April 1881

Queen's Park 3 (Smith 3)
Dumbarton 1 (Meikleham)

Attendance 10,000

1882 Scottish F.A. Cup

Semi-finals

Queen's Park vs Kilmarnock Athletic   3-2
Dumbarton vs Cartvale   11-2

Final

First Cathkin Park, 18th March 1882

Queen's Park 2 (Harrower 2)
Dumbarton 2 (Brown, Meikleham)

Attendance 12,000

Replay

First Cathkin Park, 1st April 1882

Queen's Park 4 (Richmond, Ker, Harrower, Fraser)
Dumbarton 1 (Miller)

Attendance 14,000

1883 Scottish F.A. Cup

Semi-finals

Dumbarton vs Pollockshields Athletic	5-0
Vale of Leven vs Kilmarnock Athletic	1-1, 2-0

Final

First Hampden Park, 31st March 1883

Dumbarton 2   (Paton, McArthur)

Vale of Leven 2   (Johnstone, McCrae)

Attendance 11,000

Replay

First Hampden Park, 7th April 1883

Dumbarton 2   (R. Brown (I), R. Brown (II))

Vale of Leven 1   (Friel)

Attendance 15,000

1884 Scottish F.A. Cup

Semi-finals

Hibernian vs Queen's Park	1-5
Vale of Leven vs Rangers	3-0

Final

Queen's Park were awarded the Cup. Vale of Leven asked for the Final to be postponed because of the illness of two players and the family bereavement of another. The Scottish F.A. decided that this was impossible due to other engagements, such as the international against England. Vale did not appear for the Final and the trophy was awarded to Queen's Park.

1885 Scottish F.A. Cup

Semi-finals

Renton vs Hibernian	3-2
Vale of Leven vs Cambuslang	0-0, 3-1

Final

Second Hampden Park, 21st February 1885

Renton 0

Vale of Leven 0

Attendance 3,500

Replay

Second Hampden Park, 28th February 1885

Renton 3   (J. McCall, McIntyre 2)

Vale of Leven 1   (Gillies)

Attendance 7,000

1886 Scottish F.A. Cup

Semi-finals

Third Lanark vs Queen's Park	0-3
Hibernian vs Renton	0-2

Final

First Cathkin Park, 13th February 1886

Queen's Park 3   (Hamilton, Christie, Somerville)

Renton 1   (Kelso)

Attendance 7,000

1887 Scottish F.A. Cup

Semi-finals

Hibernian vs Vale of Leven	3-1
Queen's Park vs Dumbarton	1-2

Final

Second Hampden Park, 12th February 1887

Hibernian 2   (Montgomery, Groves)

Dumbarton 1   (Aitken)

Attendance 11,000

1888 Scottish F.A. Cup

Semi-finals

Renton vs Queen's Park	3-1
Abercorn vs Cambuslang	1-1, 1-10

Final

Second Hampden Park, 4th February 1888

Renton 6   (McNee 2, McCallum 2, McCall 2)

Cambuslang 1   (H. Gourlay)

Attendance 11,000

1889 Scottish F.A. Cup

Semi-finals

Third Lanark vs Renton	2-0
Dumbarton vs Celtic	1-4

Final

Second Hampden Park, 2nd February 1889

Third Lanark 3   (Marshall, Oswald Jnr., Hannah)

Celtic 0

Attendance 18,000

The first game was later declared void due to a snow-covered pitch and was ordered to be replayed.

Replay

Second Hampden Park, 9th February 1889

Third Lanark 2   (Marshall, Oswald Jnr.)

Celtic 1   (McCallum)

Attendance 18,000

1890 Scottish F.A. Cup

Semi-finals

Queen's Park vs Abercorn	2-0
Vale of Leven vs Third Lanark	3-0

Final

First Ibrox Park, 15th February 1890

Queen's Park 1   (Sellar)

Vale of Leven 1   (McLachlan)

Attendance 10,000

Replay

First Ibrox Park, 22nd February 1890

Queen's Park 2   (Hamilton, Stewart)

Vale of Leven 1   (Bruce)

Attendance 14,000

SCOTTISH LEAGUE 1890-91

Dumbarton	18	13	3	2	61	21	29
Rangers	18	13	3	2	58	25	29
Celtic	18	11	3	4	48	21	21
Cambuslang	18	8	4	6	47	42	20
Third Lanark	18	8	3	7	38	39	15
Heart of Midlothian	18	6	2	10	31	37	14
Abercorn	18	5	2	11	36	47	12
St. Mirren	18	5	1	12	39	62	11
Vale Of Leven	18	5	1	12	27	65	11
Cowlairs	18	3	4	11	24	50	6

1891 Scottish F.A. Cup

Semi-finals

Heart of Midlothian vs Third Lanark	4-1
Dumbarton vs Abercorn	3-1

Final

Second Hampden Park, 7th February 1891

Heart of Midlothian 1   (Russell)

Dumbarton 0

Attendance 10, 836

SCOTTISH LEAGUE 1891-92

Dumbarton	22	18	1	3	79	28	37
Celtic	22	16	3	3	62	22	35
Heart of Midlothian	22	15	4	3	65	35	34
Leith Athletic	22	12	1	9	51	41	25
Rangers	22	11	2	9	59	46	24
Third Lanark	22	9	4	9	44	47	22
Renton	22	8	5	9	38	44	21
Clyde	22	8	4	10	63	62	20
Abercorn	22	6	5	11	47	59	17
St. Mirren	22	4	5	13	43	60	13
Cambuslang	22	2	6	14	22	53	10
Vale of Leven	22	0	5	17	24	100	5

1892 Scottish F.A. Cup

Semi-finals

Celtic vs Rangers	5-3
Renton vs Queen's Park	1-1, 0-3

Final

First Ibrox Park, 12th March 1892

Celtic 1   (Campbell)
Queen's Park 0

Attendance 40,000

Due to disruption caused by the large crowd, it was decided that the first game be a friendly. The final was replayed with the entrance fee doubled to reduce the attendance.

Replay

First Ibrox Park, 9th April 1892

Celtic 5   (Campbell 2, McMahon 2, Sillars (og))
Queen's Park 1   (Waddell)

Attendance 20,000

SCOTTISH LEAGUE 1892-93

Celtic	18	14	1	3	54	25	29
Rangers	18	12	4	2	41	27	28
St. Mirren	18	9	2	7	40	39	20
Third Lanark	18	9	1	8	54	40	19
Heart of Midlothian	18	8	2	8	40	42	18
Leith Athletic	18	8	1	9	35	31	17
Dumbarton	18	8	1	9	35	35	17
Renton	18	5	5	8	31	44	15
Abercorn	18	5	1	12	35	52	11
Clyde	18	2	2	14	25	55	6

1893 Scottish F.A. Cup

Semi-finals

Queen's Park vs Broxburn Shamrock	4-2
Celtic vs St. Bernard's	5-0

Final

First Ibrox Park, 25th February 1893

Queen's Park 0
Celtic 1   (Towie)

Attendance 25,000

The first game was played as a friendly due to a frozen pitch.

Replay

First Ibrox Park, 11th March 1893

Queen's Park 2   (Sellar 2)
Celtic 1   (Blessington)

Attendance 22,000

SCOTTISH DIVISION 1 1893-94

Celtic	18	14	1	3	53	32	29
Heart of Midlothian	18	11	4	3	46	32	26
St. Bernard's	18	11	1	6	53	41	23
Rangers	18	8	4	6	44	30	20
Dumbarton	18	7	5	6	32	35	19
St. Mirren	18	7	3	8	50	46	17
Third Lanark	18	7	3	8	37	45	17
Dundee	18	6	3	9	43	58	15
Leith Athletic	18	4	2	12	36	46	10
Renton	18	1	2	15	23	52	4

SCOTTISH DIVISION 2 1893-94

Hibernian	18	13	3	2	83	29	29
Cowlairs	18	13	1	4	75	32	27
Clyde	18	11	2	5	51	36	24
Motherwell	18	11	1	6	61	46	23
Partick Thistle	18	10	0	8	56	58	20
Port Glasgow Athletic	18	9	2	7	52	53	13
Abercorn	18	5	2	11	42	60	12
Greenock Morton	18	4	1	13	36	62	9
Northern	18	3	3	12	29	66	9
Thistle	18	2	3	13	31	74	7

1894 Scottish F.A. Cup

Semi-finals

Rangers vs Queen's Park	1-1, 3-1
Third Lanark vs Celtic	3-5

Final

Second Hampden Park, 17th February 1894

Rangers 3   (H. McCreadie, Barker, McPherson)
Celtic 1   (W. Maley)

Attendance 17,000

SCOTTISH DIVISION 1 1894-95

Heart of Midlothian	18	15	1	2	50	18	31
Celtic	18	11	4	3	50	29	26
Rangers	18	10	2	6	41	26	22
Third Lanark	18	10	1	7	51	39	21
St. Mirren	18	9	1	8	34	36	19
St. Bernards	18	8	1	9	39	40	17
Clyde	18	8	0	10	40	49	16
Dundee	18	6	2	10	28	33	14
Leith Athletic	18	3	1	14	32	64	7
Dumbarton	18	3	1	14	27	58	7

SCOTTISH DIVISION 2 1894-95

Hibernian	18	14	2	2	92	27	30
Motherwell	18	10	2	6	56	39	22
Port Glasgow Athletic	18	8	4	6	62	56	20
Renton	17	10	0	7	46	44	20
Greenock Morton	18	9	1	8	59	63	19
Airdrieonians	18	8	2	8	68	45	18
Partick Thistle	18	8	2	8	50	60	18
Abercorn	18	7	3	8	48	65	17
Dundee Wanderers	17	3	1	13	44	86	9
Cowlairs	18	2	3	13	37	77	7

1895 Scottish F.A. Cup

Semi-finals

Heart of Midlothian vs St. Bernard's	0-0, 0-1
Dundee vs Renton	1-1, 3-3, 0-3

Final

First Ibrox Park, 20th April 1895

St. Bernard's 2   (Cleland 2)
Renton 1   (Duncan)

Attendance 15,000

SCOTTISH DIVISION 1 1895-96

Celtic	18	15	0	3	64	25	30
Rangers	18	11	4	3	57	39	26
Hibernian	18	11	2	5	58	39	24
Heart of Midlothian	18	11	0	7	68	36	22
Dundee	18	7	2	9	33	42	16
Third Lanark	18	7	1	10	47	51	15
St. Bernards	18	7	1	10	36	53	15
St. Mirren	18	5	3	10	31	51	13
Clyde	18	4	3	11	39	59	11
Dumbarton	18	4	0	14	36	74	8

SCOTTISH DIVISION 2 1895-96

Abercorn	18	12	3	3	55	31	27
Leith Athletic	18	11	1	6	55	37	23
Renton	18	9	3	6	40	28	21
Kilmarnock	18	10	1	7	45	45	21
Airdrieonians	18	7	4	7	48	44	18
Partick Thistle	18	8	2	8	44	54	18
Port Glasgow Athletic	18	6	4	8	40	41	16
Motherwell	18	5	3	10	31	47	13
Greenock Morton	18	4	4	10	32	40	12
Linthouse	18	5	1	12	25	48	11

1896 Scottish F.A. Cup

Semi-finals

Heart of Midlothian vs St. Bernard's	1-0
Hibernian vs Renton	2-1

Final

Logie Green, Edinburgh, 14th March 1896

Heart of Midlothian 3   (Walker, King, Mitchell)

Hibernian 1   (O'Neill)

Attendance 17,034

SCOTTISH DIVISION 1 1896-97

Heart of Midlothian	18	13	2	3	47	22	28
Hibernian	18	12	2	4	50	20	26
Rangers	18	11	3	4	64	30	25
Celtic	18	10	4	4	42	18	24
Dundee	18	10	2	6	38	30	22
St. Mirren	18	9	1	8	38	29	19
St. Bernards	18	7	0	11	32	40	14
Third Lanark	18	5	1	12	29	46	11
Clyde	18	4	0	14	27	65	8
Abercorn	18	1	1	16	21	88	3

SCOTTISH DIVISION 2 1896-97

Partick Thistle	18	14	3	1	61	28	31
Leith Athletic	18	13	1	4	54	28	27
Kilmarnock	18	10	1	7	44	33	21
Airdrieonians	18	10	1	7	48	39	21
Greenock Morton	18	7	2	9	38	40	16
Renton	18	6	2	10	34	40	14
Linthouse	18	8	2	8	44	52	14
Port Glasgow Athletic	18	4	5	9	39	50	13
Motherwell	18	6	1	11	40	55	13
Dumbarton	18	2	2	14	27	64	6

1897 Scottish F.A. Cup

Semi-finals

Morton vs Rangers	2-7
Dumbarton vs Kilmarnock	4-3

Final

Second Hampden Park, 20th March 1897

Rangers 5   (Miller 2, Hyslop, McPherson, Smith)

Dumbarton 1   (W. Thomson)

Attendance 15,000

SCOTTISH DIVISION 1 1897-98

Celtic	18	15	3	0	56	13	33
Rangers	18	13	3	2	71	15	29
Hibernian	18	10	2	6	48	28	22
Heart of Midlothian	18	8	4	6	54	33	20
Third Lanark	18	8	2	8	37	38	18
St. Mirren	18	8	2	8	30	36	18
Dundee	18	5	3	10	29	36	13
Partick Thistle	18	6	1	11	34	64	13
St. Bernard's	18	4	1	13	35	67	19
Clyde	18	1	3	14	20	84	5

SCOTTISH DIVISION 2 1897-98

Kilmarnock	18	14	1	3	64	29	29
Port Glasgow Athletic	18	12	1	5	66	35	25
Greenock Morton	18	9	4	5	47	38	22
Leith Athletic	18	9	2	7	39	38	20
Linthouse	18	6	4	8	37	39	16
Ayr	18	7	2	9	36	42	16
Abercorn	18	6	4	8	33	41	16
Airdrieonians	18	6	2	10	44	56	14
Hamilton Academical	18	5	2	11	28	51	12
Motherwell	18	3	4	11	31	56	10

1898 Scottish F.A. Cup

Semi-finals

Rangers vs Third Lanark	1-1, 2-2, 2-0
Kilmarnock vs Dundee	3-2

Final

Second Hampden Park, 26th March 1898

Rangers 2   (A. Smith, Hamilton)

Kilmarnock 0

Attendance 15,000

SCOTTISH DIVISION 1 1898-99

Rangers	18	18	0	0	79	18	36
Heart of Midlothian	18	12	2	4	56	30	26
Celtic	18	11	2	5	51	33	24
Hibernian	18	10	3	5	42	43	23
St. Mirren	18	8	4	6	46	32	20
Third Lanark	18	7	3	8	33	38	17
St. Bernard's	18	4	4	10	30	37	12
Clyde	18	4	4	10	23	48	12
Partick Thistle	18	2	2	14	19	58	6
Dundee	18	1	2	15	23	65	4

SCOTTISH DIVISION 2 1898-99

Kilmarnock	18	14	4	0	73	24	32
Leith Athletic	18	12	3	3	63	38	27
Port Glasgow Athletic	18	12	1	5	75	51	25
Motherwell	18	7	6	5	41	40	20
Hamilton Academical	18	7	1	10	48	58	15
Airdrieonians	18	6	3	9	35	46	15
Greenock Morton	18	6	1	11	36	41	13
Ayr	18	5	3	10	35	51	13
Linthouse	18	5	1	12	29	62	11
Abercorn	18	4	1	13	41	65	9

1899 Scottish F.A. Cup

Semi-finals

Celtic vs Port Glasgow Athletic	4-2
St. Mirren vs Rangers	1-2

Final

Second Hampden Park, 22nd April 1899

Celtic 2   (McMahon, Hodge)

Rangers 0

Attendance 25,000

SCOTTISH DIVISION 1 1899-1900

Rangers	18	15	2	1	69	27	32
Celtic	18	9	7	2	46	27	25
Hibernian	18	9	6	3	43	24	24
Heart of Midlothian	18	10	3	5	41	24	23
Kilmarnock	18	6	6	6	30	37	18
Dundee	18	4	7	7	36	39	15
Third Lanark	18	5	5	8	31	36	15
St. Mirren	18	3	6	9	30	46	12
St. Bernard's	18	4	4	10	29	47	12
Clyde	18	2	0	16	25	70	4

SCOTTISH DIVISION 2 1899-1900

Partick Thistle	18	14	1	3	56	26	29
Greenock Morton	18	14	0	4	66	25	28
Port Glasgow Athletic	18	10	0	8	50	41	20
Motherwell	18	9	1	8	38	36	19
Leith Athletic	18	9	1	8	32	37	19
Abercorn	18	7	2	9	46	39	16
Hamilton Academical	18	7	1	10	33	46	15
Ayr	18	6	2	10	39	48	14
Airdrieonians	18	4	3	11	27	49	11
Linthouse	18	2	5	11	28	68	9

1900 Scottish F.A. Cup

Semi-finals

Celtic vs Rangers	2-2, 4-0
Queen's Park vs Heart of Midlothian	2-1

Final

Second Ibrox Park, 14th April 1900

Celtic 4 (McMahon, Divers 2, Bell)

Queen's Park 3 (Christie, W. Stewart, Battles (og))

Attendance 18,000

SCOTTISH DIVISION 1 1900-01

Rangers	20	17	1	2	60	25	35
Celtic	20	13	3	4	49	28	29
Hibernian	20	9	7	4	29	22	25
Greenock Morton	20	9	3	8	40	40	21
Kilmarnock	20	7	4	9	35	47	18
Third Lanark	20	6	6	8	20	29	18
Dundee	20	6	5	9	36	35	17
Queen's Park	20	7	3	10	33	37	17
St. Mirren	20	5	6	9	33	43	16
Heart of Midlothian	20	5	4	11	22	30	14
Partick Thistle	20	4	2	14	28	49	10

SCOTTISH DIVISION 2 1900-01

St. Bernard's	18	10	5	3	41	26	25
Airdrieonians	18	11	1	6	46	35	23
Abercorn	18	9	3	6	37	33	21
Clyde	18	9	2	7	43	35	20
Port Glasgow Athletic	18	9	1	8	45	44	19
Ayr	18	9	0	9	32	34	18
East Stirlingshire	18	7	4	7	35	39	18
Leith Athletic	18	5	3	10	23	33	13
Hamilton Academical	18	4	4	10	44	51	12
Motherwell	18	4	3	11	26	42	11

1901 Scottish F.A. Cup

Semi-finals

Heart of Midlothian vs Hibernian	1-1, 2-1
Celtic vs St. Mirren	1-0

Final

Second Ibrox Park, 6th April 1901

Heart of Midlothian 4 (Walker, Davidson (og),
Thomson, Bell)

Celtic 3 (McOustra 2, McMahon)

Attendance 12,000

SCOTTISH DIVISION 1 1901-02

Rangers	18	13	2	3	43	29	28
Celtic	18	11	4	3	38	28	26
Heart of Midlothian	18	10	2	6	32	21	22
Third Lanark	18	7	5	6	30	26	19
St. Mirren	18	8	3	7	29	28	19
Hibernian	18	6	4	8	36	24	16
Kilmarnock	18	5	6	7	21	25	16
Queen's Park	18	5	4	9	21	32	14
Dundee	18	4	5	9	16	31	13
Greenock Morton	18	1	5	12	18	40	7

SCOTTISH DIVISION 2 1901-02

Port Glasgow Athletic	22	14	4	4	71	31	32
Partick Thistle	22	14	3	5	55	26	31
Motherwell	22	12	2	8	50	44	26
Airdrieonians	22	10	5	7	40	32	25
Hamilton Academical	22	11	3	8	45	40	25
St. Bernard's	22	10	2	10	30	30	22
Leith Athletic	22	9	3	10	34	38	21
Ayr	22	8	5	9	27	33	21
East Stirlingshire	22	8	3	11	36	46	19
Arthurlie	22	6	5	11	32	42	17
Abercorn	22	4	5	13	27	57	13
Clyde	22	5	3	14	22	50	13

1902 Scottish F.A. Cup

Semi-finals

Hibernian vs Rangers	2-0
Celtic vs St. Mirren	3-2

Final

Celtic Park, 26th April 1902

Hibernian 1 (McGeachan)

Celtic 0

Attendance 15,000

SCOTTISH DIVISION 1 1902-03

Hibernian	22	16	5	1	48	18	37
Dundee	22	13	5	4	31	12	31
Rangers	22	12	5	5	56	30	29
Heart of Midlothian	22	11	6	5	46	27	28
Celtic	22	8	10	4	36	30	26
St. Mirren	22	7	8	7	39	40	22
Third Lanark	22	8	5	9	34	27	21
Partick Thistle	22	6	7	9	34	50	19
Kilmarnock	22	6	4	12	24	43	16
Queen's Park	22	5	5	12	33	48	15
Port Glasgow Athletic	22	3	5	14	26	49	11
Greenock Morton	22	2	5	15	22	55	9

SCOTTISH DIVISION 2 1902-03

Airdrieonians	22	15	5	2	43	19	35
Motherwell	22	12	4	6	44	35	28
Ayr	22	12	3	7	34	24	27
Leith Athletic	22	11	5	6	43	41	27
St. Bernard's	22	12	2	8	45	32	26
Hamilton Academical	22	11	1	10	44	35	23
Falkirk	22	8	7	7	39	37	23
East Stirlingshire	22	9	3	10	46	41	21
Arthurlie	22	6	8	8	34	46	20
Abercorn	22	5	2	15	35	58	12
Raith Rovers	22	3	5	14	34	55	11
Clyde	22	2	7	13	22	40	11

1903 Scottish F.A. Cup

Semi-finals

Rangers vs Stenhousemuir	4-1
Dundee vs Heart of Midlothian	0-0, 0-1

Final

Celtic Park, 11th April 1903

Rangers 1   (Stark)

Heart of Midlothian 1   (Walker)

Attendance 35,000

Replay

Celtic Park, 18th April 1903

Rangers 0

Heart of Midlothian 0

Attendance 16,000

2nd Replay

Celtic Park, 25th April 1903

Rangers 2   (Mackie, Hamilton)

Heart of Midlothian 0

Attendance 35,000

SCOTTISH DIVISION 1 1903-04

Third Lanark	26	20	3	3	61	26	43
Heart of Midlothian	26	18	3	5	62	34	39
Celtic	26	18	2	6	68	27	38
Rangers	26	16	6	4	80	33	38
Dundee	26	13	2	11	54	45	28
St. Mirren	26	11	5	10	45	38	27
Partick Thistle	26	10	7	9	46	41	27
Queen's Park	26	6	9	11	28	47	21
Port Glasgow Athletic	26	8	4	14	32	49	20
Hibernian	26	7	5	14	29	40	19
Greenock Morton	26	7	4	15	32	53	18
Airdrieonians	26	7	4	15	32	62	18
Motherwell	26	6	3	17	26	61	15
Kilmarnock	26	4	5	17	24	63	13

SCOTTISH DIVISION 2 1903-04

Hamilton Academical	22	16	5	1	56	19	37
Clyde	22	12	5	5	51	36	29
Ayr	22	11	6	5	33	30	28
Falkirk	22	11	4	7	50	34	26
Raith Rovers	22	8	5	9	40	38	21
East Stirlingshire	22	8	5	9	35	40	21
Leith Athletic	22	8	4	10	42	40	20
St. Bernard's	22	9	2	11	31	43	20
Albion Rovers	22	8	5	9	47	37	19
Abercorn	22	6	4	12	38	55	16
Arthurlie	22	5	5	12	37	50	15
Ayr Parkhouse	22	3	4	15	23	61	10

1904 Scottish F.A. Cup

Semi-finals

Celtic vs Third Lanark	2-1
Rangers vs Morton	3-0

Final

Third Hampden Park, 16th April 1904

Celtic 3   (Quinn 3)

Rangers 2   (Speedie 2)

Attendance 65,000

SCOTTISH DIVISION 1 1904-05

Celtic	26	18	5	3	68	31	41
Rangers	26	19	3	4	83	28	41
Third Lanark	26	14	7	5	60	28	35
Airdrieonians	26	11	5	10	38	45	27
Hibernian	26	9	8	9	39	39	26
Partick Thistle	26	12	2	12	36	56	26
Dundee	26	10	5	11	43	37	25
Heart of Midlothian	26	11	3	12	46	44	25
Kilmarnock	26	9	5	12	29	45	23
St. Mirren	26	9	4	13	33	36	22
Port Glasgow Athletic	26	8	5	13	30	51	21
Queen's Park	26	6	8	12	28	45	20
Greenock Morton	26	7	4	15	27	50	18
Motherwell	26	6	2	18	28	53	14

SCOTTISH DIVISION 2 1904-05

Clyde	22	13	6	3	38	22	32
Falkirk	22	12	4	6	31	25	28
Hamilton Academical	22	12	3	7	40	22	27
Leith Athletic	22	10	4	8	36	26	24
Ayr	22	11	1	10	46	37	23
Arthurlie	22	9	5	8	37	42	23
Aberdeen	22	7	7	8	36	26	21
Albion Rovers	22	8	4	10	38	53	20
East Stirlingshire	22	7	5	10	38	38	19
Raith Rovers	22	9	1	12	30	34	19
Abercorn	22	8	1	13	31	45	17
St. Bernard's	22	3	5	14	23	54	11

1905 Scottish F.A. Cup

Semi-finals

Airdrieonians vs Third Lanark	1-2
Celtic vs Rangers	0-2

Final

Hampden Park, 8th April 1905

Third Lanark 0

Rangers 0

Attendance 55,000

Replay

Hampden Park, 15th April 1905

Third Lanark 3   (Wilson 2, Johnstone)

Rangers 1   (Smith)

Attendance 40,000

SCOTTISH DIVISION 1 1905-06

Celtic	30	24	1	5	76	19	49
Heart of Midlothian	30	18	7	5	64	27	43
Airdrieonians	30	15	8	7	53	31	38
Rangers	30	15	7	8	58	48	37
Partick Thistle	30	15	6	9	44	40	36
Third Lanark	30	16	2	12	62	39	34
Dundee	30	11	12	7	40	33	34
St. Mirren	30	13	5	12	41	37	31
Motherwell	30	9	8	13	50	62	26
Greenock Morton	30	10	6	14	35	54	26
Hibernian	30	10	5	15	35	40	25
Aberdeen	30	8	8	14	36	48	24
Falkirk	30	9	5	16	52	68	23
Port Glasgow Athletic	30	6	8	16	38	68	20
Kilmarnock	30	8	4	18	46	68	20
Queen's Park	30	5	4	21	41	88	14

SCOTTISH DIVISION 2 1905-06

Leith Athletic	22	15	4	3	46	21	34
Clyde	22	11	9	2	37	21	31
Albion Rovers	22	12	3	7	48	29	27
Hamilton Academical	22	12	2	8	45	34	26
St. Bernard's	22	9	4	9	42	34	22
Arthurlie	22	10	2	10	42	43	22
Ayr	22	9	3	10	43	51	21
Raith Rovers	22	6	7	9	36	42	19
Cowdenbeath	22	7	3	12	27	39	17
Abercorn	22	6	5	11	29	45	17
Vale of Leven	22	6	4	12	34	49	16
East Stirlingshire	22	1	10	11	26	47	12

1906 Scottish F.A. Cup

Semi-finals

Port Glasgow Athletic vs Heart of Midlothian	0-2
St. Mirren vs Third Lanark	1-1, 0-0, 0-1

Final

Ibrox Park, 28th April 1906

Heart of Midlothian 1   (G. Wilson)

Third Lanark 0

Attendance 25,000

SCOTTISH DIVISION 1 1906-07

Celtic	34	23	9	2	80	30	55
Dundee	34	18	12	4	53	26	48
Rangers	34	19	7	8	69	33	45
Airdrieonians	34	18	6	10	59	44	42
Falkirk	34	17	7	10	73	58	41
Third Lanark	34	15	9	10	57	48	39
St. Mirren	34	12	13	9	50	44	37
Clyde	34	15	6	13	47	52	36
Heart of Midlothian	34	11	13	10	47	43	35
Motherwell	34	12	9	13	45	49	33
Aberdeen	34	10	10	14	48	55	30
Hibernian	34	10	10	14	40	49	33
Greenock Morton	34	11	6	17	41	50	28
Partick Thistle	34	9	8	17	40	60	26
Queen's Park	34	9	6	19	51	66	24
Hamilton Academical	34	8	5	21	40	64	21
Kilmarnock	34	8	5	21	40	72	21
Port Glasgow Athletic	34	7	7	20	30	67	21

SCOTTISH DIVISION 2 1906-07

St. Bernard's	22	14	4	4	41	24	32
Vale of Leven	22	13	1	8	54	35	27
Arthurlie	22	12	3	7	50	39	27
Dumbarton	22	11	3	8	52	35	25
Leith Athletic	22	10	4	8	40	35	24
Albion Rovers	22	10	3	9	43	36	23
Cowdenbeath	22	10	5	7	36	39	23
Ayr	22	7	6	9	34	38	20
Abercorn	22	5	7	10	29	47	17
Raith Rovers	22	6	4	12	39	47	16
East Stirlingshire	22	6	4	12	37	48	16
Ayr Parkhouse	22	5	2	15	32	64	12

1907 Scottish F.A. Cup

Semi-finals

Celtic vs Hibernian	0-0, 0-0, 3-0
Heart of Midlothian vs Queen's Park	1-0

Final

Hampden Park, 20th April 1907

Celtic 3 (Orr (pen), Somers 2)
Heart of Midlothian 0

Attendance 50,000

SCOTTISH DIVISION 1 1907-08

Celtic	34	24	7	3	86	27	55
Falkirk	34	22	7	5	102	40	51
Rangers	34	21	8	5	74	40	50
Dundee	34	20	8	6	70	27	48
Hibernian	34	17	8	9	55	42	42
Airdrieonians	34	18	5	11	58	41	41
St. Mirren	34	13	10	11	50	59	36
Aberdeen	34	13	9	12	45	44	35
Third Lanark	34	13	7	14	45	50	33
Motherwell	34	12	7	15	61	53	31
Hamilton Academical	34	10	8	16	54	65	28
Heart of Midlothian	34	11	6	17	50	62	28
Greenock Morton	34	9	9	16	43	66	27
Kilmarnock	34	6	13	15	38	61	25
Partick Thistle	34	8	9	17	43	69	25
Queen's Park	34	7	8	19	54	84	22
Clyde	34	5	8	21	36	75	18
Port Glasgow Athletic	34	5	7	22	39	98	17

SCOTTISH DIVISION 2 1907-08

Raith Rovers	22	14	2	6	37	23	30
Dumbarton	22	12	5	5	49	32	27
Ayr	22	11	5	6	40	33	27
Abercorn	22	9	5	8	33	30	23
East Stirlingshire	22	9	5	8	30	32	23
Ayr Parkhouse	22	11	0	11	38	38	22
Leith Athletic	22	8	5	9	41	40	21
St. Bernard's	22	8	5	9	31	32	21
Albion Rovers	22	7	5	10	36	48	19
Vale of Leven	22	5	8	9	25	31	18
Arthurlie	22	6	5	11	33	45	17
Cowdenbeath	22	5	4	13	26	35	14

1908 Scottish F.A. Cup

Semi-finals

Aberdeen vs Celtic	0-1
Kilmarnock vs St. Mirren	0-0, 0-2

Final

Hampden Park, 18th April 1908

Celtic 5 (Bennett 2, Hamilton, Somers, Quinn)
St. Mirren 1 (Cunningham)

Attendance 55,000

SCOTTISH DIVISION 1 1908-09

Celtic	34	23	5	6	71	24	51
Dundee	34	22	6	6	70	32	50
Clyde	34	21	6	7	61	37	48
Rangers	34	19	7	8	91	38	45
Airdrieonians	34	16	9	9	67	46	41
Hibernian	34	16	7	11	40	32	39
St. Mirren	34	15	6	13	53	45	36
Aberdeen	34	15	6	13	61	53	36
Falkirk	34	13	7	14	58	56	33
Kilmarnock	34	13	7	14	47	61	33
Third Lanark	34	11	10	13	56	49	32
Heart of Midlothian	34	12	8	14	54	49	32
Port Glasgow Athletic	34	10	8	16	39	52	28
Motherwell	34	11	6	17	47	73	28
Queen's Park	34	6	13	15	42	65	25
Hamilton Academical	34	6	12	16	42	72	24
Greenock Morton	34	8	7	19	39	90	23
Partick Thistle	34	2	4	28	38	102	8

SCOTTISH DIVISION 2 1908-09

Abercorn	22	13	5	4	40	18	31
Raith Rovers	22	11	6	5	46	22	28
Vale of Leven	22	12	4	6	39	25	28
Dumbarton	22	10	5	7	34	34	25
Ayr	22	10	3	9	43	36	23
Leith Athletic	22	10	3	9	37	33	23
Ayr Parkhouse	22	8	5	9	29	31	21
St. Bernard's	22	9	3	10	34	37	21
East Stirlingshire	22	9	3	10	28	34	21
Albion Rovers	22	9	2	11	37	48	20
Cowdenbeath	22	4	4	14	19	42	12
Arthurlie	22	5	1	16	29	55	11

1909 Scottish F.A. Cup

Semi-final

Celtic vs Clyde	0-0, 2-0
Falkirk vs Rangers	0-1

Final

Hampden Park, 10th April 1909

Celtic 2 (Quinn, Munro)
Rangers 2 (Gilchrist, Bennett)

Attendance 70,000

Replay

Hampden Park, 17th April 1909

Celtic 1　(Quinn)
Rangers 1　(Gordon)

Attendance 60,000

When, as stated in the rules, extra time was not played at the end of the game, the crowd rioted and over a hundred people were injured. As a result, both clubs refused to play a third match and the Scottish F.A. agreed that the trophy would not be awarded.

SCOTTISH DIVISION 1 1909-10

Celtic	34	24	6	4	63	22	54
Falkirk	34	22	8	4	71	28	52
Rangers	34	20	6	8	70	35	46
Aberdeen	34	16	8	10	44	29	40
Clyde	34	14	9	11	47	40	37
Dundee	34	14	8	12	52	44	36
Third Lanark	34	13	8	13	62	44	34
Hibernian	34	14	6	14	33	40	34
Airdrieonians	34	12	9	13	46	57	33
Motherwell	34	12	8	14	59	60	32
Kilmarnock	34	12	8	14	53	60	32
Heart of Midlothian	34	12	7	15	59	50	31
St. Mirren	34	13	5	16	49	58	31
Queen's Park	34	12	6	16	54	74	30
Hamilton Academical	34	11	6	17	50	67	28
Partick Thistle	34	8	10	16	47	59	26
Greenock Morton	34	11	3	20	38	60	25
Port Glasgow Athletic	34	3	5	26	25	95	11

SCOTTISH DIVISION 2 1909-10

Leith Athletic	22	13	7	2	44	19	33
Raith Rovers	22	14	5	3	36	21	33
St. Bernard's	22	12	3	7	43	31	27
Dumbarton	22	9	5	8	44	38	23
Abercorn	22	7	8	7	38	40	22
Vale of Leven	22	8	5	9	36	38	21
Ayr	22	9	3	10	37	40	21
East Stirlingshire	22	9	2	11	38	43	20
Albion Rovers	22	7	5	10	34	39	19
Arthurlie	22	6	5	11	34	47	17
Cowdenbeath	22	7	3	12	22	34	17
Ayr Parkhouse	22	4	3	15	27	43	11

1910 Scottish F.A. Cup

Semi-finals

Hibernian vs Dundee	0-0, 0-0, 0-1
Clyde vs Celtic	3-1

Final

Ibrox Park, 9th April 1910

Dundee 2　(Hunter, Langlands)
Clyde 2　(Chalmers, Booth)

Attendance 60,000

Replay

Ibrox Park, 16th April 1910

Dundee 0
Clyde 0　(aet.)

Attendance 22,000

2nd Replay

Ibrox Park, 20th April 1910

Dundee 2　(Bellamy, Hunter)
Clyde 1　(Chalmers)

Attendance 25,000

SCOTTISH DIVISION 1 1910-11

Rangers	34	23	6	5	90	34	52
Aberdeen	34	19	10	5	53	28	48
Falkirk	34	17	10	7	65	42	44
Partick Thistle	34	17	8	9	50	41	42
Celtic	34	15	11	8	48	18	41
Dundee	34	18	5	11	54	42	41
Clyde	34	14	11	9	45	36	39
Third Lanark	34	16	7	11	59	53	39
Hibernian	34	15	6	13	44	48	36
Kilmarnock	34	12	10	12	43	45	34
Airdrieonians	34	12	9	13	49	53	33
St. Mirren	34	12	7	15	46	57	31
Greenock Morton	34	9	11	14	49	51	29
Heart of Midlothian	34	8	8	18	42	59	24
Raith Rovers	34	7	10	17	36	56	24
Hamilton Academical	34	8	5	21	31	60	21
Motherwell	34	8	4	22	37	66	20
Queen's Park	34	5	4	25	28	80	14

SCOTTISH DIVISION 2 1910-11

Dumbarton	22	15	1	6	55	31	31
Ayr United	22	12	3	7	52	36	27
Albion Rovers	22	10	5	7	27	21	25
Leith Athletic	22	9	6	7	42	43	24
Cowdenbeath	22	9	5	8	31	27	23
St. Bernard's	22	10	2	10	36	39	22
East Stirlingshire	22	7	6	9	28	35	20
Port Glasgow Athletic	22	8	3	11	27	32	19
Dundee Hibernians	22	7	5	10	29	36	19
Arthurlie	22	7	5	10	26	33	19
Abercorn	22	9	1	12	39	50	19
Vale of Leven	22	4	8	10	22	31	16

1911 Scottish F.A. Cup

Semi-finals

Celtic vs Aberdeen	1-0
Hamilton Academical vs Dundee	3-2

Final

Ibrox Park, 8th April 1911

Celtic 0
Hamilton Academical 0

Attendance 45,000

Replay

Ibrox Park, 15th April 1911

Celtic 2　(Quinn, McAteer)
Hamilton Academical 0

Attendance 25,000

SCOTTISH DIVISION 1 1911-12

Rangers	34	24	3	7	86	34	51
Celtic	34	17	11	6	58	33	45
Clyde	34	19	4	11	56	32	42
Heart of Midlothian	34	16	8	10	54	40	40
Partick Thistle	34	16	8	10	47	40	40
Greenock Morton	34	14	9	11	44	44	37
Falkirk	34	15	6	13	46	43	36
Dundee	34	13	9	12	52	41	35
Aberdeen	34	14	7	13	44	44	35
Airdrieonians	34	12	8	14	40	41	32
Third Lanark	34	12	7	15	40	57	31
Hamilton Academical	34	11	8	15	32	44	30
Hibernian	34	12	5	17	44	47	29
Motherwell	34	11	5	18	34	44	27
Raith Rovers	34	9	9	16	39	59	27
Kilmarnock	34	11	4	19	38	60	26
Queen's Park	34	8	9	17	29	53	25
St. Mirren	34	7	10	17	32	59	24

SCOTTISH DIVISION 2 1911-12

Ayr United	22	16	3	3	54	24	35
Abercorn	22	13	4	5	43	22	30
Dumbarton	22	13	1	8	47	31	27
Cowdenbeath	22	12	2	8	39	31	26
Johnstone	22	10	4	8	29	27	24
St. Bernard's	22	9	5	8	38	36	23
Leith Athletic	22	9	4	9	31	34	22
Arthurlie	22	7	5	10	26	30	19
East Stirlingshire	22	7	3	12	21	31	17
Dundee Hibernians	22	5	5	12	21	41	15
Vale of Leven	22	6	1	15	19	37	13
Albion Rovers	22	6	1	15	26	50	13

1912 Scottish F.A. Cup

Semi-finals

Celtic vs Heart of Midlothian	3-0
Clyde vs Third Lanark	3-1

Final

Ibrox Park, 6th April 1912

Celtic 2   (McMenemy, Gallacher)

Clyde 0

Attendance 50,000

SCOTTISH DIVISION 1 1912-13

Rangers	34	24	5	5	76	41	53
Celtic	34	22	5	7	53	28	49
Heart of Midlothian	34	17	7	10	71	43	41
Airdrieonians	34	15	11	8	64	46	41
Falkirk	34	14	12	8	56	38	40
Hibernian	34	16	5	13	63	54	37
Motherwell	34	12	13	9	47	39	37
Aberdeen	34	14	9	11	47	40	37
Clyde	34	13	9	12	41	44	35
Hamilton Academical	34	12	8	14	44	47	32
Kilmarnock	34	10	11	13	37	54	31
St. Mirren	34	10	10	14	50	60	30
Greenock Morton	34	11	7	16	50	59	29
Dundee	34	8	13	13	33	46	29
Third Lanark	34	8	12	14	31	41	28
Raith Rovers	34	8	10	16	46	60	26
Partick Thistle	34	10	4	20	40	55	24
Queen's Park	34	5	3	26	34	88	13

SCOTTISH DIVISION 2 1912-13

Ayr United	26	13	8	5	45	19	34
Dunfermline Athletic	26	13	7	6	45	27	33
East Stirlingshire	26	12	8	6	43	27	32
Abercorn	26	12	7	7	33	31	31
Cowdenbeath	26	12	6	8	36	27	30
Dumbarton	26	12	5	9	39	30	29
St. Bernard's	26	12	3	11	36	34	27
Johnstone	26	9	6	11	31	43	24
Albion Rovers	26	10	3	13	38	40	23
Dundee Hibernians	26	6	10	10	34	43	22
St. Johnstone	26	7	7	12	29	38	21
Vale of Leven	26	8	5	13	28	45	21
Arthurlie	26	7	5	14	37	49	19
Leith Athletic	26	5	8	13	26	47	18

1913 Scottish F.A. Cup

Semi-finals

Falkirk vs Heart of Midlothian	1-0
Raith Rovers vs Clyde	1-1, 1-0

Final

Celtic Park, 12th April 1913

Falkirk 2   (Robertson, Logan)

Raith Rovers 0

Attendance 45,000

SCOTTISH DIVISION 1 1913-14

Celtic	38	30	5	3	81	14	65
Rangers	38	27	5	6	79	31	59
Heart of Midlothian	38	23	8	7	70	29	54
Greenock Morton	38	26	2	10	76	51	54
Falkirk	38	20	9	9	69	51	49
Airdrieonians	38	18	12	8	72	43	48
Dundee	38	19	5	14	64	53	43
Third Lanark	38	13	10	15	42	51	36
Clyde	38	11	11	16	46	46	33
Ayr United	38	13	7	18	58	74	33
Raith Rovers	38	13	6	19	56	57	32
Kilmarnock	38	11	9	18	48	68	31
Hibernian	38	12	6	20	58	75	30
Aberdeen	38	10	10	18	38	55	30
Partick Thistle	38	10	9	19	37	51	29
Queen's Park	38	10	9	19	52	84	29
Motherwell	38	11	6	21	49	66	28
Hamilton Academical	38	11	6	21	46	65	28
Dumbarton	38	10	7	21	45	87	27
St. Mirren	38	8	6	24	38	73	22

SCOTTISH DIVISION 2 1913-14

Cowdenbeath	22	13	5	4	34	17	31
Albion Rovers	22	10	7	5	38	33	27
Dunfermline Athletic	22	11	4	7	46	28	26
Dundee Hibernians	22	11	4	7	36	31	26
St. Johnstone	22	9	5	8	48	38	23
Abercorn	22	10	3	9	32	32	23
St. Bernard's	22	8	6	8	39	31	22
East Stirlingshire	22	7	8	7	40	36	22
Arthurlie	22	8	4	10	35	37	20
Leith Athletic	22	5	9	8	31	37	19
Vale of Leven	22	5	3	14	23	47	13
Johnstone	22	4	4	14	20	55	12

1914 Scottish F.A. Cup

Semi-finals

Celtic vs Third Lanark	2-0
Hibernian vs St. Mirren	3-1

Final

Ibrox Park, 11th April 1914

Celtic 0

Hibernian 0

Attendance 56,000

Replay

Ibrox Park, 16th April 1914

Celtic 4   (McColl 2, Browning 2)

Hibernian 1   (Smith)

Attendance 40,000

SCOTTISH DIVISION 'A' 1914-15

Celtic	38	30	5	3	91	25	65
Heart of Midlothian	38	27	7	4	83	32	61
Rangers	38	23	4	11	74	47	50
Greenock Morton	38	18	12	8	74	48	48
Ayr United	38	20	8	10	55	40	48
Falkirk	38	16	7	15	48	48	39
Hamilton Academical	38	16	6	16	60	55	38
Partick Thistle	38	15	8	15	56	58	38
St. Mirren	38	14	8	16	56	65	36
Airdrieonians	38	14	7	17	54	60	35
Hibernian	38	12	11	15	59	66	35
Kilmarnock	38	15	4	19	55	59	34
Dumbarton	38	13	8	17	51	66	34
Aberdeen	38	11	11	16	39	52	33
Dundee	38	12	9	17	43	61	33
Third Lanark	38	10	12	16	51	57	32
Clyde	38	12	6	20	44	59	30
Motherwell	38	10	10	18	49	66	30
Raith Rovers	38	9	10	19	53	68	28
Queen's Park	38	4	5	29	27	90	13

SCOTTISH DIVISION 'B' 1914-15

Cowdenbeath	26	16	5	5	49	17	37
Leith Athletic	26	15	7	4	54	31	37
St. Bernards	26	18	1	7	66	34	37
East Stirlingshire	26	13	5	8	53	46	31
Clydebank	26	13	4	9	68	37	30
Dunfermline Athletic	26	13	2	11	49	39	28
Johnstone	26	11	5	10	41	52	27
St. Johnstone	26	10	6	10	56	53	26
Albion Rovers	26	9	7	10	37	42	25
Lochgelly United	26	9	3	14	44	60	21
Dundee Hibernians	26	8	3	15	48	61	19
Abercorn	26	5	7	14	35	65	17
Arthurlie	26	6	4	16	36	66	16
Vale of Leven	26	4	5	17	33	66	13

SCOTTISH LEAGUE 1915-16

Celtic	38	32	3	3	116	23	67
Rangers	38	25	6	7	87	39	56
*Greenock Morton	37	22	7	8	83	35	51
Ayr United	38	20	8	10	72	45	48
Partick Thistle	38	19	8	11	65	41	46
*Heart of Midlothian	37	20	6	11	66	45	46
Hamilton Academical	38	19	3	16	68	76	41
Dundee	38	18	4	16	57	49	40
Dumbarton	38	13	11	14	53	64	37
Kilmarnock	38	12	11	15	46	49	35
Aberdeen	38	11	12	15	51	64	34
Falkirk	38	12	9	17	45	61	33
St. Mirren	38	13	4	21	50	67	30
Motherwell	38	11	8	19	55	81	30
Airdrieonians	38	11	8	19	44	71	30
Clyde	38	11	7	20	49	71	29
Third Lanark	38	9	11	18	38	56	29
Queen's Park	38	11	6	21	53	100	28
Hibernian	38	9	7	22	44	70	25
Raith Rovers	38	9	5	24	30	65	23

Greenock Morton and Heart of Midlothian played only once

SCOTTISH LEAGUE 1916-17

Celtic	38	27	10	1	79	17	64
Greenock Morton	38	24	6	8	72	39	54
Rangers	38	24	5	9	68	32	53
Airdrieonians	38	21	8	9	72	38	50
Third Lanark	38	19	11	8	53	37	49
Kilmarnock	38	18	7	13	69	45	43
St. Mirren	38	15	10	13	49	43	40
Motherwell	38	16	6	16	57	58	38
Partick Thistle	38	14	7	17	44	43	35
Dumbarton	38	12	11	15	56	73	35
Hamilton Academical	38	13	9	16	54	73	35
Falkirk	38	12	10	16	57	57	34
Clyde	38	10	14	14	41	54	34
Heart of Midlothian	38	14	4	20	44	59	32
Ayr United	38	12	7	19	46	59	31
Dundee	38	13	4	21	58	71	30
Hibernian	38	10	10	18	57	72	30
Queen's Park	38	11	7	20	56	81	29
Raith Rovers	38	8	7	23	42	91	23
Aberdeen	38	7	7	24	36	68	21

SCOTTISH LEAGUE 1917-18

Rangers	34	25	6	3	66	24	56
Celtic	34	24	7	3	66	26	55
Kilmarnock	34	19	5	10	69	41	43
Greenock Morton	34	17	9	8	53	42	43
Motherwell	34	16	9	9	70	51	41
Partick Thistle	34	14	12	8	51	37	40
Queen's Park	34	14	6	14	64	63	34
Dumbarton	34	13	8	13	48	49	34
Clydebank	34	14	5	15	55	56	33
Heart of Midlothian	34	14	4	16	41	58	32
St. Mirren	34	11	7	16	42	50	29
Hamilton Academical	34	11	6	17	52	63	28
Third Lanark	34	10	7	17	56	62	27
Falkirk	34	9	9	16	38	58	27
Airdrieonians	34	10	6	18	46	58	26
Hibernian	34	8	9	17	42	57	25
Clyde	34	9	2	23	37	72	20
Ayr United	34	5	9	20	32	61	19

SCOTTISH LEAGUE 1918-19

Celtic	34	26	6	2	71	22	58
Rangers	34	26	5	3	86	16	57
Greenock Morton	34	18	11	5	76	38	47
Partick Thistle	34	17	7	10	62	43	41
Motherwell	34	14	10	10	51	40	38
Heart of Midlothian	34	14	9	11	59	52	37
Ayr United	34	14	9	11	57	53	37
Queen's Park	34	15	5	14	59	57	35
Kilmarnock	34	14	7	13	61	59	35
Clydebank	34	12	8	14	52	65	32
St. Mirren	34	10	12	12	43	55	32
Third Lanark	34	11	9	14	60	60	31
Airdrieonians	34	9	11	14	45	54	29
Hamilton Academical	34	11	5	18	49	75	27
Dumbarton	34	7	8	19	31	57	22
Falkirk	34	6	8	20	46	72	20
Clyde	34	7	6	21	45	75	20
Hibernian	34	5	4	25	28	87	14

SCOTTISH LEAGUE 1919-20

Rangers	42	31	9	2	106	25	71
Celtic	42	29	10	3	89	31	68
Motherwell	42	23	11	8	73	53	57
Dundee	42	22	6	14	79	64	50
Clydebank	42	20	8	14	78	54	48
Greenock Morton	42	16	13	13	71	48	45
Airdrieonians	42	17	10	15	57	43	44
Third Lanark	42	16	11	15	57	62	43
Kilmarnock	42	20	3	19	59	74	43
Ayr United	42	15	10	17	72	69	40
Dumbarton	42	13	13	16	57	65	39
Queen's Park	42	14	10	18	67	73	38
Partick Thistle	42	13	12	17	51	62	38
St. Mirren	42	15	8	19	63	81	38
Clyde	42	14	9	19	64	71	37
Heart of Midlothian	42	14	9	19	57	72	37
Aberdeen	42	11	13	18	46	64	35
Hibernian	42	13	7	22	60	79	33
Raith Rovers	42	11	10	21	61	82	32
Falkirk	42	10	11	21	45	74	31
Hamilton Academical	42	11	7	24	56	86	29
Albion Rovers	42	10	7	25	42	77	27

1920 Scottish F.A. Cup

Semi-finals

Kilmarnock vs Greenock Morton	3-2
Albion Rovers vs Rangers	0-0, 1-1, 2-0

Final

Hampden Park, 17th April 1920

Kilmarnock 3 (Culley, Shortt, J.R. Smith)
Albion Rovers 2 (Watson, Hillhouse)

Attendance 97,000

SCOTTISH LEAGUE 1920-21

Rangers	42	35	6	1	91	24	76
Celtic	42	30	6	6	86	35	66
Heart of Midlothian	42	20	10	12	74	49	50
Dundee	42	19	11	12	54	48	49
Motherwell	42	19	10	13	75	51	48
Partick Thistle	42	17	12	13	53	39	46
Clyde	42	21	3	18	63	62	45
Third Lanark	42	19	6	17	74	61	44
Greenock Morton	42	15	14	13	66	58	44
Airdrieonians	42	17	9	16	71	64	43
Aberdeen	42	14	14	14	53	54	42
Kilmarnock	42	17	8	17	62	68	42
Hibernian	42	16	9	17	58	57	41
Ayr United	42	14	12	16	62	69	40
Hamilton Academical	42	14	12	16	44	57	40
Raith Rovers	42	16	5	21	54	58	37
Albion Rovers	42	11	12	19	57	68	34
Falkirk	42	11	12	19	54	72	34
Queen's Park	42	11	11	20	45	80	33
Clydebank	42	7	14	21	47	72	28
Dumbarton	42	10	4	28	41	89	24
St. Mirren	42	7	4	31	43	92	18

1921 Scottish F.A. Cup

Semi-finals

Partick Thistle vs Heart of Midlothian	0-0, 0-0, 2-0
Rangers vs Albion Rovers	4-1

Final

Celtic Park, 16th April 1921

Partick Thistle 1   (Blair)
Rangers 0

Attendance 28,000

SCOTTISH DIVISION 1 1921-22

Celtic	42	27	13	2	83	20	67
Rangers	42	28	10	4	83	26	66
Raith Rovers	42	19	13	10	66	43	51
Dundee	42	19	11	12	57	40	49
Falkirk	42	16	17	9	48	38	49
Partick Thistle	42	20	8	14	57	53	48
Hibernian	42	16	14	12	55	44	46
St. Mirren	42	17	12	13	71	61	46
Third Lanark	42	17	12	13	58	52	46
Clyde	42	16	12	14	60	51	44
Albion Rovers	42	17	10	15	55	51	44
Greenock Morton	42	16	10	16	58	57	42
Motherwell	42	16	7	19	63	58	39
Ayr United	42	13	12	17	55	63	38
Aberdeen	42	13	9	20	48	54	35
Airdrieonians	42	12	11	19	46	56	35
Kilmarnock	42	13	9	20	56	83	35
Hamilton Academical	42	9	16	17	51	62	34
Heart of Midlothian	42	11	10	21	50	60	32
Dumbarton	42	10	10	22	46	81	30
Queen's Park	42	9	10	23	38	82	28
Clydebank	42	6	8	28	34	103	20

SCOTTISH DIVISION 2 1921-22

Alloa Athletic	38	26	8	4	81	32	60
Cowdenbeath	38	19	9	10	56	30	47
Armadale	38	20	5	13	64	49	45
Vale of Leven	38	17	10	11	56	43	44
Bathgate	38	16	11	11	56	41	43
Bo'ness	38	16	7	15	57	49	39
Broxburn United	38	14	11	13	43	43	39
Dunfermline Athletic	38	14	10	14	56	42	38
St. Bernard's	38	15	8	15	50	49	38
Stenhousemuir	38	14	10	14	50	51	38
Johnstone	38	14	10	14	46	59	38
East Fife	38	15	7	16	55	54	37
St. Johnstone	38	12	11	15	41	52	35
Forfar Athletic	38	11	12	15	44	53	34
East Stirlingshire	38	12	10	16	43	60	34
Arbroath	38	11	11	16	45	56	33
King's Park	38	10	12	16	47	65	32
Lochgelly United	38	11	9	18	46	56	31
Dundee Hibernians	38	10	8	20	47	65	28
Clackmannan	38	10	7	21	41	75	27

1922 Scottish F.A. Cup

Semi-finals

Greenock Morton vs Aberdeen	3-1
Rangers vs Partick Thistle	2-0

Final

Hampden Park, 15th April 1922

Greenock Morton 1   (Gourlay)
Rangers 0

Attendance 75,000

SCOTTISH DIVISION 1 1922-23

Rangers	38	23	9	6	67	29	55
Airdrieonians	38	20	10	8	58	38	50
Celtic	38	19	8	11	52	39	46
Falkirk	38	14	17	7	44	32	45
Aberdeen	38	15	12	11	46	34	42
St. Mirren	38	15	12	11	54	44	42
Dundee	38	17	7	14	51	45	41
Hibernian	38	17	7	14	45	40	41
Raith Rovers	38	13	13	12	31	43	39
Ayr United	38	13	12	13	43	44	38
Partick Thistle	38	14	9	15	51	48	37
Heart of Midlothian	38	11	15	12	51	50	37
Motherwell	38	13	10	15	59	60	36
Greenock Morton	38	12	11	15	44	47	35
Kilmarnock	38	14	7	17	57	66	35
Clyde	38	12	9	17	36	44	33
Third Lanark	38	11	8	19	40	59	30
Hamilton Academical	38	11	7	20	43	59	29
Albion Rovers	38	8	10	20	38	64	26
Alloa Athletic	38	6	11	21	27	52	23

SCOTTISH DIVISION 2 1922-23

Queen's Park	38	24	9	5	73	31	57
Clydebank	38	21	10	7	69	29	52
* St. Johnstone	38	19	12	7	60	39	48
Dumbarton	38	17	8	13	61	40	42
Bathgate	38	16	9	13	67	55	41
Armadale	38	15	11	12	63	52	41
Bo'ness	38	12	17	9	48	46	41
Broxburn United	38	14	12	12	40	43	40
East Fife	38	16	7	15	48	42	39
Lochgelly United	38	16	5	17	41	64	37
* Cowdenbeath	38	16	6	16	56	52	36
King's Park	38	14	6	18	46	60	34
Dunfermline Athletic	38	11	11	16	47	44	33
Stenhousemuir	38	13	7	18	53	67	33
Forfar Athletic	38	13	7	18	51	73	33
Johnstone	38	13	6	19	41	62	32
Vale of Leven	38	11	8	19	50	59	30
* St. Bernard's	38	8	15	15	39	50	29
East Stirlingshire	38	10	8	20	48	69	28
Arbroath	38	8	12	18	45	69	28

* 2 points deducted for fielding ineligible players

1923 Scottish F.A. Cup

Semi-finals

Celtic vs Motherwell   2-0
Hibernian vs Third Lanark   1-0

Final

Hampden Park, 31st March 1923

Celtic 1   (Cassidy)
Hibernian 0

Attendance 80,000

1924 Scottish F.A. Cup

Semi-finals

Airdrieonians vs Falkirk   2-1
Aberdeen vs Hibernian   0-0, 0-0, 0-1

Final

Ibrox Park, 19th April 1924

Airdrieonians 2   (Russell 2)
Hibernian 0

Attendance 59,218

SCOTTISH DIVISION 1 1923-24

Rangers	38	25	9	4	72	22	59
Airdrieonians	38	20	10	8	72	46	50
Celtic	38	17	12	9	56	33	46
Raith Rovers	38	18	7	13	56	38	43
Dundee	38	15	13	10	70	57	43
St. Mirren	38	15	12	11	53	45	42
Hibernian	38	15	11	12	66	52	41
Partick Thistle	38	15	9	14	58	55	39
Heart of Midlothian	38	14	10	14	61	50	38
Motherwell	38	15	7	16	58	63	37
Greenock Morton	38	16	5	17	48	54	37
Hamilton Academical	38	15	6	17	52	57	36
Aberdeen	38	13	10	15	37	41	36
Ayr United	38	12	10	16	38	60	34
Falkirk	38	13	6	19	46	53	32
Kilmarnock	38	12	8	18	48	65	32
Queen's Park	38	11	9	18	43	60	31
Third Lanark	38	11	8	19	54	78	30
Clyde	38	10	9	19	40	70	29
Clydebank	38	10	5	23	42	71	25

SCOTTISH DIVISION 2 1923-24

St. Johnstone	38	22	12	4	79	33	56
Cowdenbeath	38	23	9	6	78	33	55
Bathgate	38	16	12	10	58	49	44
Stenhousemuir	38	16	11	11	58	45	43
Albion Rovers	38	15	12	11	67	53	42
King's Park	38	16	10	12	67	56	42
Dunfermline Athletic	38	14	11	13	52	45	39
Johnstone	38	16	7	15	60	56	39
Dundee United	38	12	15	11	41	41	39
Dumbarton	38	17	5	16	55	58	39
Armadale	38	16	6	16	56	63	38
East Fife	38	14	9	15	54	47	37
Bo'ness	38	13	11	14	45	52	37
Forfar Athletic	38	14	7	17	43	68	35
Broxburn United	38	13	8	17	50	56	34
Alloa Athletic	38	14	6	18	44	53	34
Arbroath	38	12	8	18	49	51	32
St. Bernard's	38	11	10	17	49	54	32
Vale of Leven	38	11	9	18	41	67	31
Lochgelly United	38	4	4	30	20	86	12

SCOTTISH DIVISION 3 1923-24

Arthurlie	30	21	5	4	59	24	47
East Stirlingshire	30	17	8	5	63	36	42
Queen of the South	30	14	10	6	64	31	38
Montrose	30	15	6	9	60	48	36
Dykehead	30	16	1	13	55	41	33
Nithsdale Wanderers	30	13	7	10	42	35	33
Beith	30	14	4	12	49	41	32
Mid-Annandale	30	13	5	12	59	48	31
Royal Albert	30	12	4	14	44	53	28
Dumbarton Harp	30	10	8	12	40	51	28
Solway Star	30	9	9	12	42	48	27
Clackmannan	30	10	7	13	37	54	27
Galston	30	11	3	16	53	70	25
Peebles Rovers	30	7	8	15	43	56	22
Helensburgh	30	5	7	18	46	72	17
Brechin City	30	4	6	20	28	76	14

SCOTTISH DIVISION 1 1924-25

Rangers	38	25	10	3	76	26	60
Airdrieonians	38	25	7	6	85	31	57
Hibernian	38	22	8	8	78	43	52
Celtic	38	18	8	12	77	44	44
Cowdenbeath	38	16	10	12	76	65	42
St. Mirren	38	18	4	16	65	63	40
Partick Thistle	38	14	10	14	60	61	38
Dundee	38	14	8	16	48	55	36
Raith Rovers	38	14	8	16	52	60	36
Heart of Midlothian	38	12	11	15	65	69	35
St. Johnston	38	12	11	15	56	71	35
Kilmarnock	38	12	9	17	53	64	33
Hamilton Academical	38	15	3	20	50	63	33
Greenock Morton	38	12	9	17	46	69	33
Aberdeen	38	11	10	17	46	56	32
Falkirk	38	12	8	18	44	54	32
Queen's Park	38	12	8	18	50	71	32
Motherwell	38	10	10	18	55	64	30
Ayr United	38	11	8	19	43	65	30
Third Lanark	38	11	8	19	53	84	30

SCOTTISH DIVISION 2 1924-25

Dundee United	38	20	10	8	58	44	50
Clydebank	38	20	8	10	65	42	48
Clyde	38	20	7	11	72	39	47
Alloa Athletic	38	17	11	10	57	33	45
Arbroath	38	16	10	12	47	46	42
Bo'ness	38	16	9	13	71	48	41
Broxburn United	38	16	9	13	48	54	41
Dumbarton	38	15	10	13	45	44	40
East Fife	38	17	5	16	66	58	39
King's Park	38	15	8	15	54	46	38
Stenhousemuir	38	15	7	16	51	58	37
Arthurlie	38	14	8	16	56	60	36
Dunfermline Athletic	38	14	7	17	62	57	35
Armadale	38	15	5	18	55	62	35
Albion Rovers	38	15	5	18	46	61	35
Bathgate	38	12	10	16	58	74	34
St. Bernard's	38	14	4	20	52	70	32
East Stirlingshire	38	11	8	19	58	72	30
Johnstone	38	12	4	22	53	85	28
Forfar Athletic	38	10	7	21	46	67	27

SCOTTISH DIVISION 3 1924-25

Nithsdale Wanderers	30	18	7	5	81	40	43
Queen of the South	30	17	6	7	67	32	40
Solway Star	30	15	10	5	41	28	40
Vale of Leven	30	17	4	9	61	43	38
Lochgelly United	30	15	4	11	59	41	34
Leith Athletic	30	13	5	12	48	42	31
Helensburgh	30	12	7	11	68	60	31
Peebles Rovers	30	12	7	11	64	57	31
Royal Albert	30	9	8	13	48	61	26
Clackmannan	30	10	6	14	35	48	26
Galston	30	10	6	14	39	70	26
Dykehead	30	7	11	12	30	47	25
Beith	30	9	6	15	62	74	24
Brechin City	29	9	4	16	51	61	24
Mid-Annandale	30	7	7	16	47	70	21
Montrose	30	8	4	18	39	66	20
* Dumbarton Harp	17	5	3	9	25	47	13

Dumbarton Harp's results were expunged from the records

1925 Scottish F.A. Cup

Semi-finals

Celtic vs Rangers	5-0
Dundee vs Hamilton Academical	1-1, 2-0

Final

Hampden Park, 11th April 1925

Celtic 2 (Gallacher, McGrory)

Dundee 1 (McLean)

Attendance 75,137

1926 Scottish F.A. Cup

Semi-finals

St. Mirren vs Rangers	1-0
Celtic vs Aberdeen	2-1

Final

Hampden Park, 10th April 1926

St. Mirren 2 (McCrae, Howieson)

Celtic 0

Attendance 98,620

SCOTTISH DIVISION 1 1925-26

Celtic	38	25	8	5	97	40	58
Airdrieonians	38	23	4	11	95	54	50
Heart of Midlothian	38	21	8	9	87	56	50
St. Mirren	38	20	7	11	62	52	47
Motherwell	38	19	8	11	67	46	46
Rangers	38	19	6	13	79	55	44
Cowdenbeath	38	18	6	14	87	68	42
Falkirk	38	14	14	10	61	57	42
Kilmarnock	38	17	7	14	79	77	41
Dundee	38	14	9	15	47	59	37
Aberdeen	38	13	10	15	49	54	36
Hamilton Academical	38	13	9	16	68	79	35
Queen's Park	38	15	4	19	70	81	34
Partick Thistle	38	10	13	15	64	73	33
Greenock Morton	38	12	7	19	57	84	31
Hibernian	38	12	6	20	72	77	30
Dundee	38	11	6	21	52	74	28
St. Johnstone	38	9	10	19	43	78	28
Raith Rovers	38	11	4	23	46	81	26
Clydebank	38	7	8	23	55	92	22

SCOTTISH DIVISION 2 1925-26

Dunfermline Athletic	38	26	7	5	109	43	59
Clyde	38	24	5	9	87	51	53
Ayr United	38	20	12	6	77	39	52
East Fife	38	20	9	9	98	73	49
Stenhousemuir	38	19	10	9	74	52	48
Third Lanark	38	19	8	11	72	47	46
Arthurlie	38	17	5	16	81	75	39
Bo'ness	38	17	5	16	65	70	39
Albion Rovers	38	16	6	16	78	71	38
Arbroath	38	17	4	17	80	73	38
Dumbarton	38	14	10	14	54	78	38
Nithsdale Wanderers	38	15	7	16	79	82	37
King's Park	38	14	9	15	67	73	37
St. Bernard's	38	15	5	18	86	82	35
Armadale	38	14	5	19	82	101	33
Alloa Athletic	38	11	8	19	54	63	30
Queen of the South	38	10	8	20	64	88	28
East Stirlingshire	38	10	7	21	59	89	27
Bathgate	38	7	6	25	60	105	20
Broxburn United	38	4	6	28	55	126	14

SCOTTISH DIVISION 3 1925-26

Helensburgh	30	16	6	8	66	47	38
Leith Athletic	29	16	5	8	73	41	37
Forfar Athletic	28	16	3	9	61	42	35
Dykehead	28	14	5	9	62	47	33
Royal Albert	28	16	1	11	75	61	33
Mid-Annandale	29	14	3	12	50	54	31
Vale of Leven	26	14	2	10	78	55	30
Montrose	26	12	3	11	56	58	28
Brechin City	28	12	3	13	67	73	27
Lochgelly United	29	9	9	11	58	63	27
Solway Star	29	9	6	14	50	62	24
Beith	27	9	4	14	58	68	22
Johnstone	29	7	6	16	55	74	20
Clackmannan	25	5	8	12	42	74	18
Peebles Rovers	26	9	0	17	52	76	18
Galston	15	4	4	7	38	46	12

SCOTTISH DIVISION 1 1926-27

Rangers	38	23	10	5	85	41	56
Motherwell	38	23	5	10	81	52	51
Celtic	38	21	7	10	101	55	49
Airdrieonians	38	18	9	11	97	64	45
Dundee	38	17	9	12	77	51	43
Falkirk	38	16	10	12	77	60	42
Cowdenbeath	38	18	6	14	74	60	42
Aberdeen	38	13	14	11	73	72	40
Hibernian	38	16	7	15	62	71	39
St. Mirren	38	16	5	17	78	76	37
Partick Thistle	38	15	6	17	89	74	36
Queen's Park	38	15	6	17	74	84	36
Heart of Midlothian	38	12	11	15	65	64	35
St. Johnstone	38	13	9	16	55	69	35
Hamilton Academical	38	13	9	16	60	85	35
Kilmarnock	38	12	8	18	54	71	32
Clyde	38	10	9	19	54	85	29
Dunfermline Athletic	38	10	8	20	53	85	28
Greenock Morton	38	12	4	22	56	101	28
Dundee	38	7	8	23	56	101	22

SCOTTISH DIVISION 2 1926-27

Bo'ness	38	23	10	5	86	41	56
Raith Rovers	38	21	7	10	92	52	49
Clydebank	38	18	9	11	94	75	45
Third Lanark	38	17	10	11	67	48	44
East Stirlingshire	38	18	8	12	93	75	44
East Fife	38	19	4	15	103	91	42
Arthurlie	38	18	5	15	90	83	41
Ayr United	38	13	15	10	67	68	41
Forfar Athletic	38	15	7	16	66	79	37
Stenhousemuir	38	12	12	14	69	75	36
Queen of the South	38	16	4	18	72	80	36
King's Park	38	13	9	16	76	75	35
St. Bernard's	38	14	6	18	70	77	34
Armadale	38	12	10	16	69	78	34
Alloa Athletic	38	11	11	16	70	78	33
Albion Rovers	38	11	11	16	74	87	33
Bathgate	38	13	7	18	76	98	33
Dumbarton	38	13	6	19	69	84	32
Arbroath	38	13	6	19	64	82	32
Nithsdale Wanderers	38	7	9	22	59	100	23

1927 Scottish F.A. Cup

Semi-finals

Celtic vs Falkirk	1-0
East Fife vs Partick Thistle	2-1

Final

Hampden Park, 16th April 1927

Celtic 3 (Robertson (og), McLean, Connolly)

St. Mirren 1 (Wood)

Attendance 80,070

SCOTTISH DIVISION 1 1927-28

	P	W	D	L	F	A	Pts
Rangers	38	26	8	4	109	36	60
Celtic	38	23	9	6	93	39	55
Motherwell	38	23	9	6	92	46	55
Heart of Midlothian	38	20	7	11	89	50	47
St. Mirren	38	18	8	12	77	76	44
Partick Thistle	38	18	7	13	65	67	43
Aberdeen	38	19	5	14	71	61	43
Kilmarnock	38	15	10	13	68	78	40
Cowdenbeath	38	16	7	15	66	68	39
Falkirk	38	16	5	17	76	69	37
St. Johnstone	38	14	8	16	66	67	36
Hibernian	38	13	9	16	73	75	35
Airdrieonians	38	12	11	15	59	69	35
Dundee	38	14	7	17	65	80	35
Clyde	38	10	11	17	46	72	31
Queen's Park	38	12	6	20	69	80	30
Raith Rovers	38	11	7	20	60	89	29
Hamilton Academical	38	11	6	21	67	86	28
Bo'ness	38	9	8	21	48	86	26
Dunfermline Athletic	38	4	4	30	41	126	12

SCOTTISH DIVISION 2 1927-28

	P	W	D	L	F	A	Pts
Ayr United	38	24	6	8	117	60	54
Third Lanark	38	18	9	11	99	66	45
King's Park	38	16	12	10	84	68	44
East Fife	38	18	7	13	87	73	43
Forfar Athletic	38	18	7	13	83	73	43
Dundee United	38	17	9	12	81	73	43
Arthurlie	38	18	4	16	84	90	40
Albion Rovers	38	17	4	17	79	69	38
East Stirlingshire	38	14	10	14	84	76	38
Arbroath	38	16	4	18	84	86	36
Dumbarton	38	16	4	18	66	72	36
Queen of the South	38	15	6	17	92	106	36
Leith Athletic	38	13	9	16	76	71	35
Clydebank	38	16	3	19	78	80	35
Alloa Athletic	38	12	11	15	72	76	35
Stenhousemuir	38	15	5	18	75	81	35
St. Bernard's	38	15	5	18	75	101	35
Greenock Morton	38	13	8	17	65	82	34
Bathgate	38	10	11	17	62	81	31
Armadale	38	8	8	22	53	112	24

1928 Scottish F.A. Cup

Semi-finals

Rangers vs Hibernian	3-0
Celtic vs Queen's Park	2-1

Final

Hampden Park, 14th April 1928

Rangers 4 (Meiklejohn (pen), McPhail, Archibald 2)

Celtic 0

Attendance 118,115

SCOTTISH DIVISION 1 1928-29

	P	W	D	L	F	A	Pts
Rangers	38	30	7	1	107	32	67
Celtic	38	22	7	9	67	44	51
Motherwell	38	20	10	8	85	66	50
Heart of Midlothian	38	19	9	10	91	57	47
Queen's Park	38	18	7	13	100	69	43
Partick Thistle	38	17	7	14	69	70	41
Aberdeen	38	16	8	14	81	69	40
St. Mirren	38	16	8	14	78	74	40
St. Johnstone	38	14	10	14	57	70	38
Kilmarnock	38	14	8	16	79	74	36
Falkirk	38	14	8	16	68	86	36
Hamilton Academical	38	13	9	16	58	83	35
Cowdenbeath	38	14	5	19	55	69	33
Hibernian	38	13	6	19	54	62	32
Airdrieonians	38	12	7	19	56	65	31
Ayr United	38	12	7	19	65	84	31
Clyde	38	12	6	20	47	71	30
Dundee	38	9	11	18	58	68	29
Third Lanark	38	10	6	22	71	102	26
Raith Rovers	38	9	6	23	52	105	24

SCOTTISH DIVISION 2 1928-29

	P	W	D	L	F	A	Pts
Dundee United	36	24	3	9	99	55	51
Greenock Morton	36	21	8	7	85	49	50
Arbroath	36	19	9	8	90	60	47
Albion Rovers	36	18	8	10	95	67	44
Leith Athletic	36	18	7	11	78	56	43
St. Bernard's	36	16	9	11	77	55	41
Forfar Athletic	35	14	10	11	69	75	38
East Fife	35	15	6	14	88	77	36
Queen of the South	36	16	4	16	86	79	36
Bo'ness	35	15	5	15	62	62	35
Dunfermline Athletic	36	13	7	16	66	72	33
East Stirlingshire	36	14	4	18	71	75	32
Alloa Athletic	36	12	7	17	64	77	31
Dumbarton	36	11	9	16	59	78	31
King's Park	36	8	13	15	60	84	29
Clydebank	36	11	5	20	70	86	27
Arthurlie	32	9	7	16	51	73	25
Stenhousemuir	35	9	6	20	52	90	24
Armadale	36	8	7	21	47	99	23

Bathgate resigned during the season. Arthurlie also resigned with four games to play, leaving matches against Forfar Athletic, East Fife, Bo'ness and Stenhousemuir unplayed.

1929 Scottish F.A. Cup

Semi-finals

Celtic vs Kilmarnock	0-1
Rangers vs St. Mirren	3-2

Final

Hampden Park, 6th April 1929

Kilmarnock 2 (Aitken, Williamson)

Rangers 0

Attendance 114,708

SCOTTISH DIVISION 1 1929-30

	P	W	D	L	F	A	Pts
Rangers	38	28	4	6	94	32	60
Motherwell	38	25	5	8	104	48	55
Aberdeen	38	23	7	8	85	61	53
Celtic	38	22	5	11	88	46	49
St. Mirren	38	18	5	15	73	56	41
Partick Thistle	38	16	9	13	72	61	41
Falkirk	38	16	9	13	62	64	41
Kilmarnock	38	15	9	14	77	73	39
Ayr United	38	16	6	16	70	92	38
Heart of Midlothian	38	14	9	15	69	69	37
Clyde	38	13	11	14	64	69	37
Airdrieonians	38	16	4	18	60	66	36
Hamilton Academical	38	14	7	17	76	81	35
Dundee	38	14	6	18	51	58	34
Queen's Park	38	15	4	19	67	80	34
Cowdenbeath	38	13	7	18	64	74	33
Hibernian	38	9	11	18	45	62	29
Greenock Morton	38	10	7	21	67	95	27
Dundee United	38	7	8	23	56	109	22
St. Johnstone	38	6	7	25	48	96	19

SCOTTISH DIVISION 2 1929-30

	P	W	D	L	F	A	Pts
Leith Athletic	38	23	11	4	92	42	57
East Fife	38	26	5	7	114	58	57
Albion Rovers	38	24	6	8	101	60	54
Third Lanark	38	23	6	9	92	53	52
Raith Rovers	38	18	8	12	94	67	44
King's Park	38	17	8	13	109	80	42
Queen of the South	38	18	6	14	65	63	42
Forfar Athletic	38	18	5	15	98	95	41
Arbroath	38	16	7	15	83	87	39
Dunfermline Athletic	38	16	6	16	99	85	38
Montrose	38	14	10	14	79	87	38
East Stirlingshire	38	16	4	18	83	75	36
Bo'ness	38	15	4	19	67	95	34
St. Bernard's	38	13	6	19	65	65	32
Armadale	38	13	5	20	56	91	31
Dumbarton	38	14	2	22	77	95	30
Stenhousemuir	38	11	5	22	75	108	27
Clydebank	38	7	10	21	66	92	24
Alloa Athletic	38	9	6	23	55	104	24
Brechin City	38	7	4	27	57	125	18

1930 Scottish F.A. Cup

Semi-finals

Rangers vs Heart of Midlothian   4-1
Partick Thistle vs Hamilton Academical   3-1

Final

Hampden Park, 12th April 1930

Rangers 0
Partick Thistle 0

Attendance 107,475

Replay

Hampden Park, 16th April 1930

Rangers 2   (Marshall, Craig)
Partick Thistle 1   (Torbet)

Attendance 102,479

SCOTTISH DIVISION 1 1930-31

Rangers	38	27	6	5	96	29	60
Celtic	38	24	10	4	101	34	58
Motherwell	38	24	8	6	102	42	56
Partick Thistle	38	24	5	9	76	44	53
Heart of Midlothian	38	19	6	13	90	63	44
Aberdeen	38	17	7	14	79	63	41
Cowdenbeath	38	17	7	14	58	65	41
Dundee	38	17	5	16	65	63	39
Airdrieonians	38	17	5	16	59	66	39
Hamilton Academical	38	16	5	17	59	57	37
Kilmarnock	38	15	5	18	59	60	35
Clyde	38	15	4	19	60	87	34
Queen's Park	38	13	7	18	71	72	33
Falkirk	38	14	4	20	77	87	32
St. Mirren	38	11	8	19	49	72	30
Greenock Morton	38	11	7	20	58	83	29
Leith Athletic	38	8	11	19	52	85	27
Ayr United	38	8	11	19	53	92	27
Hibernian	38	9	7	22	49	81	25
East Fife	38	8	4	26	45	113	20

SCOTTISH DIVISION 2 1930-31

Third Lanark	38	27	7	4	107	42	61
Dundee United	38	21	8	9	93	54	50
Dunfermline Athletic	38	20	7	11	83	50	47
Raith Rovers	38	20	6	12	93	72	46
Queen of the South	38	18	6	14	83	66	42
St. Johnstone	38	18	6	14	76	64	42
East Stirlingshire	38	17	7	14	85	74	41
Montrose	38	19	3	16	75	90	41
Albion Rovers	38	14	11	13	80	83	39
Dumbarton	38	15	8	15	73	72	38
St. Bernard's	38	14	9	15	85	66	37
Forfar Athletic	38	15	6	17	78	83	36
Alloa Athletic	38	15	5	18	65	87	35
King's Park	38	14	6	18	78	70	34
Arbroath	38	15	4	19	83	94	34
Brechin City	38	13	7	18	52	84	33
Stenhousemuir	38	13	6	19	78	98	32
Armadale	38	13	2	23	74	99	28
Clydebank	38	10	2	26	61	108	22
Bo'ness	38	9	4	25	54	100	22

1931 Scottish F.A. Cup

Semi-finals

Celtic vs Kilmarnock   3-0
Motherwell vs St. Mirren   1-0

Final

Hampden Park, 11th April 1931

Celtic 2   (McGrory, Craig (og))
Motherwell 2   (Stevenson, McMenemy)

Attendance 105,000

Replay

Hampden Park, 15th April 1931

Celtic 4   (R. Thomson 2, McGrory 2)
Motherwell 2   (Murdoch, Stevenson)

Attendance 98,579

SCOTTISH DIVISION 1 1931-32

Motherwell	38	30	6	2	119	31	66
Rangers	38	28	5	5	118	42	61
Celtic	38	20	8	10	94	50	48
Third Lanark	38	21	4	13	92	81	46
St. Mirren	38	20	4	14	77	56	44
Partick Thistle	38	19	4	15	58	59	42
Aberdeen	38	16	9	13	57	49	41
Heart of Midlothian	38	17	5	16	63	61	39
Kilmarnock	38	16	7	15	68	70	39
Hamilton Academical	38	16	6	16	84	65	38
Dundee	38	14	10	14	61	72	38
Cowdenbeath	38	15	8	15	66	78	38
Clyde	38	13	9	16	58	70	35
Airdrieonians	38	13	6	19	74	81	32
Greenock Morton	38	12	7	19	78	87	31
Queen's Park	38	13	5	20	59	79	31
Ayr United	38	11	7	20	70	90	29
Falkirk	38	11	5	22	70	76	27
Dundee	38	6	7	25	40	118	19
Leith Athletic	38	6	4	28	46	137	16

SCOTTISH DIVISION 2 1931-32

East Stirlingshire	38	26	3	9	111	55	55
St. Johnstone	38	24	7	7	102	52	55
Raith Rovers	38	20	6	12	83	65	46
Stenhousemuir	38	19	8	11	88	76	46
St. Bernard's	38	19	7	12	81	62	45
Forfar Athletic	38	19	7	12	90	79	45
Hibernian	38	18	8	12	73	52	44
East Fife	38	18	5	15	107	77	41
Queen of the South	38	18	5	15	99	91	41
Dunfermline Athletic	38	17	6	15	78	73	40
Arbroath	38	17	5	16	82	78	39
Dumbarton	38	14	10	14	70	68	38
Alloa Athletic	38	14	7	17	73	74	35
Bo'ness	38	15	4	19	70	103	34
King's Park	38	14	5	19	97	93	33
Albion Rovers	38	13	2	23	81	104	28
Montrose	38	11	6	21	60	96	28
Armadale	38	10	5	23	68	102	25
Brechin City	38	9	7	22	52	97	25
Edinburgh City	38	5	7	26	78	146	17

1932 Scottish F.A. Cup

Semi-finals

Rangers vs Hamilton Academical   5-2
Kilmarnock vs Airdrieonians   3-2

Final

Hampden Park, 16th April 1932

Rangers 1   (McPhail)
Kilmarnock 1   (Maxwell)

Attendance 111,982

Replay

Hampden Park, 20th April 1932

Rangers 3   (Fleming, McPhail, English)
Kilmarnock 0

Attendance 104,600

SCOTTISH DIVISION 1 1932-33

Rangers	38	26	10	2	113	43	62
Motherwell	38	27	5	6	114	53	59
Heart of Midlothian	38	21	8	9	84	51	50
Celtic	38	20	8	10	75	44	48
St. Johnstone	38	17	10	11	70	57	44
Aberdeen	38	18	6	14	85	58	42
St. Mirren	38	18	6	14	73	60	42
Hamilton Academical	38	18	6	14	92	78	42
Queen's Park	38	17	7	14	78	79	41
Partick Thistle	38	17	6	15	75	55	40
Falkirk	38	15	6	17	70	70	36
Clyde	38	15	5	18	69	75	35
Third Lanark	38	14	7	17	70	80	35
Kilmarnock	38	13	9	16	72	86	35
Dundee	38	12	9	17	58	74	33
Ayr United	38	13	4	21	62	96	30
Cowdenbeath	38	10	5	23	65	111	25
Airdrieonians	38	10	3	25	55	102	23
Greenock Morton	38	6	9	23	49	97	21
East Stirlingshire	38	7	3	28	55	115	17

SCOTTISH DIVISION 2 1932-33

Hibernian	34	25	4	5	80	29	54
Queen of the South	34	20	9	5	93	59	49
Dunfermline Athletic	34	20	7	7	89	44	47
Stenhousemuir	34	18	6	10	67	58	42
Albion Rovers	34	19	2	13	82	57	40
Raith Rovers	34	16	4	14	83	67	36
East Fife	34	15	4	15	85	71	34
King's Park	34	13	8	13	85	80	34
Dumbarton	34	14	6	14	69	67	34
Arbroath	34	14	5	15	65	62	33
Alloa Athletic	34	14	5	15	60	58	33
St. Bernard's	34	13	6	15	67	64	32
Dundee United	34	14	4	16	65	67	32
Forfar Athletic	34	12	4	18	68	87	28
Brechin City	34	11	4	19	65	95	26
Leith Athletic	34	10	5	19	43	81	25
Montrose	34	8	5	21	63	89	21
Edinburgh City	34	4	4	26	39	133	12

Bo'ness and Armadale were expelled in November 1932 being unable to meet match guarantees.

1933 Scottish F.A. Cup

Semi-finals

Celtic vs Heart of Midlothian	0-0, 2-1
Motherwell vs Clyde	2-0

Final

Hampden Park, 15th April 1933

Celtic 1   (McGrory)

Motherwell 0

Attendance 102,339

SCOTTISH DIVISION 1 1933-34

Rangers	38	30	6	2	118	41	66
Motherwell	38	29	4	5	97	45	62
Celtic	38	18	11	9	78	53	47
Queen's Park	38	21	3	14	75	78	45
Aberdeen	38	18	8	12	90	57	44
Heart of Midlothian	38	17	10	11	86	59	44
Kilmarnock	38	17	9	12	73	64	43
Ayr United	38	16	10	12	87	92	42
St. Johnstone	38	17	6	15	74	53	40
Falkirk	38	16	6	16	73	68	38
Hamilton Academical	38	15	8	15	65	79	38
Dundee	38	15	6	17	68	64	36
Partick Thistle	38	14	5	19	73	78	33
Clyde	38	10	11	17	56	70	31
Queen's Park	38	13	5	20	65	85	31
Hibernian	38	12	3	23	51	69	27
St. Mirren	38	9	9	20	46	75	27
Airdrieonians	38	10	6	22	59	103	26
Third Lanark	38	8	9	21	62	103	25
Cowdenbeath	38	5	5	28	58	118	15

SCOTTISH DIVISION 2 1933-34

Albion Rovers	34	20	5	9	74	47	45
Dunfermline Athletic	34	20	4	10	90	52	44
Arbroath	34	20	4	10	83	53	44
Stenhousemuir	34	18	4	12	70	73	40
Greenock Morton	34	17	5	12	67	64	39
Dumbarton	34	17	3	14	67	68	37
King's Park	34	14	8	12	78	70	36
Raith Rovers	34	15	5	14	71	55	35
East Stirlingshire	34	14	7	13	65	74	35
St. Bernard's	34	15	4	15	75	56	34
Forfar Athletic	34	13	7	14	77	71	33
Leith Athletic	34	12	8	14	63	60	32
East Fife	34	12	8	14	71	76	32
Brechin City	34	13	5	16	60	70	31
Alloa Athletic	34	11	9	14	55	68	31
Montrose	34	11	4	19	53	81	26
Dundee United	34	10	4	20	81	88	24
Edinburgh City	34	4	6	24	37	111	14

1934 Scottish F.A. Cup

Semi-finals

Rangers vs St. Johnstone	1-0
St. Mirren vs Motherwell	3-1

Final

Hampden Park, 21st April 1934

Rangers 5   (Nicholson 2, McPhail, Main, Smith)

St. Mirren 0

Attendance 113,403

SCOTTISH DIVISION 1 1934-35

Rangers	38	25	5	8	96	46	55
Celtic	38	24	4	10	92	45	52
Heart of Midlothian	38	20	10	8	87	51	50
Hamilton Academical	38	19	10	9	87	67	48
St. Johnstone	38	18	10	10	66	46	46
Aberdeen	38	17	10	11	68	54	44
Motherwell	38	15	10	13	83	64	40
Dundee	38	16	8	14	63	63	40
Kilmarnock	38	16	6	16	76	68	38
Clyde	38	14	10	14	71	69	38
Hibernian	38	14	8	16	59	70	36
Queen's Park	38	13	10	15	61	80	36
Partick Thistle	38	15	5	18	61	68	35
Airdrieonians	38	13	7	18	64	72	33
Dunfermline Athletic	38	13	5	20	56	96	31
Albion Rovers	38	10	9	19	62	77	29
Queen of the South	38	11	7	20	52	72	29
Ayr United	38	12	5	21	61	112	29
St. Mirren	38	11	5	22	49	70	27
Falkirk	38	9	6	23	58	82	24

SCOTTISH DIVISION 2 1934-35

Third Lanark	34	23	6	5	94	43	52
Arbroath	34	23	4	7	78	42	50
St. Bernard's	34	20	7	7	103	47	47
Dundee United	34	18	6	10	105	65	42
Stenhousemuir	34	17	5	12	86	80	39
Greenock Morton	34	17	4	13	88	64	38
King's Park	34	18	2	14	86	71	38
Leith Athletic	34	16	5	13	69	71	37
East Fife	34	16	3	15	79	73	35
Alloa Athletic	34	12	10	12	68	61	34
Forfar Athletic	34	13	8	13	77	73	34
Cowdenbeath	34	13	6	15	84	75	32
Raith Rovers	34	13	3	18	68	73	29
East Stirlingshire	34	11	7	16	57	76	29
Brechin City	34	10	6	18	51	98	26
Dumbarton	34	9	4	21	60	105	22
Montrose	34	7	6	21	58	105	20
Edinburgh City	34	3	2	29	45	134	8

1935 Scottish F.A. Cup

Semi-finals

Rangers vs Heart of Midlothian   1-1, 2-1
Aberdeen vs Hamilton Academical   1-2

Final

Hampden Park, 20th April 1935

Rangers 2 (Smith 2)
Hamilton Academical 1 (Harrison)

Attendance 87,740

SCOTTISH DIVISION 1 1935-36

Celtic	38	32	2	4	115	33	66
Rangers	38	27	7	4	110	43	61
Aberdeen	38	26	9	3	96	50	61
Motherwell	38	18	12	8	77	58	48
Heart of Midlothian	38	20	7	11	88	55	47
Hamilton Academical	38	15	7	16	77	74	37
St. Johnstone	38	15	7	16	70	81	37
Kilmarnock	38	14	7	17	69	64	35
Partick Thistle	38	12	10	16	64	72	34
Dunfermline Athletic	38	13	8	17	73	92	34
Third Lanark	38	14	5	19	63	71	33
Arbroath	38	11	11	16	46	69	33
Dundee	38	11	10	17	67	80	32
Queen's Park	38	11	10	17	58	75	32
Queen of the South	38	11	9	18	54	72	31
Albion Rovers	38	13	4	21	69	92	30
Hibernian	38	11	7	20	56	82	29
Clyde	38	10	8	20	63	84	28
Airdrieonians	38	9	9	20	68	91	27
Ayr United	38	11	3	24	53	98	25

SCOTTISH DIVISION 2 1935-36

Falkirk	34	28	3	3	132	34	59
St. Mirren	34	25	2	7	114	41	52
Greenock Morton	34	21	6	7	117	60	48
Alloa Athletic	34	19	6	9	65	51	44
St. Bernard's	34	18	4	12	106	78	40
East Fife	34	16	6	12	86	79	38
Dundee United	34	16	5	13	108	81	37
East Stirlingshire	34	13	8	13	70	75	34
Leith Athletic	34	15	3	16	67	77	33
Cowdenbeath	34	13	5	16	79	77	31
Stenhousemuir	34	13	3	18	59	78	29
Montrose	34	13	3	18	58	82	29
Forfar Athletic	34	10	7	17	60	81	27
King's Park	34	11	5	18	55	109	27
Edinburgh City	34	8	9	17	57	83	25
Brechin City	34	8	6	20	57	96	22
Raith Rovers	34	9	3	22	60	96	21
Dumbarton	34	5	6	23	52	121	16

1936 Scottish F.A. Cup

Semi-finals

Rangers vs Clyde   3-0
Falkirk vs Third Lanark   1-3

Final

Hampden Park, 18th April 1936

Rangers 1 (McPhail)
Third Lanark 0

Attendance 88,859

SCOTTISH DIVISION 1 1936-37

Rangers	38	26	9	3	88	32	61
Aberdeen	38	23	8	7	89	44	54
Celtic	38	22	8	8	89	58	52
Motherwell	38	22	7	9	96	54	51
Heart of Midlothian	38	24	3	11	99	60	51
Third Lanark	38	20	6	12	79	61	46
Falkirk	38	19	6	13	98	66	44
Hamilton Academical	38	18	5	15	91	96	41
Dundee	38	12	15	11	58	69	39
Clyde	38	16	6	16	59	70	38
Kilmarnock	38	14	9	15	60	70	37
St. Johnstone	38	14	8	16	74	68	36
Partick Thistle	38	11	12	15	73	68	34
Arbroath	38	13	5	20	57	84	31
Queen's Park	38	9	12	17	51	77	30
St. Mirren	38	11	7	20	68	81	29
Hibernian	38	6	13	19	54	83	25
Queen of the South	38	8	8	22	49	95	24
Dunfermline Athletic	38	5	11	22	65	98	21
Albion Rovers	38	5	6	27	53	116	16

SCOTTISH DIVISION 2 1936-37

Ayr United	34	25	4	5	122	49	54
Greenock Morton	34	23	5	6	110	42	51
St. Bernard's	34	22	4	8	102	51	48
Airdrieonians	34	18	8	8	85	60	44
East Fife	34	15	8	11	76	51	38
Cowdenbeath	34	14	10	10	75	59	38
East Stirlingshire	34	18	2	14	81	78	38
Raith Rovers	34	16	4	14	72	66	36
Alloa Athletic	34	13	7	14	64	65	33
Stenhousemuir	34	14	4	16	82	86	32
Leith Athletic	34	13	5	16	62	65	31
Forfar Athletic	34	11	8	15	73	89	30
Montrose	34	11	6	17	65	100	28
Dundee United	34	9	9	16	72	97	27
Dumbarton	34	11	5	18	57	83	27
Brechin City	34	8	9	17	64	98	25
King's Park	34	11	3	20	61	106	25
Edinburgh City	34	2	3	29	42	120	7

1937 Scottish F.A. Cup

Semi-finals

Celtic vs Clyde   2-0
Aberdeen vs Greenock Morton   2-0

Final

Hampden Park, 24th April 1937

Celtic 2 (Crum, Buchan)
Aberdeen 1 (Armstrong)

Attendance 146,433

SCOTTISH DIVISION 1 1937-38

Celtic	38	27	7	4	114	42	61
Heart of Midlothian	38	26	6	6	90	50	58
Rangers	38	18	13	7	75	49	49
Falkirk	38	19	9	10	82	52	47
Motherwell	38	17	10	11	78	69	44
Aberdeen	38	15	9	14	74	59	39
Partick Thistle	38	15	9	14	68	70	39
St. Johnstone	38	16	7	15	78	81	39
Third Lanark	38	11	13	14	68	73	35
Hibernian	38	11	13	14	57	65	35
Arbroath	38	11	13	14	58	79	35
Queen's Park	38	11	12	15	59	74	34
Hamilton Academical	38	13	7	18	81	76	33
St. Mirren	38	14	5	19	58	66	33
Clyde	38	10	13	15	68	78	33
Queen of the South	38	11	11	16	58	71	33
Ayr United	38	9	15	14	66	85	33
Kilmarnock	38	12	9	17	65	91	33
Dundee	38	13	6	19	70	74	32
Greenock Morton	38	6	3	29	64	127	15

SCOTTISH DIVISION 2 1937-38

Raith Rovers	34	27	5	2	142	54	59
Albion Rovers	34	20	8	6	97	50	48
Airdrieonians	34	21	5	8	100	53	47
St. Bernard's	34	20	5	9	75	49	45
East Fife	34	19	5	10	104	61	43
Cowdenbeath	34	17	9	8	115	71	43
Dumbarton	34	17	5	12	85	66	39
Stenhousemuir	34	17	5	12	87	78	39
Dunfermline Athletic	34	17	5	12	82	76	39
Leith Athletic	34	16	5	13	71	56	37
Alloa Athletic	34	11	4	19	78	106	26
King's Park	34	11	4	19	64	96	26
East Stirlingshire	34	9	7	18	55	95	25
Dundee United	34	9	5	20	69	104	23
Forfar Athletic	34	8	6	20	67	100	22
Montrose	34	7	8	19	56	88	22
Edinburgh City	34	7	3	24	77	135	17
Brechin City	34	5	2	27	53	139	12

1938 Scottish F.A. Cup

Semi-finals

Kilmarnock vs Rangers	4-3
St. Bernard's vs East Fife	1-1, 1-1, 1-2

Final

Hampden Park, 23rd April 1938

East Fife 1   (McLeod)
Kilmarnock 1   (McAvoy)

Attendance 80,091

Replay

Hampden Park, 27th April 1938

East Fife 4   (McKerrell 2, McLeod, Miller)
Kilmarnock 2 (aet.)   (Thomson (pen), McGrogan)

Attendance 92,716

SCOTTISH DIVISION 1 1938-39

Rangers	38	25	9	4	112	55	59
Celtic	38	20	8	10	99	53	48
Aberdeen	38	20	6	12	91	61	46
Heart of Midlothian	38	20	5	13	98	70	45
Falkirk	38	19	7	12	73	63	45
Queen of the South	38	17	9	12	69	64	43
Hamilton Academical	38	18	5	15	67	71	41
St. Johnstone	38	17	6	15	85	82	40
Clyde	38	17	5	16	78	70	39
Kilmarnock	38	15	9	14	73	86	39
Partick Thistle	38	17	4	17	74	87	38
Motherwell	38	16	5	17	82	86	37
Hibernian	38	14	7	17	68	69	35
Ayr United	38	13	9	16	76	83	35
Third Lanark	38	12	8	18	80	96	32
Albion Rovers	38	12	6	20	65	90	30
Arbroath	38	11	8	19	54	75	30
St. Mirren	38	11	7	20	57	80	29
Queen's Park	38	11	5	22	57	83	27
Raith Rovers	38	10	2	26	65	99	22

SCOTTISH DIVISION 2 1938-39

Cowdenbeath	34	28	4	2	120	45	60
Alloa Athletic	34	22	4	8	91	46	48
East Fife	34	21	6	7	99	61	48
Airdrieonians	34	21	5	8	85	57	47
Dunfermline Athletic	34	18	5	11	99	78	41
Dundee	34	15	7	12	99	63	37
St. Bernard's	34	15	6	13	79	79	36
Stenhousemuir	34	15	5	14	74	69	35
Dundee United	34	15	3	16	78	69	33
Brechin City	34	11	9	14	82	106	31
Dumbarton	34	9	12	13	68	76	30
Greenock Morton	34	11	6	17	74	88	28
King's Park	34	12	2	20	87	92	26
Montrose	34	10	5	19	82	96	25
Forfar Athletic	34	11	3	20	74	138	25
Leith Athletic	34	10	4	20	57	83	24
East Stirlingshire	34	9	4	21	89	130	22
Edinburgh City	34	6	4	24	58	119	16

1939 Scottish F.A. Cup

Semi-finals

Clyde vs Hibernian	1-0
Aberdeen vs Motherwell	1-1, 1-3

Final

Hampden Park, 22nd April 1939

Clyde 4   (Wallace, Martin 2, Noble)
Motherwell 0

Attendance 94,799

1945/46 Scottish League Cup

Semi-finals

Aberdeen vs Airdrieonians	2-2, 5-3
Rangers vs Heart of Midlothian	2-1

Final

Hampden Park, 11th May 1946

Aberdeen 3   (Baird, Williamson, Taylor)
Rangers 2   (Duncanson, Thornton)

Attendance 121,000

SCOTTISH DIVISION 'A' 1946-47

Rangers	30	21	4	5	76	26	46
Hibernian	30	19	6	5	69	33	44
Aberdeen	30	16	7	7	58	41	39
Heart of Midlothian	30	16	6	8	52	43	38
Partick Thistle	30	16	3	11	74	59	35
Greenock Morton	30	12	10	8	58	45	34
Celtic	30	13	6	11	53	55	32
Motherwell	30	12	5	13	58	54	29
Third Lanark	30	11	6	13	56	64	28
Clyde	30	9	9	12	55	65	27
Falkirk	30	8	10	12	62	61	26
Queen of the South	30	9	8	13	44	69	26
Queen's Park	30	8	6	16	47	60	22
St. Mirren	30	9	4	17	47	65	22
Kilmarnock	30	6	9	15	44	66	21
Hamilton Academical	30	2	7	21	38	85	11

SCOTTISH DIVISION 'B' 1946-47

Dundee	26	21	3	2	113	30	45
Airdrieonians	26	19	4	3	78	38	42
East Fife	26	12	7	7	58	39	31
Albion Rovers	26	10	7	9	50	54	27
Alloa Athletic	26	11	5	10	51	57	27
Raith Rovers	26	10	6	10	45	52	26
Stenhousemuir	26	8	7	11	43	53	23
Dunfermline Athletic	26	10	3	13	50	72	23
St. Johnstone	26	9	4	13	45	47	22
Dundee United	26	9	4	13	53	60	22
Ayr United	26	9	2	15	56	73	20
Arbroath	26	7	6	13	42	63	20
Dumbarton	26	7	4	15	41	54	18
Cowdenbeath	26	6	6	14	44	77	18

SCOTTISH DIVISION 'C' 1946-47

Stirling Albion	18	13	4	1	66	22	30
Dundee Reserves	18	12	2	4	60	37	26
Leith Athletic	18	11	3	4	57	33	25
East Stirlingshire	18	10	2	6	54	40	22
St. Johnstone Reserves	18	8	5	5	52	37	21
Forfar Athletic	18	6	2	10	32	46	14
Montrose	18	5	2	11	39	53	12
Brechin City	18	4	4	10	42	60	12
Dundee United Reserves	18	3	3	12	42	77	9
Edinburgh City	18	3	3	12	36	75	9

1947 Scottish F.A. Cup

Semi-finals

Aberdeen vs Arbroath	2-0
Hibernian vs Motherwell	2-1

Final

Hampden Park, 19th April 1947

Aberdeen 2   (Hamilton, Williams)
Hibernian 1   (Cuthbertson)

Attendance 82,140

1946/47 Scottish League Cup

Semi-finals

Rangers vs Hibernian	3-1
Aberdeen vs Heart of Midlothian	6-2

Final

Hampden Park, 5th April 1947

Rangers 4   (Duncanson 2, Williamson, Gillick)
Aberdeen 0

Attendance 82,700

SCOTTISH DIVISION 'A' 1947-48

Hibernian	30	22	4	4	86	27	48
Rangers	30	21	4	5	64	28	46
Partick Thistle	30	16	4	10	61	42	36
Dundee	30	15	3	12	67	51	33
St. Mirren	30	13	5	12	54	58	31
Clyde	30	12	7	11	52	57	31
Falkirk	30	10	10	10	55	48	30
Motherwell	30	13	3	14	45	47	29
Heart of Midlothian	30	10	8	12	37	42	28
Aberdeen	30	10	7	13	45	45	27
Third Lanark	30	10	6	14	56	73	26
Celtic	30	10	5	15	41	56	25
Queen of the South	30	10	5	15	49	74	25
Greenock Morton	30	9	6	15	47	43	24
Airdrieonians	30	7	7	16	39	78	21
Queen's Park	30	9	2	19	45	75	20

SCOTTISH DIVISION 'B' 1947-48

East Fife	30	25	3	2	103	36	53
Albion Rovers	30	19	4	7	58	49	42
Hamilton Academical	30	17	6	7	75	45	40
Raith Rovers	30	14	6	10	83	66	34
Cowdenbeath	30	12	8	10	56	53	32
Kilmarnock	30	13	4	13	72	62	30
Dunfermline Athletic	30	13	3	14	72	71	29
Stirling Albion	30	11	6	13	85	66	28
St. Johnstone	30	11	5	14	69	63	27
Ayr United	30	9	9	12	59	61	27
Dumbarton	30	9	7	14	66	79	25
Alloa Athletic	30	10	6	14	53	77	24
Arbroath	30	10	3	17	55	62	23
Stenhousemuir	30	6	11	13	53	83	23
Dundee United	30	10	2	18	58	88	22
Leith Athletic	30	6	7	17	45	84	19

SCOTTISH DIVISION 'C' 1947-48

East Stirlingshire	22	18	3	1	72	26	39
East Fife Reserves	22	16	3	3	63	38	35
Forfar Athletic	22	14	4	4	69	40	32
Kilmarnock Reserves	22	10	3	9	52	41	23
St. Johnstone Reserves	22	9	4	9	44	51	22
Dundee United Reserves	22	9	2	11	56	57	20
Montrose	22	7	5	10	43	70	19
Arbroath Reserves	22	7	4	11	45	57	18
Leith Athletic	22	7	3	12	44	60	17
Brechin City	22	6	4	12	43	54	16
Edinburgh City	22	6	3	13	54	60	15
Raith Rovers Reserves	22	3	2	17	36	67	8

1948 Scottish F.A. Cup

Semi-finals

Rangers vs Hibernian	1-0
Greenock Morton vs Celtic	1-0

Final

Hampden Park, 17th April 1948

Rangers 1   (Gillick)
Greenock Morton 1 (aet.)   (Whyte)

Attendance 131,629

Replay

Hampden Park, 21st April 1948

Rangers 1   (Williamson)
Greenock Morton 0 (aet.)

Attendance 133,570

1947/48 Scottish League Cup

Semi-finals

Aberdeen vs East Fife	0-1
Falkirk vs Rangers	1-0

Final

Hampden Park, 25th October 1947

East Fife 0
Falkirk 0 (aet.)

Attendance 53,785

Replay

Hampden Park, 1st November 1947

East Fife 4   (Duncan 3, Adams)
Falkirk 1   (Aikman)

Attendance 31,000

SCOTTISH DIVISION 'A' 1948-49

Rangers	30	20	6	4	63	32	46
Dundee	30	20	5	5	71	48	45
Hibernian	30	17	5	8	75	52	39
East Fife	30	16	3	11	64	46	35
Falkirk	30	12	8	10	70	54	32
Celtic	30	12	7	11	48	40	31
Third Lanark	30	13	5	12	56	52	31
Heart of Midlothian	30	12	6	12	64	54	30
St. Mirren	30	13	4	13	51	47	30
Queen of the South	30	11	8	11	47	53	30
Partick Thistle	30	9	9	12	50	63	27
Motherwell	30	10	5	15	44	49	25
Aberdeen	30	7	11	12	39	48	25
Clyde	30	9	6	15	50	67	24
Greenock Morton	30	7	8	15	39	51	22
Albion Rovers	30	3	2	25	30	105	8

SCOTTISH DIVISION 'B' 1948-49

Raith Rovers	30	20	2	8	80	44	72
Stirling Albion	30	20	2	8	71	47	72
Airdrieonians	30	16	9	5	76	42	41
Dunfermline Athletic	30	16	9	5	80	58	41
Queen's Park	30	14	7	9	66	49	35
St. Johnstone	30	14	4	12	58	51	32
Arbroath	30	12	8	10	62	56	32
Dundee United	30	10	7	13	60	67	27
Ayr United	30	10	7	13	51	70	27
Hamilton Academical	30	9	8	13	48	57	26
Kilmarnock	30	9	7	14	58	61	25
Stenhousemuir	30	8	8	14	50	54	24
Cowdenbeath	30	9	5	16	53	58	23
Alloa Athletic	30	10	3	17	42	85	23
Dumbarton	30	8	6	16	52	79	22
East Stirlingshire	30	6	6	18	38	67	18

SCOTTISH DIVISION 'C' 1948-49

Forfar Athletic	22	17	1	4	80	37	35
Leith Athletic	22	15	3	4	76	29	33
Brechin City	22	13	4	5	67	38	30
Montrose	22	10	5	7	59	50	25
Queen's Park Strollers	22	9	6	7	52	52	24
Airdrieonians	22	9	4	9	66	66	22
St. Johnstone Reserves	22	9	4	9	42	44	22
Dundee United Reserves	22	10	2	10	58	67	22
Raith Rovers Reserves	22	6	7	9	56	60	19
Kilmarnock Reserves	22	5	3	14	41	54	13
Dunfermline Athletic	22	4	3	15	43	84	11
Edinburgh City	22	2	4	16	26	85	8

1949 Scottish F.A. Cup

Semi-final

Rangers vs East Fife	3-0
Clyde vs Dundee	2-2, 2-1

Final

Hampden Park, 23rd April 1949

Rangers 4 (Young 2 (2 pens), Williamson, Duncanson)
Clyde 1 (Galletly)

Attendance 102,162

1948/49 Scottish League Cup

Semi-finals

Rangers vs Dundee	4-1
Raith Rovers vs Hamilton Academical	2-0

Final

Hampden Park, 12th March 1949

Rangers 2 (Gillick, Paton)
Raith Rovers 0

Attendance 57,540

SCOTTISH DIVISION 'A' 1949-50

Rangers	30	22	6	2	58	26	50
Hibernian	30	22	5	3	86	34	49
Heart of Midlothian	30	20	3	7	86	40	43
East Fife	30	15	7	8	58	43	37
Celtic	30	14	7	9	51	50	35
Dundee	30	12	7	11	49	46	31
Partick Thistle	30	13	3	14	55	45	29
Aberdeen	30	11	4	15	48	56	26
Raith Rovers	30	9	8	13	45	54	26
Motherwell	30	10	5	15	53	58	25
St. Mirren	30	8	9	13	42	49	25
Third Lanark	30	11	3	16	44	62	25
Clyde	30	10	4	16	56	73	24
Falkirk	30	7	10	13	48	72	24
Queen of the South	30	5	6	19	31	63	16
Stirling Albion	30	6	3	21	38	77	15

SCOTTISH DIVISION 'B' 1949-50

Greenock Morton	30	20	7	3	77	33	47
Airdrieonians	30	19	6	5	79	40	44
Dunfermline Athletic	30	16	4	10	71	57	36
St. Johnstone	30	15	6	9	64	56	36
Cowdenbeath	30	16	3	11	63	56	35
Hamilton Academical	30	14	6	10	57	44	34
Dundee United	30	14	5	11	74	56	33
Kilmarnock	30	14	5	11	50	43	33
Queen's Park	30	12	7	11	63	59	31
Forfar Athletic	30	11	8	11	53	56	30
Albion Rovers	30	10	7	13	49	61	27
Stenhousemuir	30	8	8	14	54	72	24
Ayr United	30	8	6	16	53	80	22
Arbroath	30	5	9	16	47	69	19
Dumbarton	30	6	4	20	39	62	16
Alloa Athletic	30	5	3	22	47	96	13

1950 Scottish F.A. Cup

Semi-final

Rangers vs Queen of the South	1-1, 3-0
East Fife vs Partick Thistle	2-1

Final

Hampden Park, 22nd April 1950

Rangers 3 (Findlay, Thornton 2)
East Fife 0

Attendance 120,015

1949/50 Scottish League Cup

Semi-finals

East Fife vs Rangers	2-1
Dunfermline Athletic vs Hibernian	2-1

Final

Hampden Park, 29th October 1949

East Fife 3 (Fleming, Duncan, Morris)
Dunfermline Athletic 0

Attendance 39,744

SCOTTISH DIVISION 'A' 1950-51

Hibernian	30	22	4	4	78	26	48
Rangers	30	17	4	9	64	37	38
Dundee	30	15	8	7	47	30	38
Heart of Midlothian	30	16	5	9	72	45	37
Aberdeen	30	15	5	10	61	50	35
Partick Thistle	30	13	7	10	57	48	33
Celtic	30	12	5	13	48	46	29
Raith Rovers	30	13	2	15	52	52	28
Motherwell	30	11	6	13	58	65	28
East Fife	30	10	8	12	48	66	28
St. Mirren	30	9	7	14	35	51	25
Greenock Morton	30	10	4	16	47	59	24
Third Lanark	30	11	2	17	40	51	24
Airdrieonians	30	10	4	16	52	67	24
Clyde	30	8	7	15	37	57	23
Falkirk	30	7	4	19	35	81	18

SCOTTISH DIVISION 'B' 1950-51

Queen of the South	30	21	3	6	69	35	45
Stirling Albion	30	21	3	6	78	44	45
Ayr United	30	15	6	9	64	40	36
Dundee United	30	16	4	10	78	58	36
St. Johnstone	30	14	5	11	68	53	33
Queen's Park	30	13	7	10	56	53	33
Hamilton Academical	30	12	8	10	65	49	32
Albion Rovers	30	14	4	12	56	51	32
Dumbarton	30	12	5	13	52	53	29
Dunfermline Athletic	30	12	4	14	58	73	28
Cowdenbeath	30	12	3	15	61	57	27
Kilmarnock	30	8	8	14	44	49	24
Arbroath	30	8	5	17	46	78	21
Forfar Athletic	30	9	3	18	43	76	21
Stenhousemuir	30	9	2	19	51	80	20
Alloa Athletic	30	7	4	19	58	98	18

1951 Scottish F.A. Cup

Semi-final

Celtic vs Raith Rovers	3-2
Hibernian vs Motherwell	1-3

Final

Hampden Park, 21st April 1951

Celtic 1 (McPhail)
Motherwell 0

Attendance 133,343

1950/51 Scottish League Cup

Semi-finals

Motherwell vs Ayr United	4-3
Hibernian vs Queen of the South	3-1

Final

Hampden Park, 28th October 1950

Motherwell 3   (Kelly, Forrest, Watters)

Hibernian 0

Attendance 64,074

SCOTTISH DIVISION 'A' 1951-52

Hibernian	30	20	5	5	92	36	45
Rangers	30	16	9	5	61	31	41
East Fife	30	17	3	10	71	49	37
Heart of Midlothian	30	14	7	9	69	53	35
Raith Rovers	30	14	5	11	43	42	33
Partick Thistle	30	12	7	11	48	51	31
Motherwell	30	12	7	11	51	57	31
Dundee	30	11	6	13	53	52	28
Celtic	30	10	8	12	52	55	28
Queen of the South	30	10	8	12	50	60	28
Aberdeen	30	10	7	13	65	58	27
Third Lanark	30	9	8	13	51	62	26
Airdrieonians	30	11	4	15	54	69	26
St. Mirren	30	10	5	15	43	58	25
Greenock Morton	30	9	6	15	49	56	24
Stirling Albion	30	5	5	20	36	99	15

SCOTTISH DIVISION 'B' 1951-52

Clyde	30	19	6	5	100	45	44
Falkirk	30	18	7	5	80	34	43
Ayr United	30	17	5	8	55	45	39
Dundee United	30	16	5	9	75	60	37
Kilmarnock	30	16	2	12	62	48	34
Dunfermline Athletic	30	15	2	13	74	65	32
Alloa Athletic	30	13	6	11	55	49	32
Cowdenbeath	30	12	8	10	66	67	32
Hamilton Academical	30	12	6	12	47	51	30
Dumbarton	30	10	8	12	51	57	28
St. Johnstone	30	9	7	14	62	68	25
Forfar Athletic	30	10	4	16	59	97	24
Stenhousemuir	30	8	6	16	57	74	22
Albion Rovers	30	6	10	14	39	57	22
Queen's Park	30	8	4	18	40	62	20
Arbroath	30	6	4	20	40	83	16

1952 Scottish F.A. Cup

Semi-finals

Motherwell vs Heart of Midlothian	1-1, 1-1, 3-1
Dundee vs Third Lanark	2-0

Final

Hampden Park, 19th April 1952

Motherwell 4   (Watson, Redpath, Humphries, Kelly)

Dundee 0

Attendance 136,274

1951/52 Scottish League Cup

Semi-finals

Dundee vs Motherwell	5-1
Rangers vs Celtic	3-0

Final

Hampden Park, 27th October 1951

Dundee 3   (Flavell, Pattillo, Boyd)

Rangers 2   (Findlay, Thornton)

Attendance 92,325

SCOTTISH DIVISION 'A' 1952-53

Rangers	30	18	7	5	80	39	43
Hibernian	30	19	5	6	93	51	43
East Fife	30	16	7	7	72	48	39
Heart of Midlothian	30	12	6	12	59	50	30
Clyde	30	13	4	13	78	78	30
St. Mirren	30	11	8	11	52	58	30
Dundee	30	9	1	8	44	37	29
Celtic	30	11	7	12	51	54	29
Partick Thistle	30	10	9	11	55	63	29
Queen of the South	30	10	8	12	43	61	28
Aberdeen	30	11	5	14	64	68	27
Raith Rovers	30	9	8	13	47	53	26
Falkirk	30	11	4	15	53	63	26
Airdrieonians	30	10	6	14	53	75	26
Motherwell	30	10	5	15	57	80	25
Third Lanark	30	8	4	18	52	75	20

SCOTTISH DIVISION 'B' 1952-53

Stirling Albion	30	20	4	6	64	43	44
Hamilton Academical	30	20	3	7	72	40	43
Queen's Park	30	15	7	8	70	46	37
Kilmarnock	30	17	2	11	74	48	36
Ayr United	30	17	2	11	76	56	36
Greenock Morton	30	15	3	12	79	57	33
Arbroath	30	13	7	10	52	57	33
Dundee United	30	12	5	13	52	56	29
Alloa Athletic	30	12	5	13	63	68	29
Dumbarton	30	11	6	13	58	67	28
Dunfermline Athletic	30	9	9	12	51	58	27
Stenhousemuir	30	10	6	14	56	65	26
Cowdenbeath	30	8	7	15	37	54	23
St. Johnstone	30	8	6	16	41	63	22
Forfar Athletic	30	8	4	18	54	88	20
Albion Rovers	30	5	4	21	44	77	14

1953 Scottish F.A. Cup

Semi-finals

Rangers vs Heart of Midlothian	2-1
Third Lanark vs Aberdeen	1-1, 1-2

Final

Hampden Park, 25th April 1953

Rangers 1   (Prentice)

Aberdeen 1   (Yorston)

Attendance 129,761

Replay

Hampden Park, 29th April 1953

Rangers 1   (Simpson)

Aberdeen 0

Attendance 112,619

1952/53 Scottish League Cup

Semi-finals

Dundee vs Hibernian	2-1
Kilmarnock vs Rangers	1-0

Final

Hampden Park, 25th October 1952

Dundee 2   (Flavell 2)

Kilmarnock 0

Attendance 51,830

SCOTTISH DIVISION 'A' 1953-54

Celtic	30	20	3	7	72	29	43
Heart of Midlothian	30	16	6	8	70	45	38
Partick Thistle	30	17	1	12	76	54	35
Rangers	30	13	8	9	56	35	34
Hibernian	30	15	4	11	72	51	34
East Fife	30	13	8	9	55	45	34
Dundee	30	14	6	10	46	47	34
Clyde	30	15	4	11	64	67	34
Aberdeen	30	15	3	12	66	51	33
Queen of the South	30	14	4	12	72	53	32
St. Mirren	30	12	4	14	44	54	28
Raith Rovers	30	10	6	14	56	60	26
Falkirk	30	9	7	14	47	61	25
Stirling Albion	30	10	4	16	39	62	24
Airdrieonians	30	5	5	20	41	92	15
Hamilton Academical	30	4	3	23	29	94	11

SCOTTISH DIVISION 'A' 1954-55

Aberdeen	30	24	1	5	73	26	49
Celtic	30	19	8	3	76	37	46
Rangers	30	19	3	8	67	33	41
Heart of Midlothian	30	16	7	7	74	45	39
Hibernian	30	15	4	11	64	54	34
St. Mirren	30	12	8	10	55	54	32
Clyde	30	11	9	10	59	50	31
Dundee	30	13	4	13	48	48	30
Partick Thistle	30	11	7	12	49	61	29
Kilmarnock	30	10	6	14	46	58	26
East Fife	30	9	6	15	51	62	24
Falkirk	30	8	8	14	42	54	24
Queen of the South	30	9	6	15	38	56	24
Raith Rovers	30	10	3	17	49	57	23
Motherwell	30	9	4	17	42	62	22
Stirling Albion	30	2	2	26	29	105	6

SCOTTISH DIVISION 'B' 1953-54

Motherwell	30	21	3	6	109	43	45
Kilmarnock	30	19	4	7	71	39	42
Third Lanark	30	13	10	7	78	48	36
Stenhousemuir	30	14	8	8	66	58	36
Greenock Morton	30	15	3	12	85	65	33
St. Johnstone	30	14	3	13	80	71	31
Albion Rovers	30	12	7	11	55	63	31
Dunfermline Athletic	30	11	9	10	48	57	31
Ayr United	30	11	8	11	50	56	30
Queen's Park	30	9	9	12	56	51	27
Alloa Athletic	30	7	10	13	50	72	24
Forfar Athletic	30	10	4	16	38	69	24
Cowdenbeath	30	9	5	16	67	81	23
Arbroath	30	8	7	15	53	67	23
Dundee United	30	8	6	16	54	79	22
Dumbarton	30	7	8	15	51	92	22

SCOTTISH DIVISION 'B' 1954-55

Airdrieonians	30	18	10	2	103	61	46
Dunfermline Athletic	30	19	4	7	72	40	42
Hamilton Academical	30	17	5	8	74	51	39
Queen's Park	30	15	5	10	65	36	35
Third Lanark	30	13	7	10	63	49	33
Stenhousemuir	30	12	8	10	70	51	32
St. Johnstone	30	15	2	13	60	51	32
Ayr United	30	14	4	12	61	73	32
Greenock Morton	30	12	5	13	58	69	29
Forfar Athletic	30	11	6	13	63	80	28
Albion Rovers	30	8	10	12	50	69	26
Arbroath	30	8	8	14	55	72	24
Dundee United	30	8	6	16	55	70	22
Cowdenbeath	30	8	5	17	55	72	21
Alloa Athletic	30	7	6	17	51	75	20
Brechin City	30	8	3	19	53	89	19

1954 Scottish F.A. Cup

Semi-finals

Celtic vs Motherwell	2-2, 3-1
Rangers vs Aberdeen	0-6

Final

Hampden Park, 24th April 1954

Celtic 2 (Young (og), Fallon)
Aberdeen 1 (Buckley)

Attendance 130,060

1953/54 Scottish League Cup

Semi-finals

East Fife vs Hibernian	3-2
Partick Thistle vs Rangers	2-0

Final

Hampden Park, 24th October 1953

East Fife 3 (Gardiner, Fleming, Christie)
Partick Thistle 2 (Walker, McKenzie)

Attendance 38,529

1955 Scottish F.A. Cup

Semi-finals

Aberdeen vs Clyde	2-2, 0-1
Airdrieonians vs Celtic	2-2, 0-2

Final

Hampden Park, 23rd April 1955

Clyde 1 (Robertson)
Celtic 1 (Walsh)

Attendance 106,234

Replay

Hampden Park, 27th April 1955

Clyde 1 (Ring)
Celtic 0

Attendance 68,831

1954/55 Scottish League Cup

Semi-finals

Airdrieonians vs Heart of Midlothian	1-4
East Fife vs Motherwell	1-2

Final

Hampden Park, 23rd October 1954

Heart of Midlothian 4 (Bauld 3, Wardhaugh)
Motherwell 2 (Redpath (pen), Bain)

Attendance 55,640

SCOTTISH DIVISION 'A' 1955-56

Rangers	34	22	8	4	85	27	52
Aberdeen	34	18	10	6	87	50	46
Heart of Midlothian	34	19	7	8	99	47	45
Hibernian	34	19	7	8	86	50	45
Celtic	34	16	9	9	55	39	41
Queen of the South	34	16	5	13	69	73	37
Airdrieonians	34	14	8	12	85	96	36
Kilmarnock	34	12	10	12	52	45	34
Partick Thistle	34	13	7	14	62	60	33
Motherwell	34	11	11	12	53	59	33
Raith Rovers	34	12	9	13	58	75	33
East Fife	34	13	5	16	61	69	31
Dundee	34	12	6	16	56	65	30
Falkirk	34	11	6	17	58	75	28
St. Mirren	34	10	7	17	57	70	27
Dunfermline Athletic	34	10	6	18	42	82	26
Clyde	34	8	6	20	50	74	22
Stirling Albion	34	4	5	25	23	82	13

SCOTTISH DIVISION 'B' 1955-56

Queen's Park	36	23	8	5	78	28	54
Ayr United	36	24	3	9	103	55	51
St. Johnstone	36	21	7	8	86	45	49
Dumbarton	36	21	5	10	83	62	47
Stenhousemuir	36	20	4	12	82	54	44
Brechin City	36	18	6	12	60	56	42
Cowdenbeath	36	16	7	13	80	85	39
Dundee United	36	12	14	10	78	65	38
Greenock Morton	36	15	6	15	71	69	36
Third Lanark	36	16	3	17	80	64	35
Hamilton Academical	36	13	7	16	86	84	33
Stranraer	36	14	5	17	77	92	33
Alloa Athletic	36	12	7	17	67	73	31
Berwick Rangers	36	11	9	16	52	77	31
Forfar Athletic	36	10	9	17	62	75	29
East Stirlingshire	36	9	10	17	66	94	28
Albion Rovers	36	8	11	17	58	82	27
Arbroath	36	10	6	20	47	67	26
Montrose	36	4	3	29	44	133	11

1956 Scottish F.A. Cup

Semi-finals
Heart of Midlothian vs Raith Rovers	0-0, 3-0
Celtic vs Clyde	2-1

Final
Hampden Park, 21st April 1956

Heart of Midlothian 3   (Crawford 2, Conn)

Celtic 1   (Haughney)

Attendance 132,840

1955/56 Scottish League Cup

Semi-finals
Rangers vs Aberdeen	1-2
Motherwell vs St. Mirren	3-3, 0-2

Final
Hampden Park, 22nd October 1955

Aberdeen 2   (Mallan (og), Leggat)

St. Mirren 1   (Holmes)

Attendance 44,106

SCOTTISH DIVISION 1 1956-57

Rangers	34	26	3	5	96	48	55
Heart of Midlothian	34	24	5	5	81	48	53
Kilmarnock	34	16	10	8	57	39	42
Raith Rovers	34	16	7	11	84	58	39
Celtic	34	15	8	11	58	43	38
Aberdeen	34	18	2	14	79	59	38
Motherwell	34	16	5	13	75	66	37
Partick Thistle	34	13	8	13	53	51	34
Hibernian	34	12	9	13	69	56	33
Dundee	34	13	6	15	55	61	32
Airdrieonians	34	13	4	17	77	89	30
St. Mirren	34	12	6	16	58	72	30
Queen's Park	34	11	7	16	55	59	29
Falkirk	34	10	8	16	51	70	28
East Fife	34	10	6	18	59	82	26
Queen of the South	34	10	5	19	54	96	25
Dunfermline Athletic	34	9	6	19	54	74	24
Ayr United	34	7	5	22	48	89	19

SCOTTISH DIVISION 2 1956-57

Clyde	36	29	6	1	112	39	64
Third Lanark	36	24	3	9	105	51	51
Cowdenbeath	36	20	5	11	87	65	45
Greenock Morton	36	18	7	11	81	70	43
Albion Rovers	36	18	6	12	98	80	42
Brechin City	36	15	10	11	72	68	40
Stranraer	36	15	10	11	79	77	40
Stirling Albion	36	17	5	14	81	64	39
Dumbarton	36	17	4	15	101	70	38
Arbroath	36	17	4	15	79	57	38
Hamilton Academical	36	14	8	14	69	68	36
St. Johnstone	36	14	6	16	79	80	34
Dundee United	36	14	6	16	75	80	34
Stenhousemuir	36	13	6	17	71	81	32
Alloa Athletic	36	11	5	20	66	99	27
Forfar Athletic	36	9	5	22	75	100	23
Montrose	36	7	7	22	54	124	21
Berwick Rangers	36	7	6	23	58	114	20
East Stirlingshire	36	5	7	24	56	121	17

1957 Scottish F.A. Cup

Semi-finals
Falkirk vs Raith Rovers	2-2, 2-0
Celtic vs Kilmarnock	1-1, 1-3

Final
Hampden Park, 20th April 1957

Falkirk 1   (Prentice (pen))

Kilmarnock 1   (Curlett)

Attendance 81,375

Replay
Hampden Park, 24th April 1957

Falkirk 2   (Merchant, Moran)

Kilmarnock 1   (Curlett)

Attendance 79,960

1956/57 Scottish League Cup

Semi-finals
Celtic vs Clyde	2-0
Partick Thistle vs Dundee	0-0, 3-2

Final
Hampden Park, 27th October 1956

Celtic 0

Partick Thistle 0 (aet.)

Attendance 59,000

Replay
Hampden Park, 31st October 1956

Celtic 3   (McPhail 2, Collins)

Partick Thistle 0

Attendance not known

SCOTTISH DIVISION 1 1957-58

Heart of Midlothian	34	29	4	1	132	29	62
Rangers	34	22	5	7	89	49	49
Celtic	34	19	8	7	84	47	46
Clyde	34	18	6	10	84	61	42
Kilmarnock	34	14	9	11	60	55	37
Partick Thistle	34	17	3	14	69	71	37
Raith Rovers	34	14	7	13	66	56	35
Motherwell	34	12	8	14	68	67	32
Hibernian	34	13	5	16	59	60	31
Falkirk	34	11	9	14	64	82	31
Dundee	34	13	5	16	49	65	31
Aberdeen	34	14	2	18	68	76	30
St. Mirren	34	11	8	15	59	66	30
Third Lanark	34	13	4	17	69	88	30
Queen of the South	34	12	5	17	61	72	29
Airdrieonians	34	13	2	19	71	92	28
East Fife	34	10	3	21	45	88	23
Queen's Park	34	4	1	29	41	114	9

SCOTTISH DIVISION 1 1958-59

Rangers	34	21	8	5	92	51	50
Heart of Midlothian	34	21	6	7	92	51	48
Motherwell	34	18	8	8	83	50	44
Dundee	34	16	9	9	61	51	41
Airdrieonians	34	15	7	12	64	62	37
Celtic	34	14	8	12	70	53	36
St. Mirren	34	14	7	13	71	74	35
Kilmarnock	34	13	8	13	58	51	34
Partick Thistle	34	14	6	14	59	66	34
Hibernian	34	13	6	15	68	70	32
Third Lanark	34	11	10	13	74	83	32
Stirling Albion	34	11	8	15	54	64	30
Aberdeen	34	12	5	17	63	66	29
Raith Rovers	34	10	9	15	60	70	29
Clyde	34	12	4	18	62	66	28
Dunfermline Athletic	34	10	8	16	68	87	28
Falkirk	34	10	7	17	58	79	27
Queen of the South	34	6	6	22	38	101	18

SCOTTISH DIVISION 2 1957-58

Stirling Albion	36	25	5	6	105	48	55
Dunfermline Athletic	36	24	5	7	120	42	53
Arbroath	36	21	5	10	89	72	47
Dumbarton	36	20	4	12	92	57	44
Ayr United	36	18	6	12	98	81	42
Cowdenbeath	36	17	8	11	100	85	42
Brechin City	36	16	8	12	80	81	40
Alloa Athletic	36	15	9	12	88	78	39
Dundee United	36	12	9	15	81	77	33
Hamilton Academical	36	12	9	15	70	79	33
St. Johnstone	36	12	9	15	67	85	33
Forfar Athletic	36	13	6	17	70	71	32
Greenock Morton	36	12	8	16	77	83	32
Montrose	36	13	6	17	55	72	32
East Stirlingshire	36	12	5	19	55	79	29
Stenhousemuir	36	12	5	19	68	98	29
Albion Rovers	36	12	5	19	53	79	29
Stranraer	36	9	7	20	54	83	25
Berwick Rangers	36	5	5	26	37	109	15

SCOTTISH DIVISION 2 1958-59

Ayr United	36	28	4	4	115	48	60
Arbroath	36	23	5	8	86	59	51
Stenhousemuir	36	20	6	10	87	68	46
Dumbarton	36	19	7	10	94	61	45
Brechin City	36	16	10	10	79	65	42
St. Johnstone	36	15	10	11	54	44	40
Hamilton Academical	36	15	8	13	76	62	38
East Fife	36	15	8	13	83	81	38
Berwick Rangers	36	16	6	14	63	66	38
Albion Rovers	36	14	7	15	84	79	35
Greenock Morton	36	13	8	15	68	85	34
Forfar Athletic	36	12	9	15	73	87	33
Alloa Athletic	36	12	7	17	76	81	31
Cowdenbeath	36	13	5	18	67	79	31
East Stirlingshire	36	10	8	18	50	77	28
Stranraer	36	8	11	17	63	76	27
Dundee United	36	9	7	20	62	86	25
Queen's Park	36	9	6	21	53	80	24
Montrose	36	6	6	24	49	96	18

1958 Scottish F.A. Cup

Semi-finals

Clyde vs Motherwell	3-2
Rangers vs Hibernian	2-2, 1-2

Final

Hampden Park, 26th April 1958

Clyde 1 (Coyle)
Hibernian 0

Attendance 95,123

1959 Scottish F.A. Cup

Semi-finals

St. Mirren vs Celtic	4-0
Third Lanark vs Aberdeen	1-1, 0-1

Final

Hampden Park, 25th April 1959

St. Mirren 3 (Bryceland, Miller, Baker)
Aberdeen 1 (Baird)

Attendance 108,591

1957/58 Scottish League Cup

Semi-finals

Clyde vs Celtic	2-4
Rangers vs Brechin City	4-0

Final

Hampden Park, 19th October 1957

Celtic 7 (Mochan 2, Wilson, McPhail 3, Fernie (pen))
Rangers 1 (Simpson)

Attendance 82,293

1958/59 Scottish League Cup

Semi-finals

Heart of Midlothian vs Kilmarnock	3-0
Celtic vs Partick Thistle	1-2

Final

Hampden Park, 25th October 1958

Heart of Midlothian 5 (Bauld 2, Murray 2, Hamilton)
Partick Thistle 1 (Smith)

Attendance 59,960

SCOTTISH DIVISION 1 1959-60

Heart of Midlothian	34	23	8	3	102	51	54
Kilmarnock	34	24	2	8	67	45	50
Rangers	34	17	8	9	72	38	42
Dundee	34	16	10	8	70	49	42
Motherwell	34	16	8	10	71	61	40
Clyde	34	15	9	10	77	69	39
Hibernian	34	14	7	13	106	85	35
Ayr United	34	14	6	14	65	73	34
Celtic	34	12	9	13	73	59	33
Partick Thistle	34	14	4	16	54	78	32
Raith Rovers	34	14	3	17	64	62	31
Third Lanark	34	13	4	17	75	83	30
Dunfermline Athletic	34	10	9	15	72	80	29
St. Mirren	34	11	6	17	78	86	28
Aberdeen	34	11	6	17	54	72	28
Airdrieonians	34	11	6	17	56	80	28
Stirling Albion	34	7	8	19	55	72	22
Arbroath	34	6	7	23	38	106	15

SCOTTISH DIVISION 2 1959-60

St. Johnstone	36	24	5	7	87	47	53
Dundee United	36	22	6	8	90	45	50
Queen of the South	36	21	7	8	94	52	49
Hamilton Academical	36	21	6	9	91	62	48
Stenhousemuir	36	20	4	12	86	67	44
Dumbarton	36	18	7	11	67	53	43
Montrose	36	19	5	12	60	52	43
Falkirk	36	15	9	12	77	43	39
Berwick Rangers	36	16	5	15	62	55	37
Albion Rovers	36	14	8	14	71	78	36
Queen's Park	36	17	2	17	65	79	36
Brechin City	36	14	6	16	66	66	34
Alloa Athletic	36	13	5	18	70	85	31
Greenock Morton	36	10	8	18	67	79	28
East Stirlingshire	36	10	8	18	68	82	28
Forfar Athletic	36	10	8	18	53	84	28
Stranraer	36	10	3	23	53	77	23
East Fife	36	7	6	23	50	84	20
Cowdenbeath	36	6	2	28	42	124	14

SCOTTISH DIVISION 1 1960-61

Rangers	34	23	5	6	88	46	51
Kilmarnock	34	21	8	5	77	45	50
Third Lanark	34	20	2	12	100	80	42
Celtic	34	15	9	10	64	46	39
Motherwell	34	15	8	11	70	57	38
Aberdeen	34	14	8	12	72	72	36
Heart of Midlothian	34	13	8	13	51	53	34
Hibernian	34	15	4	15	66	69	34
Dundee United	34	13	7	14	60	58	33
Dundee	34	13	6	15	61	53	32
Partick Thistle	34	13	6	15	59	69	32
Dunfermline Athletic	34	12	7	15	65	81	31
Airdrieonians	34	10	10	14	61	71	30
St. Mirren	34	11	7	16	53	58	29
St. Johnstone	34	10	9	15	47	63	29
Raith Rovers	34	10	7	17	46	67	27
Clyde	34	6	11	17	55	77	23
Ayr United	34	5	12	17	51	81	22

SCOTTISH DIVISION 2 1960-61

Stirling Albion	36	24	7	5	89	37	55
Falkirk	36	24	6	6	100	40	54
Stenhousemuir	36	24	2	10	99	69	50
Stranraer	36	19	6	11	83	55	44
Queen of the South	36	20	3	13	77	52	43
Hamilton Academical	36	17	7	12	84	80	41
Montrose	36	19	2	15	75	65	40
Cowdenbeath	36	17	6	13	71	65	40
Berwick Rangers	36	14	9	13	62	69	37
Dumbarton	36	15	5	16	78	82	35
Alloa Athletic	36	13	7	16	78	68	33
Arbroath	36	13	7	16	56	76	33
East Fife	36	14	4	18	70	80	32
Brechin City	36	9	9	18	60	78	27
Queen's Park	36	10	6	20	61	87	26
East Stirlingshire	36	9	7	20	59	100	25
Albion Rovers	36	9	6	21	60	89	24
Forfar Athletic	36	10	4	22	65	98	24
Greenock Morton	36	5	11	20	56	93	21

1960 Scottish F.A. Cup

Semi-finals

Rangers vs Celtic	1-1, 4-1
Clyde vs Kilmarnock	0-2

Final

Hampden Park, 23rd April 1960

Rangers 2 (Millar 2)
Kilmarnock 0

Attendance 108,017

1961 Scottish F.A. Cup

Semi-finals

Celtic vs Airdrieonians	4-0
Dunfermline Athletic vs St. Mirren	0-0, 1-0

Final

Hampden Park, 22nd April 1961

Dunfermline Athletic 0
Celtic 0

Attendance 113,328

Replay

Hampden Park, 26th April 1961

Dunfermline Athletic 2 (Thomson, Dickson)
Celtic 0

Attendance 87,866

1959/60 Scottish League Cup

Semi-finals

Heart of Midlothian vs Cowdenbeath	9-3
Third Lanark vs Arbroath	3-0

Final

Hampden Park, 24th October 1959

Heart of Midlothian 2 (Hamilton, Young)
Third Lanark 1 (Gray)

Attendance 57,994

1960/61 Scottish League Cup

Semi-finals

Rangers vs Queen of the South	7-0
Kilmarnock vs Hamilton Academical	5-1

Final

Hampden Park, 29th October 1960

Rangers 2 (Brand, Scott)
Kilmarnock 0

Attendance 82,063

SCOTTISH DIVISION 1 1961-62

Dundee	34	25	4	5	80	46	54
Rangers	34	22	7	5	84	31	51
Celtic	34	19	8	7	81	37	46
Dunfermline Athletic	34	19	5	10	77	46	43
Kilmarnock	34	16	10	8	74	58	42
Heart of Midlothian	34	16	6	12	54	49	38
Partick Thistle	34	16	3	15	60	55	35
Hibernian	34	14	5	15	58	72	33
Motherwell	34	13	6	15	65	62	32
Dundee United	34	13	6	15	70	71	32
Third Lanark	34	13	5	16	59	60	31
Aberdeen	34	10	9	15	60	73	29
Raith Rovers	34	10	7	17	51	73	27
Falkirk	34	11	4	19	45	68	26
Airdrieonians	34	9	7	18	57	78	25
St. Mirren	34	10	5	19	52	80	25
St. Johnstone	34	9	7	18	35	61	25
Stirling Albion	34	6	6	22	34	76	18

SCOTTISH DIVISION 1 1962-63

Rangers	34	25	7	2	94	28	57
Kilmarnock	34	20	8	6	92	40	48
Partick Thistle	34	20	6	8	66	44	46
Celtic	34	19	6	9	76	44	44
Heart of Midlothian	34	17	9	8	85	59	43
Aberdeen	34	17	7	10	70	47	41
Dundee United	34	15	11	8	67	52	41
Dunfermline Athletic	34	13	8	13	50	47	34
Dundee	34	12	9	13	60	49	33
Motherwell	34	10	11	13	60	63	31
Airdrieonians	34	14	2	18	52	76	30
St. Mirren	34	10	8	16	52	72	28
Falkirk	34	12	3	19	54	69	27
Third Lanark	34	9	8	17	56	68	26
Queen of the South	34	10	6	18	36	75	26
Hibernian	34	8	9	17	47	67	25
Clyde	34	9	5	20	49	83	23
Raith Rovers	34	2	5	27	35	118	9

SCOTTISH DIVISION 2 1961-62

Clyde	36	25	4	7	108	47	54
Queen of the South	36	24	5	7	78	33	53
Greenock Morton	36	19	6	11	78	64	44
Alloa Athletic	36	17	8	11	92	78	42
Montrose	36	15	11	10	63	50	41
Arbroath	36	17	7	12	66	59	41
Stranraer	36	14	11	11	61	62	39
Berwick Rangers	36	16	6	14	83	70	38
Ayr United	36	15	8	13	71	63	38
East Fife	36	15	7	14	60	59	37
East Stirlingshire	36	15	4	17	70	81	34
Queen's Park	36	12	9	15	64	62	33
Hamilton Academical	36	14	5	17	78	79	33
Cowdenbeath	36	11	9	16	65	77	31
Stenhousemuir	36	13	5	18	69	86	31
Forfar Athletic	36	11	8	17	68	76	30
Dumbarton	36	9	10	17	49	66	28
Albion Rovers	36	10	5	21	42	74	25
Brechin City	36	5	2	29	44	123	12

SCOTTISH DIVISION 2 1962-63

St. Johnstone	36	25	5	6	83	37	55
East Stirlingshire	36	20	9	7	80	50	49
Greenock Morton	36	23	2	11	100	49	48
Hamilton Academical	36	18	8	10	69	56	44
Stranraer	36	16	10	10	81	70	42
Arbroath	36	18	4	14	74	51	40
Albion Rovers	36	18	2	16	72	79	38
Cowdenbeath	36	15	7	14	72	61	37
Alloa Athletic	36	15	6	15	57	56	36
Stirling Albion	36	16	4	16	74	75	36
East Fife	36	15	6	15	60	69	36
Dumbarton	36	15	4	17	64	64	34
Ayr United	36	13	8	15	68	77	34
Queen's Park	36	13	6	17	68	72	32
Montrose	36	13	5	18	57	70	31
Stenhousemuir	36	13	5	18	54	75	31
Berwick Rangers	36	11	7	18	57	77	29
Forfar Athletic	36	9	5	22	73	99	23
Brechin City	36	3	3	30	39	113	9

1962 Scottish F.A. Cup

Semi-finals

Rangers vs Motherwell	3-1
Celtic vs St. Mirren	1-3

Final

Hampden Park, 21st April 1962

Rangers 2   (Brand, Wilson)
St. Mirren 0

Attendance 127,940

1961/62 Scottish League Cup

Semi-finals

Rangers vs St. Johnstone	3-2
Heart of Midlothian vs Stirling Albion	2-1

Final

Hampden Park, 28th October 1961

Rangers 1   (Millar (pen))
Heart of Midlothian 0 (aet.)   (Cumming (pen))

Attendance 88,635

Replay

Hampden Park, 18th December 1961

Rangers 3   (Millar, Brand, McMillan)
Heart of Midlothian 1   (Davidson)

Attendance 47,500

1963 Scottish F.A. Cup

Semi-finals

Rangers vs Dundee United	5-2
Raith Rovers vs Celtic	2-5

Final

Hampden Park, 4th May 1963

Rangers 1   (Brand)
Celtic 1   (Murdoch)

Attendance 129,643

Replay

Hampden Park, 15th May 1963

Rangers 3   (Wilson, Brand 2)
Celtic 0

Attendance 120,273

1962/63 Scottish League Cup

Semi-finals

St. Johnstone vs Heart of Midlothian	0-4
Rangers vs Kilmarnock	2-3

Final

Hampden Park, 27th October 1962

Heart of Midlothian 1   (Davidson)
Kilmarnock 0

Attendance 51,280

SCOTTISH DIVISION 1 1963-64

Rangers	34	25	5	4	85	31	55
Kilmarnock	34	22	5	7	77	40	49
Celtic	34	19	9	6	89	34	47
Heart of Midlothian	34	19	9	6	74	40	47
Dunfermline Athletic	34	18	9	7	64	33	45
Dundee	34	20	5	9	94	50	45
Partick Thistle	34	15	5	14	55	54	35
Dundee United	34	13	8	13	65	49	34
Aberdeen	34	12	8	14	53	53	32
Hibernian	34	12	6	16	59	66	30
Motherwell	34	9	11	14	51	62	29
St. Mirren	34	12	5	17	44	74	29
St. Johnstone	34	11	6	17	54	70	28
Falkirk	34	11	6	17	54	84	28
Airdrieonians	34	11	4	19	52	97	26
Third Lanark	34	9	7	18	47	78	25
Queen of the South	34	5	6	23	40	92	16
East Stirlingshire	34	5	2	27	37	91	12

SCOTTISH DIVISION 1 1964-65

Kilmarnock	34	22	6	6	62	33	50
Heart of Midlothian	34	22	6	6	90	49	50
Dunfermline Athletic	34	22	5	7	83	36	49
Hibernian	34	21	4	9	75	47	46
Rangers	34	18	8	8	78	35	44
Dundee	34	15	10	9	86	63	40
Clyde	34	17	6	11	64	58	40
Celtic	34	16	5	13	76	57	37
Dundee United	34	15	6	13	59	51	36
Greenock Morton	34	13	7	14	54	54	33
Partick Thistle	34	11	10	13	57	58	32
Aberdeen	34	12	8	14	59	75	32
St. Johnstone	34	9	11	14	57	62	29
Motherwell	34	10	8	16	45	54	28
St. Mirren	34	9	6	19	38	70	24
Falkirk	34	7	7	20	43	85	21
Airdrieonians	34	5	4	25	48	110	14
Third Lanark	34	3	1	30	22	99	7

SCOTTISH DIVISION 2 1963-64

Greenock Morton	36	32	3	1	135	37	67
Clyde	36	22	9	5	81	44	53
Arbroath	36	20	6	10	79	46	46
East Fife	36	16	13	7	92	57	45
Montrose	36	19	6	11	79	57	44
Dumbarton	36	16	6	14	67	59	38
Queen's Park	36	17	4	15	57	54	38
Stranraer	36	16	6	14	71	73	38
Albion Rovers	36	12	12	12	67	71	36
Raith Rovers	36	15	5	16	70	61	35
Stenhousemuir	36	15	5	16	83	75	35
Berwick Rangers	36	10	10	16	68	84	30
Hamilton Academical	36	12	6	18	65	81	30
Ayr United	36	12	5	19	58	83	29
Brechin City	36	10	8	18	61	98	28
Alloa Athletic	36	11	5	20	64	92	27
Cowdenbeath	36	7	11	18	46	72	25
Forfar Athletic	36	6	8	22	57	104	20
Stirling Albion	36	6	8	22	47	99	20

SCOTTISH DIVISION 2 1964-65

Stirling Albion	36	26	7	3	84	41	59
Hamilton Academical	36	21	8	7	86	53	50
Queen of the South	36	16	13	7	84	50	45
Queen's Park	36	17	9	10	57	41	43
E.S. Clydebank	36	15	10	11	64	50	40
Stranraer	36	17	6	13	74	64	40
Arbroath	36	13	13	10	56	51	39
Berwick Rangers	36	15	9	12	73	70	39
East Fife	36	15	7	14	78	77	37
Alloa Athletic	36	14	8	14	71	81	36
Albion Rovers	36	14	5	17	56	60	33
Cowdenbeath	36	11	10	15	55	62	32
Raith Rovers	36	9	14	13	54	61	32
Dumbarton	36	13	6	17	55	67	32
Stenhousemuir	36	11	8	17	49	74	30
Montrose	36	10	9	17	80	91	29
Forfar Athletic	36	9	7	20	63	89	25
Ayr United	36	9	6	21	49	67	24
Brechin City	36	6	7	23	53	102	19

1964 Scottish F.A. Cup

Semi-finals

Rangers vs Dunfermline Athletic	1-0
Kilmarnock vs Dundee	0-4

Final

Hampden Park, 25th April 1964

Rangers 3   (Millar 2, Brand)
Dundee 1   (Cameron)

Attendance 120,982

1965 Scottish F.A. Cup

Semi-finals

Celtic vs Motherwell	2-2, 3-0
Hibernian vs Dunfermline Athletic	0-2

Final

Hampden Park, 24th April 1965

Celtic 3   (Auld 2, McNeill)
Dunfermline Athletic 2   (Melrose, McLaughlin)

Attendance 108,800

1963/64 Scottish League Cup

Semi-finals

Rangers vs Berwick Rangers	3-1
Greenock Morton vs Hibernian	1-1, 1-0

Final

Hampden Park, 26th October 1963

Rangers 5   (Forrest 4, Willoughby)
Greenock Morton 0

Attendance 105,907

1964/65 Scottish League Cup

Semi-finals

Dundee United vs Rangers	1-2
Celtic v Greenock Morton	2-0

Final

Hampden Park, 24th October 1964

Rangers 2   (Forrest 2)
Celtic 1   (Johnstone)

Attendance 91,423

SCOTTISH DIVISION 1 1965-66

Celtic	34	27	3	4	106	30	57
Rangers	34	25	5	4	91	29	55
Kilmarnock	34	20	5	9	73	46	45
Dunfermline Athletic	34	19	6	9	94	55	44
Dundee United	34	19	5	10	79	51	43
Hibernian	34	16	6	12	81	55	38
Heart of Midlothian	34	13	12	9	56	48	38
Aberdeen	34	15	6	13	61	54	36
Dundee	34	14	6	14	61	61	34
Falkirk	34	15	1	18	48	72	31
Clyde	34	13	4	17	62	64	30
Partick Thistle	34	10	10	14	55	64	30
Motherwell	34	12	4	18	52	69	28
St. Johnstone	34	9	8	17	58	81	26
Stirling Albion	34	9	8	17	40	68	26
St. Mirren	34	9	4	21	44	82	22
Greenock Morton	34	8	5	21	42	84	21
Hamilton Academical	34	3	2	29	27	117	8

SCOTTISH DIVISION 1 1966-67

Celtic	34	26	6	2	111	33	58
Rangers	34	24	7	3	92	31	55
Clyde	34	20	6	8	64	48	46
Aberdeen	34	17	8	9	72	38	42
Hibernian	34	19	4	11	72	49	42
Dundee	34	16	9	9	74	51	41
Kilmarnock	34	16	8	10	59	46	40
Dunfermline Athletic	34	14	10	10	72	52	38
Dundee United	34	14	9	11	68	62	37
Motherwell	34	10	11	13	59	60	31
Heart of Midlothian	34	11	8	15	38	48	30
Partick Thistle	34	9	12	13	49	68	30
Airdrieonians	34	11	6	17	41	53	28
Falkirk	34	11	4	19	33	70	26
St. Johnstone	34	10	5	19	53	73	25
Stirling Albion	34	5	9	20	31	85	19
St. Mirren	34	4	7	23	25	81	15
Ayr United	34	1	7	26	20	86	9

SCOTTISH DIVISION 2 1965-66

Ayr United	36	22	9	5	78	37	53
Airdrieonians	36	22	6	8	107	56	50
Queen of the South	36	18	11	7	83	53	47
East Fife	36	20	4	12	72	55	44
Raith Rovers	36	16	11	9	71	43	43
Arbroath	36	15	13	8	72	52	43
Albion Rovers	36	18	7	11	58	54	43
Alloa Athletic	36	14	10	12	65	65	38
Montrose	36	15	7	14	67	63	37
Cowdenbeath	36	15	7	14	69	68	37
Berwick Rangers	36	12	11	13	69	58	35
Dumbarton	36	14	7	15	63	61	35
Queen's Park	36	13	7	16	62	65	33
Third Lanark	36	12	8	16	55	65	32
Stranraer	36	9	10	17	64	83	28
Brechin City	36	10	7	19	52	92	27
East Stirlingshire	36	9	5	22	59	91	23
Stenhousemuir	36	6	7	23	47	93	19
Forfar Athletic	36	7	3	26	61	120	17

SCOTTISH DIVISION 2 1966-67

Greenock Morton	38	33	3	2	113	20	69
Raith Rovers	38	27	4	7	95	44	58
Arbroath	38	25	7	6	75	32	57
Hamilton Academical	38	18	8	12	74	60	44
East Fife	38	19	4	15	70	63	42
Cowdenbeath	38	16	8	14	70	55	40
Queen's Park	38	15	10	13	78	68	40
Albion Rovers	38	17	6	15	66	62	40
Queen of the South	38	15	9	14	84	76	39
Berwick Rangers	38	16	6	16	63	55	38
Third Lanark	38	13	8	17	67	78	34
Montrose	38	13	8	17	63	77	34
Alloa Athletic	38	15	4	19	55	74	34
Dumbarton	38	12	9	17	55	64	33
Stranraer	38	13	7	18	57	73	33
Forfar Athletic	38	12	3	23	74	106	27
Stenhousemuir	38	9	9	20	62	104	27
Clydebank	38	8	8	22	59	92	24
East Stirlingshire	38	7	10	21	44	87	24
Brechin City	38	8	7	23	58	93	23

1966 Scottish F.A. Cup

Semi-finals

Aberdeen vs Rangers	0-0, 1-2
Celtic vs Dunfermline Athletic	2-0

Final

Hampden Park, 23rd April 1966

Rangers 0

Celtic 0

Attendance 126,559

Replay

Hampden Park, 27th April 1966

Rangers 1   (Johansen)

Celtic 0

Attendance 96,862

1967 Scottish F.A. Cup

Semi-finals

Celtic vs Clyde	0-0, 2-0
Dundee United vs Aberdeen	0-1

Final

Hampden Park, 29th April 1967

Celtic 2   (Wallace 2)

Aberdeen 0

Attendance 126,102

1965/66 Scottish League Cup

Semi-finals

Celtic vs Hibernian	2-2, 4-0
Rangers vs Kilmarnock	6-4

Final

Hampden Park, 23rd October 1965

Celtic 2   (Hughes 2 (2 pens))

Rangers 1   (Young (og))

Attendance 107,609

1966/67 Scottish League Cup

Semi-finals

Celtic vs Airdrieonians	2-0
Rangers vs Aberdeen	2-2, 2-0

Final

Hampden Park, 29th October 1966

Celtic 1   (Lennox)

Rangers 0

Attendance 94,532

SCOTTISH DIVISION 1 1967-68

Celtic	34	30	3	1	106	24	63
Rangers	34	28	5	1	93	34	61
Hibernian	34	20	5	9	67	49	45
Dunfermline Athletic	34	17	5	12	64	41	39
Aberdeen	34	16	5	13	63	48	37
Greenock Morton	34	15	6	13	57	53	36
Kilmarnock	34	13	8	13	59	57	34
Clyde	34	15	4	15	55	55	34
Dundee	34	13	7	14	62	59	33
Partick Thistle	34	12	7	15	51	67	31
Dundee United	34	10	11	13	53	72	31
Heart of Midlothian	34	13	4	17	56	61	30
Airdrieonians	34	10	9	15	45	58	29
St. Johnstone	34	10	7	17	43	52	27
Falkirk	34	7	12	15	36	50	26
Raith Rovers	34	9	7	18	58	86	25
Motherwell	34	6	7	21	40	66	19
Stirling Albion	34	4	4	26	29	105	12

SCOTTISH DIVISION 1 1968-69

Celtic	34	23	8	3	89	32	54
Rangers	34	21	7	6	81	32	49
Dunfermline Athletic	34	19	7	8	63	45	45
Kilmarnock	34	15	14	5	50	32	44
Dundee United	34	17	9	8	61	49	43
St. Johnstone	34	16	5	13	66	59	37
Airdrieonians	34	13	11	10	46	44	37
Heart of Midlothian	34	14	8	12	52	54	36
Dundee	34	10	12	12	47	48	32
Greenock Morton	34	12	8	14	58	68	32
St. Mirren	34	11	10	13	40	54	32
Hibernian	34	12	7	15	60	59	31
Clyde	34	9	13	12	35	50	31
Partick Thistle	34	9	10	15	39	53	28
Aberdeen	34	9	8	17	50	59	26
Raith Rovers	34	8	5	21	45	67	21
Falkirk	34	5	8	21	33	69	18
Arbroath	34	5	6	23	41	82	16

SCOTTISH DIVISION 2 1967-68

St. Mirren	36	27	8	1	100	23	62
Arbroath	36	24	5	7	87	34	53
East Fife	36	21	7	8	71	47	49
Queen's Park	36	20	8	8	76	47	48
Ayr United	36	18	6	12	69	48	42
Queen of the South	36	16	6	14	73	57	38
Forfar Athletic	36	14	10	12	57	63	38
Albion Rovers	36	14	9	13	62	55	37
Clydebank	36	13	8	15	62	73	34
Dumbarton	36	11	11	14	63	74	33
Hamilton Academical	36	13	7	16	49	58	33
Cowdenbeath	36	12	8	16	57	62	32
Montrose	36	10	11	15	54	64	31
Berwick Rangers	36	13	4	19	34	54	30
East Stirlingshire	36	9	10	17	61	74	28
Brechin City	36	8	12	16	45	62	28
Alloa Athletic	36	11	6	19	42	69	28
Stranraer	36	8	4	24	41	80	20
Stenhousemuir	36	7	6	23	34	93	20

SCOTTISH DIVISION 2 1968-69

Motherwell	36	30	4	2	112	23	64
Ayr United	36	23	7	6	82	31	53
East Fife	36	21	6	9	82	45	48
Stirling Albion	36	21	6	9	67	40	48
Queen of the South	36	20	7	9	75	41	47
Forfar Athletic	36	18	7	11	71	56	47
Albion Rovers	36	19	5	12	60	56	43
Stranraer	36	17	7	12	57	45	41
East Stirlingshire	36	17	5	14	70	62	39
Montrose	36	15	4	17	59	71	34
Queen's Park	36	13	7	16	50	59	33
Cowdenbeath	36	12	5	19	54	67	29
Clydebank	36	6	15	15	52	67	27
Dumbarton	36	11	5	20	46	69	27
Hamilton Academical	36	8	8	20	37	72	24
Berwick Rangers	36	7	9	20	42	70	23
Brechin City	36	8	6	22	40	78	22
Alloa Athletic	36	7	7	22	45	79	21
Stenhousemuir	36	6	6	24	55	125	18

1968 Scottish F.A. Cup

Semi-finals

Dunfermline Athletic vs St. Johnstone	1-1, 2-1
Heart of Midlothian vs Greenock Morton	1-1, 2-1

Final

Hampden Park, 27th April 1968

Dunfermline Athletic 3 (Gardner 2, Lister (pen))
Heart of Midlothian 1 (Lunn (og))

Attendance 56,365

1969 Scottish F.A. Cup

Semi-finals

Celtic vs Greenock Morton	4-1
Rangers vs Aberdeen	6-1

Final

Hampden Park, 26th April 1969

Celtic 4 (McNeill, Lennox, Connelly, Chalmers)
Rangers 0

Attendance 132,874

1967/68 Scottish League Cup

Semi-finals

Ayr United vs Celtic	3-3, 1-2
Motherwell vs St. Johnstone	0-2

Final

Hampden Park, 28th October 1967

Celtic 5 (Chalmers 2, Wallace, Lennox, Hughes)
Dundee 3 (G. McLean 2, J. McLean)

Attendance 66,660

1968/69 Scottish League Cup

Semi-finals

Celtic vs Clyde	1-0
Dundee vs Hibernian	1-2

Final

Hampden Park, 5th April 1969

Celtic 6 (Lennox 3, Wallace, Auld, Craig)
Hibernian 2 (O'Rourke, Stevenson)

Attendance 74,240

SCOTTISH DIVISION 1 1969-70

Celtic	34	27	3	4	96	33	57
Rangers	34	19	7	8	67	40	45
Hibernian	34	19	6	9	65	40	44
Heart of Midlothian	34	13	12	9	50	36	38
Dundee United	34	16	6	12	62	64	38
Dundee	34	15	6	13	49	44	36
Kilmarnock	34	13	10	11	62	57	36
Aberdeen	34	14	7	13	55	45	35
Dunfermline Athletic	34	15	5	14	45	45	35
Greenock Morton	34	13	9	12	52	52	35
Motherwell	34	11	10	13	49	51	32
Airdrieonians	34	12	8	14	59	64	32
St. Johnstone	34	11	9	14	50	62	31
Ayr United	34	12	6	16	37	52	30
St. Mirren	34	8	9	17	39	54	25
Clyde	34	9	7	18	34	56	25
Raith Rovers	34	5	11	18	32	67	21
Partick Thistle	34	5	7	22	41	82	17

SCOTTISH DIVISION 1 1970-71

Celtic	34	25	6	3	89	23	56
Aberdeen	34	24	6	4	68	18	54
St. Johnstone	34	19	6	9	59	44	44
Rangers	34	16	9	9	58	34	41
Dundee	34	14	10	10	53	45	38
Dundee United	34	14	8	12	53	54	36
Falkirk	34	13	9	12	46	53	35
Greenock Morton	34	13	8	13	44	44	34
Airdrieonians	34	13	8	13	60	65	34
Motherwell	34	13	8	13	43	47	34
Heart of Midlothian	34	13	7	14	41	40	33
Hibernian	34	10	10	14	47	53	30
Kilmarnock	34	10	8	16	43	67	28
Ayr United	34	9	8	17	37	54	26
Clyde	34	8	10	16	33	59	26
Dunfermline Athletic	34	6	11	17	44	56	23
St. Mirren	34	7	9	18	38	56	23
Cowdenbeath	34	7	3	24	33	77	17

SCOTTISH DIVISION 2 1969-70

Falkirk	36	25	6	5	94	34	56
Cowdenbeath	36	24	7	5	81	35	55
Queen of the South	36	22	6	8	72	49	50
Stirlingshire	36	18	10	8	70	40	46
Arbroath	36	20	4	12	76	39	44
Alloa Athletic	36	19	5	12	62	41	43
Dumbarton	36	17	6	13	55	46	40
Montrose	36	15	7	14	57	55	37
Berwick Rangers	36	15	5	16	67	55	35
East Fife	36	15	4	17	59	63	34
Albion Rovers	36	14	5	17	53	64	33
East Stirlingshire	36	14	5	17	58	75	33
Clydebank	36	10	10	16	47	65	30
Brechin City	36	11	6	19	47	74	28
Queen's Park	36	10	6	20	38	62	26
Stenhousemuir	36	10	6	20	47	89	26
Stranraer	36	9	7	20	56	75	25
Forfar Athletic	36	11	1	24	55	83	23
Hamilton Academical	36	8	4	24	42	92	20

SCOTTISH DIVISION 2 1970-71

Partick Thistle	36	23	10	3	78	26	56
East Fife	36	22	7	7	86	44	51
Arbroath	36	19	8	9	80	52	46
Dumbarton	36	19	6	11	87	46	44
Clydebank	36	17	8	11	57	43	42
Montrose	36	17	7	12	78	64	41
Albion Rovers	36	15	9	12	53	52	39
Raith Rovers	36	15	9	12	62	62	39
Stranraer	36	14	8	14	54	52	36
Stenhousemuir	36	14	8	14	64	70	36
Queen of the South	36	13	9	14	50	56	35
Stirling Albion	36	12	8	16	61	61	32
Queen's Park	36	13	4	19	51	72	30
Berwick Rangers	36	10	10	16	42	60	30
Forfar Athletic	36	9	11	16	63	75	29
Alloa Athletic	36	9	11	16	56	86	29
East Stirlingshire	36	9	9	18	57	86	27
Hamilton Academical	36	8	7	21	50	79	23
Brechin City	36	6	7	23	30	73	19

1970 Scottish F.A. Cup

Semi-finals

Aberdeen vs Kilmarnock	1-0
Celtic vs Dundee	2-1

Final

Hampden Park, 11th April 1970

Aberdeen 3   (Harper (pen), McKay 2)

Celtic 1   (Lennox)

Attendance 108,434

1969/70 Scottish League Cup

Semi-finals

Ayr United vs Celtic	3-3, 1-2
Motherwell vs St. Johnstone	0-2

Final

Hampden Park, 25th October 1969

Celtic 1   (Auld)

St. Johnstone 0

Attendance 73,067

1971 Scottish F.A. Cup

Semi-finals

Celtic vs Airdrieonians	3-3, 2-0
Hibernian vs Rangers	0-0, 1-2

Final

Hampden Park, 8th May 1971

Celtic 1   (Lennox)

Rangers 1   (D. Johnstone)

Attendance 120,092

Replay

Hampden Park, 12th May 1971

Celtic 2   (Macari, Hood (pen))

Rangers 1   (Craig (og))

Attendance 103,332

1970/71 Scottish League Cup

Semi-finals

Cowdenbeath vs Rangers	0-2
Celtic vs Dumbarton	0-0, 4-3

Final

Hampden Park, 24th October 1970

Rangers 1   (D. Johnstone)

Celtic 0

Attendance 106,263

SCOTTISH DIVISION 1 1971-72

Celtic	34	28	4	2	96	28	60
Aberdeen	34	21	8	5	80	26	50
Rangers	34	21	2	11	71	38	44
Hibernian	34	19	6	9	62	34	44
Dundee	34	14	13	7	59	38	41
Heart of Midlothian	34	13	13	8	53	49	39
Partick Thistle	34	12	10	12	53	54	34
St. Johnstone	34	12	8	14	52	58	32
Dundee United	34	12	7	15	55	70	31
Motherwell	34	11	7	16	49	69	29
Kilmarnock	34	11	6	17	49	64	28
Ayr United	34	9	10	15	40	58	28
Greenock Morton	34	10	7	17	46	52	27
Falkirk	34	10	7	17	44	60	27
Airdrieonians	34	7	12	15	44	76	26
East Fife	34	5	15	14	34	61	25
Clyde	34	7	10	17	36	66	24
Dunfermline Athletic	34	7	9	18	31	50	23

SCOTTISH DIVISION 1 1972-73

Celtic	34	26	5	3	93	28	57
Rangers	34	26	4	4	74	30	56
Hibernian	34	19	7	8	74	33	45
Aberdeen	34	16	11	7	61	34	43
Dundee	34	17	9	8	68	43	43
Ayr United	34	16	8	10	50	51	40
Dundee United	34	17	5	12	56	51	39
Motherwell	34	11	9	14	38	48	31
East Fife	34	11	8	15	46	54	30
Heart of Midlothian	34	12	6	16	39	50	30
St. Johnstone	34	10	9	15	52	67	29
Greenock Morton	34	10	8	16	47	53	28
Partick Thistle	34	10	8	16	40	53	28
Falkirk	34	7	12	15	38	56	26
Arbroath	34	9	8	17	39	63	26
Dumbarton	34	6	11	17	43	72	23
Kilmarnock	34	7	8	19	40	71	22
Airdrieonians	34	4	8	22	34	75	16

SCOTTISH DIVISION 2 1971-72

Dumbarton	36	24	4	8	89	51	52
Arbroath	36	22	8	6	71	41	52
Stirling Albion	36	21	8	7	75	37	50
St. Mirren	36	24	2	10	84	47	50
Cowdenbeath	36	19	10	7	69	28	48
Stranraer	36	18	8	10	70	62	44
Queen of the South	36	17	9	10	56	38	43
East Stirlingshire	36	17	7	12	60	58	41
Clydebank	36	14	11	11	60	52	39
Montrose	36	15	6	15	73	54	36
Raith Rovers	36	13	8	15	56	65	34
Queen's Park	36	12	9	15	47	61	33
Berwick Rangers	36	14	4	18	53	50	32
Stenhousemuir	36	10	8	18	41	58	28
Brechin City	36	8	7	21	41	79	23
Alloa Athletic	36	9	4	23	41	75	22
Forfar Athletic	36	6	9	21	32	84	21
Albion Rovers	36	7	6	23	36	61	20
Hamilton Academical	36	4	8	24	31	93	16

SCOTTISH DIVISION 2 1972-73

Clyde	36	23	10	3	68	28	56
Dunfermline Athletic	36	23	6	7	95	32	52
Raith Rovers	36	19	9	8	73	42	47
Stirling Albion	36	19	9	8	70	39	47
St. Mirren	36	19	7	10	79	50	45
Montrose	36	18	8	10	82	58	44
Cowdenbeath	36	14	10	12	57	53	38
Hamilton Academical	36	16	6	14	67	63	38
Berwick Rangers	36	16	5	15	45	54	37
Stenhousemuir	36	14	8	14	44	41	36
Queen of the South	36	13	8	15	45	52	34
Alloa Athletic	36	11	11	14	45	49	33
East Stirlingshire	36	12	8	16	52	69	32
Queen's Park	36	9	12	15	44	61	30
Stranraer	36	13	4	19	56	78	30
Forfar Athletic	36	10	9	17	38	66	29
Clydebank	36	9	6	21	48	72	21
Albion Rovers	36	5	8	23	35	83	18
Brechin City	36	5	4	27	46	99	14

1972 Scottish F.A. Cup

Semi-finals

Celtic vs Kilmarnock	3-1
Rangers vs Hibernian	1-1, 0-2

Final

Hampden Park, 6th May 1972

Celtic 6   (Dean 3, Macari 2, McNeill)
Hibernian 1   (Gordon)

Attendance 106,102

1973 Scottish F.A. Cup

Semi-finals

Ayr United vs Rangers	0-2
Celtic vs Dundee	0-0, 3-0

Final

Hampden Park, 5th May 1973

Rangers 3   (Parlane, Conn, Forsyth)
Celtic 2   (Dalglish, Connelly (pen))

Attendance 122,714

1971/72 Scottish League Cup

Semi-finals

Falkirk vs Partick Thistle	0-2
Celtic vs St. Mirren	3-0

Final

Hampden Park, 23rd October 1971

Partick Thistle 4   (Rae, Lawrie, McQuade, Bone)
Celtic 1   (Dalglish)

Attendance 62,740

1972/73 Scottish League Cup

Semi-finals

Hibernian vs Rangers	1-0
Aberdeen vs Celtic	2-3

Final

Hampden Park, 9th December 1972

Hibernian 2   (Stanton, O'Rourke)
Celtic 1   (Dalglish)

Attendance 71,696

SCOTTISH DIVISION 1 1973-74

Celtic	34	23	7	4	82	27	53
Hibernian	34	20	9	5	75	42	49
Rangers	34	21	6	7	67	34	48
Aberdeen	34	13	16	5	46	26	42
Dundee	34	16	7	11	67	48	39
Heart of Midlothian	34	14	10	10	54	43	38
Ayr United	34	15	8	11	44	40	38
Dundee United	34	15	7	12	55	51	37
Motherwell	34	14	7	13	45	40	35
Dumbarton	34	11	7	16	43	58	29
Partick Thistle	34	9	10	15	33	46	28
St. Johnstone	34	9	10	15	41	60	28
Arbroath	34	10	7	17	52	69	27
Greenock Morton	34	8	10	16	37	49	26
Clyde	34	8	9	17	29	65	25
Dunfermline Athletic	34	8	8	18	43	65	24
East Fife	34	9	6	19	26	51	24
Falkirk	34	4	14	16	33	58	22

SCOTTISH DIVISION 1 1974-75

Rangers	34	25	6	3	86	33	56
Hibernian	34	20	9	5	69	37	49
Celtic	34	20	5	9	81	41	45
Dundee United	34	19	7	8	72	43	45
Aberdeen	34	16	9	9	66	43	41
Dundee	34	16	6	12	48	42	38
Ayr United	34	14	8	12	50	61	36
Heart of Midlothian	34	11	13	10	47	52	35
St. Johnstone	34	11	12	11	41	44	34
Motherwell	34	14	5	15	52	57	33
Airdrieonians	34	11	9	14	43	55	31
Kilmarnock	34	8	15	11	52	68	31
Partick Thistle	34	10	10	14	48	62	30
Dumbarton	34	7	10	17	44	55	24
Dunfermline Athletic	34	7	9	18	46	66	23
Clyde	34	6	10	18	40	63	22
Greenock Morton	34	6	10	18	31	62	22
Arbroath	34	5	7	22	34	66	17

SCOTTISH DIVISION 2 1973-74

Airdrieonians	36	28	4	4	102	25	60
Kilmarnock	36	26	6	4	96	44	58
Hamilton Academical	36	24	7	5	68	38	55
Queen of the South	36	20	7	9	73	41	47
Raith Rovers	36	18	9	9	69	48	45
Berwick Rangers	36	16	13	7	53	35	45
Stirling Albion	36	17	6	13	76	50	40
Montrose	36	15	7	14	71	64	37
Stranraer	36	14	8	14	64	70	36
Clydebank	36	13	8	15	47	48	34
St. Mirren	36	12	10	14	62	66	34
Alloa Athletic	36	15	4	17	47	58	34
Cowdenbeath	36	11	9	16	59	85	31
Queen's Park	36	12	4	20	42	64	28
Stenhousemuir	36	11	5	20	44	59	27
East Stirlingshire	36	9	5	22	47	73	23
Albion Rovers	36	7	6	23	38	72	20
Forfar Athletic	36	5	6	25	42	94	16
Brechin City	36	5	4	27	33	99	14

SCOTTISH DIVISION 2 1974-75

Falkirk	38	26	2	10	76	29	54
Queen of the South	38	23	7	8	77	33	53
Montrose	38	23	7	8	70	37	53
Hamilton Academical	38	21	7	10	69	30	49
East Fife	38	20	7	11	57	42	47
St. Mirren	38	19	8	11	74	52	46
Clydebank	38	18	8	12	50	40	44
Stirling Albion	38	17	9	12	67	55	43
East Stirlingshire	38	16	8	14	56	52	40
Berwick Rangers	38	17	6	15	53	49	40
Stenhousemuir	38	14	11	13	52	42	39
Albion Rovers	38	16	7	15	72	64	39
Raith Rovers	38	14	9	15	48	44	37
Stranraer	38	12	11	15	47	65	35
Alloa Athletic	38	11	11	16	49	56	33
Queen's Park	38	10	10	18	41	54	30
Brechin City	38	9	7	22	44	85	25
Meadowbank Thistle	38	9	5	24	26	87	23
Cowdenbeath	38	5	12	22	39	73	21
Forfar Athletic	38	1	7	30	27	102	9

1974 Scottish F.A. Cup

Semi-finals
Celtic vs Dundee   1-0
Heart of Midlothian vs Dundee United   1-1, 2-4
Final
Hampden Park, 4th May 1974
Celtic 3   (Hood, Murray, Deans)
Dundee United 0
Attendance 75,959

1975 Scottish F.A. Cup

Semi-finals
Celtic vs Dundee   1-0
Airdrieonians vs Motherwell   1-1, 1-0
Final
Hampden Park, 3rd May 1975
Celtic 3   (Wilson 2, McCluskey (pen))
Airdrieonians 1   (McCann)
Attendance 75,457

1973/74 Scottish League Cup

Semi-finals
Dundee vs Kilmarnock   1-0
Celtic vs Rangers   3-1
Final
Hampden Park, 15th December 1973
Dundee 1   (Wallace)
Celtic 0
Attendance 27,974

1974/75 Scottish League Cup

Semi-finals
Celtic vs Airdrieonians   1-0
Falkirk vs Hibernian   0-1
Final
Hampden Park, 26th October 1974
Celtic 6   (Johnstone, Deans 3, Wilson, Murray)
Hibernian 3   (Harper 3)
Attendance 53,848

SCOTTISH PREMIER 1975-76

Rangers	36	23	8	5	60	24	54
Celtic	36	21	6	9	71	42	48
Hibernian	36	18	7	11	55	43	43
Motherwell	36	16	8	12	56	48	40
Heart of Midlothian	36	13	9	14	39	45	35
Ayr United	36	14	5	17	46	59	33
Aberdeen	36	11	10	15	49	50	32
Dundee United	36	12	8	16	46	48	32
Dundee	36	11	10	15	49	62	32
St. Johnstone	36	3	5	28	29	79	11

SCOTTISH PREMIER 1976-77

Celtic	36	23	9	4	79	39	55
Rangers	36	18	10	8	62	37	46
Aberdeen	36	16	11	9	56	42	43
Dundee United	36	16	9	11	54	45	41
Partick Thistle	36	11	13	12	40	44	35
Hibernian	36	8	18	10	34	35	34
Motherwell	36	10	12	14	57	60	32
Ayr United	36	11	8	17	44	68	30
Heart of Midlothian	36	7	13	16	49	66	27
Kilmarnock	36	4	9	23	32	71	17

SCOTTISH DIVISION 1 1975-76

Partick Thistle	26	17	7	2	47	19	41
Kilmarnock	26	16	3	7	44	29	35
Montrose	26	12	6	8	53	43	30
Dumbarton	26	12	4	10	35	46	28
Arbroath	26	11	4	11	41	39	26
St. Mirren	26	9	8	9	37	37	26
Airdrieonians	26	7	11	8	44	41	25
Falkirk	26	10	5	11	38	35	25
Hamilton Academical	26	7	10	9	37	37	24
Queen of the South	26	9	6	11	41	47	24
Greenock Morton	26	7	9	10	31	40	23
East Fife	26	8	7	11	39	53	23
Dunfermline Athletic	26	5	10	11	30	51	20
Clyde	26	5	4	17	34	52	14

SCOTTISH DIVISION 1 1976-77

St. Mirren	39	25	12	2	91	38	62
Clydebank	39	24	10	5	89	38	58
Dundee	39	21	9	9	90	55	51
Greenock Morton	39	20	10	9	77	52	50
Montrose	39	16	9	14	61	62	41
Airdrieonians	39	13	12	14	63	58	38
Dumbarton	39	14	9	16	63	68	37
Arbroath	39	17	3	19	46	62	37
Queen of the South	39	11	13	15	58	65	35
Hamilton Academical	39	11	10	18	44	59	32
St. Johnstone	39	8	13	18	42	64	29
East Fife	39	8	13	18	40	71	29
Raith Rovers	39	8	11	20	45	68	27
Falkirk	39	6	8	25	36	85	20

SCOTTISH DIVISION 2 1975-76

Clydebank	26	17	6	3	44	13	40
Raith Rovers	26	15	10	1	45	22	40
Alloa Athletic	26	14	7	5	44	28	35
Queen's Park	26	10	9	7	41	33	29
Cowdenbeath	26	11	7	8	44	43	29
Stirling Albion	26	9	7	10	41	33	25
Stranraer	26	11	3	12	49	43	25
East Stirlingshire	26	8	8	10	33	33	24
Albion Rovers	26	7	10	9	35	38	24
Stenhousemuir	26	9	5	12	39	44	23
Berwick Rangers	26	7	5	14	32	44	19
Forfar Athletic	26	4	10	12	28	48	18
Brechin City	26	6	5	15	28	52	17
Meadowbank Thistle	26	5	6	15	24	53	16

SCOTTISH DIVISION 2 1976-77

Stirling Albion	39	22	11	6	59	29	55
Alloa Athletic	39	19	13	7	73	45	51
Dunfermline Athletic	39	20	10	9	52	36	50
Stranraer	39	20	6	13	74	53	46
Queen's Park	39	17	11	11	65	51	45
Albion Rovers	39	15	12	12	74	61	42
Clyde	39	15	11	13	68	64	41
Berwick Rangers	39	13	10	16	37	51	36
Stenhousemuir	39	15	5	19	38	49	35
East Stirlingshire	39	12	8	19	47	63	32
Meadowbank Thistle	39	8	16	15	41	57	32
Cowdenbeath	39	13	5	21	46	64	31
Brechin City	39	7	12	20	51	77	26
Forfar Athletic	39	7	10	22	43	68	24

1976 Scottish F.A. Cup

Semi-finals

Motherwell vs Rangers	2-3
Dumbarton vs Heart of Midlothian	0-0, 0-3

Final

Hampden Park, 1st May 1976

Rangers 3   (Johnstone 2, McDonald)
Heart of Midlothian 1   (Shaw)

Attendance 85,250

1977 Scottish F.A. Cup

Semi-finals

Celtic vs Dundee	2-0
Rangers vs Heart of Midlothian	2-0

Final

Hampden Park, 7th May 1977

Celtic 1   (Lynch (pen))
Rangers 0

Attendance 54,252

1975/76 Scottish League Cup

Semi-finals

Montrose vs Rangers	1-5
Celtic vs Partick Thistle	1-0

Final

Hampden Park, 25th October 1975

Rangers 1   (MacDonald)
Celtic 0

Attendance 58,806

1976/77 Scottish League Cup

Semi-finals

Aberdeen vs Rangers	5-1
Celtic vs Heart of Midlothian	2-1

Final

Hampden Park, 6th November 1976

Aberdeen 2   (Jarvie, Robb)
Celtic 1   (Dalglish (pen))

Attendance 69,707

SCOTTISH PREMIER 1977-78

Rangers	36	24	7	5	76	39	55
Aberdeen	36	22	9	5	68	29	53
Dundee United	36	16	8	12	42	32	40
Hibernian	36	15	7	14	51	43	37
Celtic	36	15	6	15	63	54	36
Motherwell	36	13	7	16	45	52	33
Partick Thistle	36	14	5	17	52	64	33
St. Mirren	36	11	8	17	52	63	30
Ayr United	36	9	6	21	36	68	24
Clydebank	36	6	7	23	23	64	19

SCOTTISH DIVISION 1 1977-78

Greenock Morton	39	25	8	6	85	42	58
Heart of Midlothian	39	24	10	5	77	42	58
Dundee	39	25	7	7	91	44	57
Dumbarton	39	16	17	6	65	48	49
Stirling Albion	39	15	12	12	60	52	42
Kilmarnock	39	14	12	13	52	46	40
Hamilton Academical	39	12	12	15	54	56	36
St. Johnstone	39	15	6	18	52	64	36
Arbroath	39	11	13	15	42	55	35
Airdrieonians	39	12	10	17	50	64	34
Montrose	39	10	9	20	55	71	29
Queen of the South	39	8	13	18	44	68	29
Alloa Athletic	39	8	8	23	44	84	24
East Fife	39	4	11	24	39	74	19

SCOTTISH DIVISION 2 1977-78

Clyde	39	21	11	7	71	32	53
Raith Rovers	39	19	15	5	63	34	53
Dunfermline Athletic	39	18	12	9	64	41	48
Berwick Rangers	39	16	16	7	68	51	48
Falkirk	39	15	14	10	51	46	44
Forfar Athletic	39	17	8	14	61	55	42
Queen's Park	39	13	15	11	52	51	41
Albion Rovers	39	16	8	15	68	68	40
East Stirlingshire	39	15	8	16	55	65	38
Cowdenbeath	39	13	8	18	75	78	34
Stranraer	39	13	7	19	54	63	33
Stenhousemuir	39	10	10	19	43	67	30
Meadowbank Thistle	39	6	10	23	43	89	22
Brechin City	39	7	6	26	45	73	20

1978 Scottish F.A. Cup

Semi-finals

Rangers vs Dundee United	2-0
Aberdeen vs Partick Thistle	4-2

Final

Hampden Park, 6th May 1978

Rangers 2 (McDonald, Johnstone)

Aberdeen 1 (Ritchie)

Attendance 61,563

1977/78 Scottish League Cup

Semi-finals

Forfar Athletic vs Rangers	2-5
Celtic vs Heart of Midlothian	2-0

Final

Hampden Park, 18th March 1978

Rangers 2 (Cooper, Smith)

Celtic 1 (aet.) (Edvaldsson)

Attendance 60,168

SCOTTISH PREMIER 1978-79

Celtic	36	21	6	9	61	37	48
Rangers	36	18	9	9	52	35	45
Dundee United	36	18	8	10	56	37	44
Aberdeen	36	13	14	9	59	36	40
Hibernian	36	12	13	11	44	48	37
St. Mirren	36	15	6	15	45	41	36
Greenock Morton	36	12	12	12	52	53	36
Partick Thistle	36	13	8	15	42	39	34
Heart of Midlothian	36	8	7	21	49	71	23
Motherwell	36	5	7	24	33	86	17

SCOTTISH DIVISION 1 1978-79

Dundee	39	24	7	8	68	36	55
Kilmarnock	39	22	10	7	72	35	54
Clydebank	39	24	6	9	78	50	54
Ayr United	39	21	5	13	71	52	47
Hamilton Academical	39	17	9	13	62	60	43
Airdrieonians	39	16	8	15	72	61	40
Dumbarton	39	14	11	14	58	49	39
Stirling Albion	39	13	9	17	43	55	35
Clyde	39	13	8	18	54	65	34
Arbroath	39	11	11	17	50	61	33
Raith Rovers	39	12	8	19	47	55	32
St. Johnstone	39	10	11	18	57	66	31
Montrose	39	8	9	22	55	92	25
Queen of the South	39	8	8	23	43	93	24

SCOTTISH DIVISION 2 1978-79

Berwick Rangers	39	22	10	7	82	44	54
Dunfermline Athletic	39	19	14	6	66	40	52
Falkirk	39	19	12	8	66	37	50
East Fife	39	17	9	13	64	53	43
Cowdenbeath	39	16	10	13	63	58	42
Alloa Athletic	39	16	9	14	57	62	41
Albion Rovers	39	15	10	14	57	56	40
Forfar Athletic	39	13	12	14	55	52	38
Stranraer	39	18	2	19	52	66	38
Stenhousemuir	39	12	8	19	54	58	32
Brechin City	39	9	14	16	49	65	32
East Stirlingshire	39	12	8	19	61	87	32
Queen's Park	39	8	12	19	46	57	28
Meadowbank Thistle	39	8	8	23	37	74	24

1979 Scottish F.A. Cup

Semi-finals

Partick Thistle vs Rangers	0-0, 0-1
Aberdeen vs Hibernian	1-2

Final

Hampden Park, 12th May 1979

Rangers 0 **Hibernian 0**

Attendance 50,610

Replay

Hampden Park, 16th May 1979

Rangers 0 **Hibernian 0 (aet.)**

Attendance 33,504

2nd Replay

Hampden Park, 28th May 1979

Rangers 3 (Johnstone 2, Duncan (og))

Hibernian 2 (aet.) (Higgins, McLeod (pen))

Attendance 30,602

1978/79 Scottish League Cup

Semi-finals

Celtic vs Rangers	2-3
Aberdeen vs Hibernian	1-0

Final

Hampden Park, 31st March 1979

Rangers 2 (MacDonald, Jackson)

Aberdeen 1 (Davidson)

Attendance 54,000

SCOTTISH PREMIER 1979-80

Aberdeen	36	19	10	7	68	36	48
Celtic	36	18	11	7	61	38	47
St. Mirren	36	15	12	9	56	49	42
Dundee United	36	12	13	11	43	30	37
Rangers	36	15	7	14	50	46	37
Greenock Morton	36	14	8	14	51	46	36
Partick Thistle	36	11	14	11	43	47	36
Kilmarnock	36	11	11	14	36	52	33
Dundee	36	10	6	20	47	73	26
Hibernian	36	6	6	24	29	67	18

SCOTTISH PREMIER 1980-81

Celtic	36	26	4	6	84	37	56
Aberdeen	36	19	11	6	61	26	49
Rangers	36	16	12	8	60	32	44
St. Mirren	36	18	8	10	56	47	44
Dundee United	36	17	9	10	66	42	43
Partick Thistle	36	10	10	16	32	48	30
Airdrieonians	36	10	9	17	36	55	29
Greenock Morton	36	10	8	18	36	58	28
Kilmarnock	36	5	9	22	23	65	19
Heart of Midlothian	36	6	6	24	27	71	18

SCOTTISH DIVISION 1 1979-80

Heart of Midlothian	39	20	13	6	58	39	53
Airdrieonians	39	21	9	9	78	47	51
Ayr United	39	16	12	11	64	51	44
Dumbarton	39	19	6	14	59	51	44
Raith Rovers	39	14	15	10	59	46	43
Motherwell	39	16	11	12	59	48	43
Hamilton Academical	39	15	10	14	60	59	40
Stirling Albion	39	13	13	13	40	40	39
Clydebank	39	14	8	17	58	57	36
Dunfermline Athletic	39	11	13	15	39	57	35
St. Johnstone	39	12	10	17	57	74	34
Berwick Rangers	39	8	15	16	57	64	31
Arbroath	39	9	10	20	50	79	28
Clyde	39	6	13	20	43	69	25

SCOTTISH DIVISION 1 1980-81

Hibernian	39	24	9	6	67	24	57
Dundee	39	22	8	9	64	40	52
St. Johnstone	39	20	11	8	64	45	51
Raith Rovers	39	20	10	9	49	32	50
Motherwell	39	19	11	9	65	51	49
Ayr United	39	17	11	11	59	42	45
Hamilton Academical	39	15	7	17	61	57	37
Dumbarton	39	13	11	15	49	50	37
Falkirk	39	13	8	18	39	52	34
Clydebank	39	10	13	16	48	59	33
East Stirlingshire	39	6	17	16	41	56	29
Dunfermline Athletic	39	10	7	22	41	58	27
Stirling Albion	39	6	11	22	18	48	23
Berwick Rangers	39	5	12	22	31	82	22

SCOTTISH DIVISION 2 1979-80

Falkirk	39	19	12	8	65	35	50
East Stirlingshire	39	21	7	11	55	40	49
Forfar Athletic	39	19	8	12	63	51	46
Albion Rovers	39	16	12	11	73	56	44
Queen's Park	39	16	9	14	59	47	41
Stenhousemuir	39	16	9	14	56	51	41
Brechin City	39	15	10	14	61	59	40
Cowdenbeath	39	14	12	13	54	52	40
Montrose	39	14	10	15	60	63	38
East Fife	39	12	9	18	45	57	33
Stranraer	39	12	8	19	51	65	32
Meadowbank Thistle	39	12	8	19	42	70	32
Queen of the South	39	11	9	19	51	69	31
Alloa Athletic	39	11	7	21	44	64	29

SCOTTISH DIVISION 2 1980-81

Queen's Park	39	16	18	5	62	43	50
Queen of the South	39	16	14	9	66	53	46
Cowdenbeath	39	18	9	12	63	48	45
Brechin City	39	15	14	10	52	46	44
Forfar Athletic	39	17	9	13	63	57	43
Alloa Athletic	39	15	12	12	61	54	42
Montrose	39	16	8	15	66	55	40
Clyde	39	14	12	13	68	63	40
Arbroath	39	13	12	14	58	54	38
Stenhousemuir	39	13	11	15	63	58	37
East Fife	39	10	15	14	44	53	35
Albion Rovers	39	13	9	17	59	72	34
Meadowbank Thistle	39	11	7	21	42	64	29
Stranraer	39	7	8	24	36	83	22

1980 Scottish F.A. Cup

Semi-finals

Celtic vs Hibernian	5-0
Aberdeen vs Rangers	0-1

Final

Hampden Park, 10th May 1980

Celtic 1   (McCluskey)
Rangers 0 (aet.)

Attendance 70,303

1979/80 Scottish League Cup

Semi-finals

Dundee United vs Hamilton Academical	6-2
Aberdeen vs Greenock Morton	2-1

Final

Hampden Park, 8th December 1979

Dundee United 0
Aberdeen 0 (aet.)

Attendance 27,173

Replay

Dens Park, Dundee, 12th December 1979

Dundee United 3   (Pettigrew 2, Sturrock)
Aberdeen 0

Attendance 28,933

1981 Scottish F.A. Cup

Semi-finals

Greenock Morton vs Rangers	1-2
Celtic vs Dundee United	0-0, 2-3

Final

Hampden Park, 9th May 1981

Rangers 0
Dundee United 0 (aet.)

Attendance 53,000

Replay

Hampden Park, 12th May 1981

Rangers 4   (Cooper, Russell, MacDonald 2)
Dundee United 1   (Dodds)

Attendance 43,099

1980/81 Scottish League Cup

Semi-finals

Dundee United vs Celtic (1-1, 3-0)	4-1
Ayr United vs Dundee (1-1, 2-3)	3-4

Final

Dens Park, Dundee, 6th December 1980

Dundee United 3   (Dodds, Sturrock 2)
Dundee 0

Attendance 24,456

SCOTTISH PREMIER 1981-82

Celtic	36	24	7	5	79	33	55
Aberdeen	36	23	7	6	71	29	53
Rangers	36	16	11	9	57	45	43
Dundee United	36	15	10	11	61	38	40
St. Mirren	36	14	9	13	49	52	37
Hibernian	36	11	14	11	48	40	36
Greenock Morton	36	9	12	15	31	54	30
Dundee	36	11	4	21	46	72	26
Partick Thistle	36	6	10	20	35	59	22
Airdrieonians	36	5	8	23	31	76	18

SCOTTISH PREMIER 1982-83

Dundee United	36	24	8	4	90	35	56
Celtic	36	25	5	6	90	36	55
Aberdeen	36	25	5	6	76	24	55
Rangers	36	13	12	11	52	41	38
St. Mirren	36	11	12	13	47	51	34
Dundee	36	9	11	16	42	53	29
Hibernian	36	11	7	18	35	51	29
Motherwell	36	11	5	20	39	73	27
Greenock Morton	36	6	8	22	30	74	20
Kilmarnock	36	3	11	22	28	91	17

SCOTTISH DIVISION 1 1981-82

Motherwell	39	26	9	4	92	36	61
Kilmarnock	39	17	17	5	60	29	51
Heart of Midlothian	39	21	8	10	65	37	50
Clydebank	39	19	8	12	61	53	46
St. Johnstone	39	17	8	14	69	60	42
Ayr United	39	15	12	12	56	50	42
Hamilton Academical	39	16	8	15	52	49	40
Queen's Park	39	13	10	16	41	41	36
Falkirk	39	11	14	14	49	52	36
Dunfermline Athletic	39	11	14	14	46	56	36
Dumbarton	39	13	9	17	49	61	35
Raith Rovers	39	11	7	21	31	59	29
East Stirlingshire	39	7	10	22	38	77	24
Queen of the South	39	4	10	25	44	93	18

SCOTTISH DIVISION 1 1982-83

St. Johnstone	39	25	5	9	59	37	55
Heart of Midlothian	39	22	10	7	79	38	54
Clydebank	39	20	10	9	72	49	50
Partick Thistle	39	20	9	10	66	45	49
Airdrieonians	39	16	7	16	62	46	39
Alloa Athletic	39	14	11	14	52	52	39
Falkirk	39	15	6	18	45	55	36
Dumbarton	39	13	10	16	50	59	36
Hamilton Academical	39	11	12	16	54	66	34
Raith Rovers	39	13	8	18	64	63	34
Clyde	39	14	6	19	55	66	34
Ayr United	39	12	8	19	45	61	32
Dunfermline Athletic	39	7	17	15	39	69	31
Queen's Park	39	16	11	22	44	80	23

SCOTTISH DIVISION 2 1981-82

Clyde	39	24	11	4	79	38	59
Alloa Athletic	39	19	12	8	66	42	50
Arbroath	39	20	10	9	62	50	50
Berwick Rangers	39	20	8	11	66	38	48
Brechin City	39	18	10	11	61	43	46
Forfar Athletic	39	15	15	9	59	35	45
East Fife	39	14	9	16	48	51	37
Stirling Albion	39	12	11	16	39	44	35
Cowdenbeath	39	11	13	15	51	57	35
Montrose	39	12	8	19	49	74	32
Albion Rovers	39	13	5	21	52	74	31
Meadowbank Thistle	39	10	10	19	49	62	30
Stenhousemuir	39	11	6	22	41	65	28
Stranraer	39	7	6	26	36	85	20

SCOTTISH DIVISION 2 1982-83

Brechin City	39	21	3	5	77	38	55
Meadowbank Thistle	39	23	8	8	64	45	54
Arbroath	39	21	7	11	78	51	49
Forfar Athletic	39	18	12	9	58	37	48
Stirling Albion	39	18	10	11	57	41	46
East Fife	39	16	11	12	68	43	43
Queen of the South	39	17	7	15	75	56	42
Cowdenbeath	39	13	12	14	55	53	38
Berwick Rangers	39	13	10	16	47	60	36
Albion Rovers	39	14	6	19	55	6	34
Stenhousemuir	39	7	14	18	43	66	29
Stranraer	39	10	6	23	46	79	27
East Stirlingshire	39	7	9	23	43	79	23
Montrose	39	8	6	25	37	86	22

1982 Scottish F.A. Cup

Semi-finals

Aberdeen vs St. Mirren	1-1, 3-2
Forfar Athletic vs Rangers	0-0, 1-3

Final

Hampden Park, 22nd May 1982

Aberdeen 4   (McLeish, McGhee, Strachan, Cooper)
Rangers 1 (aet.)   (McDonald)

Attendance 53,788

1983 Scottish F.A. Cup

Semi-finals

Aberdeen vs Celtic	1-0
Rangers vs St. Mirren	1-1, 1-0

Final

Hampden Park, 21st May 1983

Aberdeen 1   (Black)
Rangers 0 (aet.)

Attendance 62,979

1981/82 Scottish League Cup

Semi-finals

Dundee United vs Aberdeen (0-1, 3-0)	3-1
St. Mirren vs Rangers (2-2, 1-2)	3-4

Final

Hampden Park, 28th November 1981

Rangers 2   (Cooper, Redford)
Dundee United 1   (Milne)

Attendance 53,777

1982/83 Scottish League Cup

Semi-finals

Celtic vs Dundee United (2-0, 1-2)	3-2
Rangers vs Heart of Midlothian (2-0, 2-1)	4-1

Final

Hampden Park, 2nd December 1982

Celtic 2   (Nicholas, MacLeod)
Rangers 1   (Bett)

Attendance 55,372

SCOTTISH PREMIER 1983-84

Aberdeen	36	25	7	4	78	21	57
Celtic	36	21	8	7	80	41	50
Dundee United	36	18	11	7	67	39	47
Rangers	36	15	12	9	53	41	42
Heart of Midlothian	36	10	16	10	38	47	36
St. Mirren	36	9	14	13	55	59	32
Hibernian	36	12	7	17	45	55	31
Dundee	36	11	5	20	50	74	27
St. Johnstone	36	10	3	23	36	81	23
Motherwell	36	4	7	25	31	75	15

SCOTTISH PREMIER 1984-85

Aberdeen	36	27	5	4	89	26	59
Celtic	36	22	8	6	77	30	52
Dundee United	36	20	7	9	67	33	47
Rangers	36	13	12	11	47	38	38
St. Mirren	36	17	4	15	51	56	38
Dundee	36	15	7	14	48	50	37
Heart of Midlothian	36	13	5	18	47	64	31
Hibernian	36	10	7	19	38	61	27
Dumbarton	36	6	7	23	29	64	19
Greenock Morton	36	5	2	29	29	100	12

SCOTTISH DIVISION 1 1983-84

Greenock Morton	39	21	12	6	75	46	54
Dumbarton	39	20	11	8	66	44	51
Partick Thistle	39	19	8	12	67	50	46
Clydebank	39	16	13	10	62	50	45
Brechin City	39	14	14	11	56	58	42
Kilmarnock	39	16	6	17	57	53	38
Falkirk	39	16	6	17	46	54	38
Clyde	39	12	13	14	53	50	37
Hamilton Academical	39	11	14	14	43	46	36
Airdrieonians	39	13	10	16	45	53	36
Meadowbank Thistle	39	12	10	17	49	69	34
Ayr United	39	10	12	17	56	70	32
Raith Rovers	39	10	11	18	53	62	31
Alloa Athletic	39	8	10	21	41	64	26

SCOTTISH DIVISION 1 1984-85

Motherwell	39	21	8	10	62	36	50
Clydebank	39	17	14	8	57	37	48
Falkirk	39	19	7	13	65	54	45
Hamilton Academical	39	16	11	12	48	49	43
Airdrieonians	39	17	8	14	70	59	42
Forfar Athletic	39	14	13	12	54	49	41
Ayr United	39	15	9	15	57	52	39
Clyde	39	14	11	14	47	48	39
Brechin City	39	14	9	16	49	57	37
East Fife	39	12	12	15	55	56	36
Partick Thistle	39	13	9	17	50	55	35
Kilmarnock	39	12	10	17	42	61	34
Meadowbank Thistle	39	11	10	18	50	66	32
St. Johnstone	39	10	5	24	51	78	25

SCOTTISH DIVISION 2 1983-84

Forfar Athletic	39	27	9	3	73	31	63
East Fife	39	20	7	12	57	42	47
Berwick Rangers	39	16	11	12	60	38	43
Stirling Albion	39	14	14	11	51	42	42
Arbroath	39	18	6	15	51	46	42
Queen of the South	39	16	10	13	51	46	42
Stenhousemuir	39	14	11	14	47	57	39
Stranraer	39	13	12	14	47	47	38
Dunfermline Athletic	39	13	10	16	44	45	36
Queen's Park	39	14	8	17	58	63	36
East Stirlingshire	39	10	11	18	51	66	31
Montrose	39	12	7	20	36	59	31
Cowdenbeath	39	10	9	20	44	58	29
Albion Rovers	39	8	11	20	46	76	27

SCOTTISH DIVISION 2 1984-85

Montrose	39	22	9	8	57	40	53
Alloa Athletic	39	20	10	9	58	40	50
Dunfermline Athletic	39	17	15	7	61	36	49
Cowdenbeath	39	18	11	10	68	39	47
Stenhousemuir	39	15	15	9	45	43	45
Stirling Albion	39	15	13	11	62	47	43
Raith Rovers	39	18	6	15	69	57	42
Queen of the South	39	10	14	15	42	56	34
Albion Rovers	39	13	8	18	49	72	34
Queen's Park	39	12	9	18	48	55	33
Stranraer	39	13	6	20	52	67	32
East Stirlingshire	39	8	15	16	38	53	31
Berwick Rangers	39	8	12	19	36	49	28
Arbroath	39	9	7	23	35	66	25

1984 Scottish F.A. Cup

Semi-finals

Aberdeen vs Dundee	2-0
St. Mirren vs Celtic	1-2

Final

Hampden Park, 19th May 1984

Aberdeen 2   (Black, McGhee)

Celtic 1 (aet.)   (P. McStay)

Attendance 58,900

1985 Scottish F.A. Cup

Semi-finals

Dundee United vs Aberdeen	0-0, 2-1
Motherwell vs Celtic	1-1, 0-3

Final

Hampden Park, 18th May 1985

Celtic 2   (Provan, McGarvey)

Dundee United 0

Attendance 60,346

1983/84 Scottish League Cup

Semi-finals

Dundee United vs Rangers (1-1, 0-2)	1-3
Aberdeen vs Celtic (0-0, 0-1)	0-1

Final

Hampden Park, 25th March 1984

Rangers 3   (McCoist 3 (2 pens))

Celtic 2 (aet.)   (McClair, Reid)

Attendance 66,369

1984/85 Scottish League Cup

Semi-finals

Heart of Midlothian vs Dundee United (1-2, 1-3)	2-5
Rangers vs Meadowbank Thistle (4-0, 1-1)	5-1

Final

Hampden Park, 28th October 1984

Rangers 1   (Ferguson)

Dundee United 0

Attendance 44,698

SCOTTISH PREMIER 1985-86

Celtic	36	20	10	6	67	38	50
Heart of Midlothian	36	20	10	6	59	33	50
Dundee United	36	18	11	7	59	31	47
Aberdeen	36	16	12	8	62	31	44
Rangers	36	13	9	14	53	45	35
Dundee	36	14	7	15	45	51	35
St. Mirren	36	13	5	18	42	63	31
Hibernian	36	11	6	19	49	63	28
Motherwell	36	7	6	23	33	66	20
Clydebank	36	6	8	22	29	77	20

SCOTTISH DIVISION 1 1985-86

Hamilton Academical	39	24	8	7	77	44	56
Falkirk	39	17	11	11	57	39	45
Kilmarnock	39	18	8	13	62	49	44
Forfar Athletic	39	17	10	12	51	43	44
East Fife	39	14	15	10	54	46	43
Dumbarton	39	16	11	12	59	52	43
Greenock Morton	39	14	11	14	57	63	39
Partick Thistle	39	10	16	13	53	64	36
Airdrieonians	39	12	11	16	51	50	35
Brechin City	39	13	9	17	58	64	35
Clyde	39	9	17	13	49	59	35
Montrose	39	10	14	15	43	54	34
Ayr United	39	10	11	18	41	60	31
Alloa Athletic	39	6	14	19	49	74	26

SCOTTISH DIVISION 2 1985-86

Dunfermline Athletic	39	23	11	5	91	47	57
Queen of the South	39	23	9	7	71	36	55
Meadowbank Thistle	39	19	11	9	68	45	49
Queen's Park	39	19	8	12	61	39	46
Stirling Albion	39	18	8	13	57	53	44
St. Johnstone	39	18	6	15	63	55	42
Stenhousemuir	39	16	8	15	55	63	40
Arbroath	39	15	9	15	56	50	39
Raith Rovers	39	15	7	17	67	65	37
Cowdenbeath	39	14	9	16	52	53	37
East Stirlingshire	39	11	6	22	49	69	28
Berwick Rangers	39	7	11	21	45	80	25
Albion Rovers	39	8	8	23	38	86	24
Stranraer	39	9	5	25	41	83	23

SCOTTISH PREMIER 1986-87

Rangers	44	31	7	6	85	23	69
Celtic	44	27	9	8	90	41	63
Dundee United	44	24	12	8	66	36	60
Aberdeen	44	21	16	7	63	29	58
Heart of Midlothian	44	21	14	9	64	43	56
Dundee	44	18	12	14	74	57	48
St. Mirren	44	12	12	20	36	51	36
Motherwell	44	11	12	21	43	64	34
Hibernian	44	10	13	21	44	70	33
Falkirk	44	8	10	26	31	70	26
Clydebank	44	6	12	26	35	93	24
Hamilton Academical	44	6	9	29	39	93	21

SCOTTISH DIVISION 1 1986-87

Greenock Morton	44	24	9	11	88	56	57
Dunfermline Athletic	44	23	10	11	61	41	56
Dumbarton	44	23	7	14	67	52	53
East Fife	44	15	21	8	68	55	51
Airdrieonians	44	20	11	13	58	46	51
Kilmarnock	44	17	11	16	62	53	45
Forfar Athletic	44	14	15	15	61	63	43
Partick Thistle	44	12	15	17	49	54	39
Clyde	44	11	16	17	48	56	38
Queen of the South	44	11	12	21	50	71	34
Brechin City	44	11	10	23	44	72	32
Montrose	44	9	11	24	37	74	29

SCOTTISH DIVISION 2 1986-87

Meadowbank Thistle	39	23	9	7	69	38	55
Raith Rovers	39	16	20	3	73	44	52
Stirling Albion	39	20	12	7	55	33	52
Ayr United	39	22	8	9	70	49	52
St. Johnstone	39	16	13	10	59	49	45
Alloa Athletic	39	17	7	15	48	46	41
Cowdenbeath	39	16	8	15	59	55	40
Albion Rovers	39	15	9	15	48	51	39
Queen's Park	39	9	19	11	48	49	37
Stranraer	39	9	11	19	41	59	29
Arbroath	39	11	7	21	46	66	29
Stenhousemuir	39	10	9	20	37	58	29
East Stirlingshire	39	6	11	22	33	56	23
Berwick Rangers	39	8	7	24	40	69	23

1986 Scottish F.A. Cup

Semi-finals

Hibernian vs Aberdeen	0-3
Dundee United vs Heart of Midlothian	0-1

Final

Hampden Park, 10th May 1986

Aberdeen 3 (Hewitt 2, Stark)
Heart of Midlothian 0

Attendance 62,841

1987 Scottish F.A. Cup

Semi-finals

Dundee vs Dundee United	2-3
Heart of Midlothian vs St. Mirren	1-2

Final

Hampden Park, 16th May 1987

St. Mirren 1 (Ferguson)
Dundee United 0 (aet.)

Attendance 51,782

1985/86 Scottish League Cup

Semi-finals

Dundee United vs Aberdeen (0-1, 0-1)	0-2
Hibernian vs Rangers (2-0, 0-1)	2-1

Final

Hampden Park, 27th October 1985

Aberdeen 3 (Black 2, Stark)
Hibernian 0

Attendance 40,061

1986/87 Scottish League Cup

Semi-finals

Celtic vs Motherwell	2-2
Celtic won 5-4 on penalties	
Dundee United vs Rangers	1-2

Final

Hampden Park, 26th October 1986

Rangers 2 (Durrant, Cooper (pen))
Celtic 1 (McClair)

Attendance 74,219

SCOTTISH PREMIER 1987-88

Celtic	44	31	10	3	79	23	72
Heart of Midlothian	44	23	16	5	74	32	62
Rangers	44	26	8	10	85	34	60
Aberdeen	44	21	17	6	56	25	59
Dundee United	44	16	15	13	54	47	47
Hibernian	44	12	19	13	41	42	43
Dundee	44	17	7	20	70	64	41
Motherwell	44	13	10	21	37	56	36
St. Mirren	44	10	15	19	41	64	35
Falkirk	44	10	11	23	41	75	31
Dunfermline Athletic	44	8	10	26	41	84	26
Greenock Morton	44	3	10	31	27	100	16

SCOTTISH DIVISION 1 1987-88

Hamilton Academical	44	22	12	10	67	39	56
Meadowbank Thistle	44	20	12	12	70	51	52
Clydebank	44	21	7	16	59	61	49
Forfar Athletic	44	16	16	12	67	58	48
Raith Rovers	44	19	7	18	81	76	45
Airdrieonians	44	16	13	15	65	68	45
Queen of the South	44	14	15	15	56	67	43
Partick Thistle	44	16	9	19	60	64	41
Clyde	44	17	6	21	73	75	40
Kilmarnock	44	13	11	20	55	60	37
East Fife	44	13	10	21	61	76	36
Dumbarton	44	12	12	20	51	70	36

SCOTTISH DIVISION 2 1987-88

Ayr United	39	27	7	5	95	31	61
St. Johnstone	39	25	9	5	74	24	59
Queen's Park	39	21	9	9	64	44	51
Brechin City	39	20	8	11	56	40	48
Stirling Albion	39	18	10	11	60	51	46
East Stirlingshire	39	15	13	11	51	47	43
Alloa Athletic	39	16	8	15	50	46	40
Montrose	39	12	11	16	45	51	35
Arbroath	39	10	14	15	54	66	34
Stenhousemuir	39	12	9	18	49	58	33
Cowdenbeath	39	10	13	16	51	66	33
Albion Rovers	39	10	11	18	45	75	31
Berwick Rangers	39	6	4	29	32	77	16
Stranraer	39	4	8	27	34	84	16

SCOTTISH PREMIER 1988-89

Rangers	36	26	4	6	62	26	56
Aberdeen	36	18	14	4	51	25	50
Celtic	36	21	4	11	66	44	46
Dundee United	36	16	12	8	44	26	44
Hibernian	36	13	9	14	37	36	35
Heart of Midlothian	36	9	13	14	35	42	31
St. Mirren	36	11	7	18	39	55	29
Dundee	36	9	10	17	34	48	28
Motherwell	36	7	13	16	35	44	27
Hamilton Academical	36	6	2	28	19	76	14

SCOTTISH DIVISION 1 1988-89

Dunfermline Athletic	39	22	10	7	60	36	54
Falkirk	39	22	8	9	71	37	52
Clydebank	39	18	12	9	80	55	48
Airdrieonians	39	17	13	9	66	44	47
Greenock Morton	39	16	9	14	46	46	41
St. Johnstone	39	14	12	13	51	42	40
Raith Rovers	39	15	10	14	50	52	40
Partick Thistle	39	13	11	15	57	58	37
Forfar Athletic	39	10	16	13	52	56	36
Meadowbank Thistle	39	13	10	16	45	50	36
Ayr United	39	13	9	17	56	72	35
Clyde	39	9	16	14	40	52	34
Kilmarnock	39	10	14	15	47	60	34
Queen of the South	39	2	8	29	38	99	10

Queen of the South 2 points deducted for a breach of the rules

SCOTTISH DIVISION 2 1988-89

Albion Rovers	39	21	8	10	65	48	50
Alloa Athletic	39	17	11	11	66	48	45
Brechin City	39	15	13	11	58	49	43
Stirling Albion	39	15	12	12	64	55	42
East Fife	39	14	13	12	55	54	41
Montrose	39	15	11	13	54	55	41
Queen's Park	39	10	18	11	50	49	38
Cowdenbeath	39	13	14	12	48	52	38
East Stirlingshire	39	13	11	15	54	58	37
Arbroath	39	11	15	13	56	63	37
Stranraer	39	12	12	15	58	63	36
Dumbarton	39	12	10	17	45	55	34
Berwick Rangers	39	10	13	16	50	59	33
Stenhousemuir	39	9	11	19	44	59	29

1988 Scottish F.A. Cup

Semi-finals

Celtic vs Heart of Midlothian	2-1
Aberdeen vs Dundee United	0-0, 1-1, 0-1

Final

Hampden Park, 14th May 1988

Celtic 2   (McAvennie 2)

Dundee United 1   (Gallacher)

Attendance 74,000

1987/88 Scottish League Cup

Semi-finals

Aberdeen vs Dundee	2-0
Motherwell vs Rangers	1-3

Final

Hampden Park, 25th October 1987

Rangers 3   (Cooper, Durrant, Fleck)

Aberdeen 3 (aet.)   (Bett (pen), Hewitt, Falconer)

Rangers won 5-3 on penalties

Attendance 71,961

1989 Scottish F.A. Cup

Semi-finals

Rangers vs St. Johnstone	0-0, 4-0
Celtic vs Hibernian	3-1

Final

Hampden Park, 20th May 1989

Celtic 1   (Miller)

Rangers 0

Attendance 72,069

1988/89 Scottish League Cup

Semi-finals

Aberdeen vs Dundee United	2-0
Heart of Midlothian vs Rangers	0-3

Final

Hampden Park, 23rd October 1988

Rangers 3   (McCoist 2 (1 pen), I. Ferguson)

Aberdeen 2   (Dodds 2)

Attendance 72,122

SCOTTISH PREMIER 1989-90

Rangers	36	20	11	5	48	19	51
Aberdeen	36	17	10	9	56	33	44
Heart of Midlothian	36	16	12	8	54	35	44
Dundee United	36	11	13	12	36	39	35
Celtic	36	10	14	12	37	37	34
Motherwell	36	11	12	13	43	47	34
Hibernian	36	12	10	14	32	41	34
Dunfermline Athletic	36	11	8	17	37	50	30
St. Mirren	36	10	10	16	28	48	30
Dundee	36	5	14	17	41	65	24

SCOTTISH PREMIER 1990-91

Rangers	36	24	7	5	62	23	55
Aberdeen	36	22	9	5	62	27	53
Celtic	36	17	7	12	52	38	41
Dundee United	36	17	7	12	41	29	41
Heart of Midlothian	36	14	7	15	48	55	35
Motherwell	36	12	9	15	51	50	33
St. Johnstone	36	11	9	16	41	54	31
Dunfermline Athletic	36	8	11	17	38	61	27
Hibernian	36	6	13	17	24	51	25
St. Mirren	36	5	9	22	28	59	19

SCOTTISH DIVISION 1 1989-90

St. Johnstone	39	25	8	6	81	39	58
Airdrieonians	39	23	8	8	77	45	54
Clydebank	39	17	10	12	74	64	44
Falkirk	39	14	15	10	59	46	43
Raith Rovers	39	15	12	12	57	50	42
Hamilton Academical	39	14	13	12	52	53	41
Meadowbank Thistle	39	13	13	13	41	46	39
Partick Thistle	39	12	14	13	62	53	38
Clyde	39	10	15	14	39	46	35
Ayr United	39	11	13	15	41	62	35
Greenock Morton	39	9	16	14	38	46	34
Forfar Athletic	39	8	15	16	51	65	29
Albion Rovers	39	8	11	20	50	78	27
Alloa Athletic	39	6	13	20	41	70	25

Forfar Athletic had 2 points deducted for a breach of the rules

SCOTTISH DIVISION 1 1990-91

Falkirk	39	21	12	6	70	35	54
Airdrieonians	39	21	11	7	69	43	53
Dundee	39	22	8	9	59	33	52
Partick Thistle	39	16	13	10	56	53	45
Kilmarnock	39	15	13	11	58	48	43
Hamilton Academical	39	16	10	13	50	41	42
Raith Rovers	39	14	9	16	54	64	37
Clydebank	39	13	10	16	65	70	36
Greenock Morton	39	11	13	15	48	55	35
Forfar Athletic	39	9	15	15	50	57	33
Meadowbank Thistle	39	10	13	16	56	68	33
Ayr United	39	10	12	17	47	59	32
Clyde	39	9	9	21	41	61	27
Brechin City	39	7	10	22	44	80	24

SCOTTISH DIVISION 2 1989-90

Brechin City	39	19	11	9	59	44	49
Kilmarnock	39	22	4	13	67	39	48
Stirling Albion	39	20	7	12	73	50	47
Stenhousemuir	39	18	8	13	60	53	44
Berwick Rangers	39	18	5	16	66	57	41
Dumbarton	39	15	10	14	70	73	40
Cowdenbeath	39	13	13	13	58	54	39
Stranraer	39	15	8	16	57	59	38
East Fife	39	12	12	15	60	63	36
Queen of the South	39	11	14	14	58	69	36
Queen's Park	39	13	10	16	40	51	36
Arbroath	39	12	10	17	47	61	34
Montrose	39	10	12	17	53	63	32
East Stirlingshire	39	8	10	21	34	66	26

SCOTTISH DIVISION 2 1990-91

Stirling Albion	39	20	14	5	62	24	54
Montrose	39	20	6	13	54	34	46
Cowdenbeath	39	18	9	12	64	50	45
Stenhousemuir	39	16	12	11	56	42	44
Queen's Park	39	17	8	14	48	42	42
Stranraer	39	18	4	17	61	60	40
Dumbarton	39	15	10	14	49	49	40
Berwick Rangers	39	15	10	14	51	57	40
Alloa Athletic	39	13	11	15	51	46	37
East Fife	39	14	9	16	57	65	37
Albion Rovers	39	11	13	15	48	63	35
Queen of the South	39	9	12	18	46	62	30
East Stirlingshire	39	9	11	19	36	71	29
Arbroath	39	8	11	20	41	59	27

1990 Scottish F.A. Cup

Semi-finals

Celtic vs Clydebank	2-0
Aberdeen vs Dundee United	4-0

Final

Hampden Park, 12th May 1990

Aberdeen 0
Celtic 0 (aet.)

Aberdeen won 9-8 on penalties   Attendance 60,493

1991 Scottish F.A. Cup

Semi-finals

Celtic vs Motherwell	0-0, 2-4
Dundee United vs St. Johnstone	2-1

Final

Hampden Park, 18th May 1991

Motherwell 4 (Ferguson, O'Donnell, Angus, Kirk)
Dundee United 2 (aet.) (Bowman, O'Neil, Jackson)

Attendance 57,319

1989/90 Scottish League Cup

Semi-finals

Aberdeen vs Celtic	1-0
Dunfermline Athletic vs Rangers	0-5

Final

Hampden Park, 22nd October 1989

Aberdeen 2 (Mason 2)
Rangers 1 (aet.) (Walters (pen))

Attendance 61,190

1990/91 Scottish League Cup

Semi-finals

Aberdeen vs Rangers	0-1
Celtic vs Dundee United	2-0

Final

Hampden Park, 28th October 1990

Rangers 2 (Walters, Gough)
Celtic 1 (aet.) (Elliott)

Attendance 62,817

SCOTTISH PREMIER 1991-92

Rangers	44	33	6	5	101	31	72
Heart of Midlothian	44	27	9	8	60	37	63
Celtic	44	26	10	8	88	42	62
Dundee United	44	19	13	12	66	50	51
Hibernian	44	16	17	11	53	45	49
Aberdeen	44	17	14	13	55	42	48
Airdrieonians	44	13	10	21	50	70	36
St. Johnstone	44	13	10	21	52	73	36
Falkirk	44	12	11	21	54	73	35
Motherwell	44	10	14	20	43	61	34
St. Mirren	44	6	12	26	33	73	24
Dunfermline Athletic	44	4	10	30	22	80	18

SCOTTISH PREMIER 1992-93

Rangers	44	33	7	4	97	35	73
Aberdeen	44	27	10	7	87	36	64
Celtic	44	24	12	8	68	41	60
Dundee United	44	19	9	16	56	49	47
Heart of Midlothian	44	15	14	15	37	35	44
St. Johnstone	44	10	20	14	52	66	40
Hibernian	44	12	13	19	54	64	37
Partick Thistle	44	12	12	20	50	71	36
Motherwell	44	11	13	20	46	62	35
Dundee	44	11	12	21	48	68	34
Falkirk	44	11	7	26	60	86	29
Airdrieonians	44	6	17	21	35	70	29

SCOTTISH DIVISION 1 1991-92

Dundee	44	23	12	9	80	48	58
Partick Thistle	44	23	11	10	52	36	57
Hamilton Academical	44	22	13	9	72	48	57
Kilmarnock	44	21	12	11	59	37	54
Raith Rovers	44	21	11	12	59	42	53
Ayr United	44	18	11	15	63	55	47
Greenock Morton	44	17	12	15	66	59	46
Stirling Albion	44	14	13	17	50	57	41
Clydebank	44	12	12	20	59	77	36
Meadowbank Thistle	44	7	16	21	37	59	30
Montrose	44	5	17	22	45	85	27
Forfar Athletic	44	5	12	27	36	85	22

SCOTTISH DIVISION 1 1992-93

Raith Rovers	44	25	15	4	85	41	65
Kilmarnock	44	21	12	11	67	40	54
Dunfermline Athletic	44	22	8	14	64	47	52
St. Mirren	44	21	9	14	62	52	51
Hamilton Academical	44	19	12	13	65	45	50
Greenock Morton	44	19	10	15	65	56	48
Ayr United	44	14	18	12	49	44	46
Clydebank	44	16	13	15	71	66	45
Dumbarton	44	15	7	22	56	71	37
Stirling Albion	44	11	13	20	44	61	35
Meadowbank Thistle	44	11	10	23	51	80	32
Cowdenbeath	44	3	7	34	33	109	13

SCOTTISH DIVISION 2 1991-92

Dumbarton	39	20	12	7	65	37	52
Cowdenbeath	39	22	7	10	74	52	51
Alloa Athletic	39	20	10	9	58	38	50
East Fife	39	19	11	9	72	57	49
Clyde	39	18	7	14	61	43	43
East Stirlingshire	39	15	11	13	61	70	41
Arbroath	39	12	14	13	49	48	38
Brechin City	39	13	12	14	54	55	38
Queen's Park	39	14	7	18	59	63	35
Stranraer	39	13	9	17	46	56	35
Queen of the South	39	14	5	20	71	86	33
Berwick Rangers	39	10	11	18	50	65	31
Stenhousemuir	39	11	8	20	46	57	30
Albion Rovers	39	5	10	24	42	81	20

SCOTTISH DIVISION 2 1992-93

Clyde	39	22	10	7	77	42	54
Brechin City	39	23	7	9	62	32	53
Stranraer	39	19	15	5	69	44	53
Forfar Athletic	39	18	10	11	74	54	46
Alloa Athletic	39	16	12	11	63	54	44
Arbroath	39	18	8	13	59	50	44
Stenhousemuir	39	15	10	14	59	48	40
Berwick Rangers	39	16	7	16	56	64	39
East Fife	39	14	10	15	70	64	38
Queen of the South	39	12	9	18	57	72	33
Queen's Park	39	8	12	19	51	73	28
Montrose	39	10	7	22	46	71	27
East Stirlingshire	39	8	9	22	50	85	25
Albion Rovers	39	6	10	23	36	76	22

1992 Scottish F.A. Cup

Semi-finals

Celtic vs Rangers	0-1
Airdrieonians vs Heart of Midlothian	0-0, 1-1
Airdrieonians won 4-2 on penalties	

Final

Hampden Park, 9th May 1992

Rangers 2   (Hateley, McCoist)
Airdrieonians 1   (Smith)

Attendance 44,045

1993 Scottish F.A. Cup

Semi-finals

Hibernian vs Aberdeen	0-1
Rangers vs Heart of Midlothian	2-1

Final

Celtic Park, 29th May 1993

Rangers 2   (Murray, Hateley)
Aberdeen 1   (Richardson)

Attendance 50,715

1991/92 Scottish League Cup

Semi-finals

Airdrieonians vs Dunfermline Athletic	1-1
Dunfermline Athletic won 3-2 on penalties	
Hibernian vs Rangers	1-0

Final

Hampden Park, 27th October 1991

Hibernian 2   (McIntyre (pen), Wright)
Dunfermline Athletic 0

Attendance 40,377

1992/93 Scottish League Cup

Semi-finals

Aberdeen vs Celtic	1-0
Rangers vs St. Johnstone	3-1

Final

Hampden Park, 25th October 1992

Rangers 2   (McCall, Smith(og))
Aberdeen 1 (aet.)   (Shearer)

Attendance 45,298

SCOTTISH PREMIER 1993-94

Rangers	44	22	14	8	74	41	58
Aberdeen	44	17	21	6	58	36	55
Motherwell	44	20	14	10	58	43	54
Celtic	44	15	20	9	51	38	50
Hibernian	44	16	15	13	53	48	47
Dundee United	44	11	20	13	47	48	42
Heart of Midlothian	44	11	20	13	37	43	42
Kilmarnock	44	12	16	16	36	45	40
Partick Thistle	44	12	16	16	46	57	40
St. Johnstone	44	10	20	14	35	47	40
Raith Rovers	44	6	19	19	46	80	31
Dundee	44	8	13	23	42	57	29

SCOTTISH DIVISION 1 1993-94

Falkirk	44	26	14	4	81	32	66
Dunfermline Athletic	44	29	7	8	93	35	65
Airdrieonians	44	20	14	10	48	38	54
Hamilton Academical	44	19	12	13	66	54	50
Clydebank	44	18	14	12	56	48	50
St. Mirren	44	21	8	15	61	55	50
Ayr United	44	14	14	16	42	52	42
Dumbarton	44	11	14	19	48	59	36
Stirling Albion	44	13	9	22	41	68	35
Clyde	44	10	12	22	35	58	32
Greenock Morton	44	6	17	21	44	75	29
Brechin City	44	6	7	31	30	81	19

SCOTTISH DIVISION 2 1993-94

Stranraer	39	23	10	6	63	35	56
Berwick Rangers	39	18	12	9	75	46	48
Stenhousemuir	39	19	9	11	62	44	47
Meadowbank Thistle	39	17	13	9	62	48	47
Queen of the South	39	17	9	13	69	48	43
East Fife	39	15	11	13	58	52	41
Alloa Athletic	39	12	17	10	41	39	41
Forfar Athletic	39	14	11	14	58	58	39
East Stirlingshire	39	13	11	15	54	57	37
Montrose	39	14	8	17	56	61	36
Queen's Park	39	12	10	17	52	76	34
Arbroath	39	12	9	18	42	67	33
Albion Rovers	39	7	10	22	37	66	24
Cowdenbeath	39	6	8	25	40	72	20

SCOTTISH PREMIER 1994-95

Rangers	36	20	9	7	60	35	69
Motherwell	36	14	12	10	50	50	54
Hibernian	36	12	17	7	49	37	53
Celtic	36	11	18	7	39	33	51
Falkirk	36	12	12	12	48	47	48
Heart of Midlothian	36	12	7	17	44	51	43
Kilmarnock	36	11	10	15	40	48	43
Partick Thistle	36	10	13	13	40	50	43
Aberdeen	36	10	11	15	43	46	41
Dundee United	36	9	9	18	40	56	36

SCOTTISH DIVISION 1 1994-95

Raith Rovers	36	19	12	5	54	32	69
Dunfermline Athletic	36	18	14	4	63	32	68
Dundee	36	20	8	8	65	36	68
Airdrieonians	36	17	10	9	50	33	61
St. Johnstone	36	14	14	8	59	39	56
Hamilton Academical	36	14	7	15	42	48	49
St. Mirren	36	8	12	16	34	50	36
Clydebank	36	8	11	17	43	47	35
Ayr United	36	6	11	19	31	58	29
Stranraer	36	4	5	27	25	81	17

SCOTTISH DIVISION 2 1994-95

Greenock Morton	36	18	10	8	55	33	64
Dumbarton	36	17	9	10	57	35	60
Stirling Albion	36	17	7	12	54	43	58
Stenhousemuir	36	14	14	8	46	39	56
Berwick Rangers	36	15	10	11	52	46	55
Clyde	36	14	10	12	53	48	52
Queen of the South	36	11	11	14	46	51	44
East Fife	36	11	10	15	48	56	43
Meadowbank Thistle	36	11	5	20	32	54	35
Brechin City	36	6	6	24	22	60	24

Meadowbank Thistle had 3 points deducted

SCOTTISH DIVISION 3 1994-95

Forfar Athletic	36	25	5	6	67	33	80
Montrose	36	20	7	9	69	32	67
Ross County	36	18	6	12	59	44	60
East Stirlingshire	36	18	5	13	61	50	59
Alloa Athletic	36	15	9	12	50	45	54
Inverness Caledonian Thistle	36	12	9	15	48	61	45
Arbroath	36	13	5	18	51	62	44
Queen's Park	36	12	6	18	46	57	42
Cowdenbeath	36	11	7	18	48	60	40
Albion Rovers	36	5	3	28	27	82	18

1994 Scottish F.A. Cup

Semi-finals

Dundee United vs Aberdeen	1-1, 1-0
Kilmarnock vs Rangers	0-0, 1-2

Final

Hampden Park, 21st May 1994

Dundee United 1   (Brewster)
Rangers 0

Attendance 37,450

1993/94 Scottish League Cup

Semi-finals

Dundee United vs Hibernian	0-1
Rangers vs Celtic	1-0

Final

Hampden Park, 24th October 1993

Rangers 2   (Durrant, McCoist)
Hibernian 1   (McPherson (og))

Attendance 47,632

1995 Scottish F.A. Cup

Semi-finals

Celtic vs Hibernian	0-0, 3-1
Airdrieonians vs Heart of Midlothian	1-0

Final

Hampden Park, 27th May 1995

Celtic 1   (Van Hooijdonk)
Airdrieonians 0

Attendance 36,915

1994/95 Scottish League Cup

Semi-finals

Airdrieonians vs Raith Rovers	1-1
Raith Rovers won 5-4 on penalties	
Celtic vs Aberdeen	1-0

Final

Ibrox Stadium, 27th November 1994

Raith Rovers 2   (Crawford, Dalziel)
Celtic 2 (aet.)   (Walker, Nicholas)

Raith Rovers won 6-5 on penalties

Attendance 45,384

SCOTTISH PREMIER 1995-96

Rangers	36	27	6	3	85	25	87
Celtic	36	24	11	1	74	25	83
Aberdeen	36	16	7	13	52	45	55
Heart of Midlothian	36	16	7	13	55	53	55
Hibernian	36	11	10	15	43	57	43
Raith Rovers	36	12	7	17	41	57	43
Kilmarnock	36	11	8	17	39	54	41
Motherwell	36	9	12	15	28	39	39
Partick Thistle	36	8	6	22	29	62	30
Falkirk	36	8	6	24	31	60	24

SCOTTISH PREMIER 1996-97

Rangers	36	25	5	6	85	33	80
Celtic	36	23	6	7	78	32	75
Dundee United	36	17	9	10	46	33	60
Heart of Midlothian	36	14	10	12	46	43	52
Dunfermline Athletic	36	12	9	15	52	65	45
Aberdeen	36	10	14	12	45	57	44
Kilmarnock	36	11	6	19	41	61	39
Motherwell	36	9	11	16	44	55	38
Hibernian	36	9	11	16	38	55	38
Raith Rovers	36	6	7	23	29	73	25

SCOTTISH DIVISION 1 1995-96

Dunfermline Athletic	36	21	8	7	73	41	71
Dundee United	36	19	10	7	73	37	67
Greenock Morton	36	20	7	9	57	39	67
St. Johnstone	36	19	8	9	60	36	65
Dundee	36	15	12	9	53	40	57
St. Mirren	36	13	8	15	46	51	47
Clydebank	36	10	10	16	39	58	40
Airdrieonians	36	9	11	16	43	54	38
Hamilton Academical	36	10	6	20	40	57	36
Dumbarton	36	3	2	31	23	94	11

SCOTTISH DIVISION 1 1996-97

St. Johnstone	36	24	8	4	74	23	80
Airdrieonians	36	15	15	6	56	34	60
Dundee	36	15	13	8	47	33	58
St. Mirren	36	17	7	12	48	41	58
Falkirk	36	15	9	12	42	39	54
Partick Thistle	36	12	12	12	49	48	48
Stirling Albion	36	12	10	14	54	61	46
Greenock Morton	36	12	9	15	42	41	45
Clydebank	36	7	7	22	31	59	28
East Fife	36	2	8	26	28	92	14

SCOTTISH DIVISION 2 1995-96

Stirling Albion	36	24	9	3	83	30	81
East Fife	36	19	10	7	50	29	67
Berwick Rangers	36	18	6	12	64	47	60
Stenhousemuir	36	14	7	15	51	49	49
Clyde	36	11	12	13	47	45	45
Ayr United	36	11	12	13	40	40	45
Queen of the South	36	11	10	15	54	67	43
Stranraer	36	8	18	10	38	43	42
Forfar Athletic	36	11	7	18	37	61	40
Montrose	36	5	5	26	33	86	20

SCOTTISH DIVISION 2 1996-97

Ayr United	36	23	8	5	61	33	77
Hamilton Academical	36	22	8	6	75	28	74
Livingston	36	18	10	8	56	38	64
Clyde	36	14	10	12	42	39	52
Queen of the South	36	13	8	15	55	57	47
Stenhousemuir	36	11	11	14	49	43	44
Brechin City	36	10	11	15	36	49	41
Stranraer	36	9	9	18	29	51	36
Dumbarton	36	9	8	19	44	66	35
Berwick Rangers	36	4	11	21	32	75	23

SCOTTISH DIVISION 3 1995-96

Livingston	36	21	9	6	51	24	72
Brechin City	36	18	9	9	41	21	63
Inverness Caledonian Thistle	36	15	12	9	64	38	57
Ross County	36	12	17	7	56	39	53
Arbroath	36	13	13	10	41	41	52
Queen's Park	36	12	12	12	40	43	48
East Stirlingshire	36	11	11	14	58	62	44
Cowdenbeath	36	10	8	18	45	59	38
Alloa Athletic	36	6	11	19	26	58	29
Albion Rovers	36	7	8	21	37	74	29

SCOTTISH DIVISION 3 1996-97

Inverness Caledonian Thistle	36	23	7	6	70	37	76
Forfar Athletic	36	19	10	7	74	45	67
Ross County	36	20	7	9	58	41	67
Alloa Athletic	36	16	7	13	50	47	55
Albion Rovers	36	13	10	13	50	47	49
Montrose	36	12	7	17	46	62	43
Cowdenbeath	36	10	9	17	38	51	39
Queen's Park	36	9	9	18	46	59	36
East Stirlingshire	36	8	9	19	36	58	33
Arbroath	36	6	13	17	31	52	31

1996 Scottish F.A. Cup

Semi-finals

Aberdeen vs Heart of Midlothian	1-2
Celtic vs Rangers	1-2

Final

Hampden Park, 18th May 1996

Rangers 5 (Laudrup 2, Durie 3)
Heart of Midlothian 1 (Colquhoun)

Attendance 37,730

1997 Scottish F.A. Cup

Semi-finals

Celtic vs Falkirk	1-1, 0-1
Kilmarnock vs Dundee United	0-0, 1-0

Final

Ibrox Stadium, 24th May 1997

Kilmarnock 1 (Wright)
Falkirk 0

Attendance 48,953

1995/96 Scottish League Cup

Semi-finals

Rangers vs Aberdeen	1-2
Dundee vs Airdrieonians	2-1

Final

Hampden Park, 26th November 1995

Aberdeen 2 (Dodds, Shearer)
Dundee 0

Attendance 33,096

1996/97 Scottish League Cup

Semi-finals

Dunfermline Athletic vs Rangers	1-6
Heart of Midlothian vs Dundee	3-1

Final

Celtic Park, 24th November 1996

Rangers 4 (McCoist 2, Gascoigne 2)
Heart of Midlothian 3 (Fulton, Robinson, Weir)

Attendance 48,559

SCOTTISH PREMIER 1997-98

Celtic	36	22	8	6	64	24	74
Rangers	36	21	9	6	76	38	72
Heart of Midlothian	36	19	10	7	70	46	67
Kilmarnock	36	13	11	12	40	52	50
St. Johnstone	36	13	9	14	38	42	48
Aberdeen	36	9	12	15	39	53	39
Dundee United	36	8	13	15	43	51	37
Dunfermline Athletic	36	8	13	15	43	68	37
Motherwell	36	9	7	20	46	64	34
Hibernian	36	6	12	18	38	59	30

SCOTTISH PREMIER 1998-99

Rangers	36	23	8	5	78	31	77
Celtic	36	21	8	7	84	35	71
St. Johnstone	36	15	12	9	39	38	57
Kilmarnock	36	14	14	8	47	29	56
Dundee	36	13	7	16	36	56	46
Heart of Midlothian	36	11	9	16	44	50	42
Motherwell	36	10	11	15	35	54	41
Aberdeen	36	10	7	19	43	71	37
Dundee United	36	8	10	18	37	48	34
Dunfermline Athletic	36	4	16	16	28	59	28

SCOTTISH DIVISION 1 1997-98

Dundee	36	20	10	6	52	24	70
Falkirk	36	19	8	9	56	41	65
Raith Rovers	36	17	9	10	51	33	60
Airdrieonians	36	16	12	8	42	35	60
Greenock Morton	36	12	10	14	47	48	46
St. Mirren	36	11	8	17	41	53	41
Ayr United	36	10	10	16	40	56	40
Hamilton Academical	36	9	11	16	43	56	38
Partick Thistle	36	8	12	16	45	55	36
Stirling Albion	36	8	10	18	40	56	34

SCOTTISH DIVISION 1 1998-99

Hibernian	36	28	5	3	84	33	89
Falkirk	36	20	6	10	60	38	66
Ayr United	36	19	5	12	66	42	62
Airdrieonians	36	18	5	13	42	43	59
St. Mirren	36	14	10	12	42	43	52
Greenock Morton	36	14	7	15	45	41	49
Clydebank	36	11	13	12	36	38	46
Raith Rovers	36	8	11	17	37	57	35
Hamilton Academical	36	6	10	20	30	62	28
Stranraer	36	5	2	29	29	74	17

SCOTTISH DIVISION 2 1997-98

Stranraer	36	18	7	11	62	44	61
Clydebank	36	16	12	8	48	31	60
Livingston	36	16	11	9	56	40	59
Queen of the South	36	15	9	12	57	51	54
Inverness Caledonian Thistle	36	13	10	13	65	51	49
East Fife	36	14	6	16	51	59	48
Forfar Athletic	36	12	10	14	51	61	46
Clyde	36	10	12	14	40	53	42
Stenhousemuir	36	10	10	16	44	53	40
Brechin City	36	7	11	18	42	73	32

SCOTTISH DIVISION 2 1998-99

Livingston	36	22	11	3	66	35	77
Inverness Caledonian Thistle	36	21	9	6	80	48	72
Clyde	36	15	8	13	46	42	53
Queen of the South	36	13	9	14	50	45	48
Alloa Athletic	36	13	7	16	65	56	46
Stirling Albion	36	12	8	16	50	63	44
Arbroath	36	12	8	16	37	52	44
Partick Thistle	36	12	7	17	36	45	43
East Fife	36	12	6	18	42	64	42
Forfar Athletic	36	8	7	21	48	70	31

SCOTTISH DIVISION 3 1997-98

Alloa Athletic	36	24	4	8	78	39	76
Arbroath	36	20	8	8	67	39	68
Ross County	36	19	10	7	71	36	67
East Stirlingshire	36	17	6	13	50	48	57
Albion Rovers	36	13	5	18	60	73	44
Berwick Rangers	36	10	12	14	47	55	42
Queen's Park	36	10	11	15	42	55	41
Cowdenbeath	36	12	2	22	33	57	38
Montrose	36	10	8	18	53	80	38
Dumbarton	36	7	10	19	42	61	31

SCOTTISH DIVISION 3 1998-99

Ross County	36	24	5	7	87	42	77
Stenhousemuir	36	19	7	10	62	42	64
Brechin City	36	17	8	11	47	43	59
Dumbarton	36	16	9	11	53	40	57
Berwick Rangers	36	12	14	10	53	49	50
Queen's Park	36	11	11	14	41	46	44
Albion Rovers	36	12	8	16	43	63	44
East Stirlingshire	36	9	13	14	50	48	40
Cowdenbeath	36	8	7	21	34	65	31
Montrose	36	8	6	22	42	74	30

1998 Scottish F.A. Cup

Semi-finals

Falkirk vs Heart of Midlothian	1-3
Rangers vs Celtic	2-1

Final

Celtic Park, 16th May 1998

Heart of Midlothian 2   (Cameron (pen), Adam)
Rangers 1   (McCoist)

Attendance 48,496

1999 Scottish F.A. Cup

Semi-finals

Celtic vs Dundee United	2-0
St. Johnstone vs Rangers	0-4

Final

Hampden Park, 29th May 1999

Rangers 1   (Wallace)
Celtic 0

Attendance 52,760

1997/98 Scottish League Cup

Semi-finals

Celtic vs Dunfermline Athletic	1-0
Dundee United vs Aberdeen	3-1

Final

Ibrox Stadium, 30th November 1997

Celtic 3   (Rieper, Larsson, Burley)
Dundee United 0

Attendance 49,305

1998/99 Scottish League Cup

Semi-finals

Rangers vs Airdrieonians	5-0
St. Johnstone vs Heart of Midlothian	3-0

Final

Celtic Park, 29th November 1998

Rangers 2   (Guivarc'h, Albertz)
St. Johnstone 1   (Dasovic)

Attendance 45,533

SCOTTISH PREMIER 1999-2000

Rangers	36	28	6	2	96	26	90
Celtic	36	21	6	9	90	38	69
Heart of Midlothian	36	15	9	12	47	40	54
Motherwell	36	14	10	12	49	63	52
St. Johnstone	36	10	12	14	36	44	42
Hibernian	36	10	11	15	49	61	41
Dundee	36	12	5	19	45	64	41
Dundee United	36	11	6	19	34	57	39
Kilmarnock	36	8	13	15	38	52	37
Aberdeen	36	9	6	21	44	83	33

SCOTTISH DIVISION 1 1999-2000

St. Mirren	36	23	7	6	75	39	76
Dunfermline Athletic	36	20	11	5	66	33	71
Falkirk	36	20	8	8	67	40	68
Livingston	36	19	7	10	60	45	64
Raith Rovers	36	17	8	11	55	40	59
Inverness Caledonian Thistle	36	13	10	13	60	55	49
Ayr United	36	10	8	18	42	52	38
Greenock Morton	36	10	6	20	45	61	36
Airdrieonians	36	7	8	21	29	69	29
Clydebank	36	1	7	28	17	82	10

SCOTTISH DIVISION 2 1999-2000

Clyde	36	18	11	7	65	37	65
Alloa Athletic	36	17	13	6	58	38	64
Ross County	36	18	8	10	57	39	62
Arbroath	36	11	14	11	52	55	47
Partick Thistle	36	12	10	14	42	44	46
Stranraer	36	9	18	9	47	46	45
Stirling Albion	36	11	7	18	60	72	40
Stenhousemuir	36	10	8	18	42	52	38
Queen of the South	36	8	9	19	45	75	33
Hamilton Academical	36	10	14	12	39	44	29*

Hamilton Academical had 15 points deducted

SCOTTISH DIVISION 3 1999-2000

Queen's Park	36	20	9	7	54	37	69
Berwick Rangers	36	19	9	8	53	30	66
Forfar Athletic	36	17	10	9	64	40	61
East Fife	36	17	8	11	45	39	59
Cowdenbeath	36	15	9	12	59	43	54
Dumbarton	36	15	8	13	53	51	53
East Stirlingshire	36	11	7	18	28	50	40
Brechin City	36	10	8	18	42	51	38
Montrose	36	10	7	19	39	54	37
Albion Rovers	36	5	7	24	33	75	22

1999 Scottish F.A. Cup

Semi-finals

Ayr United vs Rangers	0-7
Hibernian vs Aberdeen	1-2

Final

Hampden Park, 27th May 2000

Rangers 4   (Van Bronckhorst, Vidmar, Dodds, Albertz)
Aberdeen 0

Attendance 50,865

1999/2000 Scottish League Cup

Semi-finals

Aberdeen vs Dundee United	1-0
Celtic vs Kilmarnock	1-0

Final

Hampden Park, 19th March 2000

Celtic 2   (Riseth, Johnson)
Aberdeen 0
Attendance 50,073

SCOTTISH PREMIER 2000-2001

Celtic	38	31	4	3	90	29	97
Rangers	38	26	4	8	76	36	82
Hibernian	38	18	12	8	57	35	66
Kilmarnock	38	15	9	14	44	53	54
Heart of Midlothian	38	14	10	14	56	50	52
Dundee	38	13	8	17	51	49	47
Aberdeen	38	11	12	15	45	52	45
Motherwell	38	12	7	19	42	56	43
Dunfermline Athletic	38	11	9	18	34	54	42
St. Johnstone	38	9	13	16	40	56	40
Dundee United	38	9	8	21	38	63	35
St. Mirren	38	8	6	24	32	72	30

With 6 games of the season left, the Division was split into two groups of 6. The top half contended for the Championship while the bottom half decided relegation.

SCOTTISH DIVISION 1 2000-2001

Livingston	36	23	7	6	72	31	76
Ayr United	36	19	12	5	73	41	69
Falkirk	36	16	8	12	57	59	56
Inverness Caledonian Thistle	36	14	12	10	71	54	54
Clyde	36	11	14	11	44	46	47
Ross County	36	11	10	15	48	52	43
Raith Rovers	36	10	8	18	41	55	38
Airdrieonians	36	8	14	14	49	67	38
Greenock Morton	36	9	8	19	34	61	35
Alloa Athletic	36	7	11	18	38	61	32

SCOTTISH DIVISION 2 2000-2001

Partick Thistle	36	22	9	5	66	32	75
Arbroath	36	15	13	8	54	38	58
Berwick Rangers	36	14	12	10	51	44	54
Stranraer	36	15	9	12	51	50	54
Clydebank	36	12	11	13	42	43	47
Queen of the South	36	13	7	16	52	59	46
Stenhousemuir	36	12	6	18	45	63	42
Forfar Athletic	36	10	10	16	48	52	40
Queen's Park	36	10	10	16	28	40	40
Stirling Albion	36	5	17	14	34	50	32

SCOTTISH DIVISION 3 2000-2001

Hamilton Academical	36	22	10	4	75	30	76
Cowdenbeath	36	23	7	6	58	31	76
Brechin City	36	22	6	8	71	36	72
East Fife	36	15	8	13	49	46	53
Peterhead	36	13	10	13	46	46	49
Dumbarton	36	13	6	17	46	49	45
Albion Rovers	36	12	9	15	38	43	45
East Stirlingshire	36	10	7	19	37	69	37
Montrose	36	6	8	22	31	65	26
Elgin City	36	5	7	24	29	65	22

2000/2001 Scottish F.A. Cup

Semi-finals

Hibernian vs Livingston	3-0
Celtic vs Dundee	3-1

Final

Hampden Park, 26th May 2001

Celtic 3   (McNamara, Larsson 2 (1 pen))
Hibernian 0

Attendance 51,824

2000/2001 Scottish League Cup

Semi-finals

Celtic vs Rangers	3-1
St. Mirren vs Kilmarnock	0-3

Final

Hampden Park, 18th March 2001

Celtic 3   (Larsson 3)
Kilmarnock 0
Attendance 48,830

SCOTTISH PREMIER 2001-2002

	P	W	D	L	F	A	Pts
Celtic	38	33	4	1	94	18	103
Rangers	38	25	10	3	82	27	85
Livingston	38	16	10	12	50	47	58
Aberdeen	38	16	7	15	51	49	55
Heart of Midlothian	38	14	6	18	52	57	48
Dunfermline Athletic	38	12	9	17	41	64	45
Kilmarnock	38	13	10	15	44	54	49
Dundee United	38	12	10	16	38	59	46
Dundee	38	12	8	18	41	55	44
Hibernian	38	10	11	17	51	56	41
Motherwell	38	11	7	20	49	69	40
St. Johnstone	38	5	6	27	24	62	21

With 6 games of the season left, the Division was split into two groups of 6. The top half contended for the Championship while the bottom half decided relegation.

SCOTTISH PREMIER 2002-2003

	P	W	D	L	F	A	Pts
Rangers	38	31	4	3	101	28	97
Celtic	38	31	4	3	98	26	97
Heart of Midlothian	38	18	9	11	57	51	63
Kilmarnock	38	16	9	13	47	56	57
Dunfermline Athletic	38	13	7	18	54	71	46
Dundee	38	10	14	14	50	60	44
Hibernian	38	15	6	17	56	64	51
Aberdeen	38	13	10	15	41	54	49
Livingston	38	9	8	21	48	62	35
Partick Thistle	38	8	11	19	37	58	35
Dundee United	38	7	11	20	35	68	32
Motherwell	38	7	7	24	45	71	28

With 6 games of the season left, the Division was split into two groups of 6. The top half contended for the Championship while the bottom half decided relegation.

SCOTTISH DIVISION 1 2001-2002

	P	W	D	L	F	A	Pts
Partick Thistle	36	19	9	8	61	38	66
Airdrieonians	36	15	11	10	59	40	56
Ayr United	36	13	13	10	53	44	52
Ross County	36	14	10	12	51	43	52
Clyde	36	13	10	13	51	56	49
Inverness Caledonian Thistle	36	13	9	14	60	51	48
Arbroath	36	14	6	16	42	59	48
St. Mirren	36	11	12	13	43	53	45
Falkirk	36	10	9	17	49	73	39
Raith Rovers	36	8	11	17	50	62	35

SCOTTISH DIVISION 1 2002-2003

	P	W	D	L	F	A	Pts
Falkirk	36	25	6	5	80	32	81
Clyde	36	21	9	6	66	37	72
St. Johnstone	36	20	7	9	49	29	67
Inverness Caledonian Thistle	36	20	5	11	74	45	65
Queen of the South	36	12	12	12	45	48	48
Ayr United	36	12	9	15	34	44	45
St. Mirren	36	9	10	17	42	71	37
Ross County	36	9	8	19	42	46	35
Alloa Athletic	36	9	8	19	39	72	35
Arbroath	36	3	6	27	30	77	15

SCOTTISH DIVISION 2 2001-2002

	P	W	D	L	F	A	Pts
Queen of the South	36	20	7	9	64	42	67
Alloa Athletic	36	15	14	7	55	33	59
Forfar Athletic	36	15	8	13	51	47	53
Clydebank	36	14	9	13	44	45	51
Hamilton Academical	36	13	9	14	49	44	48
Berwick Rangers	36	12	11	13	44	52	47
Stranraer	36	10	15	11	48	51	45
Cowdenbeath	36	11	11	14	49	51	44
Stenhousemuir	36	8	12	16	33	57	36
Greenock Morton	36	7	14	15	48	63	35

SCOTTISH DIVISION 2 2002-2003

	P	W	D	L	F	A	Pts
Raith Rovers	36	16	11	9	53	36	59
Brechin City	36	16	7	13	63	59	55
Airdrie United	36	14	12	10	51	44	54
Forfar Athletic	36	14	9	13	55	53	51
Berwick Rangers	36	13	10	13	43	48	49
Dumbarton	36	13	9	14	48	47	48
Stenhousemuir	36	12	11	13	49	51	47
Hamilton Academical	36	12	11	13	43	48	47
Stranraer	36	12	8	16	49	57	44
Cowdenbeath	36	8	12	16	46	57	36

SCOTTISH DIVISION 3 2001-2002

	P	W	D	L	F	A	Pts
Brechin City	36	22	7	7	67	38	73
Dumbarton	36	18	7	11	59	48	61
Albion Rovers	36	16	11	9	51	42	59
Peterhead	36	17	5	14	63	52	56
Montrose	36	16	7	13	43	39	55
Elgin City	36	13	8	15	45	47	47
East Stirlingshire	36	12	4	20	51	58	40
East Fife	36	11	7	18	39	56	40
Stirling Albion	36	9	10	17	45	68	37
Queen's Park	36	9	8	19	38	53	35

SCOTTISH DIVISION 3 2002-2003

	P	W	D	L	F	A	Pts
Greenock Morton	36	21	9	6	67	33	72
East Fife	36	20	11	5	73	37	71
Albion Rovers	36	20	10	6	62	36	70
Peterhead	36	20	8	8	76	37	68
Stirling Albion	36	15	11	10	50	44	56
Gretna	36	11	12	13	50	50	45
Montrose	36	7	12	17	35	61	33
Queen's Park	36	7	11	18	39	51	32
Elgin City	36	5	13	18	33	63	28
East Stirlingshire	36	2	7	27	32	105	13

2001/2002 Scottish F.A. Cup

Semi-finals

Ayr United vs Celtic	0-3
Rangers vs Partick Thistle	3-0

Final

Hampden Park, 4th May 2002

Celtic 2 (Hartson, Balde)

Rangers 3 (Lovenkrands 2, Ferguson)

Attendance 51,138

2001/2002 Scottish League Cup

Semi-finals

Hibernian vs Ayr United	0-1 (aet)
Rangers vs Celtic	2-1 (aet)

Final

Hampden Park, 17th March 2002

Ayr United 0

Rangers 4 (Flo, Ferguson, Caniggia 2)

Attendance 50,076

2002/2003 Scottish F.A. Cup

Semi-finals

Inverness Caledonian Thistle vs Dundee	0-1
Rangers vs Motherwell	4-3

Final

Hampden Park, 31st May 2003

Dundee 0

Rangers 1 (Amoruso)

Attendance 47,136

2002/2003 Scottish League Cup

Semi-finals

Celtic vs Dundee United	3-0
Heart of Midlothian vs Rangers	0-1

Final

Hampden Park, 16th March 2003

Celtic 1 (Larsson)

Rangers 2 (Caniggia, Lovenkrands)

Attendance 52,000

SCOTTISH PREMIER 2003-2004

Celtic	38	31	5	2	105	25	98
Rangers	38	25	6	7	76	33	81
Heart of Midlothian	38	19	11	8	56	40	68
Dunfermline Athletic	38	14	11	13	45	52	53
Dundee United	38	13	10	15	47	60	49
Motherwell	38	12	10	16	42	49	46
Dundee	38	12	10	16	48	57	46
Hibernian	38	11	11	16	41	60	44
Livingston	38	10	13	15	48	57	43
Kilmarnock	38	12	6	20	51	74	42
Aberdeen	38	9	7	22	39	63	34
Partick Thistle	38	6	8	24	39	67	26

With 6 games of the season left, the Division was split into two groups of 6. The top half contended for the Championship while the bottom half decided relegation.

SCOTTISH DIVISION 1 2003-2004

Inverness Caledonian Thistle	36	21	7	8	67	33	70
Clyde	36	20	9	7	64	40	69
St. Johnstone	36	15	12	9	59	45	57
Falkirk	36	15	10	11	43	37	55
Queen of the South	36	15	9	12	46	48	54
Ross County	36	12	13	11	49	41	49
St. Mirren	36	9	14	13	39	46	41
Raith Rovers	36	8	10	18	37	57	34
Ayr United	36	6	13	17	37	58	31
Brechin City	36	6	9	21	37	73	27

SCOTTISH DIVISION 2 2003-2004

Airdrie United	36	20	10	6	64	36	70
Hamilton Academical	36	18	8	10	70	47	62
Dumbarton	36	18	6	12	56	41	60
Greenock Morton	36	16	11	9	66	58	59
Berwick Rangers	36	14	6	16	61	67	48
Forfar Athletic	36	12	11	13	49	57	47
Alloa Athletic	36	12	8	16	55	55	44
Arbroath	36	11	10	15	41	57	43
East Fife	36	11	8	17	38	45	41
Stenhousemuir	36	7	4	25	28	65	25

SCOTTISH DIVISION 3 2003-2004

Stranraer	36	24	7	5	87	30	79
Stirling Albion	36	23	8	5	78	27	77
Gretna	36	20	8	8	59	39	68
Peterhead	36	18	7	11	67	37	61
Cowdenbeath	36	15	10	11	46	39	55
Montrose	36	12	12	12	52	63	48
Queen's Park	36	10	11	15	41	53	41
Albion Rovers	36	12	4	20	66	75	40
Elgin City	36	6	7	23	48	93	25
East Stirlingshire	36	2	2	32	30	118	8

2003/2004 Scottish F.A. Cup

Semi-finals

Livingston vs Celtic	1-3
Inverness Cal. Thistle vs Dunfermline Athletic	1-1, 2-3

Final

Hampden Park, 22nd May 2004

Dunfermline Athletic 1   (Skerla)
Celtic 3   (Larsson 2, Petrov)

Attendance 50,846

2003/2004 Scottish League Cup

Semi-finals

Hibernian vs Rangers	1-1 (aet)
Hibernian won 4-3 on penalties	
Dundee vs Livingston	0-1

Final

Hampden Park, 14th March 2004

Livingston 2   (Lilley, McAllister)
Hibernian 0

Attendance 45,500

SCOTTISH PREMIER 2004-2005

Rangers	38	29	6	3	78	22	93
Celtic	38	30	2	6	87	35	92
Heart of Midlothian	38	13	11	14	43	41	50
Motherwell	38	13	9	16	46	49	48
Dundee United	39	9	12	18	43	59	39
Dunfermline Athletic	38	8	10	20	34	60	34
Hibernian	39	18	7	14	64	59	61
Aberdeen	38	18	7	13	44	39	61
Kilmarnock	38	15	4	19	49	55	49
Partick Thistle	36	10	9	17	38	52	39
Livingston	38	9	8	21	34	58	35
Dundee	38	8	9	21	37	71	33

With 6 games of the season left, the Division was split into two groups of 6. The top half contended for the Championship while the bottom half decided relegation.

SCOTTISH DIVISION 1 2004-2005

Falkirk	36	22	9	5	66	30	75
St Mirren	36	15	15	6	41	23	60
Clyde	36	16	12	8	35	29	60
Queen of the South	36	14	9	13	36	38	51
Airdrie United	36	14	8	14	44	48	50
Ross County	36	13	8	15	40	37	47
Hamilton Academical	36	12	11	13	35	36	47
St Johnstone	36	12	10	14	38	39	46
Partick Thistle	36	10	9	17	38	52	39
Raith Rovers	36	3	7	26	26	67	16

SCOTTISH DIVISION 2 2004-2005

Brechin City	36	22	6	8	81	43	72
Stranraer	36	18	9	9	48	41	63
Morton	36	18	8	10	60	37	62
Alloa Athletic	37	13	9	15	69	68	48
Stirling Albion	36	13	9	14	53	57	48
Forfar Athletic	35	13	8	14	49	42	47
Dumbarton	36	11	9	16	43	53	42
Ayr United	36	11	9	16	39	54	42
Arbroath	36	10	8	18	49	73	38
Berwick Rangers	36	9	9	18	40	63	36

SCOTTISH DIVISION 3 2004-2005

Gretna	36	32	2	2	130	29	98
Peterhead	37	24	9	4	83	38	81
Cowdenbeath	35	14	8	13	53	60	50
Queens Park	36	13	9	14	51	50	48
Montrose	36	13	7	16	47	53	46
Elgin City	38	12	7	19	39	65	43
Stenhousemuir	36	10	12	14	58	58	42
East Fife	36	11	7	18	41	55	40
Albion Rovers	36	8	10	18	40	78	34
East Stirlingshire	36	5	7	24	32	88	22

2004/2005 Scottish F.A. Cup

Semi-finals

Heart of Midlothian vs Celtic	1-2
Dundee United vs Hibernian	2-1

Final

Hampden Park, 28th May 2005

Celtic 1 (Thompson)
Dundee United 0

Attendance 50,635

2004/2005 Scottish League Cup

Semi-finals

Celtic vs Dundee United	3-0
Heart of Midlothian vs Rangers	0-1

Final

Hampden Park, 20th March 2005

Rangers 5 (Ross, Kyrgiakos 2, Ricksen, Novo)
Motherwell 1 (Partridge)

Attendance 50,182

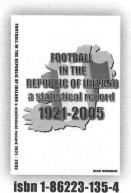

isbn 1-86223-135-4

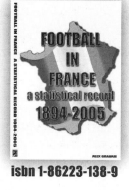

isbn 1-86223-138-9

isbn 1-86223-137-0

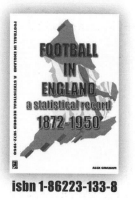

isbn 1-86223-133-8

Football in Series a statistical record

isbn 1-86223-139-7

isbn 1-86223-134-6

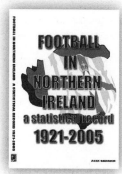

isbn 1-86223-136-2

isbn 1-86223-123-0

Supporters' Guides Series

This top-selling series has been published annually since 1982 and contains 2004/2005 Season's results and tables, Directions, Photographs, Phone numbers, Parking information, Admission details, Disabled information and much more.

THE SUPPORTERS' GUIDE TO PREMIER & FOOTBALL LEAGUE CLUBS 2006

The 22nd edition featuring all Premiership and Football League clubs.   *Price £6.99*

THE SUPPORTERS' GUIDE TO NON-LEAGUE FOOTBALL 2006

Following the reorganisation of Non-League Football this 14th edition covers all 66 Step 1 & Step 2 clubs – the Football Conference National, Conference North and Conference South.   *Price £6.99*

THE SUPPORTERS' GUIDE TO NON-LEAGUE FOOTBALL 2006 – STEP 3 CLUBS

Following the reorganisation of Non-League Football the 2nd edition of this book features the 66 clubs which feed into the Football Conference.   *Price £6.99*

THE SUPPORTERS' GUIDE TO SCOTTISH FOOTBALL 2006

The 14th edition featuring all Scottish Premier League, Scottish League and Highland League clubs.   *Price £6.99*

THE SUPPORTERS' GUIDE TO WELSH FOOTBALL GROUNDS 2006

The 10th edition featuring all League of Wales, Cymru Alliance & Welsh Football League Clubs + results, tables & much more.   *Price £6.99*

THE SUPPORTERS' GUIDE TO NORTHERN IRISH FOOTBALL 2006

Back after a long absence, this 3rd edition features all Irish Premier League and Irish Football League Clubs + results, tables & much more.   *Price £6.99*

THE SUPPORTERS' GUIDE TO EIRCOM FAI CLUBS 2005

Back after a long absence this 3rd edition features all Eircom League Premier and First Division Clubs + 10 years of results, tables & much more.   *Price £6.99*

These books are available UK & Surface post free from –

Soccer Books Limited (Dept. SBL)
72 St. Peter's Avenue
Cleethorpes
N.E. Lincolnshire
DN35 8HU